From

From Parry to Britten

British Music in Letters
1900 — 1945

LEWIS FOREMAN

A chronological anthology
including correspondence by
Bantock, Britten, Delius, Elgar,
Balfour Gardiner, Heseltine,
Moeran, Parry, Stanford and
Vaughan Williams

With an appendix identifying
families and copyright owners of
British composers of the period

B. T. Batsford Ltd · London

ISBN 0 7134 5520 9 (hardback)
0 7134 5521 7 (paperback)

Typeset by Latimer Trend & Company Ltd, Plymouth
and printed by
Anchor Brendon Ltd
Tiptree, Essex

for the publishers
B. T. Batsford Ltd.
4 Fitzhardinge Street
London W1H 0AH

CONTENTS

For those many friends whose dedicated research over many years has returned a huge repertoire of glorious music to performance.

SOURCES

A Institutional Sources

BBC Written Archives Centre, Caversham
Birmingham Public Library
Boosey & Hawkes Ltd., London
British Library, Department of Manuscripts
Britten-Pears Library, The Red House, Aldeburgh
Cape Town University Music Library, Cape Town, South Africa
Central Music Library, Westminster Public Libraries: Edwin Evans Collection
City of Birmingham Symphony Orchestra: Leslie Heward Papers
Delius Trust Archive, London
EMI Records Archive
Gloucester Public Library: Ivor Gurney Collection
Grainger Museum, Melbourne, Australia
Leeds University: Herbert Thompson Collection
Library of Congress, Washington DC.
McMaster University Library, Hamilton, Ontario, Canada
Royal College of Music: Parry Room
Royal Opera House Archives
Royal Philharmonic Society: loan collection, British Library
Royal Northern College of Music Library
University of Texas: Humanities Research Centre

B Personal Collections

Adolf Borsdorf, Gwydion Brooke, Richard Brookes, David Brown, Geoffrey Bush, Patricia Cleveland-Peck, David Deas, David Dunhill, Lewis Foreman, Michael Hurd, Lyndon Jenkins, George Lloyd, Stephen Lloyd, Raymond Monk, Miss C. N. Newbery, the late C. W. Orr, Christpher Palmer, Patrick Piggott, Dr R. K. R. Thornton, Fred Tomlinson.

C Printed Sources

Dance Research: The Journal of the Society for Dance Research Vol. II No. 1 Spring 1984
George Butterworth 1885–1916 [privately printed] 1916
GRAVES, Charles L.: *Hubert Parry: his life and works* 2 vols, Macmillan, 1926
GRAY, Cecil: *Peter Warlock – a memoir of Philip Heseltine*, Cape, 1934, 1938
GREENE, H. Plunket: *Charles Villiers Stanford*. Edward Arnold, 1935

A Man of Our Time: Michael Tippett [Exhibition Catalogue] Schott, 1977

SIMMONS, Jennifer R.: *So Deft a Builder: an account of the life and work of Sir Henry Hadow*, PhD thesis, Sheffield, 1978

Welsh Music: Winter 1980–81 vol. 6 no. 6

Reid Concert Programme 19 February 1921

VAUGHAN WILLIAMS, Ursula: *R.V.W.: a biography of Ralph Vaughan Williams*. OUP, 1964

WILD, Stephen: *E. J. Moeran – an assessment*, MA Thesis, University of Western Australia, 1967

Scrapbooks belonging to the present author (including lot 167 from Sotheby's sale of 30 June 1969), Felix Aprahamian and the late Edmund Rubbra. They contain cuttings from:
The Author, The Daily News, The Daily Telegraph, The Evening Standard, Morley College Magazine, the Morning Post, Picture Post, Radio Times, and *The Times.*

LIST OF ILLUSTRATIONS

Illustrations and Facsimiles in Text

INTRODUCTION

I have long accumulated copies of letters and other documents in support of my continuing research into the history of the music written in Britain since 1880. While my primary interest has been to hear as much of the music as possible in good performances, I have always been fascinated by the factors that bore upon the evaluation of different works and composers at different times, and the artistic assumptions on which such assessments – often the received opinion for decades afterwards – were based. Therefore, to see the developing musical scene over many years in contemporary documents is a valuable adjunct to the music.

The realization that a volume could be selected from these documents, which while interesting in itself would also ensure the availability of a wide span of source material, came one day when visiting the late Freda Swain – composer, teacher, and for many years the wife of the pianist and teacher Arthur Alexander. Miss Swain was in her sitting room, a large wastepaper basket by her full of torn letters. 'Just having a clear-out', she explained in her no-nonsense manner. She offered me refreshment and on my acceptance went out to make the tea. My attention was riveted to that wastepaper basket. I peered into the bin – were the contents purely personal or was there anything of historical significance? After all, Miss Swain had been very widely connected, as had her husband. The little I could read of the top document whetted my appetite. It appeared to be an account of London in the First World War. Miss Swain returned with the tea, and I, apologizing for my incorrigible curiosity, asked if I could see the top item. 'Have it' she said, and on piecing the fragments together I read the letter from 'Tim' Braithwaite to Arthur Alexander (No. 57 in the present collection). However, she pooh-poohed further investigation and I never learned what else went to the bonfire.

The lesson to the musical historian is that the most valuable historical documents are not necessarily those written by famous names. Our assessment of this period is only just beginning and one is never sure what may be of value. Certainly, any broad descriptive over-view is not to be missed, but in each example the sympathies of the author should be remembered by the user.

This chronological anthology of letters by and about British composers during the first half of the twentieth century underlines the tremendous growth in activity during this period, and the changing circumstances in which composers worked over this time. Apart from letters to the press (themselves difficult to trace) the letters here are largely unpublished, and in presenting this selection I have tried to achieve several objectives. Firstly, I hope it will be useful to students of British music of this period, both as a history and as a sourcebook. Secondly, I have tried to cast my net widely, and I anticipate that admirers of a wide variety of specific composers and social historians of different complexions will all find something to interest them.

Thirdly, although I have assumed a certain level of knowledge of the field in my readers, I hope that the collection succeeds both as an anthology and as a history on its own account – and that anyone dipping or reading consecutively will find things to interest and please them. In addition to letters I have also used some diary extracts, as well as BBC internal documents.

However, the reader should not expect each letter to have an equivalent weight, and there is a measure of comparative trivia which is of interest, particularly in context. While some letters discuss matters we now consider significant in the history of British music, and included are a number of set-piece sources which I suspect future commentators on the period will wish to quote and quote again, this is not primarily intended as a collection of seminal documents. There are also items concerning the ephemera of musical history – a composer seeks a publisher, a philanthropist agrees to find funds, a quarrel develops, a conductor wishes to appear as a composer, a child prodigy appears in a concert.

I have included a number of items concerning less well known figures on the musical scene. It should be made clear at the outset that this is not intended to make any particular claim for those writers, but merely to suggest that the predicament or event thus illuminated is interesting in the history of the period and its development. However, those with a bent for musical exploration may well find that the works thus mentioned may be worthy of their time.

Finally, there are a few self-promotional pieces by comparatively unfamiliar composers, including Rutland Boughton, John Foulds, Robin Milford and William Fenney. Again, while these may be of consuming interest to students of these composers or their circles – and they are certainly interesting to me – their inclusion chiefly adds to the context of a particular period, and should also be seen in the light of other letters in the book.

It has not been possible in the space available to deal adequately with performing artists, and conductors in particular are not treated in a balanced way. This is primarily a book concerned with the social history of the composer. That said, I would like to underline the fact that while the undoubted architect of the later plural musical tradition in Britain (exemplified by the international repertoire broadcast by the BBC in the inter-war years) was Sir Adrian Boult, to whom a very great debt is due, I must draw attention to the unsung hero of British music in the context of the BBC in the 1930s and 1940s: Kenneth A. Wright. Wright filled various roles in BBC music, including for several years being Boult's deputy, and under Boult's leadership he was the source of much of the wider vision that the BBC espoused in the 1930s – as becomes clear from some of the letters and documents quoted from BBC sources.

In fact, although my title would suggest that this book ends with the War, I make no apology for having actually extended my coverage to 1946. The period is more convincingly rounded off in the year following the war, with its mixture of 'business as usual' and those new forces which would shape the tremendous activity of the years that would follow.

═══ ACKNOWLEDGEMENTS ═══

The musicologist who writes in a vacuum is very unwise, for it is only sympathetic friends and colleagues who can be the patient critics that help to mould any work into its final shape, and it is here my pleasure to thank all those who have helped in the preparation of my book. This collection of chips from the workshops of many musical research interests has slowly gathered momentum over nearly a quarter of a century and I would particularly like to acknowledge those who helped in the early days, with some of whom I have since lost touch, as well as all who were involved with the more frantic final stages.

When the book was in its penultimate typescript Rosemary Dooley read it and I am most grateful to her for introducing me to my publisher. Later, Stephen Banfield read it in manuscript, and Jory Bennett, David Brown, Garry Humphreys and Stephen Lloyd read the galley proofs. For their shoals of suggestions and comments I am truly grateful – the book is much the better for their knowledge and enthusiastic criticism. Lionel Carley read those sections related to Delius and was good enough to check my texts against the Delius Trust transcripts of the Delius letters. He also specially translated for me letter no. 16 from its original German.

Of my various sources, a number have gone to special trouble to help me, and I must, in particular, draw attention to that unique source for the historian of twentieth-century music which is to be found at the BBC Written Archives Centre at Caversham, near Reading. For the historian of British music since the late 1920s it is probably the richest single source. Thanks are due to Jacqueline Kavanagh, Written Archives Officer, and to Clare Brown for their sympathetic assistance in tracing a variety of files and making them available. Letters from this source are to be found there on the Radio Contributors files for the composers concerned, except for a small self-evident number of policy documents.

Among private collections the largest single source is my own and I would like to thank those who have assisted me in acquiring many items, in particular John and Laurie May, whose antiquarian catalogues are such a joy. Raymond Monk made his own splendid collection of composers' letters available to me and allowed me to choose from them: in the event I have used five items. I am most grateful to him.

Aware that space is not unlimited and that my editor will be looking askance at the length to which these acknowledgements are stretching I must now produce an alphabetical list of the many names I wish to acknowledge. Thanks are due to:

Denis ApIvor, Felix Aprahamian, Cuillin Bantock, Helen Bainton, John Bishop, Lady Bliss, Adolf Borsdorf, Trevor Bray, Gwydion Brooke, Richard Brookes, Geoffrey Bush, Patricia Cleveland-Peck, Mrs M. V. Cranmer (Music Librarian, Kings College Cambridge), Oliver Davies, David Deas, Christopher Dyment, Ruth

Edge (EMI Music Archives), Francesca Franchi (Royal Opera House Archives), Professor David Greer, Mrs Norma Herrmann, Mr Hiatt (Gloucester County Libraries), Paul Hindmarsh, the late Dorothie Harrison, Tony Hodges (Librarian, Royal Northern College of Music), Michael Hurd, Lyndon Jenkins, Leonie Twentyman Jones (University of Cape Town Library), Jessica M. Kerr, Dr Milo Keynes, Dr E. D. Mackerness, Colin Matthews, the late Bernard Naylor, the late Helen Orr, Christopher Palmer, Patrick Piggott, Michael Pope, Richard Ralph (editor, *Dance Research*), Paul Rapoport, A. J. Heward Rees (for matters Welsh, and especially to do with Grace Williams), Dr Frank Ries, Stewart Robertson, the late Edmund Rubbra, Malcolm Smith, Charlotte A. Stewart (Director of Archives and Research Collections, McMaster University), Hugh Taylor, Kelsey Thornton, Peter Todd, Fred Tomlinson and Jane Wilson.

For formal permission to reproduce copyright material I am delighted to make acknowledgement the following. Firstly, to the BBC, who constitute my largest single source; I am most grateful for permission to reproduce Boosey & Hawkes Ltd copyright material, and to Tom Rivers, Assistant Head of Copyright for facilitating this permission. To the Sir Thomas Beecham Trust; Captain Godfrey Brewer, British Library Dept. of Manuscripts; the Rutland Boughton Trust; Malcolm Boyd (for permission to quote from his article on the Britten/Grace Williams correspondence, and most particularly for his generosity in allowing me to use his original footnotes); Benjamin Britten's letters to Grace Williams (nos 161–3 and 175) and the excerpt from his letter to Edward Clark are *c*. 1987 the Trustees of the Britten-Pears Foundation and not to be further reproduced without written permission; the Rt. Hon. Sir Adam Butler MP; Central Music Library, London; Tamara Coates; Dr D. A. Croft (Secretary, The George Butterworth Memorial Fund); the Delius Trust; Alice Dyson; Decca International; EMI Music Archives; Jean Furnivall (for letters and music by Havergal Brian); John Eliot Gardner; James Gibson (in respect of letters of Patrick Hadley); Leon Goossens CBE; Grainger Museum Board, University of Melbourne; J. R. Haines of Haines & Sumner (in respect of Ivor Gurney copyrights); item 230 is Crown Copyright, and is reproduced by permission of the controller of HM Stationery Office; Mrs Alberta Hill (in respect of her father Albert Sammons); G. & I. Holst Ltd; Elisabeth Jane Howard (in respect of her grandfather Sir Arthur Somervell); Dr Milo Keynes (for letters from Lydia Lopokova and Ninette de Valois to Sir Geoffrey Keynes); Miss Karen Heward; the John Ireland Charitable Trust; Dr Elisabeth Legge-Schwarzkopf; the Library of Congress; The William Neady Division of Archives and Research Collections, McMaster University Library, Hamilton, Ontario; Marion Milford; Walter Knott (for the letters of E. J. Moeran); the late Bernard Naylor; Miss C. N. Newbery; the late Helen Orr; the papers of Sir Hubert Parry are reproduced by permission of Lord Ponsonby of Shulbrede; Ursula Pélissier (in respect of her father Herbert Howells); Isobel Rawsthorne; Royal Academy of Music (in respect of Sir Henry Wood copyrights); the Royal College of Music; the Royal Northern College of Music; the Royal Opera House, Covent Garden; Mrs Sheila Smit; the late Edmund Rubbra; Arthur Searle (Hon. Librarian, Royal Philharmonic Society); Texas University, Humanities Research Institute; Dr Herbert Sumsion CBE; Dr Stanley Sadie (editor, *The Musical Times* for letters taken from that journal); the Society of Authors; G. L. Sudlow; Sir Michael Tippett OM; Ursula Vaughan Williams; Lady Walton; the Trustees of Sir Donald F. Tovey c/o Messrs Skene Edwards & Garson, Edinburgh; *Welsh Music* (for letters between Britten and Grace Williams); the poetry of Randall Swingler is reproduced by permission of his daughter Judith Wilson; John Wilson (Trustee of the Estate of the late Sir Walford Davies); Mrs Marybride Watt (in respect of the

Estate of John Foulds); the Herbert Thompson papers are reproduced by courtesy of the Brotherton Library in the University of Leeds and are from collection MS 361.

The photographs and illustrations are largely drawn from out-of-copyright sources in my own collection (the majority of them old picture postcards). However, I am very grateful to the following for plugging the gaps I was unable to fill myself: John Bishop (28); David Dunhill (21, 48); Pauline Gray (45); Norma Herrmann (46); Lyndon Jenkins (51); Royal College of Music (42); University of Leeds (50); Welsh Music Information Centre (43).

Robin Crofton prepared the musical examples with his customary care. The short fragment from Richard Strauss's *Don Juan* is Copyright 1904 by Jos. Albi Verlag, Leipzig. Renewal 1932 by C. F. Peters. Reproduction by permission of Peters Edition Ltd., London. The page from Christian Darnton's *Song of Democracy* by permission of Mrs Vera Darnton, and from Havergal Brian's *Cleopatra* by permission of Jean Furnivall.

Finally I must thank Tim Auger and Richard Reynolds of B.T. Batsford for making my scheme a reality.

I hope I have not forgotten to thank anyone or to make acknowledgements where they are due. If I have, I must apologise now and say that great efforts have been made to clear permissions on all material used, and in the case of any unwitting omission an appropriate acknowledgement will be printed in a later edition. As the book has been prepared for press I have corrected and amended many flaws and infelicities. Doubtless in a month I will have noticed more; but there must be an end if it is to appear at all. I hope that the book instructs and entertains. Please send me your comments and suggestions for additions or changes in later editions.

LEWIS FOREMAN
Rickmansworth
June 1987

Location of the original of each document quoted, where known

Lewis Foreman, personal collection: 46, 53, 57, 62, 67, 75, 77, 78, 79, 241; (ex May & May Catalogues 182, 184, 212, 213, 216, 217); press cuttings: 18, 23, 25, 31, 39, 58, 59, 60, 70, 72, 73, 81, 91, 98, 100, 106, 107, 110, 111, 120, 123, 130, 153, 218, 219, 220, 241

Boosey & Hawkes Ltd, London: 112, 117, 136, 148, 159, 191, 201, 221, 222

Adolph Borsdorf, personal collection: 28

British Broadcasting Corporation, Written Archives Centre, Caversham: 124, 127, 134, 135, 137, 138, 140, 142, 147, 149, 150, 166, 168, 169, 173, 174, 176, 177, 179, 180, 181, 187, 189, 193, 194, 196, 203, 204, 206, 208, 210, 211, 214, 224, 226, 227, 229, 230, 233, 236, 238, 240, 242, 243, 244, 245, 246, 247

British Library, Dept. of Manuscripts: 34 (Eg 3304); 150 (Add ms 56482); 188 (57785); 202 (57785).

Gwydion Brooke, private collection: 19, 30, 154

Richard Brookes, private collection: 2, 3, 4, 13

David Brown, private collection: 200

Dr Geoffrey Bush, private collection: 231
Cape Town University: pp 3–5
Central Music Library, London: 88, 105, 115, 116, 155, 192, 234
Patricia Cleveland-Peck: Harrison papers: 199, 207
David Deas, private collection: 143
Delius Trust Archive, London: 1, 55, 76, 89, 90, 97
David Dunhill, private collection: 113, 185
EMI Records Archive, Hayes, Middlesex: 121
Gloucester Public Library, Ivor Gurney Collection: 82, 84, 85, 86, 205
Grainger Museum, Melbourne, Australia: 41, 42, 90, 109
Leslie Heward Papers, Birmingham: 151, 178, 198, 228
Michael Hurd, private collection: 118
Leeds University, Brotherton Library: 7, 10, 11, 12, 14, 15, 17, 24, 26, 27, 35, 36, 37,
    40, 49, 50, 103, 156, 158
Library of Congress, Washington D.C. USA:
George Lloyd, private collection: 122, 171, 172
McMaster University Library, Ontario, Canada: 48, 51, 52, 68, 69, 71
Raymond Monk, private collection: 96, 98, 102, 114, 126
Musical Times: 83, 130, 223
Miss C. N. Newbery, personal papers: 239
C. W. Orr Papers: 108, 157, 165
Christopher Palmer, private collection: 144
Patrick Piggott, private collection: 195
Royal College of Music Library, London: 9, 16, 32, 33
Royal Northern College of Music Library, Manchester: 20, 22
Royal Opera House Archives, London: 139, 160, 183, 248
Royal Philharmonic Society loan collection: 29, 44, 45, 56
University of Texas, the Humanities Research Centre: 131
Dr R. K. R. Thornton, private collection: 190
Fred Tomlinson, private collection: 87, 235

Over the years some of the items that have been obtained from a given source may have ceased to be available there and in one or two cases it is not clear where the originals of documents reproduced in this book may now be found. In addition other documents have come in the form of photocopies of photocopies, and again the location of the original document is unclear. So, although letters reproduced here are authentic texts, newly transcribed from photocopies of the originals, in a small minority of cases it may not now be possible to locate the original. I would be grateful to hear from any owner of a document reproduced herein who has not been consulted in the book's preparation, so that it may be accurately located in future editions.

A NOTE ON THE TEXTS

A numbers of problems have had to be addressed in the presentation of the documents reproduced in this book, and these need to be appreciated by the reader. Owing to the varied nature of the originals, the treatment may differ from item to item. Many of the letters have been transcribed from manuscript originals, with all the problems of interpretation that this can entail. In one or two there is a word impossible to decipher, and these have been signified thus: [   ]. The majority of the letters have been transcribed by myself, though in the cases of the letters written by Britten and Delius, some by Elgar and one each by Gurney and Ireland, I have adopted the transcription of other hands. I am most grateful to the originators of these for allowing me to use the texts they have established.

Altogether the sources fall into the following categories:

Manuscripts
Typescripts
Carbon copies (hence without letterhead, salutation or signature)
Copies of letters in hands other than the original writer
Approved 'official' texts (in the cases of the Britten and Delius Estates)
BBC internal memoranda
Previously printed letters taken from their published sources
Extracts from diaries and other manuscript sources.

Most of the material included has been presented as a direct transcription of the correspondents' texts, including idiosyncrasies in grammar and punctuation. Occasional typing errors and spelling mistakes have been silently corrected, and punctuation very sparingly added where necessary for the sake of clarity. The Britten and Delius items already mentioned are reproduced unedited, and in the case of the Britten I have been asked to use rules to indicate underlinings rather than the more conventional italic.

Only when a retained error is particularly glaring have I used [*sic*] after the offending word. In order to make clear my insertions, square brackets used in originals have been changed to parentheses ( ) and square brackets reserved for editorial use. The square brackets in the Delius letters are, however, his own.

In headings and captions, correspondents have all been given the personal style or they used at the date of the item in question. Thus Adrian Boult, for example, only becomes 'Sir Adrian' in 1 February 1937. In the case of Holbrooke, who changed the spelling of his name from Josef to Joseph, his usage is adopted where appropriate.

By and large the correspondents tend not to use accents on names such as Bartók and Kodály. The usage herein reflects that in any given item. However in my commentary accents have been retained. Similarly, the spelling of names such as Rachmaninoff (Rachmaninov), and the misuse of the apostrophe have been accorded similar criteria. Finally, where the text reproduced is an extract, this has been marked by an asterisk [*] in the margin.

CHAPTER I

1900–1914
Edwardian Summer

Although Britain did not produce internationally famous composers of the first rank during the nineteenth century, there has been a tendency to discount the activities of those composers working at the time, and to ignore the dramatic increase in activity in the later part of the century. The last quarter of the nineteenth century marked a quickening of musical life in the United Kingdom, and saw the emergence of substantial creative personalities whose work was widely performed, not only in Britain but also abroad – particularly in Germany. If Britain was one of many tributaries of the Germanic musical river during much of Victoria's reign, by 1900 it was beginning to show signs of potential independence, and when the main stream was later to become blocked up, the remaining tributaries (of which Britain was but one) were ready to assume recognizable directions of their own.

The passing of Sir Arthur Sullivan, the most celebrated British composer of Victorian England, on 22 November 1900, symbolizes for us the end of a musical age in Britain. Between then and the outbreak of World War I, on 4 August 1914, there was evident a burgeoning of creative impulse – signalled by the emergence of Elgar as the pre-eminent British composer – and a new national identity began to be felt. The question of a distinctive British art was widely discussed, although the characteristics then regarded as typically British and those we would now describe in such terms may not be the same. It is only in retrospect that such qualities can be truly defined, though at the time there was a renewed pride in what British composers were achieving. The contemporary dominance of German culture maintained an artistic continuum and provided the soil for a nationalist reaction to grow in countries as varied as Czechoslovakia, Poland, Hungary, Scandinavia and the United States, as well as in Great Britain. Although the subject of polemic at the time, the true nature of these emergent national characters can only really be understood in retrospect, and only then in the context of performance of the music concerned. (The pioneering activities in many countries in the last quarter of the twentieth century by record companies, radio producers and specialist performing organizations in actually playing this forgotten repertoire, is making its appraisal possible – in many cases, for the first time.)

The Edwardian period was marked by an explosion of composition, though the composers who came to the forefront then as harbingers of the new are not necessarily those we might wish to see today as the big-name composers of the period – indeed, by and large they still await rediscovery and evaluation. Of them, Coleridge-Taylor and William Hurlstone died young, while Walford Davies, whose *Everyman* in 1904 was acknowledged as the most important choral work after Elgar, later became celebrated as a broadcaster; his serious music has been forgotten in favour of his popular ceremonial works *Solemn Melody* and *RAF March Past*. The performance of the lesser choral works of Elgar* has spearheaded the investigation, since about 1970, of the once celebrated British scores of the 25 years after 1890. This is a process that is continuing, with, for example, the BBC performances of scores such as Ethel Smyth's *Mass in D* and Bantock's *Omar Khayyam*, and other organizations' promotion of a variety of music, including operas by composers such as Stanford, Hamish MacCunn and Ethel Smyth.†

The Edwardian age was one crowned, so far as composition in Britain was concerned, with the emergence of the most fertile composers of the next generation, heralded by the appearance of Vaughan Williams's *Sea Symphony* in 1910 and his *London Symphony* in 1914. A multitude of musical developments which had been quietly gathering momentum for a generation appeared, simultaneously with a talented new generation of composers. Small wonder the next generation talked of 'Renaissance'.

The rise of British conductors and British musical institutions, especially educational establishments, ensured that there was a slowly developing audience for the works written by British composers. Nevertheless the issue that concerned young composers in 1900 was that which still concerned them in 1939 and today; the obvious one of getting their music performed. At the beginning of our period the big choral festivals were the major patrons of new works – and this explains why so many substantial choral works were written (and published in vocal score). As these festivals were financially guaranteed by private individuals it also ensured a variety of taste and opinion on the part of the composers' patrons. If the style or idiom of a particular young composer did not fit with the ideas of one cathedral city, it might be taken up by another. Later, when the BBC became the major source of patronage, for all its well-meaning attempts to put examples of all the best new work by British composers before the public, the educational background and artistic assumptions of its officials necessarily created a barrier to performance of works outside their experience which many composers found difficult if not impossible to breach.

The musical climate between 1900 and 1914 was one in which late Victorian institutions and attitudes still persisted, and the assumption of the superiority of Germanic models was endemic, in spite of the appearance of strong counter-influences from Russia and France in particular: it took an apocalypse to sweep them away.

In June 1905 the Society of British Composers was founded under the auspices of Frederick Corder and Tobias Matthay, respectively professors of composition and piano at the Royal Academy of Music in London. The introduction to the Society's first *Year Book*‡ encapsulates the young composer's dilemma at that time:

---

*The revivals of Elgar's *King Olaf, Caractacus, Lux Christi* and *The Black Knight* in the early 1970s were pioneering as far as most music lovers were concerned; the music had been forgotten for at least two or three decades; all were announced by the BBC as first broadcast performances, taking place in 1974, 1975, 1973 and 1975 respectively. In fact *Lux Christi* had enjoyed a single broadcast in March 1928.

†During European Music Year, 1985 the British Music Society sponsored and organized a competitive 'British Opera in Retrospect' during which fringe companies presented the following operas from our period: Bantock's *Caedmar* (only performed with piano accompaniment); MacCunn's *Jeanie Deans*; Stanford's *Much Ado About Nothing*; Holst's *Savitri*; Smyth's *The Boatswain's Mate*; Vaughan Williams' *Hugh the Drover*, *The Poisoned Kiss* and *Riders to the Sea*; and Rutland Boughton's *The Lily Maid*. For a full account and historical essays see:
[MEARES, Stan ed.]: *British Opera in Retrospect*. Upminster, The British Music Society, 1986.

‡The Society of British Composers: *Year Book, 1906/07*. Pinner, Mddx, the Society, 1906, pp 3–4.

The present position of the British composer of high-class music is a very deplorable one. He is encouraged to educate himself well – scholarships are even offered to tempt him to undertake the production of work which, on the author's entry into the world, is declared on all hands to be a non-saleable article. As a matter of fact, the number of new Symphonies, Concertos, Quartets and Sonatas published in London during the last ten years is quite insignificant. Other countries encourage and protect native work that is not directly remunerative. England alone does not. A few years ago even a hearing was denied to most, and poor indeed would have been the prospect without the noble efforts of Sir August Manns to brighten it. Even now, as a rule, only one performance of a new work can be obtained – thus treating it as a mere curiosity instead of a thing requiring time and attention to appreciate.

The number of talented young composers is nevertheless – strange to say – very large at the present time; so large, in fact, that it is felt that some effort must be made to put matters on a better footing. Accordingly, a number of the most energetic among them have held meetings to discuss the situation, and as a preliminary step to forward the desired ends have founded

THE SOCIETY OF BRITISH COMPOSERS

to which they invite all their fellow-musicians to seek election. The immediate aims of the Society are:

1. To facilitate the publication of such high-class works as the ordinary publisher cannot or will not undertake.
2. The protection of the British composer's interest in the matters of publishing agreements. This is a great need, as a young musician is seldom a good man of business.

The Society desires it to be clearly understood that it is far from regarding the London publishers with hostility, and it is fully appreciative of all that – to name only one – the house of Novello has done for English composers . . .

To set the scene and to show how the young composer saw the world before 1900, we have an extract from the unpublished memoirs of W. H. Bell, who finally emigrated to South Africa in 1912 and whose music is consequently almost totally unknown in Britain today. Yet whatever we may think of Bell's music, when we finally have an opportunity to hear it, his experiences will have been similar to those of many others.

William Henry Bell (1873–1946) was one of the large number of talented composers who came to maturity at this time. Born in St Albans, he left the Royal Academy of Music in 1893 and later studied with Stanford around 1901. Finding it difficult to make a living in England, he emigrated to South Africa on being appointed Principal of the South African College of Music, Cape Town. His music is forgotten outside South Africa, yet he remained by conviction and idiom a member of the varied group of self-proclaimed British composers who grafted elements of impressionism on to a Germanically-rooted idiom to produce a music of national character.

From W. H. BELL'S REMINISCENCES

Always the organ, whether as student or Church organist was with me a 'pis aller'. By the terms of my Scholarship it was obligatory, and afterwards for many years it was a means, almost the only means, of earning a living. I kept my activities then – and for twenty years afterwards – in water tight compartments, an organist when I had to be, but always under stress of circumstances, and without any affection for the instrument, the people who professed it, or the priests at the churches where I had, perforce, to officiate.

Frederick Corder was a very interesting personality, and musically speaking, the strongest influence on my early musical life. He had a very striking face, rather Mongoloid in type [sic], due to the upward curve of his bushy black eyebrows, and a rather clumsy gait. His hair was rather long, black and straggly, and together with Tobias Matthay, a great friend of his and I believe formerly a fellow pupil in Germany, was the most 'advanced' influence in the Academy.

He had been, and still was, one of the most ardent disciples and propagandists of the Wagner, Liszt cult, and was well known not only as one of the most prominent of the younger composers, but as a very trenchant writer of articles in the musical press. His opera Nordisa performed by the Carl Rosa Company, had recently achieved as near a success as any English opera could at that time – or it seems can ever – achieve. Looking back on the five years I spent in his class I don't think that at that time he had gained the experience or skill as a teacher that was afterwards to make him, together with Sir Charles Stanford, one of the two finest teachers of composition England ever had – especially at the time when at the same time he had a class of such brilliant pupils as Arnold Bax, Benjamin Dale, von Ahn Carse [later known as Adam Carse], York Bowen and Felix Swinstead. In the literary world he was famous as the author, in collaboration with his wife, of the first English version of the text of the Wagner operas, and had also written opera libretti for Goring Thomas.

In conjunction with Mackenzie he was taking a strong lead in modernising the RAM, and breaking down the old reactionary Macfarren* influence. To him were gradually being attracted all the young composers who were to carry on 'the Royal line' that had gone on unbroken from the days of Cipriani Potter & Charles Lucas; men like Sterndale Bennett, Mackenzie, Sullivan and Edward German. At the time I entered his class his most prominent students were Granville Bantock, and a brilliant but rather erratic genius named Learmont Drysdale. The Royal College with its brilliant line of composers had hardly got into its stride at the time; though the name of Hamish MacCunn was beginning to be heard abroad.

Corder's methods were in direct opposition to those which I afterwards learned were practised by Stanford, and I think both suffered somewhat from the faults of their qualities; the two methods, could they have been fused into one, would I think have made the ideal system, and though too late perhaps to benefit to the full by this combination (it was only when I was much more mature that I came under Stanford's influence), I perhaps am the only English composer who came under the influence of both men. To put the matter bluntly, I think Corder actually 'taught' too little; he relied almost entirely on the student's own enthusiasm, which he fostered in every way, to find out for himself the way to do things. Stanford on the other hand imposed, perhaps too much, his own very strong predilections on his pupils, he gave them models to copy, he insisted on a kind of 'historical' progression in his students' work, with the result that, with I admit some very brilliant exceptions, his students' work all showed a strong family likeness. There are a few things in composition, points of established technique which are the result of the experience of all the great composers combined through the ages, that can be 'given' to the student, as it were, ready made for his handling. Most of these, I have to confess, I had to find out for myself chiefly with criticism – at least at the time I was

*Sir George Macfarren (1813–1887), Principal of the RAM 1876–1887. The composer of 12 operas and 8 symphonies among many other works, he was undoubtedly thought very reactionary and old fashioned by the emerging young composers at the end of his life.

with him – and I have no memory of ever being really guided to a way out of a difficulty when I got 'stuck'. As I began to get into my stride as a composer, I think there must have been something in my work and outlook that disturbed him in some way for, towards the end of my career at the RAM, I often did not show him my real compositions for months on end, but contented myself with bringing to him academic exercises, fugues and what not, keeping my compositions to myself.

However, here I was started on my career as a composer! Had I known what that career involved I might have had many nightmares but luckily I didn't, and anyway it has been the only side of musical activity that has ever really interested me, and I have got more pleasure out of it than out of anything else in Life. In this as in every thing else, I have asked very little from Life, and Life has given me far more than I ever asked for. To me creative work has always been purely a means of self-expression, a subjective affair that satisfies some need in my nature and without which I feel I am drifting at a loose-end. Under the best circumstances the rewards possible to a British composer, even the most eminent, other than the satisfaction of doing the work itself, are not worth having. I was to taste the sweets of success, and the bitterness of disappointment, and the successes were just big enough to give one a sufficiently wide reputation to enable me to leave England and take up important work 6000 miles away at the other side of the globe. I have seen the rise of composer after composer in England; I have seen all of them the victims of profound disillusionment in old age, and I have seen their works and even their names forgotten and neglected. Within the last few years I was told by the wife of one of the most beloved and sought after English composers, that a year after his death his income from his royalties amounted to just seventeen shillings, and I heard one of our most brilliant young composers of today say that every Englishman born a musician was a life wasted.

Today, for the most part, the composers who filled the musical horizon when I started my career are as if they had never been. Who in England gives a thought today to that brilliant trio – who we used irreverently to call the 'Mandarins', Parry, Stanford, Mackenzie; what of MacCunn and Cliffe? Où sont les neiges d'antan? . . .

In 1910 I met and had tea with Edward German in his charming little retreat in St John's Wood. He had just heard an orchestral work of mine, *The Shepherd*, in the same programme as a brilliant early work of his own. I asked him why he had not gone on writing the same kind of music, and he said 'They let me starve when I wrote that music, they don't want it. Let them have muck! It's all they care for.' I may say I don't agree with this bitter estimate of his light operas and incidental music, but I merely mention it as characteristic of the kind of thing from which at any rate I was saved.

The climate in musical London in 1899, seen in retrospect, was dominated by the first performance of Elgar's Enigma Variations *at St James's Hall on 19 June 1899: it marked the beginning of twentieth-century British music as later audiences came to know it. Possibly of equal importance was the concert Frederick Delius had promoted of his own music in that same hall shortly before, on 30 May. That event was managed for Delius by R. Norman-Concorde with whom he corresponded during 1899, though the later part of the correspondence when the less than satisfactory financial outcome of the concert was being faced, grew somewhat strained.**

However, Concorde clearly believed in what must have appeared a very exotic idiom at the time, and acted as the focus of a scheme to promote an album of Delius's songs.

*See: CARLEY, Lionel: *Delius – a life in letters* vol. I 1862–1908. Scolar Press, 1983.

(1)
R. NORMAN-CONCORDE to
FREDERICK DELIUS

The Concorde Concert Control,
... and ...
Orchestra, Entertainments and Lecture Bureau,
186 Wardour Street,
(Corner of Oxford Street),
London w

7 Feby, 1900

Dear Delius

As I said in my last letter the sale of your songs has been extremely small, about 39 in all. Augener's have reaped the benefit of our advertising. Singers think considerably before they spend any money and they find on inquiry that they can get the songs cheaper at Augener's. Augener's also kindly devoted the window to your songs some time ago! I am sorry that you are suffering from the prevailing epidemic of shortness of funds. You know I was badly hit over the concert and it is only my method of business and the good name people have been kind enough to give me that has induced my friends to help me out of my difficulty. It is, however, certain that no agency can live on 10% commission business, that is 10% on the *ordinary* engagements of artists. One would have to book £10,000 worth of engagements in order to get £1,000 worth of commission, and it would take a staff and offices that would cost nearly this to book such engagements. *Concerts* moreover are a loss as I do them. It is only out of private speculations and *Hungarian* Bands that one can make profit! Such is the prejudice against English musicians that I find that when I offer an orchestra of first class players at the same price as men who are not fit to play at a dog fight and are dressed up like monkeys, the society lady prefers to engage the monkeys at a high price and thinks the competent musician only worth a few shillings.

I am glad to hear you are hard at work on your new opera.

I am sending you fresh copies of the Songs – I sent you some when they first came out. I certainly think I could get your music played in different centres but you have never given me a chance to do so; and those you have had faith in have done nothing. You must know I only do such things out of friendship as 'where should I come in?' I would even take a run through the country for you at the end of this month (I must have a few days rest I'm fearfully overworked) to see a lot of conductors – & all for nix!

My wife sends her love – she will I hope shortly resume her work – lecturettes & recitals from the Poets – & then you will see a success! She's one of these lucky beggars that always succeeds.

Yours Ever

RNC

*

(2)
CAROLINE ALICE ELGAR to
ALICE KILBURN

12th February 1900

... Last week was a memorable one, we stayed with a friend for the Richter Concert in Birmingham. When the 'Variations' were given they had a splendid success but Mr. Richter wd. take no refusal, so we went to Manchester for the next evening when he repeated them. He sd. it wd. be a better performance & that Edward must hear them there, & he was of course right, the performance was magnificent & created an immense sensation ... The 'Sea Pictures' are to be given at the London Philc. on May 10.

(3)
EDWARD ELGAR to NICHOLAS KILBURN

29th June 1900

Craeg Lea
Wells Road
Malvern

My dear Kilburn
I am so very glad you have broken silence – I wondered if I'd done anything wrong!

Now: your letter is good to have but it echoes some sadness – this is not my practical concern but I must send a line to say how I feel very deeply in a friend's – is it? – trouble.

I hope all is over and past that has been disagreeable. No more. My work is good to me and I think you will find Gerontius far beyond anything I've yet done – I *like* it – I am not suggesting that I have risen to the heights of the poem for one moment – but on our hillside night after night looking across 'Mimitable' horizon (Pleonasm!) I've seen in thought, the Soul go up and have written my own heart's blood into the score.

You must hear it at Birmingham.

You asked me this or I wd not have talked about myself or doings.

Deo Gratias: we are all well and flourishing after influenza and much love from us all to you all.

Yours ever

ED: ELGAR

*

(4)
CAROLINE ALICE ELGAR to
ALICE KILBURN

3 August 1900

... It seems to me that E. has given a real message of consolation to the world & that dread & terror are soothed by the infinite sweetness & mercy which penetrate one's soul with intense emotion, I think human hearts will owe him a debt of gratitude. I cannot help writing this because I feel it so intensely & as if a new path opened out in hearing his setting (variations) ... We are here in the woods (Birchwood Lodge, Malvern) which is very lovely, E. loves orchestrating here in the deep quiet hearing the 'sound of summer winds amidst the lofty pines'.
... He has written his 'Dream of Gerontius' from his very soul ...

The choral festivals held in such cities as Birmingham, Leeds, Cardiff, Norwich and Sheffield were high points of the concert season in Victorian times, a popularity which extended up to the outbreak of war in August 1914. One of the most prestigious was the Leeds Festival, and when their conductor Sir Arthur Sullivan died in 1900 it was natural that they should look for a leading figure in British music to take his place.

Charles Villiers Stanford was appointed and remained for ten years. Although remembered particularly as the Professor of Composition at the Royal College of Music, and hence the teacher of more than two generations of British composers, Stanford was pre-eminently a composer and his considerable achievement is increasingly being recognised in the 1980s as the music is performed again. In his time Stanford was also a celebrated conductor and his proposals for programme planning at Leeds were considered almost revolutionary in their day.

*

(5)
CHARLES VILLIERS STANFORD to
W. S. HANNAM

28 November 1900

It will *never do*, I tell you candidly, to substitute the *Revenge* or anything of mine for the *Golden Legend*. The present conductor must not dis-establish the last by anything of his own ... The main thing really wanted is a brilliant thing instead of the old *Elijah*. Why not such a programme as Handel's *St. Cecilia Ode*, and the Brahms *D Major Symphony* with perhaps Bach's *Singet dem Herrn* between them? Compare that programme with the *Elijah*!! Get out of this eternal rut of *Messiah* and *Elijah*. Set the example of what ought to be done at a Festival like yours. *Elijah* is done about 1,000 times a year. Leeds comes once in three years ... Gluck's *Orpheus* might be a delightful Sunday evg. It is lovely in the concert-room.*

* Stanford is discussing the Leeds Festival, of which Hannam was a committee member.

*

(6)
CHARLES VILLIERS STANFORD to
W. S. HANNAM

Jan 18, 1901

If it is to be a representative 19th-century progr: you *must* do a big Verdi and a big Berlioz. I quite understand people who don't like them. But there are many things I don't like but other people do and they have to be done . . . I daresay I should not do either the *Requiem* or the *Harold* [i.e. *Harold in Italy*] at an ideal concert for my own enjoyment. But you represent big men with big things, and take a broad view of it all. Recollect, that if attention is drawn to the programme being illustrative of the 19th century, everyone will look out for the representatives chosen and their works.

(7)
A. J. JAEGER to HERBERT THOMPSON

16 Margravine Gardens
West Kensington w.

March 4/01

My dear Thompson
Very many thanks for your letter. Stanford wrote to me re Bell: 'Impossible', but he asked me to send Bell to him with his 'Toil', & since then he devotes 2 mornings or portions of 2 mornings a week to introduce the young fellow into the mysteries of the ancient modes. Bell can't make it out. He had rather a prejudice against C.V.S. but he came back to me with an expansive grin on his merry face, saying: 'I say, Stanford was *awfully decent*!' Since then C.V.S. has been going on being awfully decent and Bell quite enjoys going to 50 Holland Street — composing Kyries and Sanctuses & masses in the mixo-this & that mode, especially as the Professor charges the poor fellow nix for his trouble. I say to myself: what can it mean! Of course I felt sure on one thing viz: that C.V.S. must think highly of Bell to devote his valuable time to giving him gratis lessons. Needless to say, because Bell has plenty of the right stuff in him, says something *poetic* &, to a certain extent, un-hackneyed, Novello's Editors won't see anything in him, say he 'can't write' is 'crude', can't score etc etc. The idea of 2 bally (excuse slang) English organists sitting in Judgement on a young genius (more, or less) like Bell makes me curse dreadful cusses. Bell has written tons of stuff, more volumes than West has written pages I should think, but of course he doesn't write in the 'English Church Style!!' Excuse me, if I said all this before, but I can't write calmly on this preposterous state of affairs, which obtains, alas', at the chief English publishers. (This quite between ourselves, *please*! But J[ohn] E W[est] and F[rederik] G[eorge] E[dwards] ruling over the destinies of musical young England *is* a funny idea.)
    I'm now trying hard to induce Brewer to try Bell and he seems half-inclined. It is all very well for you to say that Bell's turn will come at Leeds after he has begun to 'go the round of Festivals!' It is just the *Beginning* which is so darned difficult. One has

to move mountains of prejudices and 'reasons' (so called). Brewer followed my advice re Coleridge Taylor & he turned out trumps. He may safely try Bell; for though he may lack Taylor's easy invention of Tune, has certainly vastly more meaning than the young Blackie, & more depth & poetic imagination. Why I should bother about these youngsters at all I don't know. It takes a great portion of my (*few*) spare hours and I get no satisfaction out of the affair except the feeling that perhaps I have done a fellow a good turn.

I fear you won't like Taylor's Leeds cantata much. I leave him severely alone now, for he is too big a celebrity now to ever come near me. He sent me the other day another new choral work to this address without even a letter of explanation & I haven't even looked at it yet. I'll teach *that* youngster manners yet, *though* his Hiawatha sells like hot cakes. It is I should think the biggest success Novello's have had since the Elijah.

Your remarks on Mendelssohn make me laugh. Why this fury? I daresay living as you do in *the* singing county in England, you have a regular bellyful of Mendelssohn every year & this must be somewhat sickening.

You are as bad as Elgar!

By the way the Dr (EE) was in town the other day & I saw a good deal of him. Have you read anything of his 'Cockaigne' & the string Sextet! I have, more than once. You must really come to London when they do 'Cockaigne' at the Phil. It's big, *important* stuff & full of fun in parts.

Alas what a chatter-box I am. Forgive this too easy, clumsy pen. Keep my remarks private as far as they effect N & Co. & Taylor.

Parry has just written an 'Ode to Music' words by Mr Benson (son of Archbishop B) of Eton College. We are printing it now. Will be sung at the opening of the new Concert Hall at the College in May . . .

Very truly, yours

A J JAEGER

John E. West (1863–1929) and Frederick George Edwards (1853–1909) were both musical advisers to Novello & Co for whom Jaeger also worked. Both were organists and church composers, and Edwards edited the Musical Times from 1897 to 1909. Clearly they were seen by the young generation as the voices of reaction and the status quo, during the Edwardian period, and even in 1923 when the composer Benjamin Dale wrote his A Song of Praise for the 269th Festival of the Sons of the Clergy, he looked to John E. West for an academic model in order to be appropriate for a stuffy occasion and produced some Parryesque opening pages redolent of many British choral works of similar intention.

*

(8)
CHARLES VILLIERS STANFORD to J. H. GREEN

15 March 1902

When I say this [about the failure to consult him about works to be performed; not confined, apparently, to the Festival Committee] I say so especially with regard to the apparently curt dismissal of Elgar's Dream of Gerontius.

A work which is the first English composition to be given at a Lower Rhine Festival (in consequence of which Sheffield upsets its programme to include it) *is not a work to be simply dismissed because A or B don't personally care for it.* It is the duty of a great choral society in a great town to let its public form their own judgement on such an important composition which has even reached with success Germany in its most Anglophobic temper. It is this spirit of private prejudices overriding public duties which has been at the root of the difficulties which so many composers have had during their lives. Look at Berlioz! Fancy a Philharmonic Committee in the '60's voting a performance of Faust! I can hear the easy way in which it would have been ruled out of Court. Surely it is for a choral society such as yours to lead and not to follow.

Stanford, an Irish Protestant, had no time for the Catholic theology of Elgar's The Dream of Gerontius, *about which he made his oft-quoted remark that 'it stinks of incense'. It is therefore of particular interest to find him championing performance of the work from the outset. Stanford was too intelligent and magnanimous to let sectarian differences prevent him from acclaiming genius when he saw it; this remark to Thomas F. Dunhill, a pupil, was probably just a witticism which Elgar's detractors later fell on with delight.*

(9)
CHARLES VILLIERS STANFORD to HANS RICHTER

50 Holland Street
Kensington w

March 26 1902

Lieber Hans,
Can you do me a kindness, you will I am sure if you can. But if you cannot, please do not mind. The 1st Irish Rhapsody for orchestra (Hans R *mit Erlaubniss gewidmet!*) is finished: & the premiere is to be at the Norwich Festival. I want to have it published in score and parts, otherwise it is as you know buried. There are no publishers in England for such music, and those that partially publish it do not make the works known abroad. Perhaps you would not mind writing a line to Schott about it? I do not know any of the members of his firm, only Volker who is their London Manager: & I would rather get headquarters than go to him.

The work ought to be profitable, & would also do as a piano piece if Busoni for example wd arrange it or some such person.

I am assuming of course that they would make some payment for it, either by percentage which is fairest, or otherwise. I am no longer in a position to or desirous of giving things away!

But I know that your influence with them in such matters would be very great, & I think you would not mind being my Godfather in this. It will not I think disgrace you musically!

Can you write me a line when you get this, as I go to Leipzig on April 5th for my opera, & I want if possible to set matters going before then. I have begun Rhapsody

No 2. But that can wait till we see what befalls No 1. If the Irish Symphony is any guide, it would pay a publisher well to publish this, especially at not too costly a price. And orchestras are multiplying here now as well as abroad, which want such pieces.

Forgive me for troubling you on your Blackpool holiday, and give my love to all the friends and family: including Klingsor.

Yrs ever

C. V. STANFORD

Later both Stanford's second and fourth Irish Rhapsodies were to be conducted by Mengelberg at their first performance. Klingsor was Richter's dog.

(10)
CHARLES VILLIERS STANFORD to HERBERT THOMPSON

Hotel Hauffe
Leipzig

Ap 27 1902

My dear H.T.

I dare say you will like to know about Much Ado here. It came out last Friday the 25th. The performance was *quite admirable*. You will also be glad to hear that it was quite an extraordinary reception, for CVS had to come out 16 times & the singers about 16 more. This for Leipzig is I am told quite unusual. It is to be done again next Wednesday, after when we go home arriving on May 2. The public & the theatre people have been most kind & enthusiastic. Now I don't want to tell you all this to blow my own trumpet, but I do think it is only right that English people should know how appreciative Leipzig was to the first English opera (of our generation at any rate) given on their stage.

You would have a good time on the Press notices! They are Professor to a man here, & they can't exactly fly in the face of a strong verdict, so they say that the applause was immense (stürmisch) thanks to a concourse of English who arrived from everywhere. (Two ladies came from Dresden, & the English here are mostly Conservatorium [ie students at the Leipzig conservatoire] & were at the Birthday Concert for the King which was on the same evening! So if the English make any noise clapping, it will have to be next Wednesday!) Then they say that they liked very much this & that & the other, but that of course it won't last. It's really funny. But on the whole they have been in print much less abusive than I was led to anticipate & some articles read between the lines are really appreciative. The future of the thing depends upon whether the public come to hear it, & next Wednesday will tell a good deal about that.

This reads like a confoundedly egotistical letter, but I thought you would like to know how generous and warm both the artists & the public here were to me.

Yrs ever

C.V. STANFORD

A resident here told me that the Wagnerians were taken aback at not having 6 horns 4 trombones & a couple of tubas blazing away all through!

When produced the previous year at Covent Garden, Stanford's opera Much Ado About Nothing *had only run for two performances.*

(11)
GRANVILLE BANTOCK to HERBERT THOMPSON

Birmingham and Midland Institute
School of Music
Paradise Street
Birmingham

June 3rd 1902

Dear Mr. Thompson

Many thanks for your kind letter of the 2nd inst. I will send you a few particulars in the form of an analytical synopsis and argument from the Poem, but in case it might be advisable for you to see the score, I hope to see Atkins at Worcester after Coronation week & will ask him to send the score on to you, so that you can compare my notes with the ms.

I was at the Strauss Concert in London last night, hence the delay in answering your letter. What a wonderful genius the man is!

Yours very truly

GRANVILLE BANTOCK

Bantock's 'Tone-Poem No. 5' The Witch of Atlas *was to be given at the Three Choirs Festival at Worcester on 10 September 1902. The Strauss Concert had been at Queen's Hall on 2 June, the second of two, at which* Don Juan, Till Eulenspiegel *and* Tod und Verklärung *were heard. Later in the year Bantock was bowled over by the first British performance of Strauss's* Ein Heldenleben, *a work which he later produced himself when conductor of the Liverpool Orchestral Society, on 6 February 1904. He had, meantime, with the Wolverhampton Festival Choral Society given Strauss's* Wandrers Sturmlied, *which he reported the chorus found a decided strain.*

(12)
EDWARD ELGAR to HERBERT THOMPSON

The Langham Hotel,
Portland Place,
London, w.

Dictated

5th June 1902

My dear Thompson
Very many thanks for your letter which I find here on my return from Germany.
We only arrived this morning early.

Thanks for all your congratulations. I wish you had been present. The performance was extremely good and uplifting.

As to the notes for "Gerontius', I quite appreciate the fact that the description for Worcester must be brief.

Yager's analysis is practically authorised by me as far as the choice of themes is concerned, but not always the actual naming of them.

There is a new shorter Führer by a German, which seems to be very practical. I forget who publishes it, but it was on sale during the 'fest', Dusseldorf. Yager would tell you where it might be procured. I am glad you were pleased about the Sheffield chorus for the Coronation Ode. I think I did the best thing, but we shall see.

If you would really prefer some of my own remarks concerning 'Gerontius,' I would be very glad to help you later; but at present I am extremely busy, and therefore do not write in my own hand.

Kind regards to Mrs. Thompson and yourself, in which my wife joins.

Yours always

ED: ELGAR

I think the shorthand writer's *spelling priceless* so I do not touch it.

(13)
EDWARD ELGAR to NICHOLAS KILBURN

Craeg Lea
Malvern

June 7:02

My dear Kilburn
We only reached home last night after our long German rambles: we had a complete rest and no letters forwarded – I fear you have been thinking evil things of me (don't) on acct. of my silence. 'High Tide' is impossible now, as I am, when permitted, engaged on mightier stuff. I should have delighted in assisting in your Middlesborough fest: but I cannot permit a new work.

We had a glorious time at Dusseldorf – Strauss' speech has been misunderstood (deliberately?) by the village organist type in England.*

Thanks for all you say.

My wife is tired and is resting in bed, but joins me in much love to you all.

Yours ever

EDWARD ELGAR

Strauss is absolutely great – wonderful and terrifying, but somewhat cynical – his music I mean. *He* is a real clever good man.

(14)
H. WALFORD DAVIES to HERBERT THOMPSON

Segenbalm
21 Fawley Road
W Hampstead
NW

June 10th 1902

Dear Mr Thompson

Thank you for your letter. I hope Novellos will soon send you a proof copy which will make my 'Temple' clear. I do not want to be my own analyst. But if the following explanations are any help, I shall be glad.

The Temple is laid out for three soloists, two choruses (a great and small), orchestra & organ. It is Narrative & Reflective, and only dramatic within the limits of graphic story-telling. Although the Soprano usually *narrates*, the chorus *reflects*, the tenor sings *Solomon's* words and the baritone *David's*, yet the chorus frequently at exciting places takes the narrative and occasionally echoes Solomon's words; and similarly the soloists share in the purely reflective numbers. All are treated as one organism, existent not to act scenes or impersonate characters but to simply tell the tale appropriately and give expression to the human emotions, thoughts, aspirations, or whatever they are to be called, which are created by the narrative.

The so called 'Narratives' of which there are six, are interspersed with reflective movements which are either suggested by the story or form an inseparable part of it (as in David's Thanksgiving and Solomon's Prayer). In these movements, as well as in the narratives, I have naturally tried to let the text dictate the musical form. This was my greatest problem, and called into existence abstract forms which are rather new, experimental and consequently imperfect. Two movements – a Choral Overture and Solomon's Prayer – combine variation-form with binary and ternary respectively, without actually being either. David's Thanksgiving with the people is first a combination of impassioned recit. with rondo, and finally an extended ternary. The Finale is combined fugue and ternary form, with a coda which almost amounts to a separate movement. Which then seem to me right and inevitable, – from the public and from critics I anticipate for my newness no welcome and for my

*See p. 22.

experiments no praise. I hope sometimes that this problem may be sufficiently solved to neither attract attention nor annoy. But my want of experience in large forms is against this.

You will know better than I at how much of this to hint in an analysis. It would seem best to infer that the little work attempts nothing new, and let it find its own feet. It may be that my own difficulties and ignorance have exaggerated the newness, and in that it humbly emulates Bach's methods, it is sufficiently old-fashioned to earn the blame of some or retrogress.

I hold a presumptuous belief that Opera and Wagner has damaged our wits while they enriched our language; that they have had (temporarily) vicious influence on the highest abstract forms; and that the Bach of 1985 will write symphonies not symphonic poems, oratorios not dramatic somethings; or – better still – new and undreamt of abstract choral works, of the lineage of Bach, Beethoven & Brahms. When Parry's "Blest Pair" will still be treasured as a great and early example of some new choral school.

I give myself away, perhaps, tediously to you. I need hardly ask you to keep this gift confidentially, and forgive a certain flavour of implied self-importance.

Very truly yours

H WALFORD DAVIES

Walford Davies's The Temple *was produced at the Coronation Three Choirs Festival at Worcester, during a meeting that included Elgar's* The Dream of Gerontius *(still the subject of comment for its Catholicism) and also the visit of the American composer Horatio Parker to conduct his* Legend of St Christopher, Part III. *Walford Davies's score did not have sufficient rehearsal time allotted to it, and although it was more or less 'all right on the night' it received some adverse criticism, and was thus sufficiently cast into the shade by the rest of the festival that it was not taken up elsewhere. When his short oratorio* Everyman *became a great hit two years later this earlier score was eclipsed. Walford Davies made no secret of his antipathy to opera, a negative influence which later may have reached a wide audience through his broadcasts about music. Yet in his dozen or so big choral works it is the uninhibited elements of the drama which he needed to project to ensure their success. A modern performance of* The Temple, *playing up the dramatic narratives in contrast with its broadly tuneful Choral Overture and effective choruses might well reveal a score which choral societies would find worthwhile: it is yet another work of the Edwardian period for which there is no substitute for a good modern performance.*

(15)
EDWARD ELGAR to HERBERT THOMPSON

[Paper with Worcestershire Philharmonic Society letter-head]

Malvern

Sep 1st 02

My dear Thompson

I am so very sorry to have kept you so long without definite news of the ode [i.e. *The Coronation Ode*]: Mr Bennett's analysis is not ready yet.

My idea was to write the ode on broad majestic lines without undue complication – you will see my trail however in passages like 3 to 4 & much else. The piano score gives, as usual, little idea of the orchestration & still less of the employment of the Military Band – in one place at least there is a device which will delight your soul – that is the uncritical part of it – at 66 where the choir sing the big tune the M. Band suddenly bursts in with 32 ! See score.

You will see I have used the Trio of 'Pomp & Circumstance' No. 1 as the climax of the first number 25 . The whole thing (the first No) is of course an 'address' to Sovereignty in the abstract – very different is No. 2. We are allowed to show a personal affection to our Queen – Turning the [same direction] in harmony at 'Northern Sea'.

No 3 is frankly military, or rather naval & military & means 'fight'. At 36 'So shalt thou rest in *Peace*' I have kept the audacious military tread going in the background and the whole idea is 'if you are ready to fight there will be peace'! – which is true I believe: It looks, at first, as though the vows sh^d have been set *peace*fully – but I don't think so – the promised peace in this case depends upon the military preparedness, hence the setting.

Nos 4 & 5 are obvious in construction. Page 56 – I did not make a great burst on 'great' because here the 'greatness' seemed to depend upon wisdom, truth & blessing more than the military aspect. The movement is of course 'the' tune again & fraction of the 1st movement.

You will notice that as a 'link' I use the phrase 1 in several places.

You must forgive my writing however. I have just at this moment heard that my dear old mother has passed away after long and weary suffering.

Yours ever

EDW^d ELGAR

Elgar's Coronation Ode *was the most extended of many patriotic works written to celebrate the Coronation of Edward VII, postponed from the previous year owing to the King's operation for appendicitis. It incorporated the tune of the first* Pomp and Circumstance *march set to the words of* 'Land of Hope and Glory'.

(16)
SIR CHARLES VILLIERS STANFORD to HANS RICHTER

[*Original letter in German, see facsimile. This translation by Lionel Carley.*]

Nov 14 1902

Dear Hans

I have written to Forsyth regarding a solo quartet rehearsal (for the Te Deum). But he tells me that the tenor & bass are in Manchester, and that a piano rehearsal here is impossible. Now look! The quartets are *very difficult*, and without a piano rehearsal you will have a bad time of it. Albani (with Crossley, Lloyd & Santley)* had *three*!! In Cambridge too, where the quartets were very nicely sung by four virtually unknown singers, I had 3 piano rehearsals. Please send the tenor & bass here for at least one rehearsal. Forsyth could arrange it with Sillinger, and I will rehearse the quartets at the piano myself. I know the difficulties in them, and consider it *just about impossible* to get the quartets to come off without a piano rehearsal.

Forgive me for troubling you. The work is quite unknown in Manchester. I intend to come to Manchester on Wednesday afternoon 26th. If there is a choir rehearsal on Wednesday evening, I would come earlier, if not, then in the evening. So please send me a postcard.

Ever yours

C.V. STANFORD

Stanford's Te Deum, *Op 66, had been written for the Leeds Festival of 1898, in commemoration of the sixtieth year of Queen Victoria's reign. It is an extended work in six movements, in which the solo quartet is always used together as a group, and in the second and fourth movements appears without the chorus.*

*Probably the leading quartet of vocal soloists of their day: Emma Albani (sop) (1874–1930); Ada Crossley (cont) (1874–1929); Edward Lloyd (ten) (1845–1927); Charles Santley (bar) (1834–1922). Lloyd officially retired in 1900, the year in which he created the role of Gerontius at the premiere of Elgar's score. Santley was knighted in 1907 and did not finally retire until 1915.

50, HOLLAND STREET.
KENSINGTON. W.

Nov 14. 1902

Lieber Hans! ich habe an Forsyth über ein Soloquartett Probe (für das Te Deum) geschrieben. Er schreibt mir aber dass der Tenor u. Bass, sind von Manchester, und dass eine Clavier Probe hier unmöglich ist. Guck einmal an! Die Quartetten sind <u>sehr</u> <u>schwer</u>, und ohne Clavier-probe Du wirst eine schlechte Zeit haben. Albani (mit Crossley Lloyd u. [illegible]) hat <u>drei</u> platt!! Auch für Cambridge wo die Quartetten von vier ziemlich unbekannten Sänger sehr hübsch gesungen waren, habe ich 3

(a) Stanford's original German text

Clavier Proben gehabt. Bitte schicke Sie den Piano à Vier wenigstens für ein Probe hierher. Forsyth könnte es mit Billiger arrangieren, und ich werde die Quartetten selbst probieren am Clavier. Ich kenne die Schwierigkeiten davon, und halte es brauche für unmöglich die Quartetten ohne Clavier-Probe wirken zu machen. Verzeih' dass ich dich belästige. Das Werk ist in Manchester ganz unbekannt.

Ich beabsichtige am Mittwoch
Nachmittag 26th nach Manchester zu
kommen. Wenn es eine Chor
Probe Mittwoch Abend giebt
ich würde früher kommen, wenn
nicht, abends. Bitte also um
eine Postkarte.

Immer dein

C.V. Stanford

(17)
CHARLES MANNERS to HERBERT THOMPSON

[*Letterhead of Moody-Manners Opera Company Limited*]

Tyne Theatre
Newcastle-on-Tyne

3rd March 1903

Dear Mr Thompson
I cannot let our visit to Leeds pass without thanking you most sincerely from the bottom of my heart for your very kind help last week. As you are aware, it was nothing to me whether one person came in or a million from the Box Office point of view but of course I am intensely interested in trying to raise Grand Opera to that position which it has never had before, and by your fair criticism I could see that you

quite understand my efforts. If I may be allowed to say so what I do so like about your criticisms is that while pointing out where we are wrong, you at the same time point out the difficulties that we have to contend against. Mr Johnson of the Manchester Guardian damms [sic] our efforts no matter what they are and in my opinion he says everything is bad and never gives a helping hand in any way whatever. The last visit to Manchester we certainly had more help from the press than we ever had before but I am afraid it is too late now and it will take years to get Manchester in any way interested because, hard as the press are on us I think the public partly through their own fault and partly through the press are perfectly indifferent. After all I don't think it is conceited for me to state what is the fact viz: – That no other Company has ever travelled so large before and yet no other Company of anything like the size has ever yet played to such low prices. Again we have successfully conquered the low pitch and our Costumes are better than what have been done before. I think this is all true and fact. Naturally I have ideas and ambitions that I hope to fulfil in Cities like Leeds but they are no good talking about until they are fulfilled, or at any rate nearly being fulfilled.

In the meantime let me again offer you my most sincere and heartfelt thanks and Believe me.

Very Truly Yours

CHARLES MANNERS

(18)
*EDWARD ELGAR to THE DAILY TELEGRAPH

24 March 1903

I have rarely heard such finished musicianly singing, and have never had less trouble to get my exact reading – often a difficulty with one rehearsal; this was made easy for me by the splendid training of Mr. Whewall, and by the alert, attentive and friendly attitude of the chorus. The tone is magnificent – silvery, yet solid, well-balanced and sonorous, and the 'attack' fine: the infinitesimal trifles – not shortcomings – which did occur were caused merely by the want of more time in rehearsals with the orchestra. I place the chorus in the highest rank, and I thank the members for giving me the opportunity of hearing a performance of my work almost flawless.

It is well known that the first performance of The Dream of Gerontius *was something of a disaster, though ultimately even that performance was of a masterpiece recognized. Yet gradually the work was performed: the* Prelude *and* Angel's Farewell *at Queen's Hall conducted by Henry Wood in February 1901; a cut version without the Demon's chorus in Part II at Worcester in May 1901. The breakthrough came with the celebrated performances at Düsseldorf, first in December 1901 (at a time of virulent anti-British feeling owing to the Boer War) and secondly on 19 May 1902 after which Richard Strauss made his celebrated toast to Elgar 'the first English progressivist'. It started an Elgar boom in Germany – and for instance the* Prelude *and* Angel's Farewell *opened the first of Busoni's concerts of new works in Berlin on 8 November 1902. In England Gerontius was still slow to take off. There were, particularly, doubts expressed about performing such a Roman Catholic work in an Anglican*

Cathedral. *This performance was by the North Staffordshire Choir trained by James Whewall – the same choir that had given the first performance of* King Olaf *seven years before. The performance was before an enthusiastic capacity audience in the Victoria Hall Hanley, under Elgar's baton. It finally established the score as a repertoire work in the United Kingdom.*

(19)
WILLIAM WALLACE to JOSEF HOLBROOKE

75 Chelsea Gardens
SW

24.3.03

Dear Holbrooke

I hope you are satisfied with the results of last night – artistically at any rate it is a long time since I have seen so many musicians at a concert of the kind, and certainly there was no lack of interest in or of approval of your work. The only paper I have seen is the DT, a cutting from which I enclose tho' you may have seen it already. Taken in connection with what has been written of other men I think it is very complimentary.

I hope you will not have any letters to write to critics! If you are inclined to do so, write the letters by all means but do not send them!

A very great change has come over criticism since Bantock's concert in /96 when there was a slating all round, so thank your stars that the pioneer work has made critics alive to the necessity of speaking respectfully of British music!

I am heartily glad all went off so well. You had the entire sympathy of your audience, and I did not hear a word *spoken* of your work that you would have taken objection to. Let me know when & where we can meet to discuss things. *This* week I am pretty fully engaged but on or after the 30th we might have a meeting somewhere.

All good luck to you. You know I am at one with you in all you do.

Yours always

WILLIAM WALLACE

Josef Holbrooke, composer and pianist, as well as trying to launch himself as composer, spent much energy in promoting chamber concerts of music by his young contemporaries. In fact the concert mentioned, at Steinway Hall, was of music by Holbrooke himself. The Daily Telegraph *reviewed it as follows:*

> *Mr Josef Holbrooke, who began last night at Steinway Hall a series of chamber concerts of modern British music, has an honourable place among our younger composers. For his years he has accomplished a great deal of work, serious in its complexion and elevated in its aim. That acknowledgment of his talent has only come thus far from the few is quite in accordance with the established rule in this country. But Mr Holbrooke need not despair. If England is also to appreciate her musical sons when their purpose is an earnest one, appreciation may be all the warmer when it does come. Last night no less*

than seven works, large and small, gave evidence of Mr Holbrooke's capability and taste in the direction of chamber music. A Trio in G minor, a Serenade for 'cello and pianoforte, a Ballade for violin and pianoforte, and a Quintet in F minor were the more important of the composer's offerings. For all these it would be both easy and pleasant to find words of praise, seeing that Mr Holbrooke does not shape his music in the crabbed and pedantic style affected by some of the younger generation of composers. We do not think that this musician's ideas lend themselves too happily to the limited medium of the string quartet and the pianoforte. His themes often seem to yearn for the fuller expansion of the orchestra. Still, for all that, Mr Holbrooke's music is skilfully written and one can never term it uninteresting. This means much in the case of a young and aspiring composer, and more should be said later on, if present auguries hold good. Mr Holbrooke's associates last night were Miss Fanny Eveleigh, Miss Emmeline Chant, Mr John Saunders, Mr Charles Woodhouse, Mr B. Withers, and Mr Charles Winterbottom.

(20)
SIR HUBERT PARRY to ADOLPH BRODSKY

Royal College of Music
Prince Consort Road
South Kensington
London s w

Sept 28 1903

Dear Mr. Brodsky
We are going to start a new scheme for the encouragement of native talent, and hope to give an Orchestral Concert of works by young British Composers early next term. Compositions are to be submitted and chosen by experts for performance. Do you happen to know any young composers who would like to submit compositions to be considered by the experts? If so please let me know.

Yours very sincerely

C.HUBERT H.PARRY

Brodsky was the Principal of the Royal Manchester College of Music in Manchester. Similar letters were sent to the Heads of other Music Colleges in the U.K.

*

(21)
SIR CHARLES VILLIERS STANFORD to
W. S. HANNAM

Nov. 15 1903

The whole situation is ludicrous and unprecedented in any Festival. The result of the programme is a long series of solemn funeral music, without a single point of relief. The mornings would have been excellent (with the substitution of *Israel* for *Elijah*) and if the evenings had had one brilliant or lively *piece de resistance* in each. But you have got *Everyman* (the deepest of tragedies), *The Burial March of Dundee* (another tragedy) and *The Witch's Daughter* which sounds like a third. It is all Black-edged, and it will be damnably depressing. *Tod* without *Verklärung* and ending with *Golden Legend* which is dead played out.

A little timely consultation would have prevented it; but as they made their own programme, I said nothing beyond suggesting alterations when they wanted them: and I must be content to take, and I shall have to, whether the Committee think so or not, the severe criticisms which will be most certainly made, on my own shoulders ... The report will probably say that the programme has been arranged 'after consultation with me'. This must not be allowed to pass uncorrected. In no important particular was I consulted at all.

(22)
SIR HUBERT PARRY to ADOLPH BRODSKY

Royal College of Music
Prince Consort Road
South Kensington
London s w

Private

Jany 7 1904

My Dear Mr Brodsky

I am driven by circumstances over which I have no control to appeal to you for a candid and confidential opinion on Miss Neruda's* powers and ability as a teacher of pianoforte.

She appears to be a great favourite of the Queen's and I have had a communication from His Majesty's Secretary which necessitates my getting some really trustworthy information about her – And I don't know where I am likely to get it if not from you. So I hope you will excuse the liberty I am taking. I am told she is your principal teacher of the pianoforte at Manchester and I shall be most grateful if you can tell me whether you find she is a successful teacher; whether she is thoroughly mistress of her subject and competent to take charge of the most advanced pupils;

---

*Neruda was the name of a distinguished Czech musical family, of which Wilma Neruda (1839–1911) was celebrated in England as a violinist. First married to Frederick Norman, she performed as Norman-Neruda. Norman died in 1885, and in 1888 she married Sir Charles Hallé. She was conferred 'Violinist to the Queen' by Queen Alexandra, and this must explain the interest of the Queen.

whether her pupils find her sympathetic and inspiring, and whether the results of her teaching are thoroughly satisfactory. I must beg you to treat this as purely confidential, as so far the matter is entirely between me and Their Majesties, and no one ought to know anything about it – yet. I hope you are well and wish you a happy New Year.

Yours very sincerely

C HUBERT H PARRY

Parry did not appoint Miss Neruda. In a letter dated 30 Sept 1907 now in the Parry Room Library at the RCM, he wrote to Charles Cecil 'I had strong reasons for delaying'. The King supported Parry but later the Queen persuaded both the King and the Prince of Wales to support her. 'The most hopeful way of avoiding a crisis is to appoint no one' wrote Parry.

*

(23)
WILLIAM WALLACE to THE TIMES

Published in the issue dated 30 May, 1904*

75, Chelsea Gardens
s w
May 23 [1904]

Sir,—As the first concert under the auspices of the Palmer Fund has just taken place, the present seems the moment opportune for discussing the plan and purpose of the gift. I offer no apology for inquiring into the matter. Were it one that concerned solely the Royal College of Music, criticism would be silenced; but as the programme states that it is 'the wish both of the council of the Royal College of Music and of the founder that the influence of the fund should be far-reaching, and in a sense national,' I accept the aim as being towards the advancement of British music, and feel that I am in order in commenting on this or any other 'national' endowment.

When the fund was announced in your columns about a year ago, it was welcomed by musicians as the first serious step on the part of a private benefactor towards doing for the composer what had already been done to an extravagant extent for the instrumentalist and singer. One hoped that it would be truly national without any gloss as to its being 'primarily applicable for the benefit of past and present pupils of the Royal College of Music.' One felt, too, that the absolutely unknown composer was at last to have his chance. Unfortunately, the first concert has not justified these hopes. The programme states that no fewer than 42 compositions were sent in, some in reply to invitation, some no doubt unsolicited. The chosen composers, including those reserved, number 11, three of whom have distinctly foreign names. The majority hail from the Royal College of Music, and only two are names which have not been met with on any programme. Two works, moreover, out of the 12 have already been performed at Royal College of Music

*Although very long, this is an abbreviated transcript of the published letter, from which some 10 column inches have been omitted.

concerts, which invited public criticism. It is also known that certain composers did not send in any work, while others declined the invitation to submit compositions which might have to compete with purely student efforts. The terms of the 'invitation' duly emphasized the fact that 'the fund is primarily applicable for the benefit of past and present pupils of the Royal College of Music.' With this I have no quarrel. When the Royal College of Music is fortunate enough to obtain a gift such as Mr. Palmer's munificence and public spirit have prompted him to devote to the one out of the many schools of music, it is only right that the Royal College of Music should favour 'primarily' if not entirely its own pupils. But the extension of the fund so as to patronize (shall I call it?) students from other schools seems to me to set the Royal College of Music in a position to which it is scarcely entitled—namely, that of being the authoritative body *par excellence* to be entrusted with the future of British music.

That certain of the younger school have chosen to lose the chance of a public performance, a considerable sacrifice on their part, rather than acknowledge this assumption of supreme jurisdiction—this seeming assertion that the Royal College of Music above all her sister schools *suprema indicat orbes terrarum*—is significant of much. The programme refers to a committee of 'experts' of the Royal College of Music and the Royal Academy of Music. I cannot but regret that the older school should have consented to act on any conditions whatsoever with the one to which the trust was 'primarily applicable,' so long as any invidious distinction was to be made as to what students had the prior claim. Such a gift, in order to be truly 'national,' should have been entrusted to all the musical bodies in the country, and not to one merely, no matter what its standing was, with power to include at its own sweet will some other.

No musician can close his eyes to the fact that the Royal College of Music is associated with a certain phase of thought which is academically antagonistic, if not openly inimical, to every modern tendency. It is idle to point to the performance of a work by Wagner, Tchaikovsky or Richard Strauss at some college concert. That no more affects the cardinal policy of the college than a cut finger affects a man's backbone; for even though at future Palmer concerts there may occasionally be produced works showing touch with later developments of music, the Royal College of Music traditions may prove irresistible, and, when the novelty of the thing has worn off, we may find the fund devoted to the production of works which perpetuate the particular style affected by the Royal College of Music, a style which many of us feel has appreciably retarded the advancement of the art in this country. . . .

Let us consider how the matter affects the young composer. It is almost a truism to assert that the more original a musical work is, the more incomprehensible it will be to the mandarin class of imagination. He who hears new sounds, whose mind is occupied with the pure *pensée musicale*, must, from the very nature of his thought, produce work that seems chaotic to the more 'orthodox' intellect. The original thinker in music is scarcely likely to be content with platitudes; the technique of modern composition and orchestration has been carried even beyond what only a few years ago one considered the extreme limits of possibility. Whether this is the swing of the pendulum, the reaction which follows one phase and precedes a new static quality in the art, I am not prepared to say. It is sufficient to recognize its existence. Considering the uncertain state of equilibrium in which music is at present, what man would venture to declare that a work outside the frankly obvious was not of 'sufficient merit'? Suppose such a work were rejected, and subsequently met with favour from some conductor or some festival committee resolved to be independent of Kensington-gore—suppose it were hailed as a great achievement—in what position would the 'experts' find themselves? The fund is quite old enough for such a contingency to have arisen; it may yet arise; I feel safe in saying that it will surely arise.

I have spoken plainly as to my views of the fitness of the Royal College of Music for administering any fund which shall have for its goal the advancement of British music. For aught I know, the Palmer Fund may be founded upon the canon law of music as laid down by the academics, and the college may claim sanctuary owing to its being builded upon what it fondly imagines to be the impregnable rock of classicism—the shifting sands of the obsolete, as many of us think. Music, however, is eternally a new thing and demands an unselfish fostering to bring it into full maturity and honour. It is not by means of one annual concert of British music that we shall discover the new voice among us. It is not by the help of 'experts' that the blythe spirit will find wings to challenge the sun. The fund has been inaugurated with a flourish of trumpets; it will collapse like a pricked bagpipe unless some vigour, some healthy, active energy is driven into its administrators, so that they will have ever before them the truly 'national' aim of its founder and not the petty and 'primary' exaltation of the efforts of those who are 'present and past students of the Royal College of Music.' We want British music not Royal-College-of-Music music; and, until the principle of liberty of thought finds its due acknowledgment in the prospectus issued by the trustees of the fund, we shall certainly gain nothing by Mr. Palmer's generosity. I am convinced that the newer and better spirit of music exists at the present moment, and I am equally sure of the way to discover it.

I am, yours,

WILLIAM WALLACE

The Patron's Fund was founded in 1903 by Mr S. Ernest Palmer who handed the Council of the Royal College of Music the sum of £20,000 (supplemented in 1906 by a further £7000), the income from which was to be devoted to the selection and performance of works by British composers, the assistance of British performers, the provision of travelling scholarships and helping with the publication of works. The fund, though primarily for past and present pupils of the RCM, could be extended to any other British subjects. The pattern was an orchestral concert in the Summer and a chamber concert around Christmas. We saw Parry inviting the submission of scores in letter 20 above. In the concert under discussion, which took place at St James's Hall on 20 May 1904, eight composers were represented, three – Bridge (twice), Hurlstone and Holst – from the College, three – Carse, Bowen and Paul Corder – from the Academy, and Henry Geehl from the profession at large. Geehl was later well-known in brass band circles and scored Elgar's Severn Suite in 1930.

William Wallace, later to be the Secretary of the Royal Philharmonic Society and reputedly the composer of the first British orchestral tone-poem, canvassed support for his views from Robin Legge of The Daily Telegraph who sympathised, off the record, and Herbert Thompson of The Yorkshire Post who declined to discuss it in print. In fact Wallace's proposal, which was to abolish the public concerts and substitute trial rehearsals, came to pass after World War I when the arrangements for the concerts were reformed (see letter 94). Nevertheless, Wallace's antagonism to the College resulted in them taking a 'strong view' of his protest. Arnold Bax's account of a try-out session, before the works were chosen for the actual concert* suggests that the trial rehearsals that Wallace desired actually took place on this occasion before the concert ensued.

*In his autobiography *Farewell, My Youth* (pp 25–27) Arnold Bax describes the trial run-through at the RCM of the submitted scores.

(24)
JOSEF HOLBROOKE to HERBERT THOMPSON

Kelvin
Rotherham
Mon/Oct. 4 04

Dear Mr Thompson
Altho' I can not claim any acquaintance with you of an extended order, I would like to tell you how I feel regarding Q[ueen] Mab. The band has run it thro' *once* in London, and I have another rehearsal in Leeds on Thursday at *10.45*. Now without being ungrateful to *anyone* in this matter, I must say, that having been *asked* for a work, it is the duty of all concerned to give me the *instruments* I want, and 4 rehearsals if necessary. What is the use of the work being performed if it is 'ambled thro'? – no credit is given to anyone, and I am of course the chief sufferer. Naturally I take a lot of this to heart, there is no *Dulcimer, Xylophone,* & 2 horns short. I have to bring Mr Henry Wood's *Tenor Drum myself* to Leeds else I should not have had that. Is this the customary treatment to young composers? – Of course I need not impress upon you how grateful I am to Mr Spark, that I have clearly shown I think, but I feel quite upset at the orchestral aspect, the work is complicated to a degree, unless these men have much rehearsal, it matters not a whit abt the individual players – the ensemble I want, and I feel antagonism from the players, and I need not say, not much co-operation from the conductor.

All this sounds bad, but it is better for one to speak, than to wait, and say that I am far from satisfied with my work.

The chorus was splendid for me on Sun[day] as I knew they would be.

I have written to Mr Spark abt. this, but I fear he is in a difficult position. I wonder whether to withdraw my work if it does not go to my satisfaction?

Apologizing for writing to you at such length, but I feel a friend in you!

ever yours

JOSEF HOLBROOKE

Queen Mab, *for an extravagantly large orchestra and* ad lib. *chorus, was inscribed to Frederick Spark, the secretary of the Leeds Festival committee. The title-page of the vocal scores, extravagantly printed in mauve and crimson with very 'modern' lettering, underlined the aura of an* avant garde *work for the audience of the day.*

(25)
RALPH VAUGHAN WILLIAMS to THE MORNING POST

Published in the issue dated Monday September 26 1904 p 6

Sep 24 [1904]
10 Barton Street
Westminster

Sir
Your correspondent, Mr Stewart Gowe, is of the opinion that there are no folk-songs left in Essex. Last Spring I spent a fortnight in an Essex village only twenty miles from London, and there and in the neighbourhood I noted down over fifty genuine folk-songs. Most of the songs had beautiful and interesting tunes. As to the words, some were old ballads such as "Robin Hood and the Pedlar" or "The Green Glove", some came off the ballad sheets, as for instance "The Lost Lady" and others were regular country songs such as "The Painful Plough". Has Mr Gowe carefully explored his own district and made sure that the traditional songs have died out?

Yours etc

R. VAUGHAN WILLIAMS

The village in which Vaughan Williams made his collection was Ingrave, near Brentwood, where the Misses Heatley of Ingrave Rectory discovered elderly residents of the parish who could still sing the 'old ballads' and introduced Vaughan Williams to them. He noted that 'they had no idea that the folk song still survived there until I suggested the possibility to them'. (See Vaughan Williams's subsequent letter to The Morning Post *printed in Ursula Vaughan Williams's biography* R.V.W. A Biography of Ralph Vaughan Williams *(OUP, 1964) pp 69–70).*

(26)
GEORGE BENNETT to HERBERT THOMPSON

Lincoln Triennial Festival [letter head]
June 28th and 29th 1905

Nov 13 1904

Dear Mr Thompson
From the enclosed you will see that we have fixed the dates for our Festival, & that Elgar & Cowen are coming to conduct works. I wanted to get Stanford but he could not promise to come, although he said he would come if he could get away. I have taken out the Unfinished Symphony from afternoon Cathedral service to make way for Elgar's Prelude etc. from Gerontius, & had put down Schubert's Sym. in C to precede Israel in Egypt in the evening, but I am now inclined to think that the

Unfinished (although so much played, it has never been done in the Cathedral here) would be better as I think it must be quite 20 minutes shorter than the C major (in either case I should leave out the repeats), & as Israel has so many low Choruses (& we then also have two Jubilant Hymns) the Unfinished might make a pleasant contrast. Further I shall not have probably more than 12. 10. 8. 8. 8. strings & the C major seems to require such a strong body of them. But the principal question is that of length of Programme. Can you tell me what is the length in performance of Israel, my impression is that it is something between 1–45 & 2 hours.

Have you a copy of your analysis of Dvorak's Te Deum that you would kindly let me see. For the *Cathedral* books we shall only insert short notes *without* music type, if you would let me use a *shortened* form of your analysis (if it is a *full* analysis) I should be very glad. I am just in the throes of employing the soloists & band –

With kind regards

Yours sincerely

GEORGE BENNETT

(27)
HERBERT BREWER to HERBERT THOMPSON

Palace Yard
Gloucester
March 16 1905

My dear Thompson

It was awfully good of you to take the trouble over the words of my Worcester tune. I got a copy of the book & digested the poem. I like it very much, especially the last two stanzas, but I have my doubts about the Worcester folk taking to it as kindly as we should, they are queer folk over there, I mean the parson element. You remember 'Gerontius' in 1902! If it had been for the Festival proper I shouldn't have hesitated, but the Sunday performance is a *Service*. I shall keep these words up my sleeve for a future occasion. I have just come across Dryden's 'Te Deum', this seems most suitable. Do you know of any setting of this? I wish you would say on a p.c. if it has been done. I saw Atkins & *The* baby on Tuesday, the latter I kissed for you, which delighted the fond parents he was so overcome & so excited that he kissed him three times! It would be impossible to kiss their nurse by mistake, she is about 120, this entre nous. . . .

Brewer's work for Worcester was A Song of Eden. *The baby is Wulstan Atkins, later a celebrated Elgarian and author of a study of the friendship between his father Sir Ivor Atkins and Elgar; based on family papers.*

(28)

SIR EDWARD ELGAR to ADOLF BORSDORF

Plas Gwyn
Hereford
February 17, 1906

Dear Mr. Borsdorf,
Forgive me for troubling you but you are always kind to students and I am one. Will you tell me if it is 'asking too much' of four horns in unison to play this passage, in moderate *tempo*: they have clarinets, violas, 2nd violins *with* them & the chorus is against them.

[In fact from *The Kingdom*]

I want the tone as firm and rich* as it can be: I think it feels good (to me) but it looks rather formidable.

Kindest regards,

Yours sincerely

EDWARD ELGAR

*and '*squeezed out*'.

F. A. Borsdorf (1854–1923) was the first horn of the London Symphony Orchestra at the time of this letter. The passage quoted by Elgar comes from The Kingdom, *and will be found near the beginning of the chorus 'In the Name of Jesus Christ' at cue 113 (p. 110 of the vocal score).*

(29)

TOBIAS MATTHAY to THE PHILHARMONIC SOCIETY

21 Arkwright Road
South Hampstead
N W
28th January 1907

To the Directors of the Philharmonic Society
London
Gentlemen,
Mr Berger, in reply to a letter of mine which I asked him to lay before you, begs me to re-consider my decision to sever my connexion with the Society.

As I have also been appealed to by one of the Directors, privately, I feel compelled to state my reasons to you, although these must have been self-evident.

The Society has consistently ignored its DUTIES towards British Art all through its career. Lately this has been so accentuated that to every out-sider it must appear as a deliberate *boycott* of the British Instrumentalist.

This year's prospectus, instead of showing any improvement in this respect, is worse than ever, seeing the number of British Pianists and String Artists now so prominently before the public of this country, Germany and America, and whose great 'drawing' powers cannot be questioned.

For this reason I felt it my duty, as a Patriot, to take the step I did. Since, however, I now learn from my personal friends on the Directorate that there is an intention to repair the slights thus inflicted upon native talent, I will suspend my intention to resign for another month, and will await the publication of the Society's amended prospectus.

Believe me,

Yours faithfully

TOBIAS MATTHAY

Francesco Berger was the Philharmonic Society's Secretary from 1884 to 1911. The Philharmonic Society, London's senior concert promoting body, had been founded in 1813, and in 1912 became the Royal Philharmonic Society. In 1907 the Society was successfully attempting to resolve the financial crisis caused by the competition of Henry Wood with the Queen's Hall Orchestra, and the newly founded London Symphony Orchestra, by engaging famous soloists and distinguished guest conductors.

(30)
WILLIAM WALLACE to JOSEF HOLBROOKE

10.11.07

Dear Holbrooke

You are not to blame *me* for the tardy acknowledgement of your guinea, but rather that unbusinesslike organisation which calls itself the Society of British Composers.

Mrs Delius was here yesterday afternoon, and Delius himself turned up late. As far as I could make out nothing definite has been done about his scheme beyond getting Elgar as President of his New Society. Apparently he has not the ghost of a notion how to form a committee or to arrive at some way of making it a working affair. The great meeting that was to have taken place, of which Legge was to have given me notice, has not come off yet, and another that D[elius] talked about, is likely to be as mythical as the other.

I do not think any of these men will get beyond the talking stage if they go on as they are doing. I have given D[elius]. one practical suggestion after another. He has not criticized them – nor adopted them nor even rejected them. He has just said they are good, and there we stick! And he comes here & tells me – ME – ME – that no one has ventured to protest against any of the notorious abuses!!!

It is my conviction that the moral courage of the composer is nil, and that he is only too glad to see some one else doing the job while he runs away and hides! They are a fearsome lot!

Yrs always

WW

For most of the second half of the nineteenth century, the young British composer had to turn to August Manns at the Crystal Palace in the hope of a performance of his orchestral works, and indeed, a large number of new scores were first heard in this way. In the 1890s other centres of performance began to grow up, including the Bournemouth Municipal Orchestra conducted by Dan Godfrey and the New Brighton Tower Orchestra at the Merseyside pleasure resort of New Brighton, conducted by Granville Bantock. Slightly later, an outstanding promoter of private concerts was the Duke of Devonshire, whose private orchestra at Eastbourne conducted by Pierre Tas also performed many British works of the period.

There were many attempts to promote British music as a recognizable entity after 1900, possibly the earliest being the British music evenings which Henry Wood introduced in the Promenade Concerts from 1902 onward. Apart from Balfour Gardiner's concerts of 1912–13 (see pages 46–7) the two most effective such initiatives were the Society of British Composers (see pages 2–3), which lasted for ten years, and the shorter-lived but more prestigious Musical League. The latter was apparently Delius's idea and it resulted in two festivals being promoted. The first was given in September 1909 in Liverpool, when three concerts were given. The second was in Birmingham, where from 30 December 1912 to 3 January 1913, four concerts took place.

(31)
THE MUSICAL LEAGUE to THE TIMES

Published in the issue dated 23 March 1908, p. 12

TO THE EDITOR OF THE TIMES

Sir, –
We ask you to give publicity to the fact that we, the undersigned, have formed a new musical society, to be known as the Musical League. The objects of the league may be summarized as follows:–

(a) To hold an annual festival of the utmost attainable perfection in a town where conditions are favourable.

(b) To devote the programmes of these festivals to new or unfamiliar compositions, English and foreign.

(c) To make use, as far as possible, of the existing musical organisations of each district, and of the services of local musicians.

(d) To establish a means by which composers, executive musicians, and amateurs may exchange ideas.

While fully aware that much good has been done in this direction, we feel there is still room for a body which will make such performances its principal aim, and that the Musical League can accomplish this without in any way prejudicing the institutions already established in this country.

It is hoped that the support of municipal authorities in carrying out the aims of the league will be secured.

The conviction that this league will exercise a beneficial influence on the progress of music in this country is based on the knowledge of the work accomplished by the Tonkünstler–Verein, which has done so much to foster an interest in the art throughout Germany by raising the standard of musical culture in provincial towns, by the encouragement of local enterprise and by affording musicians invaluable opportunities for social intercourse.

The Musical League can only be established on a broad basis by the hearty co-operation of all who are interested in the art, whether as composers, executive artists, teachers, or amateurs; and to all these we now make appeal.

We are able to announce that Dr. Hans Richter has kindly consented to direct the first festival of the league, which, it is hoped, may be held at Manchester in the autumn of this year.

The subscription for membership will be one guinea per annum.

Those who are in sympathy with the aims of the Musical League may obtain further particulars from the hon. secretary, to whom application for admission to membership should be made.

We remain, Sir, yours truly,

EDWARD ELGAR (President).
FREDERICK DELIUS (Vice-President).
ALEXANDER C. MACKENZIE.
ADOLPH BRODSKY.
W.G.MCNAUGHT.
HENRY J. WOOD.
GRANVILLE BANTOCK.
PHILIP L. AGNEW.
PERCY PITT.
NORMAN O'NEILL.
HARRY EVANS.
C. COPELY HARDING, Hon. Secretary, 11 Waterloo-street, Birmingham.
J.D. JOHNSTON, Hon. Treasurer, 14, Chapel-street, Liverpool.

(32)
SIR CHARLES VILLIERS STANFORD to HANS RICHTER

50, Holland Street,
Kensington. W.

Dear Richter

I wrote to you some time since a letter introducing to you a young English musician of very great gift. I expected some kind of reply, but have had none. In my letter I told you of his very remarkable talent for composition, and asked you to get him to play something of his own for you; and I laid stress on the fact that he was very shy and modest, and would need encouraging treatment at your hands if you wanted to see the best of him. As far as I could gather from his own very guarded account of the interview, you did not go further about his own music than to ask him whether he wished to play as a composer or as a pianist, a question which, as my letter made clear to you, would certainly result in your not hearing any work of his own, and that your reception of him was exactly the reverse of what I asked, and as I could see made him uncomfortable and nervous.

Even if you think this the proper attitude to take to a young artist, it was not exactly courteous to his master and friend who sent him, and made me much regret that I had taken any steps in the matter. He told me that you were annoyed at his coming late for the appointment. He arrived at the Queen's Hall at 12.25, and the hour fixed by Mr Forsyth [Neil Forsyth, General Manager of the Royal Opera House, Covent Garden] in a letter to me was 12.30. You began therefore by blaming him for an unpunctuality which did not exist, and to start with undeserved reproach was not exactly calculated to encourage him or steady his nerve.

I am sorry about this, but I cannot say that I am surprised. Your position in this country, gained primarily by your own gifts, was assured by the unflinching support of men like myself, whose goodwill has now become unnecessary to you, and which you therefore have dispensed with.

But there would be no great harm done (from a personal as distinct from an artistic standpoint) if you kept up even so much show of respect for them, as to acknowledge important letters when they write them, or to fall in with such small requests as personal kindliness to a boy, in whom several of those on whose opinion in musical matters you apparently used to get some value, are exceptionally interested.

CHARLES V. STANFORD

Stanford's mercurial temperament, and his proneness to passing squalls, led him unwittingly to upset many friends, of which his break with Elgar is probably the best known. In letter 32 his irritation was almost certainly over his Scottish pupil James Friskin. Stanford spent much time and energy on those of his pupils in whom he detected what he considered to be exceptional talent. Probably the first of these had been Samuel Coleridge-Taylor, followed by William Hurlstone (whose tragic death in 1906 at the age of 30 must have caused Stanford much grief), and later Ernest Farrar (destined to be killed in the last days of World War I) whose glorious choral setting of Rossetti's The Blessed Damozel *Stanford conducted in 1908. There was also, as we have seen, W. H. Bell who subsequently made a career in South Africa.*

James Friskin (1886–1967) had been at the Royal College of Music since 1900, becoming a pupil of Stanford in 1905. He produced a Piano Quintet in C minor (published by Stainer & Bell) in his twenty-first year, which Thomas Dunhill assessed as 'one of the most brilliant op. 1's in existence', and Cobbett reports a conversation with Stanford in which Friskin's teacher remarked that he 'envied the young composer his gift of melody'. After producing a number of highly successful chamber works, Friskin went to the USA a little before the outbreak of the war and appears to have given up composition. His subsequent career was as a pianist and a teacher at the Juilliard School of Music. Later he married the viola player and composer Rebecca Clarke.

(33)
HANS RICHTER to SIR CHARLES VILLIERS STANFORD

Royal Opera Covent Garden
23rd April 1908

Dear Sir Charles

Your letter was an unexpected, nay an unpleasant surprise to me: and I regret you should have considered it necessary to write it. I imagine that it would have been worth your while to make some enquiries, to have satisfied yourself that the state of things was not such as you describe, before writing in this fashion, for I can only assure you that the young man has misrepresented things entirely. I had to finish at 12 o'clock upon the day in question because the members of the orchestra had other business which demanded their attention and simply remarked to your protegé that I was sorry the half hour between this and the time of his appointment should have been wasted, thereby meaning that had I known of this, I could have arranged to let him come earlier and thus hear more of him; it could certainly not have been a question of impatience or discourtesy as I had myself fixed the hour of meeting.

I further asked him whether he wished to be heard as a soloist or as a composer and this because I should be more able to help him in the former capacity than in the latter. He elected to play for me and after he had done so, I told him that it was unfortunately too late to make him a definite promise of engagement because many of the next season's arrangements had already been settled, adding however, that I would bear him in mind in the event of any date becoming free; upon my return to Manchester, I likewise asked Mr Forsyth to take a note of his name.

Unfortunately, I deserve to be called a negligent correspondent, but my busy life and numerous journeys are to a great extent answerable for this; in any case intentional under-estimation has nothing to do with the present case.

Your remark 'I am sorry about this, but I cannot say I am surprised. Your position in this country, gained primarily by your own gifts, was assured by the unflinching support of men like myself, whose goodwill has become unnecessary to you, and which you therefore have dispensed with' contains the undeserved accusation of ingratitude. As far as my memory of our correspondence of earlier days serve me, I always proved myself worthy of your goodwill. That you however permit yourself to write 'but I cannot say that I am surprised' throws a curious light upon our relations, for you insinuate that you have always regarded me as an ungrateful egotist, one who was open to accept favours but never to return them.

Now, I *know* that it is not necessary for me to tell you that I have never used my friends in this way: on the contrary, I have always tried to help them to the best of my ability and as far as it lay in my power. Your letter has robbed me of an illusion, but it has enriched my experience – which is a bad exchange! And in order to avoid future misunderstandings of this sort, I may add that in spite of the unpleasant effect of your letter, I shall always be at your service musically if I can do so without prejudice to my artistic feelings.

Yours truly

[HANS RICHTER]

(34)
H. V. HIGGINS to PERCY PITT

ROYAL OPERA HOUSE COVENT GARDEN
Proprietors: The Grand Opera Syndicate Ltd
General Manager, Mr Neil Forsyth
16 February 1909

My dear Mr Pitt

I have been thinking very seriously over my interview with the Doctor [i.e. Hans Richter] and you on the subject of English Opera and before you invite any of your friends to give pecuniary guarantees I strongly urge you both to look the facts fairly and squarely in the face.

On the basis of this year's results you may take it from me that you will not succeed in raising the curtain under £550 per night and I think it is more probable that that figure will be increased to £600, because it is very improbable that you will again succeed in securing the services of the artists on such good terms as this year. Furthermore you must recollect that in this calculation there is practically no provision at all for new scenery costumes, etc. etc. and if you were carrying on the season as an enterprise quite separate from the Syndicate who provide all these and charge them to their Summer expenses, they would amount to a considerable sum.

The mounting of Rienzi alone would be a serious item.

Now although you can get subscriptions for cycles of the Ring and special Wagner performances in limited numbers, it is quite certain to my mind that for the other performances such as Orfeo, Samson, Fidelio, etc. if your receipts average anything over £300. you will be lucky. This has been the experience not only of this season, but of the Italian autumn seasons in which the only performances that were ever given at a profit were those in which artists like Caruso, Melba or Tetrazzini appeared. There is always a market for stars here and indeed in most countries.

English people only come to the Opera to hear something sensational or unusual. Don Giovanni with a good ensemble of English artists but without stars would not draw £300. and it would cost £500 to give it.

After all, what opera houses are there in Europe that do more than just pay their way in spite of subventions, free opera houses without rent, exemption from taxation, insurance premiums, and very often free heating and light. No where in Europe as far as I know do the receipts average £600 per night excepting at Covent Garden in the summer, and unless they do you must lose money.

It is not a question of language at all; the fact is that unless for some very special attraction, the London public will not come to the opera in sufficient numbers to make it pay. In the summer it is a different story, but if you deducted the private subscriptions for boxes and stalls which depend to a great extent on fashion, and the seats paid for by foreigners, who certainly constitute nearly forty per cent of our audience, I do not believe that the patronage of the British public proprement dit exceeds £300 per night on average even then.

Under these circumstances I am not prepared to recommend my colleagues who rely to a great extent on my judgment to run their heads against a brick wall. I advise you strongly not to make an appeal for financial assistance without making it quite clear that in all human probability a loss would result.

If the Doctor likes I am quite willing in 1911 to introduce English opera as a feature of the summer season in place of German. It will be an experiment, but one that we can afford to make. If anything will give an impetus to opera in English, that will, but to continue to lose money on English autumn and spring seasons, when there is not even a remote prospect of the enterprise paying its way, is worse than useless and will injure the cause you have at heart.

My conviction is that there is very little demand for Opera at all outside the season, and that outside a small circle of those who have an axe of their own to grind, the idea that a craving exists for opera to be given in English is an absolute delusion.

If we can do Wagner better in English than in German by all means let us do it in English; I don't believe the summer public will care one way or the other. We shall see how they receive the Valkyrie in May. But beyond that I am not prepared to go unless someone can give me very good reasons for thinking that my conclusions are wrong.

Please show this letter to the Doctor.

Yours Sincerely

H.V. HIGGINS

The last Meistersingers resulted in a house of £300. Of this figure the libraries had subscribed £60 & did not sell the greater part of their seats. They also lost considerably on their deal for the Ring. You may therefore be advised that on another occasion there would be a considerable falling off in the nightly receipts.
HVH

(35)
HAVERGAL BRIAN to HERBERT THOMPSON

11 Gordon Street
Stoke-on-Trent
1909
July the ninth
Friday

Dear Mr Thompson

I thought you would like to know what is happening to my work since I had my first show in the Leeds Town Hall – with the Municipal orchestra. The committee of the Musical League have selected my 'By the Waters of Babylon' for their first Festival in Liverpool in September next. The Southport Triennial Festival will produce my 'Vision of Cleopatra' in October next. Landon Ronald has been specially engaged to produce this work. I've had many troubles over it. Just on the eve of publication the Committee refused to produce it unless the language was modified – I wouldn't give way on all points but I've had to fight Committee *and* publisher over it. It is strange that in this country the various versions of the 'Song of Songs' in the Bible are glibly swallowed considering that a shudder passes through the community when a poem by a *living* writer happens to be not half so sensuous and passionate. I am daily expecting copies of the 'Vision of Cleopatra' and will forward one along with some part songs I have written. I have recently perpetrated a long satirical orchestral work, 'Humorous Legend on Three Blind Mice'. *My*

B. & Cº 13211

(b) Page from the vocal score of Brian's *Cleopatra*

version differs from most others in that I introduce a policeman and the Farmer's wife to carry on the dramatic idea. It is in three movements & lasts 45 minutes.

Ist movement
A *The blind mice*
B *The Chase by the farmer's wife*
C *Enter the Policeman* who
D *Makes Love to Farmer's Wife* (all Caruso)
E *Chase resumed*
F *Capture*
G *March to the Scaffold, execution. Apotheosis*

II Scherzo – 'The Bogey Man'

III Finale – 'Dance of the Farmer's Wife'

I've also completed a setting of a poem by Scott for chorus and orchestra. It is in four movements, but *without* break and this lasts forty minutes. I hope my long epistle will not bore you.

With kind regards
Yours V Sincerely

HAVERGAL BRIAN

At this time Havergal Brian was supported financially by a patron who admired his talent and wanted to allow him time to develop it. Brian's first performance at Leeds Town Hall had been of his First English Suite *on 12 January 1907, Brian himself conducting. His* Vision of Cleopatra *was a setting of a text specially written by Gerald Cumberland for a prize offered by the Norwich Festival. The winning score was by Julius Harrison, but Brian's was considered to be sufficiently impressive to be offered production at the Southport Festival. Harrison later repudiated his luxuriant setting and destroyed the orchestral score, while that of Brian's setting was also destroyed, owing to enemy action during World War II. Thus both works survive only in vocal score. The orchestral work Brian describes in his letter was ultimately named* Fantastic Symphony, *but after the outer movements had been published separately – as* Fantastic Variations on an Old Rhyme *and* Festal Dance *– the middle one was lost. It is impossible to identify Brian's Scott setting; all trace of the score is lost and this letter constitutes the only extract reference to it.*

(36)
RALPH VAUGHAN WILLIAMS to HERBERT THOMPSON

13 Cheyne Walk
s.w.
[Summer 1910]

Dear Mr Thompson
[About *A Sea Symphony*] I will tell you all I can – I think it best to put down anything that occurs to me and then you can select anything out of it which you want.

(1) With regard to the name 'Symphony' – I use the word because the treatment of the words is symphonic rather than dramatic – that is to say the words are used as a basis on which to build up a decorative musical scheme. I have therefore felt justified in repeating the words a good deal – especially in the 1st movement.

(2) As regards your enquiry about 'significance of themes' – I can only think of two –

(a) the harmonic progression which starts the work & comes again pp 6, 47, 49 (letter E), 56, 62 (letter F), 87 etc. –

(b) the phrase

which is part of the opening theme and comes again several times in the 1st & last movements. These two themes (for no particular reason) seem to suggest the sea to my mind!

(3) As regards its history – it has been gradually growing in my mind for about 7 years – the sketch was completed in 1907 and revised and scored in 1908 and 9 – when the festival Ctee accepted it last year it had another clean up & finally during the last 6 months I have been revising the full score which meant re-copying most of it.

I don't know from your letter whether you want my 'general' history – but in case you do.

I was born in 1872

General education Charterhouse School & Trinity College Cambridge – musical education RCM & also with Charles Wood at Cambridge, also 6 months in Berlin with Max Bruch.

For some years I was organist of a church in South London.

I am sending a copy of the vocal score with a few indications – wd you kindly return it when you have done with it as it is the only one I have.

Yrs vy Tly

R VAUGHAN WILLIAMS

PS The full score is now being copied – otherwise I shd have been delighted to send it to you.

*

(37)
SIR CHARLES VILLIERS STANFORD to HERBERT THOMPSON

County Hotel
Rothbury
Aug 7 1910

My dear Thompson

... I am concerned to hear from you that the serials [i.e. repeat bookings] are below the level. But it really is not surprising when people like Legge who ought to know better slang the programme in the DT & when there are 12 English to 12 German works in the programme, curse the Cttee for asking Rachmaninoff. All these things tell. Considering that one can't get everything really as one wants with a body of men of wildly different tastes, I think the programme is wonderfully interesting & representative. I expect Legge's programme wd be this:–

Wed	Elektra. Strauss
Wed	New Symphony. Cyril Scott
	Choral Symphony. Mahler
Thur	New Oratorio 'The Loan Guarantee Assn Bankruptcy'.
	Granville Bantock
Thur	Sinfonia Domestica. Strauss
	New Choral Work 'The Fens'. Hathaway
Friday	Act 1, II, 3 Pelleas & Melisande Debussy
Friday	Act 4, 5 Pelleas & Melisande Debussy
Sat	New Oratorio 'The Black Country' Rutland Boughton
	Part I Smoke
	– II The Pit Mouth
	–III The Explosion
Sat	Cantata 'The Diversion of Messaline' Julius Harrison
	Concerto for Penny Whistle and Tuba A. Bax
	'God Help the Audience'

receipts for the Festival £1.13.4. But joking apart, it's serious if Leeds follows in Birmingham's wake financially, & it wants a long strong pull to keep its public up to the importance of its Festival from a national point of view. Also everything must have its (basic) line like the barometer, & if they stick to it the aneroid will rise when times get better: if they keep the performances at high level. *Private* I fear that abolishing the guarantors was a mistaken step, for they had a personal interest which wd cease to be dominant as soon as the receipts showed signs of filling. However with help it will turn out at least as well as last time. Certainly I never heard such a chorus, or know of one so responsive or so intelligent.

This was the Festival at which Vaughan Williams's A Sea Symphony *had its first performance under the composer's baton; in the same programme was Rachmaninov as the soloist in his* Second Piano Concerto *which Stanford conducted. The Festival also included Rachmaninov conducting his own* Second Symphony *and the first performance of Stanford's* Songs of the Fleet.

(38)
H. WALFORD DAVIES to FRANCESCO BERGER

Temple Church
E.C.
Oct 30 1910

Dear Mr Berger
The work Von Holst sent contains interesting experiments in orchestral colouring. But I am sorry to say I did not discover in it that which wd make it suitable for his introduction to the Philharmonic.

yours very truly

H WALFORD DAVIES

The essential step to performance for any composer, then as later, is the sympathies of those who are used as referees and expert readers by performing organizations. Thus Francesco Berger, Secretary of the Philharmonic Society, did not place Holst's newly composed suite Beni Mora. *Its first performance came in May 1912, in one of Balfour Gardiner's celebrated concerts of British music, conducted by the composer. Holst conducted an excerpt from* Beni Mora *as a Royal Philharmonic Concert organized by Balfour Gardiner in November 1913.*

*

(39)
EGON PETRI to THE DAILY NEWS

January 1911

I feel I am born to *play* the pianoforte, not to *teach* it, and I have come to the conclusion that I never shall make my way as a pianist as long as I am in Manchester.

Why this should be so I do not know; but the fact is there, nobody will engage you as long as you hold a provincial post. The circle of towns where I played has become smaller and smaller during those five years, till now I play merely in Manchester and suburbs—becoming a sort of local slum-pianist. In England they do not want me, because I am in England; on the Continent they do not want me either—also because I am in England. . . .

I have no appointment in view, and, for all I know, I may be selling matches or grinding an organ in the streets of Berlin next winter. But even so, I shall risk it. Berlin is the town where a pianist has a chance—it is also the town where I have friends, and my best friend, Busoni. . . .

And then I may get on. They may even engage me in Liverpool or London, which they have not done a single time in the last five years, as, for concert-agents, the distance between Liverpool and Berlin is smaller than the distance between Liverpool and Manchester.

The thirty year old Egon Petri had been Professor of the Piano at the Royal Manchester College of Music since 1906.

1 R. Norman-Concorde

2 Queen's Hall

top left **3** Sir Charles Villiers Stanford
above **4** Sir Edward Elgar (left) and Granville
Bantock

5 Josef Holbrooke

above **6** H. Walford Davies
top right **7** Sir Hubert Parry

8 Havergal Brian

top left **9** H. V. Higgins
above **10** Hans Richter

11 H. Balfour Gardiner

12 Percy Pitt

13 A. J. Jaeger

top left **14** Percy Grainger
above **15** Arthur Alexander

16 Frederick Delius

17 Landon Ronald and The New Symphony Orchestra

18 Michael Balling

19 Lena Ashwell

20 Dunhill's *Die Eiskönigin* at Hamburg, December 1937

21 A Lena Ashwell concert party

(40)
HENRY WOOD to HERBERT THOMPSON

Sheffield,
Jan.18, 1911.

Dear Mr. Thompson,
At the forthcoming Sheffield Festival we give the Grail Scene Finale of Act I. Parsifal, with English words by Margaret H. Glyn, and this selection is published separately by Schott & Co.

It starts with Gurnemanz' [*sic*] line 'From bathing doth the King wend home.' There is no cut and it runs straight on until the end of the Opera, but we do leave out the voice part on pages 38 and 39, so that you will not insert the following words in your Programme:– 'Why standest here still, knowest thou what thou sawest, thou art then nothing but a fool, Hie thee hence, on thy way be gone, yet heed well Gurnemanz, do thou henceforward our swans let alone and seek to the Gander a Goose'

The alto solo from above 'By pity awakened' is sung.

Kindly note that we carry out Wagner's intentions in the concert room as regards the placing of the three choirs. The full chorus of tenors and basses sing the parts allotted to the Knights of the Grail. The youths' voices consisting of altos and tenors will sing from a mid-height above the organ and, of course, out of sight and the boys' voices, with a few contraltos, page 12, will be sung from the roof over the Orchestra to give it its proper distant effect. I am naturally very proud and happy that with the assistance of the architect and the committee, the Albert Hall, Sheffield, is being specially arranged to get the right effect.

Previously all concert performances have been given with all the material in front of the organ and in sight of the public.

Any further information you desire, please write to me.

With kind regards,

Sincerely yours,

HENRY J. WOOD

Stage productions of Parsifal *were restricted to performances at Bayreuth until thirty years after Wagner's death. However concert performances were heard widely, and the work had been first heard thus in London in 1884. It was first staged in Great Britain at Covent Garden on 2 February 1914.*

(41)
BALFOUR GARDINER to PERCY GRAINGER

Ashampstead Green
Pangbourne
Berks
23.5.11

Dear Percy

You have got the dates of my concerts, haven't you? March 13. 27. April 17. May 1.
Please keep yourself free for all these dates, & in the case of the first & last, for some
days before. March 13 falls on a Wednesday, & the only possible time for the
rehearsal of the chorus is the previous Saturday afternoon. I have not arranged about
a chorus yet, but hope to get Fagge's.* Then as regards May 1st, the Queen's Hall
cannot let me have a rehearsal the same morning, & the exact time has to be
arranged.

I should like you to play for me, if you will, at the last concert, May 1st: your
choral works will be done at the first concert, the Hillsong at the second, & Green
Bushes at the third.

Austin is staying with me; & we have been scoring Cyril's 'Helena'. I have never
come across a work with such possibilities of instrumentation. Needless to say Cyril
has missed them all.

Could you & Mrs G[rainger] come down for a night or two, & I would ask Cyril
also.

Ever yours

H. BALFOUR GARDINER

*H. Balfour Gardiner was one of the 'Frankfurt Gang' – a group of British composers all of
whom studied at the Hoch'sche Konservatorium, Frankfurt, in the late 1890s. Of those
mentioned in letter 41, Balfour Gardiner, Cyril Scott and the Australian Percy Grainger
were included, while the others were Norman O'Neill and Roger Quilter. In 1911 Balfour
Gardiner was preparing for the first of two series, each of four concerts, that he promoted
between March 1912 and March 1913, and in which the music of a whole generation of
British composers were introduced to a wide public for the first time. Frederic Austin,
celebrated English baritone, was also a composer, twice represented in Gardiner's concerts,
and later became known for the success of his version of* The Beggar's Opera *in 1920.*

---

*Arthur Fagge (1864–1943) was at first the organist of several London churches. He founded the London
Choral Society in 1903, and paid special attention to modern British music and in the immediate pre-
World War I period had notable successes with Bax's *Enchanted Summer* and the first complete
performance in England of Bantock's *Omar Khayyam* and Ethel Smythe's *Hey Nonny No!*.

(42)
BALFOUR GARDINER to PERCY GRAINGER

7 Pembroke Villas
Kensington w
Sept 5th 1911

Dear Percy

Austin was to have sung for me on March 27th; but he finds that the opera season for which he is engaged includes that date and wants me to give him May 1st instead. I could only do so if you would not mind playing the concert on March 27th. Have you any objection to this arrangement? The Hill-Song, which was to be included in the programme of the 27th of March, would then be shifted to May 1st. Please let me have a line about this, so that Austin can have his date fixed definitely.

I am in town for a couple of days & am just going off to your house to get your scores & your present address. Attended a rehearsal of Shepherd Fennel's Dance this morning & liked it very much. Austin has come back from Ireland very fit, & with splendid sketches for what he calls a Symphonic Lark, & a tune in it that is ravishing. And Novello's are publishing my Comedy Overture & two part songs – so everything is going on very well indeed. I met Smith this morning who said he had got you a London engagement for December. If that is so, we must have some choral rehearsals while you are here. I hope you & Mrs G, are enjoying Norway: with my love to both of you.

Yours affectionately

H BALFOUR GARDINER

Balfour Gardiner's Shepherd Fennel's Dance *became one of the most popular short orchestral pieces of its generation. Frederic Austin's* Symphony in E *was performed in Balfour Gardiner's last concert on 18 March 1913.*

(43)
R. LEIGH IBBS to WILLIAM WALLACE

Ibbs and Tillett,
10 Hanover Square,
London w.
Nov 21st 1911

Dear Sir

In confirmation of my telephone message, we duly secured the license [sic] (magistrate granted permission) for Sigmund Feuermann [aged 10] to appear at your Concert on Thursday next, conditionally that he is not playing later than 9.30pm and I felt safe in giving this assurance.

I have sent the second licence to the Chief Clerk of the London County Council, and as you will notice the enclosed copy has to be exhibited in the artists' room on the night of the Concert, if you will kindly see to this.

You will notice there is a paragraph regarding the necessity of a matron to be provided to look after the youth, but I was given to understand that this was not a point likely to be pressed, and were an inspector to insist upon the carrying out of every condition, I should think one of the attendants from the Ladies' Cloak Room could be brought in for the purpose!

I am very truly

R. LEIGH IBBS

(44)
WILLIAM WALLACE to R. H. LEGGE

Royal Philharmonic Society
Feb 15 1912
Private

Dear Legge,
One of the Philharmonic Directors has sent me a cutting from the [Daily] Telegraph of the 13th, and has asked me to deal with it. I prefer to do so privately, for after the dead-set made by the press against the Phil. it is impossible to expect any fair treatment in public.

Last Sunday an official letter was sent to the Telegraph stating the circumstances that led up to the withdrawal of Bantock's work. The Directors hoped that its publication would put a stop to the campaign of misrepresentation that is going on in the press against the Phil. and had it been printed in full it would have been, in the eyes of all straightforward men, a complete vindication of their action. If the letter was shown to you according to the use and wont of journalism, I cannot understand your paragraph of the 13th. If you did not see the letter, surely it would have been the simplest thing in the world for you to have asked me directly why the work had been withdrawn.

It is scarcely playing the game to say that the Phil. 'confessed' that Bantock's new (?) work had been 'shelved' owing to the fees required by the composer, 'etc'. Why the 'etc'? If you saw the official letter you must have realised that it was not the question of fees alone that influenced the Directors' decision.

The facts are clear,and the Phil. has nothing to be ashamed of, for it played the game. I will give you the facts.

Bantock accepted the invitation of the Phil. in February 1911, and confirmed the date of the concert in July, 1911. He had therefore ample time in which to raise the question of fees. Since the end of October, 1911, he and I were meeting and corresponding, and it would have been an easy thing for him to have asked me frankly what the Society was disposed to do. Further, when I wrote to him in the second week in January about the final arrangements of the concert, he said nothing about his own fees, and referred me to Breitkopf for details about the extras and analysis. This letter I received on January 19, within fourteen working days of the first rehearsal, and it was only on that morning that I was told by Breitkopf that acting upon Bantock's instructions certain fees were demanded. I cannot understand why Bantock, when writing to me on official business, did not disclose the question of fees, instead of leaving me to find out, almost by accident, what his terms were.

The fact is not in dispute that he sprang his demand upon the Society at the last moment, and backed it up with a formal letter in which he left it to the Directors to accept his terms or to withdraw his work. At the same time he further embarrassed the Directors by saying that he was going to Manchester, and by giving no address he put himself out of reach of any communication, thus preventing the possibility of a compromise.

Had Bantock raised the question of fees at a reasonable time, the Directors would have met it as honourable men meet a business proposition, but as he practically 'held up' the Society at the eleventh hour, the Directors, who wished only to pay him the highest compliment, had no choice but to accept his own alternative.

There was no public demand to hear the work, for on the day on which it was withdrawn the booking was practically nil, and had the Directors accepted his terms, the guarantors would rightly have declined to be saddled with the loss on the concert, and would have insisted on the Directors meeting it themselves.

Never at any time has it been the policy to refuse a composer a reasonable fee when asked for – when my first work was performed the Society offered me my expenses, but these I declined – but surely the Directors have the right to administer the finances of the Society without interference by outsiders who have not a penny at stake in its concerns.

No one seems to take the trouble to remember that by its constitution the Society's Directors and officials must be professional musicians, and it should not require a severe mental effort to reckon the time they must give up voluntarily, not to speak of the pecuniary guarantee which they must find out of their own pockets, in order to run the society. The press has ignored this, and instead of recognising the public spirit that they display by their disinterested efforts on behalf of the Society, has disparaged and misrepresented every step that they have taken.

It was grossly unfair to refer to the withdrawal of Bantock's work without mentioning the exceptional circumstances under which he asked for his fees, and no Society would be worth a rap or have the slightest justification for its existence had it done what the press maintained it ought to have done. The support of the public is so small that it barely pays for the conductors, performers and rent. The orchestra and all the other expenses are met by the subscriptions of members, associates and fellows, and by a heavy call on guarantors. These calls cannot go on much longer, and if the press does not play the game it will kill the Society.

The fee that Bantock asked was far in excess of any that was or will be paid this season, and nearly one half of those engaged, including foreigners, are volunteering their services as a compliment to the Centenary of the Society.

I may point out that your statement that the cheapest seat at the Phil is 5/- is misleading and requires qualification. Numbers of students – last year show 220 – pay half a guinea for a season ticket, which entitles them to a stall for the season. This works out at 1/6 per concert, and members and associates pay 3/- per concert. I have received no complaints as to the prices charged to the public.

Seeing that some of us are giving up our entire time to help the Phil. and are compelled to put our own work on one side, a little less crabbing on the part of the press, and a recognition of our difficulties, would make our task more easy. It is all well enough to criticise – when you don't know the facts, but now that you have been informed of the situation perhaps you will suggest a course that will be financially as well as artistically sound.

The Directors deeply regretted having to discuss publicly the situation that arose in connection with Bantock's work, but having been forced to do so, they were at least entitled to state their own case. The action of the press in refusing them this while continuing to criticise them is incomprehensible. It is maybe 'good journalism', but emphatically is not 'cricket'.

I have thought it best to write to you privately about all this, because from the Minute books I find that continual protests were sent to the proprietors of various papers complaining of the terms in which the Society was referred to. I have no desire to add to my official duties in this way, and you must realise how disagreeable it has been for me to find myself, in the first three months at this job, at variance with the very man for whom I wanted to do everything that was pleasant. Every Director wants to pay the composer, and had Bantock given them time he would have had his fee, I do not say all he claimed, but he could have had something. In fact, had he hinted to me that he expected a fee, I am certain that there would have been no difficulty about an arrangement. Fortunately he understands the position and does not hold me responsible for it. But I would have given anything that it had not arisen.

Yours ever,

WILLIAM WALLACE

William Wallace acted as Secretary to the Royal Philharmonic Society between 1911 and 1913. The work in question was Bantock's Fifine at the Fair, *which was finally given its first performance at what was to be the last Birmingham Festival in October 1912. Relations between Bantock and the Royal Philharmonic were smoothed over the following year when, on 9 January 1913 they performed his comedy overture* The Pierrot of the Minute. Fifine at the Fair *was finally produced at a Royal Philharmonic concert conducted by Beecham on 26 November 1917.*

(45)
MICHAEL BALLING to PERCY PITT

Royal Station Hotel
Hull
February 14th 1912

My dear Pitt
Many thanks for your letter, as you say you should like to put my name before your direktors [*sic*] I beg you to take the trouble and do it – on the advice of Richter I ask for a fee of 50 Guineas for each performance. – I recommend you if you have not got a Sieglinde already to take Miss Easton of the Royal Opera Berlin and Mr Maclennan for Tristan or Siegfried – they are both very good especially Miss Easton. May I ask you one other question which has nothing to do with Covent Garden. Would you be so kind and give me the names (and publishers) of a few young English composers who have written some Concert music? – of course I don't mean the names of already famous composers Elgar, Bantock, Sibelius [*sic*] etc. – have you written an Overture or Suite or something.

I am making now the programme for the next Hallé Concert Season and I should like to bring out in each Concert one new piece and of course as many as possible of

English or better British composers. I would be very obliged to you if you got the time to tell me what you know about the matter.

Sandberger whom I saw at Munich sends you his kindest regards.

Believe me

Yours
very truly
MICH[AEL] BALLING

Michael Balling (1866–1925), one of the principal conductors at the Festival Theatre at Bayreuth from 1906 to 1914, was Hans Richter's successor in England, conducting an English-language cycle of The Ring *in Edinburgh in 1910 and being appointed conductor of the Hallé Orchestra in 1912. It is worth noting that the fee he is asking is substantially more than any of his British contemporaries, including instrumentalists and most singers, could have commanded at this date.*

We turn to a far more personal correspondence, in which a young composer explores the nature of his own musical individuality for the first time. The influences both of nature and of the Russian Ballet which had first taken London by storm in the Summer of 1911 are very much of the period, an influence which was to be reinforced by the postwar seasons. Rosalind Thorneycroft, daughter of the sculptor Sir Hamo Thorneycroft, later married Godwin Baynes ('Tiny') who was to be Jung's assistant in the 1920s. Paul was Paul Corder, composer and the son of Arnold Bax's composition teacher Frederick Corder, and Olga was Olga Antonietti subsequently an actress, who had accompanied Arnold Bax on an extended visit to Russia in the Spring of 1910.

(46)
ARNOLD BAX to ROSALIND THORNEYCROFT

10 Bushy Park Rd
Rathgar
Co. Dublin
Thursday
[16 Feb 1912]

Dearest Rosalind

I hope your cold is better again now. I was so disappointed not to see you that night, not alone because I would like you to have heard my sonata (one of my most intimate and Bax-y compositions) but also because I missed the 'you-ness' in the room. Also afterwards when Tiny, Paul, and Olga came home and we talked round the fire.

I was indeed glad to see you sitting at the dining table on Sunday evening and so pleased not to feel the constraint that sometimes comes when one meets someone whom one has come to know by correspondence. But I did not feel anything of that, but only that you radiated a wonderful sympathy all the evening.

Rosalind dear, this is a great and by no means common gift that you possess – a gift I think only possible in its perfection to a woman, for men are usually so obsessed by a sort of gross egotism and abstract altruisms that they are rarely capable of giving forth an atmosphere of individual sympathy.

I was very pleased with my sonata. It did not sound at all like anything else, and I realized for the first time that my harmonic scheme is unlike that of other modern composers – an interesting thought. Also I realized an illuminating paradox, i.e. that one cannot know one's own work until one gets entirely outside it, which I did then as I listened to it from the next room. Now I am full of dreams about my ballet – as to the possibility of the Russians taking it up – if only I knew how to get hold of them. I feel in such splendid creative form just now and must go on making something in one form or another. Yesterday and today the first foreshadowing of the spring has crept into the soft air and the trees seemed covered with the evanescent and scarcely perceptible phantasmal veil – which is perhaps only an effect of light with which the spring begins. But it is sufficient to get all kinds of shadowy tumults stirring in the heart – a mood changed with a strange blending of gaiety and regret.

I often wonder about you, Rozie, and frequently want to know what you are thinking and dreaming. You often surprize me by your wonderful intuitive understanding of very subtle matters in music – which as a rule only composers recognize, and not many of *them* – and that means I know a very deep emotional life hidden under the calm exterior that you show to the world – and this not only in those sides of life in which I know you feel deeply, but in other and more unusual aspects. When I come to London again at the beginning of March I hope you will come as often as you can. You are one of the few people with whom it is possible to communicate intimately in a crowd, just by the fact of your presence in the room if you know what I mean.

I wonder if you ever write things now. If not you should, I am sure. Well goodbye for the present, Rosalind dear. I want you always to think of me as a person to whom you can talk at any time and one who is always in the mood.

Always your friend

ARNOLD

(47)
*FREDERICK DELIUS to GRANVILLE BANTOCK

Grez sur Loing
(S&M)
3 June 1912

Wood wrote to me that he is doing 'Sea-drift' at the Birmingham Festival – On the Programme I see they have put it on the 4th day morning at the very end of a 4 hours Concert – Who is responsible for this friendly act? Sea-drift is unknown in Birmingham & requires some mental effort, & ought to be at the end of the first part or at the beginning of the 2nd Part – after the interval . . .

This Festival also saw the first performance of Elgar's The Music Makers *and Sibelius's* Fourth Symphony. *Bantock records in his diary how Delius, Sibelius and he sat together for the Elgar. Whether Sibelius heard the Delius is not known. In the last concert Sir Henry Wood was to have introduced Scriabin's* Prometheus: poem of fire *to England but it was cancelled after the programme had been announced.*

The contrast between the plight of those with positions in the musical world before World War I, and those trying to become established is nowhere more strongly seen than in the case of Havergal Brian, who in 1913 was already a seasoned musical journalist, though without a post and finding it increasingly difficult to make a living from music. This prompted him to biting sarcasm in his references to the entrenched names of the critical establishment.

Brian was particularly scathing when asked to compose potboilers, particularly those for church usage. In the following letter Brian refers to William McNaught (1849–1918), who had been the editor The Musical Times since 1910. Caleb Simper (1856–192?) was a typical butt of Brian's cutting wit, being the composer of church and Sunday school music which in the later nineteenth century had attained remarkable popularity. Scriabin's Prometheus reached London in the early summer of 1913, and with its demands for vast forces including piano, organ and chorus in addition to a very substantial orchestra, also required colour light effects produced by what was called a 'colour organ'. The music was conducted by Sir Henry Wood, who played it twice in the same programme, but the light effects were not undertaken, even though Scriabin was in London for the occasion. However, the work caused a considerable stir in musical circles, owing to what was considered to be a very exotic harmonic style, and for the startling theosophist cover to the score, painted by Jean Delville.

(48)
HAVERGAL BRIAN to GRANVILLE BANTOCK

Trentham
1913
Feby 10th

My dear Uncle
Please tell our Grandpa Sir Edward, that I will do my best, though suffering acutely from general obstruction. I have recently received an important commission through John Elvet to compose 20 anthems in the style of Caleb Simper commencing with 'In the beginning' and finishing with 'As was is now and ever shall be' 'Glorify me' – and I am very much taken up with my task.

By the way, dear uncle, have you heard the latest? If not, don't repeat it unless you tell grandpa!! It is quite true that McNaught purchased a copy of Scriabine's [*sic*] 'Prometheus'. He went to hear it and got so frightfully excited that he rushed to the office and in his excitement to get away he left the copy behind. John E West happened to come in as McSnuffle went out, and he seized the copy. Not having heard it, but quite well understanding it, *he* became full of excitement & went rushing all over the place shouting 'Miracle' 'Miracle' 'Messiah' 'Messiah'. McSnuffle reached home still full of excitement, but to find he had left its cause behind him. He rushed back only to find John E West gone mad, with a copy of 'Prometheus' in his hand beating the heads of some old men, shouting 'Miracle' 'Messiah' 'Glory to God'; McSnuffle feeling for his excitement and his copy plunged into the melee, a free fight ensued and McSnuffle is credited with getting back a much mutilated copy but only after he had knocked out a tooth. I give you the story for what it is worth. No doubt our grandpa has heard of it.

Love to Sir Edward & yourself

WILLIAM WALLACE [i.e.: Havergal Brian]

SYMPHONY CONCERTS

(SEVENTEENTH SEASON, 1912-13.)

QUEEN'S HALL.

(Sole Lessees - Messrs. Chappell & Co., Ltd.)

SATURDAY AFTERNOONS :

Feb. 1, 15; March 1, 15; April 5, 19, 1913.

The Queen's Hall Orchestra

(Augmented to 110 Performers).

Conductor—

Sir HENRY J. WOOD.

SATURDAY, FEBRUARY 1st, at 3 o'clock.

OVERTURE - -	Alceste - -	*Gluck*
SYMPHONY in B flat (B. & H. Edition, No. 98) -		*Haydn*
CONCERTO in D for Violin and Orchestra - -		*Beethoven*

CARL FLESCH.

PROMETHEUS (A Poem of Fire), for Orchestra, Pianoforte,
and Organ   *Scriabine*

(First performance in England.)

Solo Pianoforte - Mr. ARTHUR COOKE.
Grand Organ - Mr. FREDK. B. KIDDLE.

Solo Violin—

Herr CARL FLESCH.

Single Tickets : Reserved, 10s. 6d., 7s. 6d., & 5s.; Unreserved, 2s. 6d.
(All the Area (1/-) Tickets have already been applied for.)

MAY BE OBTAINED FROM

THE QUEEN'S HALL ORCHESTRA, Ltd., 320 Regent Street, W.
ROBERT NEWMAN, Manager.

(c) Programme for first performance of Scriabin's *Prometheus* in London

(49)
GEORGE BUTTERWORTH to HERBERT THOMPSON

8 Keble Road
Oxford
June 3 [1913]

Dear Mr Thompson
Details as follows –
Orchestral Prelude 'The Cherry Tree' by George Butterworth. Scored for full orchestra with Cor Anglais, Bass Clarinet, full brass, & Harp – about 9 minutes.

The chief theme is taken from a song of mine, to the words 'Loveliest of trees, the cherry now' (A E Housman) no 1 in 'A Cycle of Songs from "A Shropshire Lad"' (Augener).

Hence the title of the piece – the title has no other significance, & has no more concern with cherry trees than with beetles' (I wish you could suggest a better one). If it has any "meaning" at all, it is more in the nature of a meditation of the exiled Shropshire Lad.

Analysis

First a short introductory section, consisting of a two bar phrase tossed about between violas & clarinets – (A minor) Then (letter A) an anticipation of the 'Cherry' theme. Then the introd. section again (a semitone higher – leading to (letter B) the 'cherry' theme in full (E flat). After some development of this, there is a middle section (B minor) beginning quietly & gradually increasing until (letter F) with a change of tonality the 'cherry' theme returns ff on the trumpets.

Then some more development, and a climax (bar before G) which resolves itself into a long-sustained chord of E flat major. Then after further gradually receding references to the 'cherry' theme, the bass clarinet finally topples over the precipice into the original key of A minor, & a short restatement of the introductory sections brings the work to a well-deserved close.

This seems a fearfully long explanation for so short a piece, & I expect it will be quite enough to draw attention to
    (a) the introductory section
    (b) the main theme.
However, if you can wait till Tuesday next, I will send you the score. (Mr Hannam has got a piano version which he would lend you.)

Yours sincerely

GEORGE BUTTERWORTH

P S I think the tonality is less involved than it might seem. The piece is really in two keys instead of one –
(a) A minor, introduction & coda
(b) E flat major, which is the key of the main theme.

Please explain that it is not a description of orchards – I'm sorry to be so misleading.
G B

(50)
GEORGE BUTTERWORTH to HERBERT THOMPSON

8 Keble Road
OXFORD

Dear Mr Thompson

I hope I have not inconvenienced you by this delay; the fact is I have been trying without complete success, to come to some conclusion as to the title.

I don't really like any of these descriptive titles, such as the 'Exile'. On the other hand 'Prelude in A minor' sounds just as bad. I think 'Prelude' is wrong – & 'Rhapsody' better – On the whole I think this would do – A 'Shropshire Lad' Rhapsody, for Full Orchestra (be careful of the inverted commas). That is fairly vague, and yet gives a clue, which you can expand in your notes.

This will be the second change of title since the piece was accepted, and I don't know what the Committee will think, but perhaps your influence will be sufficient to calm them, if you think the change worth making.

Yours sincerely

GEORGE BUTTERWORTH

P S On thinking it over, it seems to me that the title I have suggested is distinctly the best one –

The Rhapsody A Shropshire Lad *was first performed at the Leeds Musical Festival on Thursday 2 October 1913 under the baton of Artur Nikisch. The Times critic wondered if 'Fantasy' would have been a better title than 'Rhapsody'. Its third performance in a Promenade Concert on 6 September 1917 followed the composer's death, and the Morning Post noted the 'immense promise in the work'; today one can but regret that there was no possibility of its fulfilment.*

(51)
HAVERGAL BRIAN to GRANVILLE BANTOCK

8 Lidlington Place
N.W.
1914
January 6th

My Dear BG [*sic*]

Today has been mostly wasted in seeing Legge and Curwens. The former is generously disposed (by the way he said – 'when I saw you before, you were sitting in the winter garden at the 'Midland' Manchester, alone, smoking – but you had a black beard & resembled Nikisch – where is the beard now?') but it was all talk, about people he had met, what a rich man his daughter had married & that the man had failed to get into the army because of his left eye. That his wife has had more training in singing than any other woman in London. How he met Von Bülow Rubinstein, tales of Richter. This went flowing on without hesitation – save when he lighted a cigarette. And then we were interrupted by a caller, I was introduced – and he resumed. He told funny tales, repeated a funny one dropped by Arnold Bennett at the 'Omar Khayyam' Club dinner. Ejaculated 'By jove there are a lot of you provincial chaps coming up to London just now. Three have come to me with letters of introduction from Ernest Newman'. I nearly killed myself with suppressed laughter, at this procession of the 'expecting' going to Legge as grand paterfamilias. Have heard nothing more from any of the London press chaps beyond an invitation to tea at a club on Saturday next.

Larry has not written.

Vaughan Williams writes from Italy enclosing letters of introduction, but I've put them in the fire, only keeping one directed to Gatty of the 'Pall Mall'.

I noticed that Legge had his prints framed & mounted in just the same manner as I had mine. I felt a bit mad – that I had been compelled to lose mine.

Curwens show not a little cheek in their first transaction. Of course I've hit myself one by having to go round seeking work and begging for it. They only offer 3 guineas for the two [–] a two part setting of one of Herricks childrens lyrics and a unison setting of a Tennyson child's poem. For my setting of the whimsical partsong – 'He was a rat' they offer four guineas. I told Curwen that I had never been paid less than five guineas & he must tell his uncle so. Curwen refuses Kevlaar & the Herrick as being 'out of their line'. I'm asking Kling to send all my recently published stuff to Elgar. I shall then tell Elgar what I've done & who I've seen & ask *him* to get me some work at Novellos. I cannot believe but that there is something to be had in a big concern like theirs, besides I cannot go on like this running about all over the d—— place, wasting time, & if I'm to have a contented mind I must have a permanent job. I cannot obtain anything satisfactory from R – he is silent on everything I ask about. I've just paid the landlady £1/–/9 and it pays for nothing else but the room, fuel & light for one week, and our six breakfasts, which she brings in the room each morning at 8.30. Sixpence a time for tea & breadbutter! It is at the rate of £52 per year and there isn't a bath at that! Legge said this morning I was out of it altogether living here, why didn't I live in Chelsea. But I daren't move anywhere for the reason that R will make no promises.

I cannot get to know anything as to the safety of my books – Mrs B is a devil incarnate & will neither say whether she has them or where they are. Do you know that the first few days I was up here after leaving you I walked down street after street trying to find a place where revolvers were to be bought? I couldn't find such a place & obviously daren't ask. Last week when coming into Fleet Street from seeing Cumberland I passed a place where the window was simply lined with them, and you cannot imagine the awful sense of sickness or faintness which went through me at the sight of them. But I had only 10/– in my purse and the intense longing to possess simply turned to disgust because *I had no money!* I have entered upon a phase of insomnia; I never knew what it was until recently – & the struggle I have at night to master a kind of mad tugging – which goes on making such a wreck of the nerves – to get one & use it, is horrible. I suppose this is the hell the ancients passed through when they coined the word. But I'll toast Mrs B *before* using it. I'm sending Curwen's letter to R to show I've not been idle since I came up here. Fancy their refusing 'Kevlaar' & the 'Herricks' & taking rubbish!! *Up* goes the apple cart of high art, there is no such thing, nobody wants it – and nobody understands it. We must seduce a natural instinct for the high & noble and descend to the muck heaps. I wonder which of the two R thinks is the greatest crime – my having seduced a servant maid – as *he* terms Hilda – or having seduced my own mind into writing the blasted muck Curwen's publish? I wish hell would quake & thunder & smash the whole place to smithereens.

Love to you

BRIAN

(52)
HAVERGAL BRIAN to GRANVILLE BANTOCK

14 Wykeham Mansions
West Dulwich
1914
April 30th

My dear BB
I do hope you will be fortunate enough to help me to something. I dont mind much what kind of work it is. I am on the scragend of R's last £5 & don't know where the next £1 is to come from unless Augeners or B & H take some things which they have.

I have no news from Beecham. Strecker talked, the other day, of articles, but my dear B, nobody reads them. Do you think any sane person reads an article by Newman or Cumberland and is afterwards influenced by it? Not a bit!

Do you know that when I came to move a chest at Hartshill before moving to Trentham, I found inside a double bottom a copy of an uncut 'Musical Standard' which had lain there since my enthusiastic days of youth. I cut it open and read! Do you think that one of the prophetic things mentioned there has happened even now – NO!

The thing is write fiction! and my idea at present is to complete a dozen episodes like the two I sent you – I can do a 1000 of them – and take them to Austin Harrison who might, on the strength of it give a commission for a serial work. Failing Harrison I would try publishers direct. I don't wish to go to Bennett with it – for he would find the whole thing most excellent copy & that is what he is out for.

But I want *your* 'thinks' on this. If I can only get sufficient work to enable me to live decently and without a perpetual misery of wondering where the next pound is coming to pay rent & – I could have no difficulty of mixing fiction with music. But one cannot do any continuous thinking under these cruel conditions – spasmodic jerks of enthusiasm for work intermittent by keen longing to cut one's throat or blow one's brains out.

Musical articles are no use and serve no purpose.

The only articles of any use are contained inside an original piece of music which its composer forces, himself, on the public. Then I told you of what Coates said of Newman – but enough! I would rather be the author of 'The City of beautiful nonsense', than the *condemned* writer, of all the d— articles on music ever written.

You go round – disguise yourself and try it – and meet the idiots that I've had to go to and ask 'please help' – listen to their conversation, measure their minds, &

think of 'these' my dear chap controlling the destiny of an artist with his public. You've no idea what a crass lot of unimaginative empty headed but otherwise cynical devils they are. To think that your work must go before this jury of imbeciles – and that what they say must be enframed & then circularised. Come and look at the empty baboons and think of it all.

And I am recommended to join them. Not as long as I've breath in my body.

I would rather work in the open, on a farm and have my mind free to roam undisturbed and unbridled, than join this motley army. You know of the ass Kalisch. I was told the other day by a man whom I sought for work – that following on the performance of a new work – he was known to sit down and write for 4 papers, smoking a cigarette and drinking a whisky. The latter seems the MC's talisman. Whilst doing this he would carry on a conversation – and if any one interrupted he would say – 'You don't disturb I can both write and talk'! Just think of a jew drawing his money for this kind of prostitution – and they are all alike jews & giles. Do you think McNaught any better? Not a bit!

They are all a lot of jackals.

Yours B

(53)
OTTO KLING to GRANVILLE BANTOCK

Breitkopf & Härtel
Music Publishers
Bear Building
54 Great Marlborough Street
London, w.

May 8th 1914

Dear Mr Bantock
With reference to the MS of 'In the Garden' by William Fenney, I have just heard from the Leipzig house that the cost of producing this in quarto size, the same as our Edition Breitkopf, printed on the best paper, with plain but artistic title page in one colour, would be:–

    300 copies . . . . £18–0–0.
    500   ”   . . . . £21–0–0.

Carriage and copyright fees extra.
Should it be preferred in folio size (sheet music) the cost would be

    300 copies . . . . £19–2–0.
    500   ”   . . . . £22–6–0.

It is understood that the name of my firm would be printed on the copies and that it would be included in our catalogues, also that we should keep copies on sale, with the usual commission. I am holding the MS pending further instructions.

Now, with regard to the question of title page, concerning which we spoke yesterday, perhaps you will be so kind as to place the proposals before Mr Harper, and the same might possibly be made use of for the above mentioned work!

With kindest regards,
I am,
Yours sincerely,

O H KLING.

CHAPTER II

August 1914–June 1919

The Great War

World War I, initially received in some quarters with a euphoric outburst of jingoistic feeling, was seen by almost all connected with music as a financial catastrophe from the start. The war was especially traumatic for the musical profession, for in almost no other aspect of British life were German practice and German practitioners so fully integrated into daily life. The necessity of making a living was, of course, most musicians' concern, in view of the apparent disaster that faced most of them in August 1914: nothing less than the total cessation of British musical life for the duration. The five major choral festivals due that autumn were cancelled, as were the main competitive festivals. Yet, surprisingly quickly, stability was achieved. The Promenade Concerts carried on – much against expectations – and, noted *The Musical Times* in its 1st September issue, 'the success that has so far attended the Queen's Hall Promenade Concerts is one of the most encouraging signs of the times'.

Initially anti-German feeling resulted in attempts to suppress the German music of the previous fifty years, and the first night of the Proms saw Tchaikovsky's *Italian Caprice* substituted for Strauss's *Don Juan*, and a Franco-Russian programme for a Wagner night. But this phase soon passed and, by the time of the first Queen's Hall Symphony Concert on 17 October, a traditional 'safe' programme of Beethoven, Brahms and Tchaikovsky was offered, though 'patriotic' programmes were also being given everywhere.

There was what in retrospect now appears to be amusing anti-German feeling extending to such matters as the use of British rather than 'German' fingering on the piano! The much publicized renouncing of his English honorary degrees by Hans Richter elicited the response 'it would be impossible for him to resign the degree, though he can cease to use the title of Doctor of Music of this University which was conferred upon him'. The war gave the British piano industry an unprecedented opportunity to develop in the absence of German competition, and leading musicians were favourite targets if they performed on German instruments. Unfortunately, without German competition prices rose as quality deteriorated.

In a profession in which continental attitudes had previously had so long-standing a leadership, many individuals found themselves the unwitting victims of the new situation. Several British musicians, including Edgar Bainton, Benjamin Dale and Frederick Keel, on holiday in Germany in August 1914 were interned for the duration. In Britain, where for years many performing artists had taken Germanic names for professional purposes, those with German names suddenly found themselves hounded by over zealous patriots, and even very long established and highly placed figures in the artistic life of the country found they had to leave.

Many young composers enlisted, although a small number of now famous names

– including Bax, Ireland and Heseltine – did not. Lists were quickly published of those who had joined the forces.

It is interesting to contrast the opposing views at the time, as stated by Arthur Bliss and Philip Heseltine. Only three years separated Arthur Bliss from the younger Philip Heseltine (later known as Peter Warlock). Bliss wrote: 'The crash of a European War on our very beaches sucked me into its undertow without my ever probing the consequences. My action was purely automatic, sparked off by a feeling of outrage at the cause of the war, of a debt owed, and added to this was the spirit of adventure and the heady excitement which the actions of my own contemporaries engendered . . . at that time its vague unknown possibilities made it remote from realistic definition'.* Heseltine expressed his thoughts at about the time war broke out in 1914, in a letter to his mentor Frederick Delius: 'I have never been able to understand the sentiment of patriotism, the love of empire; it has always seemed to me so empty and intangible an idea, so impersonal & so supremely unimportant as regards the things that really matter – which are all the common heritage of humanity without distinction of race or nationality . . .'†

Possibly Sir Hubert Parry best expressed the position occupied by many fair-minded artistic people when he confessed that he had 'been for a quarter century or more a pro-Teuton. I owed too much to their music and the philosophers & authors of former times to believe it possible that the nation at large could be imbued with the teaching of a few advocates of mere brutal violence & material aggression. . . . We know now that it is the hideous militarism of the Prussians that has poisoned the wells of the spirit throughout Germany.'‡

(54)
GEORGE BUTTERWORTH'S DIARY

Wednesday, September 2nd.
9 a.m. The four of us, as instructed, met at the Horse Guards Parade, where there were many hundreds of recruits assembled; after considerable delay – due to the distribution of pay and railway passes – the Bodmin men were sorted out, and marched off triumphantly to Charing Cross Underground Station, headed by a brass band and much stimulated by the cheers of the crowd.

On arriving at Paddington we were allowed to scatter for lunch, and rallied again for the train to Bodmin at 1–30. We decided unanimously that the transport arrangements were not creditable to the Committee of Railway Managers. The train was an ordinary one, and the amount of space reserved quite insufficient, many having standing room only. Notwithstanding, the journey down was a hilarious one – beer and singing ad lib – it was many days before we were so cheerful again. We had two changes, and did not reach Bodmin till after dark. There we were met by a sergeant and marched up without delay to the Barracks. Our reception there was not encouraging; at the gate we were each presented with one blanket, and told that the sleeping accommodation was already over-full, and that we must do as best we could in the open. Some 20 of us accordingly stationed ourselves under a small group

*BLISS, Sir Arthur: *As I Remember*. Faber, 1970, p. 30.

†GRAY, Cecil: *Peter Warlock – a memoir of Philip Heseltine*. Jonathan Cape, 1934, 1938, p. 94.

‡GRAVES, Charles L: *Hubert Parry – his life and works*. Vol II Macmillan & Co, 1926, p. 70.

of trees. Food was the next question; although we had been given no opportunity for a meal since Paddington, nothing was provided for us. Luckily, the canteen was still open, and by dint of much pushing we managed to secure a tin of corned beef and bottled beer. Considering the situation in which we found ourselves – the night was a distinctly cold one for September – it was not surprising that certain of the rougher specimens partook rather freely. Anyhow the result was the most extraordinary night I ever remember. Few made any attempt to sleep, and those who tried were not given much chance. It so happened that we shared our 'pitch' with a rabble from Handsworth, Birmingham – a district which is, I believe, notorious. These worthies kept us supplied with a constant stream of lewdness, mostly of a very monotonous kind; there was one real humorist who made some excellent jokes, but they are scarcely repeatable. At about 2 a.m. we were joined by several unfortunates who had found their tents already occupied (by lice), and preferred the open air and the wet grass. Altogether it was a remarkable experience, the most surprising thing about it being the complete absence of any attempt at discipline.

Thursday, September 3rd.
Morning found most of the crowd considerably sobered – not to say depressed. Breakfast was long delayed, and when it came consisted of loaves of bread thrown about indiscriminately, and large dishes of tea (mixed with milk and sugar) one dish to eight men. We eked out this allowance with the remains of last night's supper.

The proceedings of the day were irritating and futile in the extreme – endless 'parades', and very little business done. Amongst other things we were all medically inspected again; this time to see if we were fit for foreign service. But, curiously enough, this inspection was much less thorough than the one in London.

Meals were a great difficulty and the conditions generally pretty bad, and I believe not a few actually deserted on their second day of service. The hopeless lack of organization is not difficult to explain:–

(1) The maximum accommodation in the barracks is for 500, and we were about 1,500.
(2) There were only four or five N.C.O.'s to manage the lot.
(3) Fresh batches of recruits were arriving daily, and corresponding detachments were being drafted to training camps.

The only pleasant thing about the barracks was the good temper of the N.C.O.'s, who, though hopelessly overworked, yet managed to be patient with all – or most.

The conditions, however, can only be described as disgraceful; after all, if the Government say they require half a million men, they must be prepared to receive them in large numbers. If they have no room they ought to start a waiting list. I understand that Bodmin was not by any means the worst of the depots; at Reading, for instance, men had to sleep in the open without even a blanket. The conditions were all the worse because recruits had been specially told to bring next to no luggage, as they would receive their full kit directly on reaching the depot, whereas, in fact, many received nothing for days, and even weeks, and thus had absolutely no change of clothing.

In the evening general leave to go out was granted, and there was a lively time in the town. Our party took the opportunity to have a good wash and supper in the best hotel – much to the amusement of an officer who was dining at the next table. Our relations with officers are evidently going to be amusing; in normal circumstances I should be against using our comparative wealth for acquiring luxuries which are denied our comrades, but considering the shortage of supplies of all kinds, there is no alternative.

I ought to mention that during the day we were joined by the rest of our company – augmented by an eleventh hour recruit, i.e. E.G. Toye – so that our party now was

P.A. Brown, University Teacher
G. Butterworth
F.B. Ellis, Musician
R.A. Ellis, Engineer and Farmer
F.H. Keeling, Journalist
R.O. Morris, Musician
E.G. Toye, Musician
R.C. Woodhead, Civil Servant

For the night we were put into a tent – immune from vermin of the grosser kinds – and were comparatively comfortable.

In England in 1914 the war was for many still a distant happening about which it was possible to be idealistic. For Delius living in France, its proximity quickly presented him with a less pleasant reality.

(55)
FREDERICK DELIUS TO NORMAN O'NEILL

Grez-sur-Loing · Seine et Marne
15th Sept. 1914

My dear Norman –
I received yesterday your letter & 2 papers dated 14th & 15th August – I had received once before another envoi – Many thanks! We have been seeing life since I wrote you last. From towards the end of August up to the 7th of September there was an ever-growing panic here – The high road to Fontainebleau was a terrifying sight[.] as you know it is the chief road from Paris to the South & all day & all night it was one stream of fleeing refugees – Belgians, peasants from the North of France – rich parisians – big 'camion militaires' filled with wounded – Autos filled with Officers & soldiers – it was a fearful sight – We sat every afternoon for a couple of hours watching this stream of terrified humanity rush bye. [sic] Then suddenly the news came that all the depôts of Fontainebleau had been evacuated in order to make room for the english army – & that General French had established his headquarters at Melun only 20 Kilometers from here – We then began arranging our house for a flight – We buried the silver & about 1000 bottles of our best wine – took all the valuable paintings down – took them off their chassis & rolled them up to take with us – I had had up to now 4 english flags on the house & the villagers began coming & imploring me to take them down as the Uhlans might suddenly turn up & qu'ils en voudraient plus aux anglais qu'aux francais. However we only took down our flags on the morning of our departure Saturday the 5th. We took a train for Orleans via Malesherbes intending to go to Nantes & then by boat to England – In Bourron we got standing room in a luggage van with 40 or 50 others & got to Malesherbes fairly quickly, there we had to wait 4 hours & at last were crowded with 60 others into a wagon à bestiaux which had just been evacuated by horses. There was at least 2

inches of horse droppings on the floor & we had to sit on our portmanteaus: we left Malesherbes at 5 pm & arrived at Orleans at 3–30 a.m. a distance of 60 Kilometers – there was not a room to be had in Orleans – the station was crowded with refugees sleeping on the floor everywher[e]—at last we resigned ourselves to our fate & passed the rest of the night on a bench not far from the station. When the hotels opened we luckily were able to get some café au lait at the Grand Hotel d'Orléans & the proprietor promised us the first room that should become free – This we got at night & we both felt as if we had been saved from a great catastrophe. We determined not to quit this hotel until we were bombarded out of it & so we stayed a week & had a most interesting time & very good food & coffee & wine – at our table were several officers, so we got the news before the rest of the town. There are at least 100,000 soldier[s] in Orleans – train after train of english passed thro' going to the front and the high road was one long cavalcade of English Camions with supplies – By the by the organisation of the English army is admirable & the admiration of everyone – I spoke to a wounded english soldier who had been at Mons & Charleroi: he had a bullet thro his elbow & a shrapnel wound in the heel. He said that out of 1500 there were only 50 left – The most heartrending of all was to see the trains with wounded arrive. Only then does one realise what war is – We saw soldiers on stre[t]chers – with both legs shot off. There are 55,000 wounded men in Orleans & fresh coming night & day. As soon as we heard of the German defeat & repulse we determined to go back to Grez & started yesterday morning at 9.50: at Ma[r]les-herbes we had 7 hours to wait: & we saw a train full of German wounded come thro' – They looked awfully sick & some must have had fearful wounds as they were lying side by side in the straw – there were also 2 spies that had been taken – one was a big thick set looking german – bound hand & foot guarded by 4 soldiers – The other was a young fellow dressed as an English soldier. I spoke to him in English but he only knew two or 3 words – he spoke french like a french man – I suppose they are both dead by this time. On our way from Orleans to Grez we had a first class carriage entirely to ourselves – No one seems to be going in that direction – I shall never forget the look in the eyes of that big german spy – He seemed to know that he was already as good as dead & seemed to take no interest whatever in anything anymore – Everybody, of course, wanted to have a look at him & one after the other they crowded up on to the marche pied to have a look at him – Just like a menagerie. After giving a look the women generally said – Ah! qu'il est drôle! Whilst the battle of the Marne was being fought, we distinctly heard the *boum-bou-bou-boum* of the canons here in Grez so we thought it was about time to get – as the Americans say – & not be caught in a déroute – we had of course no idea that it would be a great french victory – We can only hope now that the allies will follow up their victory & drive the Germans home again & end this fearful carnage – If, then, the Germans will only get rid of their Café Concert Kaiser & his numerous family & become a peaceable nation once more I think there will be no more war in Europe ever again – But they've got to be smashed first & the sooner the better – The french have been showing qualities which I never suspected in them – a tremendous soberness & earnestness – I saw regiment upon regiment marching to the railway station on their way to the front – No military music – no tambours – silence but every man looked in dead earnest & as if he were determined to do his best to the last – Write to me & let me know how things are in England – send me the D.T. war Corresp. account of the 5 days battle of the Marne – We have begun digging up our treasures – With love to you both from Jelka & me, –
I remain,
yrs ever

FREDERICK DELIUS

(56)
LANDON RONALD to STANLEY HAWLEY

The Guildhall School of Music
October the Second 1914

Private and Confidential

My dear Stanley Hawley

If you haven't made all your arrangements with the Philharmonic, I think it might interest you to know that I had intended giving the first performance in London of Rachmaninoff's 2nd Symphony at one of my own Symphony Concerts, but for reasons I need not enter into it has practically been decided not to give these concerts this season.

The work is a stupendous one and ought to be heard here. I have done it with enormous success at Birmingham – so much so that I had to repeat it twice in one week – and I am doing it at Liverpool on Tuesday and giving the first performance of it in Manchester a little later on.

It is a work that delights the public and the musician alike, and I am wondering if you would care to arrange for me to do it at one of your concerts? It takes about 35 to 40 minutes.

Ever yours,

LANDON RONALD

Stanley Hawley was Secretary of the Royal Philharmonic Society from 1913 to 1915. In fact, the Rachmaninov Second Symphony had already been given in London, at a Philharmonic Society concert in May 1910, when it had been conducted by Nikisch. Ronald refers to the cut version of Rachmaninov's symphony. (See also letter 37.)

At the outbreak of the war many musicians, particularly those of foreign or Empire extraction, went abroad for one reason or another. The young pianist and composer Arthur Alexander, a New Zealander, had already been committed to a concert tour in Australia and New Zealand. A close friend of Arnold Bax and his circle at the Royal Academy of Music, Alexander's friends in England wrote to keep him up to date with the progress of the war and its impact on musical life.

(57)
S. H. BRAITHWAITE to ARTHUR ALEXANDER

Irton
Cromer Road
Bournemouth
Dec 5th/14

My dear Arthur
At last your long looked for letter! And I am the most envied of all your friends in London, with seven pages of particulars of the tour! I was glad enough to have them, and to know you had safely crossed all those miles of water, and arrived whole on

your native soil. You do not mention your people, or the reception given you, so I conclude your opinion of the former is not yet settled, and that the latter was not a thing to talk about. Your voyage was much as I expected; but Teneriffe [*sic*] will be remembered for a long time, and I dare say you enjoyed some other mornings, with the sun overhead and the salt breezes in your nose. But if you did not enjoy the passage as a whole, it must have done you good, and I am sure you are a great deal saner than you were when you left Hampstead.

Now for the news. I will begin with the war and work back to myself. Just what is happening you will know as well as I do, but I can perhaps tell you a little bit about London: – Soldiers everywhere, drilling, marching, eating, drinking, riding in trains, trams & 'buses, – you can't escape them, and there is no need to, as they are a fine, wholesome looking lot of men, – and mostly well behaved & pleasant to meet. The male civil population is rather small, but millions of women have come to the front (I wish they had gone) so that London is about as full as ever. After sunset most of the lights are either lowered or out, so that it is almost dark. Search lights at Hyde Park Corner, the Admiralty, and at other points, search for Zeppelins, and I believe other games much favoured by darkness go on in and around the Squares of Leicester & Soho – but of this I have no personal knowledge, and I only have the support of rumours. The Theatres are mostly open and 'business as usual' is the generally accepted motto. We travel in trains with the blinds down (here again you'll see possibilities) and on foot under the protection of bomb-proof umbrellas, or so Truth had it a fortnight or so ago. Mr. Shaw has written a long pamphlet entitled 'Common sense about the war' which seems to have upset a lot of sober minded people, though I believe that when the air has cleared and we can see by the cold light of day we shall find in it a lot more truth than malice; in fact, most of it reads, for me, as very clear, cool-headed common sense, though some of it I can't swallow. A number of Irish newspapers have been writing rather nasty things, or so I believe, but on the whole we are more or less unanimous, and all most hopeful & cheery. Now as to how the war has affected music. The Promenade Concerts were held as usual, & the Symphony & Philharmonic are on again. A few British compositions have figured in the programmes, including Arnold's [Bax] Fatherland, a new piece by Delius, & some less interesting things; but Bach, Beethoven, & Brahms still hold the field. Patriotic concerts are being given in most parts of England, & a host of vulgarities bearing Union-Jack covers come for review in the Music Student, and get very small shrift from me. Mackenzie is giving an all British orchestral concert this term, when one can absorb the subtle beauties of Cowen, Edward German, Eric Grant, Parry, & F. Corder; the latter having unearthed an Operatic Aria of the mid-Victorian era, containing a martial strain accompanied (in short chords) by the whole band! I believe that German & Austrian musicians have been banished from our large orchestras, & that all the Blue Hungarian bands have become Pink Belgian, without undergoing any other change, which matters not at all, as the players are, & were, all English! Cesar Franck's Symphony is to be done in January, Beecham conducting, Psyche I heard at the Promenades, and Eolides was done one Sunday in October. Dale is a prisoner now in Berlin; he went a Germanying for his summer holidays & was captured at Munich when war broke out. Kastner, Beringer & Wesseley are still with us; Cole & Bell have gone to fight; there is no change otherwise at the Institution. I dare say, we shall feel the pinch next term, but we are all busy so far.

Now about your friends.

Harriet [Cohen] has taken a room near Swiss Cottage, where she is living the higher life, to the accompaniment of a gas stove, & the rapping of the neighbour's knuckles on the wall whenever too much music goes on of a night. Prester John is doing special constable's duty, guarding the reservoir on Hampstead Heath! Arnold has got into the house in Regent's Park. Mrs. Matthay still owes me 5/–; and Alfred goes his rounds leaning on a stick *and an umbrella*. Now about myself. I think I told you I got an attack of influenza – you came to say goodbye when I was developing – and I got more & more in the train coming down here & after I arrived. So that I was unfit for about a month. Still, I got to Swanage, Studland, Ringwood, and many other places, and in spite of doctors & dentists managed to get well again. Early in September Mother, Nellie & I set out for Windermere, with many misgivings, for the country at that time had rather lost its head; but we arrived all right & spent a fortnight together which was enjoyed very much. There is no place quite like that. I stayed on after they had left & did some sketching. [Percy] Heming & his wife were at Ambleside, and I met a pupil in Coniston Church. When I returned I decided to stay in Town only four nights during the week, & to come down here for the week ends; so I took a room in Upper Gloucester Place & remained for three rather restless weeks. Then Heming rescued me & I was installed in his flat in Parkhill Road. This was really very nice, but it could not be allowed to continue, and in a month Heming got an engagement to go touring with Clara Butt, so I found myself homeless and adrift in the Euston Road, where eventually I anchored at the Gower Hotel! One evening I chanced to stray into the Settlement, & then I was persuaded by Greenslade & others to return to the fold; so there I am again, much as I was two years ago! Odd, isn't it? In September Pole advised me to call at the School of Music here, which I did, with the result that I was put on the staff, so you see I get my weekends for nothing & put a few shillings into my pocket. I have been ill quite half the term with colds & stomach trouble, but I have worked and turned pianist again – I appear in a Beethoven Cello Sonata at the Winter Gardens on the 22nd! The idea of my playing Beethoven is really too ludicrous, but I assure you I do it quite well. I am also supposed to appear in Tonsbillon & the Scherzo (Saint-Saëns) Mrs Farrell-Watson doing the other half, but no date is fixed as yet – Mrs Farrell-Watson is a pupil of Tobias [Matthay]. Now for the Scherzo. It is finished; 108 pages; 32 staves to the page; 2 piccolos, 2 flutes, 2 oboes, cor anglais, 2 clarinets, one E♭ clarinet & one bass, 2 bassoons, one contra bassoon, four horns, 2 trumpets, 3 trombones, tuba, tympani, bass drum, cymbals, tambourine, glockenspiel, celesta, a large bell, 2 harps, & strings. I believe it is all good, and I am sure a few pages will sound remarkable. Last Tuesday night I went to Bax's to dinner. Bax was quite excited over the score, which he seemed to think quite as good as the piece. He seemed very surprised, and could not understand how I could score so well, having had no opportunity of judging my own works. He suggested one or two additions, such as a pizzicato chord here & there to enforce an occasional climax, & a little thickening for a bar or two after some forte chords, all of which I took readily enough, as I am always open to all rational suggestions; but they will really make only a little difference. Of course Balfour Gardiner is not giving any more concerts at present, and Bax does not think it safe to entrust my one score to Beecham; so there is little chance of my hearing it for some time. Still, it is done, and that's something. Arnold has written five new songs (Roumanian Peasant Songs) which are extraordinary. [*The Bard of the Dimbovitza* for soprano and orchestra]. One, called 'The Well of Tears', is simply astounding. Now it is time to stop, & when I write again I'll give you more news. Mother is in bed with a cold, Nellie, Harry, & I have them too, my aunt has a swollen face, so you see Bournemouth is not living up to its reputation. The term ends on Friday & I am looking forward to more composition & drawings. Well, a merry Christmas to you & the best of good luck at other times.

Yours ever

TIM

(58)
PRIVATE H. TOMPKINS to A FRIEND

When the lines are very quiet during the day, as they often are, our telephone operator in the fort sometimes gives a mouth-organ concert into the receiver, and by the connexion of instruments the concert is heard in every trench throughout the whole division, covering an area of nearly 15 miles. It is quite interesting, and sounds just like a gramophone. The performances are quite looked forward to.

(59)
SIR CHARLES VILLIERS STANFORD to THE TIMES

Published in the issue dated 12 December 1914 p. 9

50 Holland Street
Kensington, London w.
Dec. 11, 1914

Sir,—May I be allowed to write a word of strong protest against the postponement of the Birmingham Festival next October? The forefathers of the Festival Committee took no such step during the Napoleonic wars of a century ago when the Empire and Birmingham alike were much smaller and poorer than they are now.

To drop the Festival means a loss to the musical profession, already disastrously hit by the war, of not less than some £5,000. To hold it as usual might or might not mean a loss at this juncture of about £2,500. Is not the rich capital of the Midlands prepared to risk that sum rather than fine the players and singers who have worked so loyally for her in the past a sum of nearly treble the amount? There never was a greater claim for 'business as usual'.

I venture to hope for a reconsideration of the decision, and for a wide public request that it should be cancelled and the Festival restored.

Yours faithfully,

CHARLES V. STANFORD.

A correspondence on this subject continued during December 1914, Stanford publishing a further two letters in the issues of 17 and 24, but the Festival was not revived and indeed no further festival was held in Birmingham until 1968.

(60)
Capt. A. CORBETT-SMITH to THE TIMES

Published in The Times dated 18 Jan 1915 p. 9

Expeditionary Force
Jan. 14, 1915

Sir,–'Referring to the interview with Sir Charles Stanford upon the above subject [the choice of appropriate songs for use by the army], as recorded in your issue of January 13, will you very kindly allow me to point out that one of the main objects for which the Naval and Military Musical Union was founded some years ago is the encouragement of the singing of good songs upon the line of march? From its inception the union has met with whole-hearted support from all ranks in the Navy and Army, from naval and military authorities in the Overseas Dominions, from the Press, and finally from his Majesty the King, who, in July last, officially recognized its work by graciously according to the union the Royal patronage.

At the outbreak of the war there were represented upon the central council every military command in the United Kingdom, the several Fleet units, and certain of the overseas commands, and a renewed organization was fully in train for the adequate propagation of the union's aims and objects. Unfortunately for the union the central council and executive committee, from General Sir H. L. Smith-Dorrien, the president, down to the hon. secretary-general, left, I believe, *en masse*, for active service and the work came to a standstill so far as home units are concerned.

Sir Charles Stanford's wholly admirable suggestion with regard to the revival of folk-songs, in connexion with the Services, was fully considered by the committee some five years ago, and we approached the English and Irish folk-song societies on the subject. A new official song-book was in preparation in which many of the best and most representative folk-songs were to be included. Further, a pocket book of marching songs was being compiled and edited by Mr. Harold Boulton (also a member of the committee).

I feel sure that I voice the opinion of members of the central council in saying that the active participation in the movement of those gentlemen whose names you mention would be most cordially welcomed in furthering by any means the objects which we have so long had in view. I have ventured to adduce the above details to indicate to all would-be helpers that an officially recognized organization is already in existence, and that it would probably prove of no little value in simplifying further activities. I shall be happy to reply (so far as active service permits) to any communications addressed to the offices of the union, 37, Russell-square, London.

I am, Sir, your obedient servant

(61)
SIR HUBERT PARRY to RALPH VAUGHAN WILLIAMS

19 January 1915

As to your enlisting, I can't express myself in any way that is likely to be serviceable. There are certain individuals who are capable of serving their country in certain exceptional and very valuable ways, and they are not on the same footing as ordinary folks, who if they are exterminated are just one individual gone and no more. You have already served your country in very notable and exceptional ways and are likely to do so again: and such folks should be shielded from risk rather than be exposed to it.

We may admit the generosity of the impulse, and feel – I will not say what.

(62)
ETHEL H. BAINTON to GRANVILLE BANTOCK

Bornholme
Moorside
Fenham
Newcastle-on-Tyne
March 21st 1915

Dear Sir
I am writing to you on behalf of my husband (Edgar L. Bainton) who is a civilian prisoner in Germany.

I am requiring a lady teacher of singing for Conservatoire in Newcastle & wondered if you had anyone at the Institute or in Birmingham who would care to start an opening in the north.

If you should know anyone really good I should be most grateful for her name and address that I may communicate with her.

I should like someone to commence next term. Apologizing for troubling you –

Yours faithfully

ETHEL H. BAINTON

The composer Edgar Bainton, later to emigrate to Australia, spent the First World War as a prisoner in Ruhleben Camp near Berlin. His wife maintained the activities of the Newcastle Conservatoire of which he was Principal, until he returned.

(63)
SIR HUBERT PARRY'S DIARY

March 18 1915

To Queen's Hall at 10.30. Very good rehearsal of [Parry's tone poem] From Death to Life. Band played up most amiably. Got back to College soon after 11. Heavy correspondence. At 1 to say good-bye to Aveling's nephew who is going off to the front to-night. Back to College for luncheon. In afternoon letters and preparation for Executive at 5. Finished soon after 6. Found Dolly had arrived at 17 Kensington Square: she had been hearing Darke play the Chorale Preludes on his organ. To Philharmonic with her and Maud. 'Death to Life' went capitally, but I could feel it was not a success.

(64)
FREDERICK S. KELLY to DONALD FRANCIS TOVEY

Hood Battalion
H.M.T. Grantully Castle
Skyros
Friday, April 23rd 1915

The events of to-day made a deep impression on me. Rupert Brooke died on board the French hospital ship at 4.45 p.m., and in view of the ship's orders to sail at 5 a.m. the following morning, arrangements were at once made to bury him on the island he loved so well ... It was about a mile from the shore to the grove, over very difficult stony ground, and the petty officers who bore the coffin had to go very slowly. We reached the grove at 10.45 p.m., where, in the light of a clouded half-moon, the burial service was read ... It was a most moving experience. The wild sage gave a strong classical tone, which was so in harmony with the poet we were burying that to some of us the Christian ceremony seemed out of keeping. When all the others had gone back to the boats, Lieut.-Commander Freyberg, Ock Asquith, Charles Lister, Denis Browne, and I covered the grave with stones and as many pieces of marble as we could find ... The body lies looking down the valley towards the harbour, and, from behind, an olive-tree bends itself over the grave as though sheltering it from the sun and rain. No more fitting resting-place for a poet could be found than this small grove, and it seems as though the gods had jealously snatched him away to enrich this scented island. For the whole day I was oppressed with the sense of loss, but when the officers and men had gone, and when at last the five of us, his friends, had covered his grave with stones, and took a last look in silence – then the sense of tragedy gave place to a sense of passionless beauty, engendered both by the poet and the place.

This makes an interesting parallel with the composer W. Denis Browne's better-known account, in a letter of 25 April to Edward Marsh, which is quoted in the Collected Poems of Rupert Brooke.* *The French Hospital Ship was the Duguay-Trouin, where Brooke had died of blood poisoning without having seen action. Within six weeks Browne was dead, and Kelly and Lister were both killed later.*

(65)
SIR HUBERT PARRY'S DIARY

3 May 1915

... To College at 12. Aveling gave me the distressing news that his nephew had died in Hospital of severe wounds received in the recent fighting. It depressed me so much that I could hardly get through the address without breaking down. So it was a very bad one.

(66)
SIR HUBERT PARRY'S DIARY

20 May 1915

... Poor Mr. B, Novello's head engraver, called to see me in great distress about being repatriated which he didn't want at all. I tried to comfort him. After lunch to see Frank and Helen [Pownall, whose only son George had been killed in Gallipoli a fortnight before]. Found him very low, lingering over old photographs. She fiercely brave. Tried to cheer them up.

(67)
GEORGE GARDNER to GRANVILLE BANTOCK

2 Vicarage Road
Handsworth
Birmingham
June 6 1915

My dear Mr. Bantock,
Curwens write – 'We are much impressed with your Te Deum & should like to publish it, if you are willing to let us do so, on a royalty of one-sixth. There are of course not many choirs that will tackle so difficult a work, but it is so distinct from anything else we have seen that we should like to have it on our list'.

This is due to your kind encouragement & I am most grateful.

The Clergy at our Diocesan Chapter last week took very kindly to the idea of a Festival Service & appointed a small sub-committee to co-operate.

Poor G. von Holst has been harrassed by the police, & I have had to write saying that his father was, & he is, as English as I am!

---

*'Death' *in* 'Memoir by Edward Marsh' pp cliii–clv *In The Collected Poems of Rupert Brook.* Sidgwick & Jackson Ltd., 2nd edition 1928, pp cliii–clvi.

(68)
HAVERGAL BRIAN to GRANVILLE BANTOCK

17 Wykeham Mansions
West Dulwich
1915 June 16th

My dear BB

If you are likely to be in town this weekend, please let me know! I am *not* likely to have much time after this weekend. My money has been made to £2 per week in the Canadian Record Office but as you know how very low the purchasing power of a sovereign now is – the slight increase makes very little difference. Nor is this all! A notice appeared in the 'Daily Orders' this morning that after Friday the staff would have to work overtime. From enquiries I've made it seems we are in for it from 9am to 11pm. My wife will never see me at this rate. Everything is chaos and arrears. The particular staff to which I belong moved to a special office this morning at 36 Victoria Street. I see a lot of the inner working of things in connection with the Canadian Force. A lieutenant who works with me got his commission for bravery at the last big battle at Ypres. A lady called at the office last Friday morning at noon for news of her husband. She was handed a slip of paper – 'Killed in action': at 2 o'clock when I went in after lunch she had not recovered from the shock. Small as the Canadian Force appears in comparison with the whole – would you believe the staff at Westminster totals 517?

There are some things I want to talk about as soon as I may see you. The 'Festal Dance' you ought to hear: the New Symph Orch is a gorgeous instrument. I heard a most extraordinary performance of Cesar Franck's Symphony under Beecham the other night. Perhaps as fine a performance has never taken place. It will long live in my memory. How shallow Tchaikovsky appears by the side of Franck! Almost an imposter! It is a strange thing that just at the time when my smash took place two years ago I had Franck's Organ Preludes on order & was about to make an exhaustive study of all he had written. The symphony is the first thing I have heard – and my study of Franck never began. But how serenely beautiful is this symphony.

Dale's Suite for Viola & Orchestra was a pleasant surprise for me. He has an exclusive temperament – as much so as the little chap (Henry?) who played his work at your concert in Nov last for Piano & orchestra. Really I must cease – I'm tired.

Always your

BRIAN

After joining up at the outbreak of the war, Brian spent part of the war working in a clerical capacity in the Canadian Record Office in London.

(69)
HAVERGAL BRIAN to GRANVILLE BANTOCK

17 Wykeham Mansions
West Dulwich
1915 June 20th

My dear BB
Beecham gave a brilliant performance of the dance last night and it was well received. Now accept my thanks, dearest friend, for the part I feel you have played in it. Curiously enough it was the strongest thing in the programme & Berlioz rather helped to emphasise this. I wish you could have heard it. No further opportunity has occurred for a chat with Beecham, so I can only be thankful that he has done something which may lead to more. I should think he would be happy with 'Merryheart' or some of the things lying in my box. Judging from what is happening the salvation of English music appears to have passed into his hands.

I like Ronald less each time I see him & he gets more crusted & old fashioned. Tchaikowsky is his biggest gun & although I must have learned something from this composer, his 'Romeo & Juliet' made me laugh the other night.

Heart-tugs my brother
Always your

BRIAN

The Beecham-Ronald Promenade concerts had included Brian's Festal Dance. (See also p.100.)

(70)
LENA ASHWELL to THE TIMES

Published in the Issue dated 5 July 1915 p. 9

Sir,—I should like to be allowed to endorse every word in Dr. Walford Davies's article 'Music and Men'. I have just returned from a tour in France through the camps and hospitals where we (the Three Arts Club Bureau) have already given nearly 400 concerts, visiting 11 centres in cooperation with the Y.M.C.A. Though we have also given a large number of concerts in England, we have realized the greater necessity to be at the front, and our committee has decided to leave other organizations to deal with the work at home, while we concentrate on France (with an eye on the Dardanelles). Hundreds of thousands of men in the Expeditionary Force look forward to these concerts as red-letter days which make them feel that they are remembered by those at home, for whom they are fighting and enduring lives of danger, monotony and suffering.

As Dr. Walford Davies says. 'Music has already proved itself a necessity, and even one of the means of winning a nation's battles.' This is my firm conviction after a great deal of personal experience in France. Every human being needs a little happiness besides boots and rations to help him on with his work. The ideal would be that national support should be guaranteed for this vital necessity, but in the meantime it is left to personal effort to raise the necessary money. Although there are many calls on our purses at this time, yet surely there is a little money left for work which, as an Army chaplain says, 'is worth much physic and not a few sermons.'

We are sending out our eighth party this month, and unless we can get support it must, alas! be our last. This would be a very bitter disappointment to hundreds of thousands of men, who are waiting for the help and encouragement which we bring them. As one colonel said. 'They have been through Hell, and are getting ready to face it again'; and all who have love and gratitude for those who are sacrificing so much cannot let this appeal fall on unresponding hearts. We are glad of anything, however small, and I will receive and personally acknowledge all donations.

(71)
HAVERGAL BRIAN to GRANVILLE BANTOCK

2 Rainbeck Mansions
West Dulwich
1915 Aug 11th

My Dear BB
I was extremely glad to find your letter here when I returned this evening. Now that my wife is away if you *do* write again, never sign your name to anything you write – because flats are flats and proprietors of furnished flats have master keys. I am living in a flat recently occupied by a now interned German. I have always dreaded the efficiency of the Germans and it is more than confirmed by what I hear – only yesterday I talked with a brawny Scotsman who arrived in London from the front at 4 a.m. yesterday morning. But what sacrifices it has demanded! As little as it may appear, do you know that my feet are of little use since the drill in the H.A.C. I walk a mile from Vauxhall Station to Millbank and it is about as much as I can comfortably manage.

Then look at my little wife having to go. I know you think I am sentimentally silly – but let us try it on you. Supposing circumstances separated you from Helen & the children. Do you think you would become sentimental or would you harden your feelings and screw tight and say 'I must not forget I'm strong – I'm a philosopher'. I know you would try, for the sheer sake of trying but you would cave in. You have never experienced the sensation yet & you cannot realise what it all means until you have. But what is the underlying feeling which has brought all these fine men from the dominions? Go through the ledger sheets & note how man after man is dotted – 'Born in England'. It is sentiment my dear boy which has brought them here. The man who sits a few feet away from me is the Speaker in the House of Parliament of Ottawa – his wife & 4 children are in Canada. Have you ever thought of what we shall be like if we live and become old? I don't think it possible that anything can break our friendship – unless it is your beastly temper. But then you only sulk for a while. Can you think of anything more simply beautiful than the picture of your uncle & your father meeting in Lime St Station Hotel. Both old and white – white beards and chuckling over early days – standing, and a beautiful pair, with their backs to the Hall fireplace. They are both gone & your beard is getting white! Ronald had the impertinence to remind me that *I* was 'awfully grey'.

Yet life is very cheap.

The chap I told you I was interested in because he happened to be so much like Harry Evans is dead. He came home from his office feeling ill, was advised to Broadstairs, came back feeling strong & well. Went straight to the operating theatre, came out a corpse. A grieving widow & child live to continue his memory. I saw a paybook yesterday in which was written just before the man went into the trenches – 'if any accident should happen to me I wish to claim the difference between £1 which I have received & £5 – my rate of pay. This will amount to a considerable sum in course of time'. Signed . . .

He never came back again, was found killed in the trenches, so his pay ceased almost as soon as he wrote his claim. Many of these pay books arrived soaked in blood. But the sad things I think of are those hearts weeping. Wives, mothers, children. Pause, then, my dear boy & try to take in the whole world – there is not a corner but where someone is either now, living in dread of some awful news reaching them, or now actually weeping.

It really is dreadful – & man's ever living curse, selfishness, is the cause. It was happening a hundred years ago is now and ever shall be. It is fate! We live to scourge ourselves.

Always your

BRIAN

During 1915 the monthly periodical The Musical Herald *ran a series of contributions on the theme 'The effect of the War on British music'. Here are two examples:*

(72)
Capt. CYRIL JENKINS to THE MUSICAL HERALD

Officers' Ward
Military Hospital
Bulford
Wilts
[Sept 1915]

The ideal of the true artist lies within himself; he does not consciously go to external surroundings for inspiration, but seeks only to express his own innermost feelings. It is true, of course, that his character and temperament are influenced by his education and environment, and numerous instances could be quoted – Grieg and Dvorak, to mention only two – to show that the national spirit may be so strong an influence as to colour and, indeed, become the chief characteristic.

This lack of national element in our own music cannot be denied, and the reason is that our composers, with few exceptions, have been content to build upon and even imitate the work of various foreign composers and schools as each one came into prominence. One thing is certain and that is that the German school will not be for many, many years the fountain head to which our young composers will go for their inspiration. Alas, it may be the case of out of the frying-pan into the fire, and developments in the future may lead us to more mere copy-work and artificiality than in the past.

No; it is not a question of 'wide sympathies' checking our national spirit in composition, *but a lack of real originality in our composers.* I feel sure all of them would be only too thankful could they write music distinctly British in idiom and character, but it cannot be denied that most of our modern music is the fruit of a foreign tree.

The *Times* statement of July 10th leads one to ask the question, if Englishmen were 'to shut themselves up to the contemplation of their local concerns.' etc., would our music improve? It would most probably limit the matter expressed and lead to artificiality in the manner of expressing it.

I do not think it wise for a creative artist to have to twist his tongue into manners or idioms of speech foreign to his nature, and I am convinced that music which is to live must be the expression of a composer's innermost ideals. For these reasons let the British composer still retain his 'wide sympathies', and let him but express that which within him lies, and it may not be long before we have a composer among us whose music is truly great because sincere. Should the national spirit have so influenced his temperament as to be a characteristic unconsciously reflected in his music and not artificially dragged in, then we shall hail him as a truly British composer.

(73)
GUSTAV HOLST to THE MUSICAL HERALD

[Sept 1915]

The present time is hardly a fit one for discussing this question, not that it is an important one. Some questions are important because they need an immediate solution, such as the one confronting Europe at the present moment; but the importance of the question of national art lies not in the finding of the solution, but rather in the attitude of mind which is brought to bear on it. It is useless to approach the question without an entire absence of prejudice and a delicate sense of artistic values. During the last eleven months we have been told on the one hand that Bach and Beethoven are not German, and on the other that Shakespeare and Dante are. If this be the fate of long established names, what hope is there in discussing the works of living men?

Critics write glibly about British composers being too frequently inspired by foreign subjects, and suggest that they are less British when they do so, forgetting that 'In art everything matters except the subject'. Wagner is Wagner whether writing of Cornwall or of Nuremberg. Elgar is Elgar whether writing of Poland or of the Severn Valley. Gounod showed his nationality most clearly in a German subject, Bizet in a Spanish one. We should be tempted to say that the great characteristic of English artists is their inability to 'shut themselves up to the contemplation of their local concerns', if we did not find the same characteristic everywhere else.

Moreover, it is interesting to note that when this breadth of outlook is most apparent in English history – as in the 16th century – English music flourishes.

For national character is always changing. Contrast the Elizabethan, a brilliant linguist, a poet and musician, with the Englishman of the 18th century. No wonder there is so much difference between the madrigal and the glee.

Finally, the problem is sufficiently elusive even when confined to one period. It is agreed that modern France possesses a national idiom in music. Then it must include Saint-Saëns and Debussy. To trace the subtle connection between two such composers is easy only to the ignorant, while to those who know and feel, such problems are to-day impertinent.

(74)
*GEORGE BUTTERWORTH to HIS FAMILY

Sept. 20. [1915]

And so the Zepps have been to London at last; such things seem small out here, where the sounds of destruction are audible all day and night. It is extraordinary how long one may manage to keep out of it. I have been three times up to the front line, and so far have seen only one shell burst, and have not seen a single
  (a) dead man,
  (b) wounded man,
  (c) German,
  (d) gun.
I have sent the General [Butterworth's father] two instalments of news; will you please ask him to see that nothing I send home gets into print. The authorities are getting nasty about it, even when the matter is harmless.

(75)
ARNOLD BAX to ARTHUR ALEXANDER

The Crossways
Station Rise
Marlow-on-Thames
Oct 10th or thereabouts – anyway it will make little difference [1915]

My dear Sasha
When am I going to hear your present view of this benighted and decidedly delirious world? I suppose the mental confusion in the Colonies is not quite so appalling and desolating as it is over here, but I take it there is quite enough even there.

For my own part I have been swaying backwards and forwards between two courses – that of entering the army (and becoming bold and British thereby, or pretending to be) and that of plunging into a narcotic ocean of creative work. The result of these vagaries is a very disconcerting dizziness of the nerves. I have gone through and survived the London Zeppelin event (which was totally lacking in charm) and have attempted (and failed) to detect some shadow of sober fact about the war from the wild performances of the English press. And so in the quixotic search for a moderately balanced state of mind I am down here in Marlow where the river at least sings the same ancient romantic poem that it sang in 1913 – and I expect in 1313. Tim* is staying with us and goes up by day to the abode of Vice (I refer to the R.A.M.) He and I have become great friends. He is really a delightful person and so perversely humorous about his pessimisms and complaints – one of the few people who have any inkling as to what is worth while in life and what he really wants. We had a great time by the shores of his adored Windermere in April.

I think you will be pleased to hear that I have had my 'annus mirabilis' as far as work is concerned – some of it – piano-stuff – is already published by Augener who until Strecker [the manager] was interned appeared to sit with open mouth for anything one cared to send them. One of these – a piece called 'In a Vodka Shop' – was performed by Myra at a recital with what I understand from Augener's catalogue was 'a sensational success'. I shall now proceed to brag of my other performances. They include

> Six orchestral songs from the 'Bard of the Dimbovitza'
> Three Chaucer Songs
> The last movement of the quintet
> A new last movement to my violin sonata
> A Second Violin Sonata
> 'Nympholept' *2nd* edition (an orchestral effort)
> About ten piano pieces
> and a longish piece for violin and piano

This is not so bad, is it? I am now going gently crazy in an attempt to orchestrate the 'Garden of Fand'.

Hitherto I note that this letter has been an exhibition of unexampled egotism which must have wearied you abominably. Are you likely to come back soon? I hear scraps of news about you from time to time chiefly from Tim. I wish you would send me a line one day and tell me all you have been doing. I expect you have had a highly successful career in New Zealand at which you probably laughed cynically. Do you know I have not played a piano duet since you left – because nobody will do after yourself for that form.

I wonder if you ever think affectionately as I often do of a certain sultry summer twilight in Well Walk when we played 'Antar' and felt damned young and deliciously melancholy – 'King George' (that egregious ass) was sitting on the sofa – but he was quite swamped in the mood. There were many good music-times – but somehow I think that was the best. There is an equally mellow mood out of doors to-day though the eyes of Autumn are very melancholy and behind every mood that would other-wise be beautiful one feels in danger of the mental and moral landslides that the present hideous social upheaval is so apt to occasion. Life is abominably nervy and all the old values are disused. Art seems an anomaly, though deep within one there is the conviction that if beauty is true at all it is always true and the only normal pursuit of the soul.

I don't know how the present chaos will effect you when you return to England. Perhaps with a fresher mind you will be able better to withstand it. Hard work in one form or another is the only anodyne to the fever. Also nature, which retains her impassive indifference whilst 'civilisation' foams at the mouth and gibbers.

However I suppose there must be an end some day.

Every good wish to you, old Sasha. If you are not yet returning let me have a letter some day.

always your affectionate friend

ARNOLD
*i.e. S. H. Braithwaite

(76)
*PHILIP HESELTINE to FREDERICK DELIUS

c/o D.H. Lawrence
Porthcothan
St. Merryn
Padstow
Cornwall
Jan. 6th, 1916

I have made five or six abortive attempts to write to you, but during these first days in a new environment I feel completely at a loss, mentally, and cannot write one coherent page. So you must pardon an apparent reticence, an apparent lack of enthusiasm and vitality, which I think and hope is only temporary and superficial. The past months have been full of anxieties and small nagging worries, each petty in itself individually, but en masse powerful and wearing to one's nervous vitality. At the moment I am completely exhausted, as though I had been dragged, insensible, out of the sea. And although I trust that with 1915 I have put behind me for ever a great deal of foolish and harmful stock-in-trade with which my life was encumbered, I have not yet gained enough positive energy to set out on the forward track again. Like the man out of whom Jesus cast seven devils, I feel 'swept and garnished' but empty, awaiting the arrival of the soul's new tenants (which in the case instanced were, I believe, seven more devils worse than the first! However, one can but hope for the angels!)

At any rate this is the beginning of a fresh start. Here on this stormy coast the winds blow through and through one from mid-Atlantic, and the waves surge and thunder and break right over the cliffs, and the spray falls on one's face with a chill, cleansing moisture. It is a wild, open country of vast expanses, giving a great sense of freedom and openness. The morning and evening twilights are incredibly beautiful. Yesterday, as I was walking home, into the sunset, I was haunted all the while by the Dance from the *North Country Sketches*, which seems most perfectly to express the Stimmung of Cornwall . . .

I asked Lawrence to write to you a few days ago, to give you this exposition of our plans. However, I don't want to identify myself with him in anything beyond his broad desire for an ampler and fuller life – a real life as distinct from the mere mouldy-vegetable existence which is all that is possible here. He is a very great artist, but hard and autocratic in his views and outlook, and his artistic canons I find utterly and entirely unsympathetic to my nature. He seems to be too metaphysical, too anxious to be comprehensive in a detached way and to care too little for purely personal, analytical, and introspective art. His views are somewhat at variance with his own achievements. But he is, nevertheless, an arresting figure, a great and attractive personality, and his passion for a new, clean, untrammelled life is very splendid.

. . . There are many other things I should like to talk to you about, but I feel too unclear to broach any of them at present. A few days will, I hope, bring both clarity and developments. I wish so much that I could have come over to you at Grez this New Year, but it appears to be quite impossible to get a passport. . . .

(77)
CECIL GRAY to GRANVILLE BANTOCK

12h Cheyne Walk
Chelsea
London s.w.
Sunday Feb 13th [1916]

Dear Mr. Bantock,
I wonder if you still remember me? It is now about a year since I saw you last in
Birmingham, and I remember on that occasion that you said you would be very glad
if I were to send you anything I wrote.

Since then I have been working at a poem for orchestra which I have just recently
finished, and I was wondering if it would be presumptuous for me to ask you if I
might send it to you for criticism. I naturally would not venture to do this without
writing to you first, knowing how busy you always are – And in any case knowing
that you would be much more profitably occupied in creation yourself than in
wasting time over the crude and possibly worthless productions of aspiring
composers. And if you also feel like that about yourself, I do sincerely hope you
would write and say so. I know that many great musicians such as Liszt have
unsparingly given their time and help to the younger generation, but it is very much
open to question if they were really justified in so doing!

The work is scored for ordinary orchestra (cor anglais and tuba included).
Mindful of your advice I intended at first to score it for small orchestra, but it
couldn't be done. It is in one fairly long movement – ie about 20 mins in
performance I should imagine.

It is not a symphonic poem in the true sense of the word – that is, it has no definite
programme, but is simply the expression of a mood. Being myself a Celt, I have
been largely inspired in it by the old Celtic legends of Deirdre, Cuchulain and these
other glorious myths, and in large part by the Celtic mysticism, and love of nature.

The musical idiom is of course anything but modern – chromaticism is absolutely
opposed to the conception of the work, although on rare occasions I have made use
of it –

– But I am afraid I am writing as if you really had expressed a desire to see it – an
impression I did not mean to give.

With kind regards
Yours sincerely,

CECIL GRAY

(78)
THE CHIEF CONSTABLE OF BIRMINGHAM to GRANVILLE BANTOCK

CHIEF CONSTABLE'S OFFICE
Corporation Street
Birmingham
16th February, 1916

Sir.
In the event of a hostile air raid, I have been asked to inform you that as soon as a public warning is given an intimation should at once be made by those in authority to the audiences or congregations, as the case may be, advising that all persons should proceed expeditiously to their homes, and that as all railway, tramway, and other traffic facilities will be at a standstill, they must walk home.

Yours faithfully
CHARLES HAUGHTON RAFTER
Chief Constable

(79)
HOWARD CARR to GRANVILLE BANTOCK

Adelphi Theatre
Strand London wc
March 20th '16

My dear Mr. Bantock
I am deputed to lay before you the reports of two meetings recently held by a group of London conductors.

It was not thought desirable to approach you until some concrete proposals could be stated to you. Now that it is agreed to form an association for the mutual protection of conductors' interests, it is desired to enlist your sympathy and support. You will see that the immediate reason for the discussions was the proposed action of the National Orchestral Association – which, if allowed to mature, would mean the submission of the orchestral director to his orchestra's union. This arrangement it is believed, would be highly prejudicial to the good relations so necessary to good work, which now exists between the great majority of conductors and their men.

There are other aspects of our professional position which it is hoped will be materially improved by the existence of a strong association of conductors. These will be discussed in due course.

You, who know so well the difficulties of a musical career in England, will, I am sure, give your serious consideration to this movement, which aims at ameliorating the conditions under which a number of earnest musicians are suffering at present. The sympathy and support of the leaders of our profession are essential to the permanent success of the association.

The meeting would be grateful, therefore, if you would address to it a letter stating your views.

Yours faithfully With kind regards.

HOWARD CARR
Hon. Sec. protem.

Enclosed with this letter were the cyclostyled minutes of the first two meetings:

CONFIDENTIAL
An informal meeting of Orchestral & Theatrical Conductors took place on March 10th in the Manager's room at the Coliseum (by courtesy of Mr. Croxton).

The object of the meeting was to discuss certain tendencies likely to prejudice the independence and free action of musical directors.

There were present Sir Edward Elgar, and Messrs. Norman O'Neill, Hubert Bath, Howard Carr, Percy Fletcher, Sidney Jones, Howard Talbot, J.M. Glover, Walter Hayne, Christopher Wilson, Napoleon Lambelet, Aubrey Kennett, Gustave Ferrari, Leon Bassett, Kennedy Russell, Walter Greco, Julian Jones, Albert Cazabon, Ernest Bucalossi, Arthur Wood, Albert Fox, and J. Weaver.

Letters regretting previous engagements and expressing their willingness to attend later meetings were received from Sir Frederic Cowen and Messrs. Landon Ronald, H. Quick and Cuthbert Clarke. Mr. A. Dove was prevented from attending by illness. Mr. J.M. Glover was elected to the chair.

Mr. Carr explained the chief reason of the meeting: the alleged intention of the N.O.A. to bring pressure to bear upon theatrical conductors to join that union.

Discussion followed, which was contributed to by Sir Edward Elgar, Hubert Bath, J.M. Glover, Howard Carr, Aubrey Kennet, Leon Bassett and Christopher Wilson.

A resolution, proposed by Mr. Howard Talbot, and seconded by Mr. Sidney Jones, that 'in the opinion of the undersigned, it is expedient to immediately form an association of Musical Directors for protective interests' was carried unanimously.

CONFIDENTIAL
A further meeting of Orchestral Conductors, and Musical Directors, took place at the Club Room, Gatti's Restaurant, on the 17th March.

There were present Sir Frederic Cowen, Messrs. L. Bassett, E. Bucalossi, H. Carr, A. Cazabon, A. Dove, G. Ferrari, H. Finck, P. Fletcher, J.M. Glover, E. Jones, A. Kennett, M. Klein, A. Maclean, N. O'Neill, and C. Wilson.

Letters and telegrams, regretting previous engagements, and expressing full sympathy with the objects of the meeting were received from Messrs. Landon Ronald, Percy Pitt, Julian Jones, A. Fox, H. Talbot, W. Hague, J. Weaver, and O. Willis.

Sir Frederic Cowen was elected to the Chair.

The alleged intention of the N.O.A. to insist upon Conductors joining the Union was discussed. Further consideration was also given to the question of forming an Association for the mutual protection of the professional interests of Orchestral and Theatrical Conductors.

Sir Frederic Cowen, Mr. Manuel Klein, Mr. Edward Jones, and Mr. Howard Carr expressed their views.

Mr. J. M. Glover proposed the following motion which was seconded by Mr. L. Bassett, and Mr. A. Kennett, that:–

1. An Association of Musical Directors be formed.
2. That a General Committee be formed, with a small Executive Committee with power to act to form a set of rules to cover legally our various activities.

The motion was carried unanimously.

It was decided to call a General Meeting of Musical Directors and Orchestral Conductors at 12, noon the 22nd March, at the Knight Room, Simpson's Restaurant, Strand, W.C.

A large attendance is expected, and every Orchestral Conductor and Musical Director is urged to make an effort to be present.

(80)
BRIGADIER-GENERAL H. PAGE CROFT
to SIR ALEXANDER KAYE BUTTERWORTH

August 13th, 1916

I feel I must write you a note to tell you how deeply I grieve with you and yours for the loss of your gallant son. He was one of those quiet, unassuming men whose path did not appear naturally to be a military one, and I had watched him doing his duty quietly and conscientiously. When the offensive came he seemed to throw off his reserve, and in those strenuous 35 days in which we were fighting off and on, he developed a power of leadership which we had not realised that he possessed. As you know, I recommended him for an earlier action near Contalmaison for the Military Cross, which, alas! he could not wear. When in front of Pozières he was reported to me to have done excellent work under very heavy fire in getting his men to dig a new trench right in front of the Germans, from which, later, the Australians were able to successfully attack that village. Later we went into a line on the right of the Australians, S.E. of Pozières.

Here we were about 450 yards from the Germans, and I gave orders to dig a trench within 200 yards of them so that we could attack with some chance of success.

This trench was dug in a fog, and was a very fine deep trench which saved many lives in the days to follow, and your son again superintended the work, and it was called Butterworth Trench on all the official maps.

Three days afterwards the 13th D.L.I. attacked Munster Alley just N.W. of Butterworth Trench. They won 100 yards after a very hot fight, and I went up there at 4 a.m. in the morning to find the bomb fight still progressing, but the 13th holding their own. Your son was in charge, and the trench was very much blown in and shallow, and I begged him to keep his head down. He was cheery and inspiring his tired men to secure the position which had been won earlier in the night, and I felt all was well with him there. The Germans had been bombing our wounded, and the men all round him were shooting Germans who showed themselves. Within about a minute of my leaving him he was shot, as I heard by telephone on my return. I could ill afford to lose so fine a soldier, and my deepest sympathy goes out to his relations, for I know that the loss of one so modest and yet so brave must create a gap which can never be filled.

Plan attached.

(81)
ARTHUR BLISS to THE PALL MALL GAZETTE

Published in the issue dated 11 Oct. 1916

Sir,

As one of those musicians who have fought German aggression in France, I should like to express my thanks to Edwin Evans and 'Musicus' for their championship of English music and their fight against the predominating influence of Germany at home.

It seems to me unseemly that a fine institution like the London Symphony Orchestra should have to put its financial security in front of its national feelings – if all had followed suit we should never have declared war. Moreover, by its choice of works it has missed a signal opportunity of showing its appreciation and gratitude to those of the profession who are fighting to maintain all the cherished institutions of this country.

The names of two such occur instantly to my mind. One is Dr. R. Vaughan Williams, who for eighteen months had been through the drudgery of a private's work in the R.A.M.C.; the other is Lieutenant G.S.K. Butterworth, M.C., who was killed in action. The works of either would add to the prestige of the English orchestra that included them in its programme; nor do I think that a performance of Vaughan Williams's Symphony in London would be altogether unfitting at this time. I am delighted to think that Dr. Allen is doing the 'Sea Symphony', together with works by Stanford and Parry later in the season to commemorate those of the Senior Service who have died. All honour and success to him!

I do not know whether as a class musicians have been less affected (except financially) than other professions, but when straight from being wounded on the Somme I went into a London concert hall and heard a public vociferously applauding a German soloist, it gives me furiously to think.

As the casualty lists grew and grew, and particularly during the time of the Battle of the Somme, attitudes hardened. Yet for two cultures that had been so inextricably intertwined, many practices long continued. Throughout the War British newspapers could be purchased in Berlin and in London as we have seen, after an initial reaction, German works continued to be performed. Small wonder then that the 25-year-old Arthur Bliss, less than a fortnight after his brother Kennard had been killed at Thiepval (on 28 September) should write in strong terms about London music. In fact Bliss's attitude was permanently coloured by the view he took then, a very positive influence in his activity after the War as a champion of the new and in the development of a highly personal style which took little if anything from Germanic models.

(82)
IVOR GURNEY to HERBERT HOWELLS

?Feb 1917

My dear Howler,
It is too bloody cold to write almost in this barn, but you having been sick and polite
to my 'Flanders' barge, deserve a note longer than this will be.

I hope old chap your health is not more shaky than the weather might excuse; our
promising young genius must not fade away as a flower; we have not enough seeds.

And thanks for playing commercial traveller to me. By the way has Allen* seen
your Concerto? Very much I wish to hear that again, being bon and far from na
pooh finis encore.

Here the country is fine and marked with 1870 earthworks. A huge rock towers
out above the town which being interpreted is the star. Quite a revelation of beauty
after grey desolations.

What stunt are you on now? I wait for the Violin Sonata clear fairly simple with
the romantic slow movement singing of Western things. Show us Tintern and sunset
across the Malvern and Welsh Hills. Make us see the one evening star among the
trees. And the Scherzo of this String Quartett – a great Spring Wind blowing the
hair of the exultant traveller wandering without purpose save to find beauty and to
be comrade with the wind.

O to be back with you . . .

Well, what is Germany's game now? What will come of the clash of the Turpitz
and Bethmann Hollweg parties?

General January has fought for us, though a hard master he was, but le General
Fevrier is even more terrible.

I want you to see a thing just sent by me to Miss Scott, called either 'Beauty' or
'Winter Beauty'. In this two lines you will like.

'Yet O, the star-born passion of Beethoven,
Makes consolation on the quivering strings'.

Pencil bust. Time to finish.

Good luck,
Plenty tuck,
Tunes in the noddle
For Concert-stück
Yours ever

IVOR GURNEY

* Sir Hugh Allen (1869–1946). He succeeded Parry as Director of the Royal College of Music in 1918.

(83)
FREDERICK CORDER to THE MUSICAL TIMES

Published in the issue dated October 1917.

13 Albion Road
S. Hampstead, N.W.6
September 3, 1917

Sir,
My attention has been drawn to the following sentence in the brief notice of a Royal Academy Students' Concert in your August number:
'B. J. Dale's Fantasia for six violas was an item. It is difficult to see why a composer should write for such a combination'.

The matter seems to demand explanation, and as the composer is a prisoner of war and the other person responsible for the work too modest to tell his share, elucidation seems to fall on me. The proper title of the work is 'A short piece (Introduction and Andante) for six Violas', and it was written at the special request of Mr. Lionel Tertis and produced by him at his lecture-recital on June 19, 1911, to testify to the interesting fact that in the short time that he had honoured his *Alma Mater* by teaching there this great artist had produced five first-class players of his beloved instrument. Through his efforts also were half a dozen other additions made to the meagre repertory of the viola, all of great interest and mostly now published. The Sestet, however, is a work of such remarkable beauty, power, and originality that it has received first and last about a dozen public performances, one last year at a de Lara Concert being by a wonderful team of executants. It is difficult, indeed, to see why a composer should ever enter the realms of concerted chamber music, considering the limited public interest even in quartets; but it is the nature of the true artist to love to grapple with difficulties, and where would you find a more striking instance than the present? The six instruments have all highly independent parts, they imitate the sounds of other instruments, they do things that one would have thought impossible for any viola player, and the effect of the whole is of an almost Beethovenish majesty and grandeur and a melodic sweep such as none of the present generation of string-writers seems able to approach. I should not omit to mention that Mr. Tertis gave the whole proceeds of his first concert towards the publication of the Sestet by the S.B.C., and if this has been so long delayed the causes are firstly the well-known fastidiousness and love of revision of the composer, and then – the War! A remarkably fine gramophone record of a special performance of the Sestet has been made, and the people who are empowered to lay hands on a composer's works without leave are trying to make a pianola roll out of it. This is an even more fatuous undertaking than murdering the 'Siegfried Idyll'. It is also interesting to note that the performance so kindly noted in the *Musical Times* was a repetition, by desire, of one given a month before, which was thought a veritable *tour de force* on the part of six young girls.

I am, &c,
F. CORDER

(84)
HERBERT HOWELLS to IVOR GURNEY

Bath Villa
Lydney
Glos.
[1918]

My dear friend,
So they have told you about this silly Army Business of mine! And perhaps you have been conjuring up wild conceptions of H.H. as a soldier! Well: I could have wished it had been possible to keep the knowledge from you altogether: but that was impossible, of course.

It is very, very kind of you to want to write to Sir Hubert about it. But Sir Hubert knows. For I told him about it in a letter which I had to write to him asking for a testimonial for Oxford. He seemed kindly perturbed about the news – and about the welfare of those who are actually in the thick of the fray. I hesitated whether I would tell him or not: but I felt, it would have been wrong to take any great new departure (even a compulsory one) without his knowing it . . . I reasoned likewise with Sir Charles. But in his case, it was like pouring oil on smouldering embers! He is bent on preventing my getting into the Army if possible: and has actually addressed a very urgent letter to Mr. Lloyd George (sent thro' his friend Mr. Butcher, M.P. for York) asking if it be possible for me to be given work in the Censoring Department in London. (Be a Greek, and keep an ox on your tongue!!) I hope good may come of his kindness; for I feel that I could so much better help with my poor brains than with my infinitely poorer body. I frankly feel altogether unfit for actual military duties. I have just discovered that unless I attest not later than tomorrow, I shall be a Conscript. No warning to this effect has been issued by our kindly recruiting officials! So tomorrow I become virtually an Army man! How extraordinarily amusing! But Rumania is a better recruit than I shall ever be!

Meanwhile: I will come on the 18th, if the authorities with further kindness of heart, allow of my being examined before then.

Meanwhile again: 'Sir Patrick'* – (God rest his soul) – is at the bottom of the sea, "Wi' the Scots lords at his feet". I finished him off yesterday. The work takes only 15 minutes to perform, so you will by that judge of its conciseness. Presently, I'm going to snatch a few hours of freedom on Bredon Hill, with *Doctor* Denke and will show him this latest microscopic fancy of mine. And I shall be glad if in the near future I may be able to show it to you too.

I'm so glad you accomplished the Surrey journey without hurt. May you continue towards complete recovery: and forgive Fate for troubling you with such a worrying friend as

HERBERT H.

---

*Howells's setting of the traditional Scottish ballad 'Sir Patrick Spens' had first been envisaged as a work for vocal quartet, string quartet and piano, but during 1917 and 1918 had been recast for chorus and orchestra.

(85)
IVOR GURNEY to HERBERT HOWELLS

Pte Gurney C Coy 4th Reserve Bat
Gloucester Regt
Seaton Delaval
March–May 1918

Mr Dear Howells
Your very jolly letter cheered me up no end: and the news that you had so good a time at Easingwold was the very best of news. Glad am I to hear there is music on the stocks, in preparation for great doings in the future, for there will be great musical doings surely once this war is over and we can settle down to ordinary life again.

But that is looking forward; meanwhile I am very glad to hear you are not yet dried up.

I am glad to say that the weather for two days has been beautiful indeed and Tyne Side has looked quite like South Country. The sea in Whitby Bay was quite wonderful, and would have given you leaping thoughts and rhythms for something very great in the future. Lets have some Sea Music out of you someday old chap will you?

Or what of the Forest of Dean Symphony? What of the opening pages of the sight from Newnham-on-Severn looking across the valley to the hills. An A major beginning surely . . .

What have they done to Shepstow river? Is it still beautiful and a whole, or is it spoiled for ever? What are your future plans, what have you settled to do with yourself? Dear old Howler, be glad they have not called you up as they have called so many, and let off steam in a Symphony, but not yet, for your health will not permit.

Do the Elizabethan Manuscripts still go strong, or are you putting them aside for the time, and waiting till the power of driving yourself all day has returned?

Poor chap, you must find it very hard work all this continual waiting. But how well you have stuck it! I wish I could stick it half so well as you for I am still crockey from my heart and a nervous breakdown from working too much at Brancepeth Castle.

Try and see as much of our County as may be while splendour of Spring lasts, which will be longer down there than up here. May you soak in something into your music, old chap, and give a delighted world your view of Gloucestershire as may clothe it in Beauty. O to see May Hill rising above the plains again, and to look at its glorious purple against the sunset skies; to drink in the hush of still evenings and feel that God is very present and is intensely alive in everything that moves or stays silent.

Well, well, you know all this old chap; and much more I do not write, for it is probable you see far more than I ever did. Why, to think of the C minor Concerto* makes me tremble; it is so much above me in everything save (I believe) pure beauty. There is a sun tonight, but I've seen better suns walking Kensington High St together old boy, or in Glostershire [sic] together. Bless you my child, and be as

---

*Howells's First Piano Concerto, which had been performed in July 1914 at Queen's Hall, with Arthur Benjamin as soloist and Stanford conducting.

happy as circumstances will let you be, for they are not too kind and it is a strain on your pluck, which will not fail never.

Best wishes
from your ever

I B G

(86)
IVOR GURNEY to HERBERT HOWELLS

No 2 (?) West
Lord Derby's War Hospital
Warrington
Lancs
[June 1918]

Dear Howells
Thank you so much for your trouble about my songs. Here is a rumbustious ending though common-place; and personally I should prefer the other. It is hard lines indeed you should have neuralgia, and that it should be so bad as to stop music – especially your music. Miss Scott's news about Dr Hull's wishing to study that gave me great pleasure. I hope he will appreciate it, and give you a good leg up, and that you will manage to squeeze something out of yourself, Herbert Norman – for you are a son of Gloucestershire, and the county deserves worthy celebration. No, I am not quite as my wish could have me, but far better, thank you. It was jolly to get your letter, and to hear that actually in Brewer's drawing room – that sacred spot – you rehearsed our songs! Strange happenings after 1904–1912! Do you remember one day when I rode over to Lydney and was simply astonished by the quantity of work you did? That was in 1912, I think.

A long time ago, and you have advanced since then by leaps and bounds indeed. You are sick now, but Thank Goodness in a lovely part of the world, where you can soak in Beauty, and feel music grow in you where your body is not too sick. What pluck you have Herbert Norman and how you have stuck it in spite of all difficulties!

Is your brother well whom I met with you at Queen's Hall one time? I hope so, for he was a very decent chap, and ought to do well. Have you heard from Evans at all? I owe him a letter yet, I fear, and must write at once.

Goodbye with best wishes and thanks

I B G

Gurney enclosed a 13-bar music manuscript.

(87)
BALFOUR GARDINER to PHILIP HESELTINE

Brook Cottage
Kerry
Newtown
Wales
Aug 12 '18
Dear Phil

On my first two attempts to read van Dieren's [*Chinese*] Symphony, I suffered acute mental distress. Subsequently [it] became easier, and I grasped at least a good bit of the Interlude: but fagged out as I am, without a piano & without any time to study it save odd quarters of an hour, it is impossible for me to obtain a thorough understanding of the work. I am most disappointed, but it cannot be helped.

What I have got to say therefore does not amount to any essential criticism at all, but I have just one or two remarks to make that may interest you, some favourable & some unfavourable. I am much struck by the freedom, resource & beauty of outline of the polyphonic parts, & believe that if I could grasp what they sounded like in combination (which I can do in many cases & cannot do in many others) I should find a novel fascination in them. Whether it would be anything more than fascination, I cannot at present tell. Up till now, owing to my defective apprehension, I have been unable to arrive at any emotional result. On the other hand, in passages where the harmonic aspect dominates others, he uses combinations that I cannot imagine I shall ever bring myself to tolerate – for example this sort of thing:

[*Chinese Symphony*: V Interlude (*Night Picture*) starting at the 8th bar.]

As regards the instrumentation he constantly robs the players of all freedom of tone by constant use of mp, mf, for singing parts, & I know only too well from actual experience what the first rehearsal of this work will be like – it will appear as if the orchestra is miserable & not trying: & all over the score there are unnecessary p, pp, & pppp. All this – or most of it – can be remedied, perhaps, with considerable trouble: but unfortunately there is only too much evidence, from what I have read, that his sense of orchestral values is defective. Take a simple passage –

[*Chinese Symphony*: V Interlude (*Night Picture*) starting at the 6th bar after Ⅴ]

This will sound atrocious. The bassoon against the buzz of the ponts will sound blurred & ineffectual: the pizz on the other hand will be too heavy in proportion. The Cymbal will begin to roar just when the violas set in passionately, & their tone, already too weak, will appear all the weaker because of the Cymbal (on the other hand if the Cymbal is kept down – & he is very difficult to regulate – one will only have the impression of a man working a machine fruitlessly) and at the very moment when the violas enter, the drum (I can see him so well) will make an absolutely futile remark quite indifferently. The violas having made their remark, it will be echoed grotesquely by the senile tones of the bassoon, but their efforts will be blurred partly by the cymbal, which cannot be damped quickly when it has once attained any volume of tone, and partly owing to a psychological reason, the inability of the mind to adapt itself to the demands made on it by a fresh entry while still in a state of bewilderment as to the general tenor of the passage.

I have grasped something of the unity of the work which you have mentioned in your letter & without really understanding what I was reading, I derived a formal satisfaction from the simple manner in which v. D. contrives the Ending. I really wish I had time to study the work properly. Are the parts to the Interlude written out? If I can have my rehearsal in October, I might be able to give v. D an hour of it.

It may interest you to know that Cyril Scott has set an English version of the Drunkard's song – one of his Chinese Songs – & I believe it is published. You might possibly find translations of other poems either in Professor Giles 'Chinese Poems'* (I think that is the title of the book from where C.S. took his text) or in Cranmer-Byng, & entitled I believe 'The Wisdom of the East'; 'A Lute of Jade' is the name of one of them.

In great haste
Ever yours

H. BALFOUR GARDINER

*Herbert Allen Giles published many books on Chinese and translations of its literature between 1874 and the 1920s. HBG probably refers to (*Chinese Poetry in English Verse*), 1898.

Van Dieren's Chinese Symphony *is entitled just 'Symphony Op 6' on the title page of the full score, which is in Philip Heseltine's hand. The score itself is headed: 'Symphony, based on Chinese poems translated into German by Hans Bethge'.† Bethge's volume was also Mahler's source for his Das Lied von der Erde, and in fact, Van Dieren does set one of the poems Mahler used: Li-Tai-Po's 'Der Trinker im Frühling'. The symphony probably dates from 1914, though it is not clear whether a full score in Van Dieren's hand ever existed. Heseltine's full core is undated, but was probably the score Heseltine sent to Balfour Gardiner, and was later used by Constant Lambert when he conducted the first performance in 1936, and again by Myer Fredman for his 1972 BBC performance. The symphony is in eight movements: I Preludio (chorus and orchestra); II Recitativo (baritone and orchestra); III Duettino (soprano, tenor and orchestra); IV Duetto e Coro (contralto, tenor and orchestra); V Interludio (Night-picture) (orchestra); VI Cavatina (baritone and orchestra); VII Aria (basso and orchestra); VIII Quintetto e Coro.*

† *Die chinesische Flöte: Nachdinctungen chinesischer Lyrik*, Leipzig, Insel-verlag, 1907.

(88)
GUSTAV HOLST to EDWIN EVANS

St Pauls Girls School
w6
Sep 22 [1918]

Dear Evans
My 'Planet' pieces are to be done at Queen's Hall next Sunday morning Sep 29 10.30
to 1.30. From 12.15 to 1.30 will be the best time. Boult is conducting. It will be a
purely private affair but please tell anyone who you think would care to come.
Entrance North door.

I am going to Salonica for the YMCA and in order to be more help to them I am
dropping my 'von'.

Yr faithfully

G.T. Holst

(89)
JELKA DELIUS to ROSE GRAINGER

44 Belsize Park Gardens
London N.W.3
14.1.1919

Dearest Mrs Grainger,
We were both perfectly delighted with your letter from Dec 13th received this morning – It was such *good* news that 'Life's Dance' was performed with such success. How I should have loved to applaud with Percy and you – I once sat next to him at a Delius-performance and it was so splendid to see him love it so!! The people here are always *so heavy*! We came to London [at the] beginning of Sept. and were thoroughly tired of our 3 years exile in France, entirely away from music. Since the big german push last spring poor little Grez has been in the War-Zone and life became intolerable and anyhow Grez was *all but* invaded by the enemy and without the Americans there was really no hope left. Fred had been writing such beautiful music during the quiet years of war – quiet at least at Grez – So we took all the manuscripts, our beautiful Gauguin pictures and left our home once more – perfectly sick at heart – We went right down to Biarritz where we soon got the good news of the turning tide – none too soon! America had done *wonderfully* reconstructing all France nobody here in England appreciates it enough. But we who have lived in France know it and shall never forget it. Also our eyes are turned to Wilson now. Our house in Grez was commandeered by the french military – and has been full of officers, and an officers mess part of the time and is still full of them. We only came back to lock away and save what could be saved and left the house to them and came here. Fred was *thirsting* for music. We are living in a furnished flat up in Hampstead and by special permission brought a little french maid along – I crossed the sea wearing a swimming tricot and the manuscripts I had tied up in watertight bags and would have swum with them fixed on to a life-belt! But, almost: alas! nothing happened after all these preparations.
   Things here looked rather dull when we came – Only dear old Wood was valiantly doing his Prom's. But Beecham has entirely thrown up Concert-conducting – He only cares for his opera-schemes – and there even he is more Impresario than conductor. He has Pitt young Goossens and Harrison as conductors. As they give all the dull old operas it is really not very interesting. He is also not conducting at the Philharmonic any more – He was too erratic and the Public became less and less. Now Norman O'Neill has made a great effort to reconstruct the Phil. Balfour Gardiner has helped financially and they have Geoffrey Toye Landon Ronald and Boult as conductors. Boult is to conduct Fred's new Violin Concerto there on the 30th Jan – Sammons playing it. They have put in an extra rehearsal, as Fred otherwise would have not allowed it to be performed – He can-not bear the way they have here of preparing so insufficiently. A few days ago Wood gave a new Orchestral Work of Freds 'Eventyr' (once upon a time) It is based on the norwegian-folk tales of Ahbjørnson. It is a charming, most beautiful work and Wood took enormous trouble over it and did it really awfully well. Of course all *could not* perhaps be quite realized in this first performance, but it was a spirited performance and the music is quite adorable – so norwegian – the little trolls cantering along on the "Vidder's", the Huldre, the Peasant's – The spirit of the whole thing was there out in that beloved nature. I think he has realized all that so

well in the very longing of his heart to go to Norway – impossible on account of the War. There was an enormous audience and the piece was awfully well received – I felt as if I was at last throwing off the war – breathing the Queen's Hall rehearsal – atmosfere [sic] – then the public, the enthusiasm and all quite thrilled me.

Fred has also written a beautiful Violin-Cello Sonata. It is all of a swing, lovely. Beatrice Harrison has already played it twice at her 2 recitals. Winthrop-Rogers is editing* it. I think it will be a great success when Beatr. Harr. takes it over to America. The Harrisons are also studying Fred's Double Concerto Violin and Cello – and it will probably be played in March. Hamilton Harty conducts quite often now. He did the 2 short pieces (Cuckoo and Summernight) rather well. Fred would like and probably will found a new Concert-Society – appealing to a more democratic public, as they certainly seem to appreciate music more than the Society people; they are deadly.

Balfour G. is still in Wales, guarding a Prisoner's camp; I hope, tho' he won't be very long now. They are woodcutters and he does not dislike the work – walking far thro' the woods to look after them. He came to see us here and was awfully nice – so sincere and real – Cyril Scott we met once at Lady Cunards he looked rather tired, but seemed quite alright. The O'Neills are bringing up their new baby. Austin is in the Beecham Opera, Bax has inherited no end of money from his father and Goeffrey Toye also lots from a brother officer.

16.1.19 Dear Mrs Grainger – will you ever find time to read all this? Since I began this letter Percy's splendid letter arrived and we just loved it. It was so awfully nice of him to collect all the cuttings and send them, it gives us such a good idea of it all – We hope most fervently that Percy will *soon soon* be given back to you and to his glorious artistic career How lucky they did not send him over here. It has been too dreadful – Fred's nephew, only 19 and an only son was killed just before the end.

We are *awfully keen* about going to America. If it were only possible to earn a little money, either by conducting or editions of Fred's works – as the cost of everything over there is so formidable. For instance I am sure Fred could conduct his piano Concerto *very well* – Financially we have had a very trying time, as most of our money is in a german Bank – on account of editors etc – and altho' lots of it is in N. Am. Railways and South America – we cannot get it, as it is in the name of the Bank. So we must hope for a speedy conclusion of peace and then see how we stand – It has been a great worry and I hope it will soon be over. Is'nt it glorious that Fred has composed such lots of lovely things during the war?

If we could we should like best to have a *little* furnished flat or rooms in N.Y. where we could cook simple food like you seem to do. Good healthy food is so essential for Fred. I must stop now dear friends, let us hear again soon!

Most affectionately yours

JELKA DELIUS

---

*Delius nearly always wrote 'edit' when he meant 'publish'.

(90)
FREDERICK DELIUS to PERCY GRAINGER

44 Belsize Park Gardens NW.3
16th Jan 1919

Your letter, dear old pal, arrived here like a flash of sunshine & I cannot tell you what pleasure it gave me. I was delighted to hear that 'Life's Dance' was so well performed by Stransky & his Orchestra & also so well received. Wood gave the first performance of my new Orchestral Ballad – Eventyr (Once upon a time) after Asbjørnsen – He gave a ripping good performance & took no end of trouble with it – I have a wild shout in it (20 men behind) which came off very well. I shall bring all my new works to America when I come – Your letter encouraged me very much to come out next season 1919–20 – Say in October or November. My new manuscript works are –

1) Requiem (in memory of all young artists fallen in the war. – *Not religious*) for Baritone & Soprano solo, Mixed Chorus & Orchestra
2) Concerto for Violin, Violoncello & Orchestra
3) Violin Concerto
4) Eventyr (once upon a time) (after Asbjørnsen)
5) Sonata for Violoncello
6) Dance Rhapsody No 2.
7) Poem of Life & Love Orchestra
   all manuscript

Then there are several works published, but awaiting a first performance –

1) Song of the high hills Orchestra & chorus (small)
   published by F.E.C. Leuckart, Leipzig
2) an Arabesk (J.P. Jacobsen) Baritone Solo, Chorus & Orchestra
   published by the Universal Edition Vienna –

It would be splendid if some of these works could be produced whilst I am in America. Your energy & enthusiasm is so wonderful & such a contrast to these dull countrymen of mine Oh! how dull & unresponsive this country is – I am just longing for a bit of American alertness and vivacity – I also want to visit California & have a look at the Pacific Ocean. We are both just longing for a change of climate & scenery & surroundings –
   I forgot 1 new work – quite short –

8) Song before Sunrise for small orchestra

& my Violin Sonata has not been played in America – & then there are 4 Elizabethan Songs: published by Winthrop Rogers & 2 à capella Chorus's
   To be sung a summer night on the water –
   My wife is writing to your dear Mother & telling her all the news – I am looking forward hugely to being in America with you What a time we shall have – Ill conduct the Concerto & you play it – Hurrah!!

Ever your loving friend

FREDERICK DELIUS

(91)
GUSTAV HOLST to HIS PUPILS AT MORLEY COLLEGE

8.30 p.m., January 25th, 1919
In a tent near the ruins of a shelled city on the borders of Bulgaria

Dear Friends,
I have just been lecturing and playing to some soldiers for an hour and a half, and am now sitting in my tent wondering how the concert is going on and trying to imagine the sound of your voices and instruments. In time I hope I shall get heaps of letters from you letting me know how it all goes, and whether Dr. Terry is pleased with you.

On the whole I am having a very good time. But the army is scattered over an enormous area, and even when you reach a place very often you find the camp breaking up and very few men left. Of course one is very glad that things like that are happening, but it is sometimes a little disconcerting. I am nearly a hundred miles north of Salonica, and have come all the way by motor car along with a sleeping bag, two blankets, lots to eat and drink, and about a dozen parcels of music. I had to cross the Struma valley, where so much fighting took place. Also I have had a long walk through the ruined city out on to the hills beyond, jumping over trenches, avoiding – or not avoiding – barbed wire, exploring dug-outs and gun emplacements, finally visiting an ancient Acropolis, the ruins of which were cleverly used by the Bulgars in a manner which was as horrible as it was clever. But the greatest sight I saw was also the greatest sight I have ever seen; indeed, I felt I was witnessing the greatest scene on earth: I saw Greek peasants and their oxen ploughing the battlefield for the first time since the fighting ceased!

Good luck to them and to you.
Yours sincerely

G T HOLST

P.S. – Jan. 27th. I returned to Salonica last night, and have been out all day motoring in a 'tin Lizzie' with the Pardar wind blowing – a really cold job. After making arrangements to form a choir in one camp, ditto plus a harmony class in a second, settling final arrangements for a lecture at a third, discussing the possibility of forming a sing-song during a cinema show by throwing the words of a song on the screen (owing to the non-arrival of song books) at a fourth, and finally conducting the Unfinished Symphony and the Mendelssohn violin concerto with the splendid Artillery School orchestra founded by Captain Colles, the musical critic of the *Times*, who is now in England. The orchestra was led by a Morleyite – Gunner Keyes, who sends his greetings to you all.

(92)
BALFOUR GARDINER to PERCY GRAINGER

Kerry
31.3.1919

Dear Percy

I have quite a lot to write about. I have two letters from you & two from your mother & have really treated you rather badly in not answering them before. I am still in the Army & have not much time for correspondence & all efforts to obtain my demobilisation are fruitless. I even heard yesterday that they are looking for interpreters to go to France, so that even when the prisoners leave this country I may have to go with them. I am heartily sick of military life & am longing to get out. I am so glad you have escaped, & know you will welcome the change in spite of your reluctance to leave the band. I was delighted to hear of all your plans, especially those for concerts in N.Y. & I wish I could attend them. But it is a long way & I hate sea journeys & am not particularly anxious to go to the USA are far as anything else but seeing you & helping with your concerts is concerned. It is nice of you to wish to do some of my works. If I could choose which I would have performed, I should say 'News from Whydah' without hesitation. This is by far the best, most effective & most popular work I have written. The Comedy Overture is no good at all, & for the English Dance (how we hanker after our old works!) I made it into a new piece which was done at the Proms about four years ago. It was not very successful, and I really have no patience to rework it once more – I had better get on to something new.

Then there is my Ballad which you do not know yet. It is still in M.S. and Geoffrey Toye is going to play it through for me at a Philharmonic rehearsal in a few weeks' time. I generally get tired of my stuff soon after it is finished, but I have constantly thought of this Ballad during my three years' military service & I like it as much as ever – so much so that I want to get it published as soon as ever I have heard it at rehearsal. And as regards this I want your advice. It is unfortunately not a popular work & will not make its way by itself like Shepherd Fennel, and I don't think it is likely to be played much even if it is pushed. It will certainly have no chance whatever if it is *not* pushed, & I must get it brought to the notice of all the prominent conductors as soon as it is printed. How would you set about it if you were in my place? I don't much mind the cost of publishing. Can I get hold of a publisher reliable enough to advertise it & send it to all the conductors, or can I get hold of a list of the conductors & send them free copies myself? Do let me know what you advise. I am so fond of the work that I do not want it to be entirely wasted, & as long as it is published & has a tolerable number of performances that is all I care. There are one or two other works I have the same sort of feeling about – Bax's 'In the faery hills', Austin's 'Spring Rhapsody' & your own first version of the 'Hillsong' (the one that was done in the little room in Percy Street). If they could all be published together they would make more effect than if they appeared separately, & if the expense is not too great, I think I should be willing to bear it. Let me know what you think of the scheme. We might even include a new work by Delius. Everybody tells me that what he has been writing lately is splendid. Unfortunately I have no opportunity of hearing or seeing anything of it myself: I have had no leave at all (except for a couple of days now & then) for the past 18 months.

To return to the other works of mine that it is possible to perform – I have done no chamber-music for years – but there are one or two partsongs that are good, including the Three Ravens & the Hunt is Up, both of which were published a few days ago. I am sending these to you under separate cover. I shall have nothing else to give you till I can get out of the Army & settle down to composition again. I am very anxious to see what sort of stuff I shall write after all these years. It has been impossible for me to do anything while I have been in the Army.

Give my love to your mother & tell her that I have given up my London house to which she sent one of her letters. My only permanent address now is Ashampstead Green, Pangbourne, Berks. I enclose the article you wished me to return & also a letter from Holst (formerly Gustav von Holst) which he asked me to forward to you. All best wishes from your affectionate

H. BALFOUR GARDINER

& let me have a further letter about your plans and also about the publication of the Ballad, etc as soon as you have time to write.

(93)
SIR HENRY WOOD to GRANVILLE BANTOCK

Apple Tree Farm House
Chorley Wood Common, Herts
21st April, 1919

My dear Bantock,
Many thanks for your letter. I rehearsed Brian's 'Festal Dance' and as you say, it will make an excellent finish to a concert. I shall put it into one of the earliest Sunday Concerts. I am enclosing you a cheque for three guineas, which I should imagine to be about the right price for such a work, but if you think otherwise, please let me know. Of course I could not pay Chester & Co. a half guinea performing fee every time I do it, as well.

Please don't tell Brian who has purchased the material of his Dance, as he does correspond at such length.

With kindest regards – and come and see us here if you can,

Yours ever,

HENRY J WOOD

(94)
BALFOUR GARDINER to PERCY GRAINGER

Ashampstead Green
Pangbourne
Berks
June 25 1919

Dear Percy

Here I am, demobilised, and sitting at my desk in the sunshine, feeling much the same, except for a slight restlessness, as I did four years ago. The wasted years in the Army have gone by leaving hardly any mark, &, after three or four days musical thought I find myself, as regards capability & the quality of the stuff, just where I was. Thank goodness, nothing has been lost, though much might have been gained, in the wasted years.

I was pleased with your letter of May 11. If I publish, I will take your advice, and moreover, avail myself of your Kindest offer to bring the works artistically under the noses of various conductors. I have not seen Bax, & von Holst is in Constantinople, as you know; & as regards my own Ballad, Geoffrey Toye only had 25 minutes to play it through & the orchestra was tired & not very keen as it was not for the concert. I shall have a better opportunity of judging its effectiveness (so I hope) in the autumn.

The Patron's Fund have at last done the sensible thing & decided to hold rehearsals instead of giving concerts, & I have sent in my Ballad which is almost sure to be accepted. I can then try various versions of places I am doubtful of, & if I think the work a success can proceed with publication.

I have a certain influence with the Philharmonic now, & suggest giving 'In a Nutshell' but there seems to be difficulty about the percussion instruments and a pianist is engaged for the concert in question who would hardly play the piano part in your suite as well as his own concerto: on the other hand we can hardly have two pianists. Have you any other work, or would you not let us do the Fast Hillsong in the Percy Hall, Percy Street version? or the third, slow one, if it is ready & for a suitable combination. We are thinking about the formation of a Philharmonic Choir too in conjunction with the Philharmonic concerts & hope to put in at least one of your choral works.

It is splendid of you to do so much for my piano pieces, & for Cyril's [i.e. Cyril Scott] & during the last few days my thoughts have been turning towards the possibility of writing more: those that are published already are very old. Two days ago I wrote a splendid small march, the most thrilling piano piece I have ever done, though it wants a big martellato piano technique.* I want to score it for military band. Then I must wait until one or two others are finished & publish them all together.

Where can I get Goldmark's Requiem that you mention? Have you any more small unaccompanied choruses for the Oriana? I want to do the Merry Wedding, and no doubt can persuade Kennedy Scott to put it on for next season. Of course we might do it with the large Philharmonic Choir, but I rather think it would be better

---

*This is 'The Joyful Homecoming' published in piano score, though once available as an orchestral piece and performed thus during the 1919 Proms.

for the smaller combination. Keep me posted about all your works & plans, & tell me what you would most like to have done over here & I will try to carry it through.

With affectionate remembrances & all best wishes to you & Mrs G

Ever yours

H. BALFOUR GARDINER

CHAPTER III

1919–1931

A New Beginning

Many commentators have characterized the 1920s as being frivolous, in reaction to the horror and strain of World War I and the excesses of the Edwardian period that preceded it. As far as music was concerned this was certainly true on the Continent where *Les Six* and other apparently irreverent movements reacted against the self-importance of much pre-war Germanic art and proclaimed the influence of jazz and other popular idioms. In Britain probably the most widely felt influence was that of Diaghilev's Russian Ballet composers, and certainly the mood in some artistic circles shared the European reaction. Arthur Bliss, for example, for two or three years the *enfant terrible* of English music, could outspokenly reject the great classical masters (see Walter Damrosch's letter, page 120). Holst, too, in his *Perfect Fool* opera, mocks the conventions of romantic grand opera, and later Lord Berners and Constant Lambert in their ballets proclaim their sympathy with the new. But it was remarkable how quickly this phase passed, and although in 1929 Lambert's *The Rio Grande* could be hailed by the press as 'Jazz changed into music of genius', and Walton's succès de scandale, *Façade*, quickly became an established popular work; neither is indicative of the style and approach of their young composers' more extended works. Certainly the overwhelming influence to impinge on composers in Great Britain between 1925 and 1935 was that of Sibelius. Frivolity was all well and good in its place, but serious issues demanded a serious idiom and Sibelius was found to offer a way out of the stylistic impasse that some composers felt themselves faced with at that time.

Those born in the 1870s, including Holst and Vaughan Williams, were producing some of their biggest works in the mid-1920s. Bax, ten years their junior, had only been launched as a major force in British music after 1920, and in 1925 was immersed in the orchestration of his *Second Symphony*. Frank Bridge, a composer then much admired for his pre-war romantic orchestral suite *The Sea*, and for his chamber music, began to embrace expressionist trends, and alienated himself from many of his former admirers: only in the impressionistic orchestral score *Enter Spring*, first played at the 1927 Norwich Festival, did he find anything approaching acceptance. Although greatly admired by the young Benjamin Britten this work was quickly forgotten and not generally appreciated until revived by Britten himself in the 1960s and subsequently recorded by Sir Charles Groves. Even as non-avant garde a figure as Herbert Howells – then 33 – seen from the 1980s to have been assuming the mantle of Vaughan Williams, did not have a good reception for his Piano Concerto op. 39. That was at a Royal Philharmonic Society concert on 27 April 1925, a concert representative stylistically of what was then new in British music. Besides Howells's concerto it included Bax's impressionistic tone poem *The Garden of Fand*, John Ireland's orchestral rhapsody *Mai-Dun*, Vaughan Williams's *Pastoral Symphony* and Lord Berners's post World War I send-up of folk-influenced styles, *Fantaisie Espagnole*.

At the time, all the composers in question would have doubtlessly thought of themselves as 'modern', rather than 'romantic'. Although not necessarily overtly programmatic, much of this evocative art was inspired by place or mood, and in some cases works were actually autobiographical in origin. Although at the time most composers appeared to have put the war behind them, looking back we can see that probably the most widely felt recent images that needed to be laid to rest were those from the war. Works which attempt this include such varied scores as Vaughan Williams's *Pastoral Symphony*; Bridge's Piano Sonata, and his later masterpiece for cello and orchestra, *Oration*; a number of piano works by Ireland; Bax's *First Symphony* (though most probably concerned more with the Easter Rising in Ireland than Passchendaele or the Somme); Bliss's epic choral symphony *Morning Heroes*; and at the time of writing it has been persuasively argued that E. J. Moeran's Symphony in G minor was in fact a war-requiem too.*

There is, also, of course, a whole literature of settings of the poetry of A. E. Housman in the context of the War, of which the work of Ivor Gurney – himself a war casualty to be confined to a mental institution for much of the inter-war period – is possibly the most poignant. These composers are now loosely referred to by some commentators as the 'British Romantic School', and exhibited colourful and expressive, largely orchestral, languages, which were ideally suited to this poignant subject matter. They encompassed a host of highly personal styles, all distinctive.

The generation that was emerging was sharply contrasted with the established names at the turn of the century, being trained almost entirely in British institutions, by British teachers of composition (themselves the pioneers of the previous generation). British performing artists played their music, and there was a marked rise in the assimilation of British works into the regular repertoire.

After the war there was a quite noticeable falling-off in the standing and importance of the great pre-war Choral Festivals, and the financial problems of performing organizations in general were a worrying preoccupation in the 1920s, with the loss of many of the rich pre-war patrons who had then been personal guarantors. The problems were brought sharply to the public's notice by the demise of the Beecham Opera Company (from which emerged the British National Opera Company) and the necessity of the Henry Wood Promenade Concerts being rescued from failure in 1927 by the BBC. But it was only later, in the 1930s, that the BBC emerged as a major patron of music, and the effects of a supreme musical bureaucracy impinges on the way works were chosen for performance, and the assessment of individual composers' music.

Yet for all the practical problems, the rise of British opera continued in the 1920s, initially promoted by Sir Thomas Beecham, later joined as conductor in the opera house by such vigorous young talents as Albert Coates and Eugene Goossens. Coates had returned to England from Russia in 1919, when he gave his revealing interview to Robin Legge of *the Daily Telegraph* –

In very sooth Albert Coates has arisen to find himself famous, a prophet honoured in his own country! Less than three months ago he lay, in Petrograd, at death's door, suffering from very severe blood poisoning induced by bad food when there was even that – salt herrings cost 18 and 20 roubles a piece! – and none at all on other occasions. Now he has been in England a few short weeks, and has, in that time, become perhaps the most talked-of native musician since

*SELF, Geoffrey: *The Music of E J. Moeran*. Toccata Press, 1986.

the rise of Sir Thomas Beecham on the production of Elgar's first symphony! One reason for this, no doubt, apart altogether from his outstanding ability and experience, is the fact, announced in the Daily Telegraph last Tuesday, that he has become an integral part, as it were, of the strongest power for musical progress in our midst – Sir Thomas Beecham and all and sundry of his musical works and projects.

To my thinking this is the greatest assurance possible that our national musical, not only operatic, life is to be kept in a state of perpetual motion in a forward direction. Beecham and Coates are much of an age, the latter some three years the junior; both are intensely imbued with the native spirit. In point of fact, long before the war Albert Coates and I had many talks on the subject of English music, not merely music in England, quite another affair; and very devoutly we wished that that should happen which actually has happened – a Beecham-Coates combination, than which after its kind there can be none other so strong. I mention this merely to show that Coates's love for British music, and his intense keenness for its development, is no new thing bred of a more or less enforced return here, but that it has been with him, to my knowledge, for many a long weary year. Nor must it be thought that Coates's joining up with Sir Thomas Beecham is a case of sheer necessity. I betray no secret. I trust – nay, I know – when I say that I am personally aware of at least half a dozen very lucrative offers of permanent engagements from American societies or companies made to Coates since his return; and, mirabile dictu, he received also the specific offer of the conductorship of the once famous Opera at Mannheim – a fact, of very considerable psychological significance.

During the past week I have had several talks with Coates, and the gist of them I give here in his own words; they speak for themselves and require no comment.

'I count myself today a happy man, for that has happened to me which seldom falls to the lot of mankind – the realisation of one of the great dreams of my life. It has always, ever since I have been a musician, been one of my dearest wishes that there should some day be real national opera in England – opera sung in English, performed by English artists, and listened to with appreciation by an English audience, and that when that time came it should be my happy lot to help in this great work with all that is in my power. This wish went so far with me that when the director of the Petrograd opera, about six months before the revolution, offered me a new contract for five years, I told him that I could not bind myself for so long, as I was convinced that after the war there would be a strong national movement in music in England, especially as regards opera, and that, should my supposition prove true, I, as an Englishman, would feel it both my duty and my privilege to do all I could to help music in my native country. Moreover, I said, it would be no use my staying in Russia, as I should not be able to give my mind properly to music there because my whole heart would be in England with the English work. I was never able to believe the theory that was so often and so mercilessly dinned into one's ears in former days, that it would be impossible to give opera in English, because nobody would go to hear it. I never could see why, since in France, in Russia, in Italy, and in all other countries, the whole repertoire is sung in the native language with perfect success, it should not be able to be done in England.

'I came back from Russia about three weeks ago, and a great surprise awaited me. One of the first things I did was to go to Drury Lane to hear the English opera. It was one of the happiest evenings of my life. I heard a performance of [Gounod's] "Romeo and Juliet" that was excellent in every way – singers with splendid voices, all evidently in love with their work, singing well, acting well, an absolutely first class orchestra and chorus all perfectly at home in opera, and Sir Thomas Beecham conducting as I have never heard "Romeo and Juliet", which I always considered a dull opera, conducted before. This opera in fact always bored me, so that I not only never wanted to conduct it, but I had never even been able to sit through a performance of it. Under the leadership of Sir Thomas Beecham I sat with the utmost pleasure, interested in every bar, and my only regret at the finish was that I was not sitting up in the gallery that I might shout hurrah with the best.

'There can be no appreciation too high for the work that Sir Thomas Beecham has done. He has put English opera on its feet – a monument that will stand, and I can see no reason why this opera should not in time become one of the best in the world. Of course there is still much to be done, and I consider this remark no disparagement to the work done already; in fact Sir

Thomas Beecham agrees with me in this. We have not only to build up a large repertoire of foreign operas in English, but an English national opera, to be perfect, must have an English national repertoire, works written by English poets with music composed by English musicians. That it should be my happy lot to help in the great work of English national opera, and, the foundations having been so firmly and well laid, to be called on to help in the further building up, is a thing that I shall always be grateful for. My dream has come to pass, and it is with a heart full of deep and sincere happiness that I take up my duties as conductor of the English national opera.'

Later, when Coates arrived in New York at the beginning of 1923, with the promise of including Vaughan Williams's *London Symphony*, Holst's *Perfect Fool* ballet music and Bax's *First Symphony*, he was reported as saying – 'There were not many new compositions obtainable in London because the composers were so poor they could not afford to have them copied.' Some of the young English composers had offered the original manuscripts to bring over, but he had declined to take the risk. 'England has revolted against the material of war ... we have been thrown back upon ourselves with the result that while heretofore we have been an interpretive nation in matters musical, now in Vaughan Williams and Holst and Bax we are creating a new school ... they are distinct to themselves.'

(95)
BALFOUR GARDINER to ROSE GRAINGER

Ashampstead Green
Pangbourne
Berks
Sept 11 1919

Dear Mrs G,
I was delighted to get your letter of July 30th, & it is quite time I answered it; but I seem to be busy all day long. Especially during the last month I have been at work from morning till night (& in the *middle* of the night, too), composing hard: there is very little to show for it, as usual, but I don't care as long as that little is good. I have been at the Ballad again, the one I wrote to Percy about: this is the 5th or 6th time I have altered it, and it gets considerably better each time – I have come to the conclusion that it must have been *very* bad at first. I shall not score it now, but put it by for six months, or until I am certain there is absolutely no more to be done to it.

You ask about the Fagges & Austin & Kennedy Scott*. I have not seen Fagge, but the Austins came here about a month ago for a brief visit & I was very pleased to see them. Old Fred is still in the Beecham Company, touring the English towns. I see a good bit of Kennedy Scott: as well as the Oriana, he is taking on the new Philharmonic Choir which I am supporting, and tomorrow, when I go to town, I shall hear how the Choir is forming. I hope it will be a good one: we have put down Morning Song in the Jungle & Father & Daughter for performance. I cannot send

---

*Charles Kennedy Scott (1876–1965) English choral conductor and composer. He founded the Oriana Madrigal Society in 1904 and formed the Philharmonic Choir in 1919, both setting high standards of performance, and pioneering as to repertoire. He was associated with Beecham, Balfour Gardiner and the Glastonbury opera productions of Rutland Boughton, and was thus an important figure in the development of British music, particularly between the wars.

you even sketch programmes, as they are not published yet, but I enclose another copy of the Promenade programmes, as you requested. I forget whether I wrote to Percy about the trouble he had in getting my piano-pieces from Schonberth: anyway I have written to Forsyth's on the subject, & no doubt they will take action.

Music does not seem to be very flourishing in London at present: the price of everything goes up & there is no increase of audiences, but rather the reverse, so that the loss on concerts is greater than ever.

Cyril wrote me a nice letter the other day (I sent the cuttings as you asked me to). I have not seen him for a long time, but I believe he is quite well & flourishing, & I hear he has written an opera.

I must now close this hastily written letter. I expect to hear from Percy in a few days' time about the piece I sent him.

Ever yours

H. BALFOUR GARDINER

(96)
PHILIP HESELTINE to BERNARD VAN DIEREN

35 Warrington Crescent w.9
14/11/19

My dear Friend

I was so pleased to hear from Frieda [van Dieren's wife] on Tuesday that you had got through the operation successfully and were well enough to write letters and make jokes as usual!

I have felt sure all along that as soon as you were in the hands of really competent doctors everything would go well. My only anxiety was on the score of the pain you might still have to suffer, but nothing could shake my firm conviction of your eventual recovery. I believe you *are* Cagliostro after all and will outlive all of us your friends! Besides, no such master-work as the third string quartet was ever yet in this world left unfinished – and before long there will be four enthusiastic players clamouring for the last movement!

It is very satisfactory to know that the operation proved the correctness of the doctors' original diagnosis. We shall see you again very soon, I am certain. Compared with the triple miracle of writing a book about sculpture in English while suffering such pains as I know you have been having, the task of getting well after an operation seems a little one which you will very easily accomplish. I received your telegram on Sunday morning and sent a reply by the boy who brought it. Afterwards, however, on referring to your telegram to note down your address I had an uneasy feeling that in my reply I had omitted a word from the address, since it seemed much longer than what I had written. I hope it did not go astray. In any case I shall, of course, be only too pleased and interested to read through the MS for you, and the proofs also, and to do anything else you want done in this connection. In fact your telegram was really quite unnecessary since you must know that it is for me a great pleasure and privilege to be able to help you in any way whatever. My only regret is that I am not capable of doing much that is of any real use; certainly not enough to repay you a tithe of the immense debt of gratitude which I owe you, both in musical and in most other matters as well.

It has been a source of enormous interest and delight to have your manuscripts here and to go through them again. I copied the score of the Overture* and took the copy to Busoni but did not see him as he was occupied when I called. The autograph copy of this work is at present in the hands of Adrian Boult, as it seemed that there was a remote chance of getting him to do it at one of the Philharmonic Concerts. These programmes appear to be more or less in the hands of Balfour Gardiner who is, however, difficult to deal with and very prejudiced. My only achieved success in this direction was the inclusion of Meyerbeer's 'Struensee' Overture in one of Geoffrey Toye's programmes. Herzka, of Universal-Edition, went to Frankfurt for the production of 'Fennimore' and Delius very warmly recommended him to publish your piano pieces; and from Delius' letter I gather that H. appeared very sympathetic towards the proposition. I despatched the MS by registered post on October 30th, enclosing a beautiful letter to H. which Frieda wrote for me, and took the precaution of writing to Busoni at the same time, asking him to write a further recommendation of the pieces to Herzka; which I am told he very promptly did.

I have given the scores and parts of the 2nd Quartet, first movement of the 3rd Quartet, 'Cenci' and 'Levana' etc to one Arthur Bliss, a rich enthusiast who gives Sunday evening chamber concerts at the Lyric Theatre, Hammersmith, and seems eager to devour every piece of modern chamber-music he can lay hands on. I met him with Dent. He is a Cambridge man. He seemed very excited over the quartets and said that, since he would no doubt find himself quite incapable of reading the scores, he would have a private rehearsal of them all so that he might hear them and get a better impression of their character. This rehearsal, I understand, is to take place at the house of M. Jean Aubry (!!) and I shall especially request the presence of our distinguished colleague Mr Edwin Evans! I also gave Mr Bliss the Béla Bartók quartet which pleases him greatly: and I did not fail to point out to this apostle of 'the modern spirit in music' the enormous indebtedness of Stravinsky to this excellent work, giving chapter and verse – a fact with considerable reluctance, he was compelled to admit. He has produced some very good work at Hammersmith, including a lot of Purcell which he has performed admirably. The present series of concerts concludes tomorrow with a stage production of 'La Serva Padrona' with harpsichord and strings. The next series starts in February.

There is an immense deal of musical activity in London at the moment – ballet at the Empire, opera at Covent Garden, Philharmonic, London Symphony and Queen's Hall Orchestras, South Place concerts, Hammersmith concerts, not to mention innumerable recitals.

I have heard so far at the opera 'Prince Igor', 'Falstaff', 'Tristan', 'The Nightingale' and 'Susanna's Secret'. The first two are most wonderful works, I think. More and more it seems to me that Borodin, with all his limitations, was one of the most *perfect* composers, as regards workmanship, that ever lived.

I read through his two quartets the other day and was simply staggered by the quiet, unostentatious mastery with which they are made. He has what one might call a kind of *pianissimo virtuosity* – always to be found and admired by those who look for it, never forcing itself upon the attention of those who are simply listening to the

---

*Van Dieren's *Overture*, for a chamber orchestra of sixteen players, had been first presented in a concert organized by Philip Heseltine and Cecil Gray which took place at the Wigmore Hall, London, on 20 February 1917, and which included only one other work, the nearly hour-long *Diaphony* for baritone solo and twenty two players. The final outcome of the concert was financially disastrous – receipts were only £5 against expenses of £110. Later, in November 1922, the overture was played in Berlin.

music. The first quartet, in A, seems to me the best – that is as regards invention, for both are beautifully worked. It has an absolutely Mozartean clarity and precision. With such models of workmanship before them, it is no longer surprising that Glazounoff and company should have been able to work up 'Prince Igor' and make it sound a complete and homogenous whole. Coates conducted the work at Covent Garden with the most admirable verve and complete command not only of the orchestra but of the immense crowd of singers which fills the stage from time to time. The choruses were wonderfully done, the difficult chattering chorus in 5/4 for the women being especially good.

There is no doubt that Coates is the only English conductor who can really *control* his forces, whether orchestral or choral: one may find his interpretations a bit coarse and unsubtle but of his command over the players there can be no question.

How different was the performance of 'Falstaff' two nights later under E. Goossens Junior! This marvellous score, so dexterously arranged that every word ought to be heard and heard clearly, was handled with the elasticity of an elephant and the delicacy of the Diplodocus Carnegii. When the orchestra has a bar's rest one could hear that the singers, bad as they were quâ singers, were really taking a great deal of trouble over their diction and were wonderfully clear: but then down fell the baton, bang went the big drum and everybody else went roarin' away regardless. Falstaff himself, however, was very good indeed. Frederick Ranalow played him and not only sang well but acted with a real Shakespearean spirit. The next night I went to 'Tristan': I didn't intend to, but having bought a ticket for something else, only discovered the mistake in the date when I got home, so I couldn't change it. *Never again!!* With the exception of the first five minutes of Act II and the first half-hour of the last act, this work seems to me a perfect monstrosity. I don't understand how anyone can sit through it unless the aphrodisiac which is so solemnly quaffed in Act I affects the audience as well as the protagonists of the drama. To me it certainly does not seem to be a glorification of love, but rather a glorification of death. The 'love', (such as it is and on the plot's own showing it is artificially produced) seems an absolute sham and it is only when death appears on the horizon in Act III that the piece seems to wake up, emotionally, into any kind of reality. The tastes of the British public are indeed hard to fathom. This was the worst performance of all: but the audience was much larger than that which had assembled for 'Falstaff' or for 'Igor', and although the performance began at 7.30 and ended three minutes before midnight, the upper portion of the house remained in their places applauding and cheering for quite five minutes after the fall of the curtain: whereas three nights before, the same section of the house showed obvious signs of restlessness during the last act of 'Igor' (which had been extensively cut) and scarcely gave the performers one recall when the curtain fell on this melodious and enchanting work at 11.40. (It began at 8).

Of 'Susanna's Secret' the less said the better. It is a modern imitation of the Italian 'intermezzo', three times too long for its subject and about 42 times too heavy. The 'Nightingale' is a charming piece to see on the stage and the music has agreeable moments which surprise one in Stravinsky: but most of it is sheer 'tub-thumping' and 'wrong-note-craze!' I understand that Stravinsky has now thought better of it and rewritten the work in his latest 'style' as a ballet – to the exclusion, no doubt, of the agreeable moments.

This morning I saw the dress rehearsal of 'Parade', a very amusing kind of cubist harliquinade with a comic horse and all the usual appurtenances. The music by Erik Satie is exactly right for the purpose, very simple and effectively grotesque without any of the pretentiousness and overloading that one finds in Stravinsky. A typewriter figures among the orchestral instruments! One of the numbers is a real rag-time which is as good as Irving Berlin – though, of course, deliberately modelled after him. I enjoyed the production far more than most of their 'seriously artistic' ventures.

I enclose an amusing notice of Warlock and Wurricoe. It appears that the reviewer rang up Rogers and asked 'Quis est ille Toad-in-the-Hole'? and the good publisher, having no evidence to the contrary, replied that he was no doubt the very person he appeared to be, to wit one Peter Warlock. It gives me great satisfaction to reflect what the 'Daily Telegraph' would have said about these same compositions had they been signed Philip Heseltine!*

Following on this Rogers immediately took up six more songs to send off to the printers, but, wishing to publish them in various keys, sent for Anthony Bernard to come and transpose them, so that he might hear in which key they went best. Anthony, whom I had not seen for months and whom I had no chance of warning, appears to have recognized my handwriting and given the show away! However Rogers has taken it very well and has promised faithfully to keep the secret: and indeed it is as much to his own interest, as regards the sales, as to mine that he should do so. I hear that Gervase Elwes, John Coates and Muriel Foster are studying the songs with enthusiasm, and I received a word of approval and kindly encouragement from no less a personage than (I tremble to write his exalted name) Frank Bridge!!!

Now however that the secret is out, as far as W.R. himself is concerned, I shall have the satisfaction of telling him, as I told Anthony Bernard to-day, that whatever is good in the workmanship of these little tunes is due to prolonged study of the works of one B. van D – and also I shall probably be able to get a few better things printed on the strength of the popularity of these 'little Peterisms'. Frederick Laurence is 'considering' the publication of a little work of mine for small orchestra by the firm of Goodwin and Tabb for which he is reader. But all these things are so utterly trivial that I feel more inclined than ever to go to Germany or Vienna at the earliest opportunity and _learn music from the very beginning_, as I feel still so hopelessly incompetent.

Well, I must end now. I do hope you are going on well and that you have less pain. You are continually in my thoughts and all my hope goes out towards your speedy recovery.

With love and every good wish I am

Yours always affectionately and gratefully

PHILIP HESELTINE

It is very difficult to decide whether Heseltine's enthusiastic hero-worship of van Dieren was the result of a genuine admiration of the music, or was primarily engendered by van Dieren's magnetic personality and his unbroken spirit in the face of illness. In a letter dated 15.5.18 Heseltine had written to Delius.

---

*Having been unsuccessful in placing his songs under his real name, Philip Heseltine adopted the pseudonym of 'Peter Warlock' and, as an apparent newcomer, succeeded in having songs accepted where previously they had not found favour. This passage describes how he was found out.

*

(97)
PHILIP HESELTINE to FREDERICK DELIUS

. . . Van Dieren, however, is a man of miraculous genius for whose music my love & enthusiasm grows by what it feeds on. It would be well worth your while to journey to England only to see this wonderful man and his works: he is still so ill that it seems impossible to predict whether he will live another year or another day. He has long ago passed the stage at which a normal man would have died—and this baffles his doctors; his will to live is all that he has to rely on, and he is working feverishly day and night whenever he has enough strength to hold a pen . . .

(98)
SIR CHARLES VILLIERS STANFORD to THE TIMES

9 Lower Berkeley Street
Portman Square
London WI
Nov. 15, [19] 19

Sir.—You announce this morning that the "Berlin Court Opera is to be exploited as a cooperative company under stage masters Richard Strauss and Leo Blech, with a leading singer." Baireuth [*sic*] is gone; the Court operas in every State in Germany are in liquidation. The Germans know, as our Allies the French have long known, the great power of and necessity for opera in humanizing and elevating the taste of the masses. Is England, the chief factor in winning the war and in the stability of peoples, going to let this great moment slip from her grasp? Or will she at last throw aside the *rôle* of follower of exotic taste and assert herself as one of the leaders in that great department of music which her sons have so long fought for at home?

Yours faithfully

CHARLES V. STANFORD.

(99)
PHILIP HESELTINE to BERNARD VAN DIEREN

35 Warrington Crescent w.9
November 22nd 1919

My dear friend
I cannot tell you how I rejoiced to read the good news of your health. It is wonderful: you must surely feel as though you had passed through the grave into a resurrexion. I always felt certain of your eventual recovery but it is good to know that the cause of all your pains has been at last discovered and removed. Knowing the works that you have written under such severe handicaps of illness, one wonders with positive awe what achievements will not be possible for you now that your full bodily vigour is likely to be restored.

I have just finished copying out in score the second and third movements of the third string quartet and the more I study them the more I am overwhelmed first of all by their wonderful poignancy of expression and deep emotion and then by the astonishing intellectual mastery with which they are made. The slow movement especially has that quality of profound serenity and detachment which one finds in the last quartets of Beethoven but in no other music that has been written since. This third work is very much clearer to me than the second of which, I must confess, I can form but a hazy notion of the eventual sound from study of the written page. However I hope to hear them both in a very short while. Bliss is at present playing the piano with the Philharmonic String Quartet in Paris but he will be back in a week's time, and by then I shall have finished copying the parts of the 3rd Quartet. The last movement, I take it, you have not yet completely written out? I found a sketch – a very hilarious-looking fugue in C major – which I liked immensely but unfortunately it comes to an end abruptly on the second page.

Could you, when you feel inclined to write, indicate to me approximately the tempo of the opening of the Menuetto movement and at the same time tell me whether you wish a sudden slowing-off when the demisemiquavers begin or a gradual rallentando – so that I may be able to rehearse the players properly?

The manuscript of 'Epstein' arrived safely and I am going through it with the greatest care. Of course that monstrous letter of 'Mr. Epstein' was simply a put-up job organised by the ever-diabolical Scotchwoman – surely she is a wurricoe if ever there was one! I went at once to see the manager of John Lane and Co. and he was as pleasant as could be, most sympathetic about your illness and he begged me to assure you that there was no need to overstrain yourself to finish it quickly as in any case it would not be published before February *owing to the difficulty of pleasing Mr. Epstein with the reproductions*!

I asked, by way of seeing how the land lay, whether they wished to impose any restrictions on the length of the text, and he hastened to say that they wanted as much as Mr. Van Dieren would give them for his money, adding that they were not sparing expense as they wished to make a really fine and important book of it. So much for the 'sinister reports'! We know now who it is that 'disapproves of you'!!

I heard from Busoni the other day. He wrote, in reply to my letter asking him to write to Herzka about the piano pieces, saying that he had done so and enclosing a copy of what he had written – a two page letter in which he speaks of your work in the highest possible terms.

Delius is confident that Herzka will print them. He and Jelka arrived late on Saturday night, very green after much sea-sickness. I managed to procure them a nice room at the Eiffel Tower, after endless scouring of hotels great and small, where they seem very happy. He has forbidden the performance of the 'Village Romeo' since he found that nobody concerned knew anything whatever about the piece and it was duly announced for next Wednesday!

Delius and Fox-Strangways met – can't you see them together? I nearly choked with laughing. Fox-Strangways began at once, in the jocular-schoolmaster-out-of-school-hours manner, with his interminable and pointless conundrums – whether the respective lengths of violin bows and cello bows affected the phrasing with regard to the sex of the performer, etc, etc – or something of the sort. After a few minutes Delius smiled benignly and exlaimed: 'I don't know what you're talkin' about. You might as well be talkin' *Chinese*'! Whereat the musical critic of London's leading newspaper (who I must add has previously enquired of Delius, with his usual amazing tact, *where his music was published*!) perceptibly blushed through his bronzed and assuredly pachydermatous hide and muttered something about 'Mere small-talk, you know: don't *you* ever use small talk?' (!!!) . . .

. . . By the way I forgot to mention that Lane does not want the MS in instalments but prefers to send it all to the printer at the same time. However it will facilitate matters if I pass it on to Epstein in sections so that he may read one portion and get it typed while the next is being corrected and so on. I await the next instalment with the greatest eagerness.

Much love and every good wish from your affectionate

Φ.

A. H. Fox-Strangways (1859–1948) was at this time a music critic on the staff of The Times. *In 1925 he would become the music critic of* The Observer. *He is probably best-known as the author of* The Music of Hindustan *(1914), written after an eight month field trip in 1910/11. He founded the journal* Music & Letters *in 1920 and edited it from then until 1937. Van Dieren's book on Epstein was published in 1920.*

(100)
C. J. HOLMES to THE TIMES

Union Club
17 February 1920

Sir,—From time to time we read suggestions for the establishment by private or public endowment of a national opera house and a national theatre. The success of *Abraham Lincoln* at Hammersmith would seem to prove that there is an educated public large enough to support a well-managed theatre. But if the supporters of opera are an equally strong body, how is it that the operas now being given at the Surrey Theatre and well noticed a few days ago by your musical critics have not had better backing? The conditions are exactly those which are usually thought to be ideal—when found, say, in Germany. The repertory includes old favourites and new operas by British composers. The scale of production is modest, the price of seats within the reach of every one, while the two performances I have seen were always spirited, and sometimes surprisingly good. Yet on neither occasion was the theatre more than half full. Must we conclude that the desire for a national opera house, unlike that for a national theatre, is a patriotic fiction?

I am Sir, your obedient servant

C. J. HOLMES

The short-lived Fairbairn-Miln opera seasons started in February 1920 and included British operas by John Barkworth (1858–1929) (Romeo and Juliet) *and Nicholas Gatty (1874–1946)* (The Tempest).

*

(101)
HENRY HADOW to WILLIAM ROTHENSTEIN

20th July, 1920

By the way, when you are writing you might let me know if you can, approximately, when we shall have the pleasure of seeing you here in the autumn. I want to know, not only to get some lectures arranged, but for a more selfish purpose – to have a great talk with you about Matisse's *Chapeau de cuir*, and all that it seems to me to stand for. I think that I could have made something out of it, though nothing with which I could very much sympathise, if it had not been for the laudatory articles which were distributed about the room and which seem to me to praise it for just the qualities that it lacked.

I am really distressed at being out of sympathy with so many artists whom intelligent people regard as great. I have a great liking for much of the new poetry, and much of the new music, and where I do not like it I can put my finger on the point where the artists and I are at variance. This, of course means that one's sense of appreciation is steadily widening, because where one disagrees with an artist it nearly always (not quite always) happens that the artist has got the best of it. That, at any rate, is what I find in the two arts of words and tones with which I am most familiar. By analogy, I expect that the same thing is true with modern painting and modern sculpture, but here, with me, the proportion is reversed. I like a very little of it intensely, with the vast majority I am so bewildered that if you told me it was a practical joke I should accept that as a solution – and the worst of it is that to discuss these things with an expert nearly always appears to take the form of an attack, and very probably an ignorant attack. Now I do not want to attack anybody. I want to find out what they are driving at (so far as my eyesight and intelligence will serve), how much of it is deliberate reaction and defiance (both of these seem to me to be bad art, because they have some other end in view than the pure service of beauty), and how much of it is a genuine attempt to reach beauty in a new and interesting way. I think, for instance, that I understand something about significant line – at any rate, it suggests some definite analogies to me in melody and in the measure of verse – but surely one pays far too high a price for this when it means representing the human frame as distorted or diseased; that is, to me, frankly, a blasphemy which no excuse in the world can condone. And then, again – but I am making this letter far too long. What I want is to talk the whole thing over with somebody who will be sympathetic with my shortcomings, and who will understand, even if he disapproves of my point of view. It is very disheartening to find a whole lot of people interested and enthusiastic about something, and oneself outside in the passage.

All kindest remembrances to Mrs. Rothenstein and the family.

Yours ever,

W.H. HADOW

(102)
PHILIP HESELTINE to JOHN GOSS

The Sackbut
18 Berners Street
London
W1
July 20th 1920

My dear Goss
Here are seven songs. You have already, I think,

(a) 'Do not, o do not prize thy beauty at too high a rate' by ROBERT JONES
(b) 'I die when I do not see my mistress' by JOHN DANYEL

Enclosed are:– (1) DOWLAND 'Awake sweet love'
(2)   "   "   'Weep you no more, sad fountains'
(3) BARTLET 'Wither runneth my sweetheart'
(4)   "   "   'When from my love I looked for love'
(5) JONES 'What if a day'
(6) Anon. 'Willow willow'
(7) PELHAM HUMPHREY 'Willow, willow'

These, with the Dolmetsch and Rosseter volumes, give you a fairly representative selection. I have not touched Campion but I am told that a volume issued by Schott called 'From Campian (sic) to Lawes' (edited by Anna Rutle Pry) contains accurate transcripts of him. I have not examined it myself. The versions I send you are all as near as possible to the originals. Only in one case ('Awake sweet love') have I attempted a free transcription. This is one of the world's immortal melodies – it so transcends the letter of its poem that it seems to call for bigger treatment than Dowland has given it. It is a tune to be sung for its own sake, almost regardless of the words – whereas the majority of songs of this period should be sung very freely, quasi parlando. But I have added the original version so that you can use or discard my accompaniment as you like. It is curious how this tune anticipates some of the loveliest melodies of the great masters of later date:– Handel's 'Ombra mai fu' (or 'Largo'), this of Bach

[In fact from J. S. Bach: *Double Violin Concerto*.]

(I forget where it occurs – a Concerto I think), the slow movement of Beethoven's 4th Symphony, the E♭ Intermezzo of Brahms – to say nothing of 'The First Nowell' which is probably earlier. The Bartlet song 'When from my love I looked for love' is a particular favourite of mine, a song you would always make a success with. It was published in one of the Keel volumes but maltreated in that gentleman's very worst style so that it lost all its grace and humour. The present accompaniment is pure Bartlet save for the ritornello which I have added. This is one of the cases where the words can be almost spoken, to give the right characterization. Don't worry about the bar-lines: in the XVII century no one had yet arrived at the strange idea of unconsciously accenting the first note of the bar, and so on. Speak the words 'trippingly on the tongue' as though they were prose and the accents will take care of themselves – even if you have to anticipate a note or two by a semiquaver. The 'Willow, willow' phrase in Humphrey's setting is another example: There is no need to accent the word in two different ways, though by the barring (to modern eyes) it looks inevitable.

May all success attend your recitals: if I can be of any further use in transcribing or suggesting songs, please command me. I feel I never half thanked you enough for your generous appreciation and enthusiasm for my little efforts: it cheered me a great deal and remains a bright spot in a very black period.

No, I don't think you will see me in Glastonbury – unless the committee invite me to come and lecture to them on the history and function of music, which seems unlikely!

With every good wish I remain

Yours ever

PHILIP HESELTINE

(103)
E. W. NAYLOR to HERBERT THOMPSON

49 Bateman Street
Cambridge
Feb: 20 1921

My dear Thompson

Thank you for writing again. I am indeed sorry you are not likely to be in Leeds at the right time. I do not remember if I told you the *Angelus* will be done twice at Hull, Grand Theatre, on March 9 and 15. Perhaps one of those dates might be possible. I thought that after missing Aberdeen and Sheffield, it was almost a duty to go to Manchester. So my wife & I went, on Friday. I never was there before. They tell me the Opera House holds 3000, and is seldom filled in consequence. I don't know the *number* of my audience, but they took between £500 and £600 at the door; 'called' me enthusiastically, & I was induced to 'say a few words' at the close.

The cutting from an irreconcilable Manchester Guardian, I enclose for your perusal. It smells of malice. My manager tells me that the M.G. allowed a statement to appear that the 'Angelus' was given in London last year, *with but moderate success.* This is truly premeditated slander, for everybody knows it has never been done anywhere, since 1909.

They asked me to conduct my new Entr'acte (before Act iii) at Hereford. I can't say how it sounded, for the band were half covered up beneath the stages & I could not even *see* some of them. But they applauded it – so long, I had to get before the curtain and take a call after 'booing' several times from the conductor's stand.

Most of the singers were very *good*: esp. the tenor & soprano.

Yours ever

E W NAYLOR

NB I have not *seen* the statement named above, so am not telling others.

Edward Naylor's opera The Angelus *won the prize offered by the publisher Ricordi for an English opera in 1907, beating Holst's opera* Sita *into third place. First produced at Covent Garden on 27 January 1909, it was given a concert performance in Cambridge in 1914 and was to reappear at Covent Garden on 1 December 1921.*

*

(104)
HENRY HADOW to ALLEN MAWER

The function of a department of Music in a University is not that of training for a professional career but that of giving Music its due place in a liberal education. The course of study which it proposes may be considered as analogous to that of language and literature: the notation is an alphabet, the technical rules are those of accidence and syntax, musical composition is poetry, musical history is a part of the general civilisation of mankind. To restrict them to students who intend to become composers or executants is as unreasonable as to restrict the study of Shakespeare to those who are going to be actors or dramatists. A special gift will always find its own outlet; of more importance to the University is the education of the cultivated man.

Here two objections present themselves. First that music is a recreation, that, apart from technical training, it is play rather than work, that it appeals to the senses and the emotions and that it affords little scope for the higher faculties of intelligence and judgement. Second, that however wide-spread its enjoyment its study is confined to a small minority of 'musical' people who claim a particular sensitiveness denied to the world at large and compare their experience in an esoteric language which they alone can understand. Both these assumptions I believe to be wrong.

The first rests upon a false antithesis. It is not true to say that 'Music appeals to the emotions and literature to the intellect': both alike may appeal to both. No doubt a man who knows nothing of music may gain physical pleasure from a concert: that is no more than to say that the sound of music is physically pleasant. But it is equally true that admiration grows as knowledge grows; not only that the trained ear detects beauties which to the untrained are non-existent, but that the trained intelligence can follow the structure of a melody or a madrigal or a fugue or a sonata in exactly the same way, and to exactly the same purpose as it can follow the stanza of a lyric or the plot of a drama. Nor is it only a matter of artistic form – though if that were all it would be enough. The significance of good music is as real as that of good poetry, you cannot translate one into the other, Palestrina into Dante or Bach into Milton, but each has its own inherent and spiritual truth.

The second error is due to historical reasons which have already passed away. During the Elizabethan age we were supreme in music: at the Restoration we still held an honourable place: then came two hundred years of bad tradition in which we allowed ourselves to be overcome with foreign influence and treated it with irrational contempt because it was foreign. In the sixteenth century Dowland could be compared, on equal terms, with Spenser, in the eighteenth Handel and Buononcini were the Tweedledum and Tweedledee of Byron's epigram. It is no wonder that our musicians, attacked by popular disdain, huddled together for self-protection and defended themselves behind a zareba of technical terms. Now the whole of that unhappy warfare has ceased. Music is once more taking its due place in the life of the nation, and all educational institutions can bear their part in its advance and development.

A University department of Music, should, at full growth, employ the services of (1) a Professor (2) at least one full-time lecturer, and (3) such part-time assistance from Musicians in the city as will on occasions be found necessary. At first, however, it may be possible to restrict it to a Professor with such external help as he requires. The number of teachers will clearly depend on the extent of ground covered and this may well begin within comparatively narrow limits and extend as opportunity arises. The minimum of equipment should be (1) adequate classroom accommodation which as far as possible, should be isolated from the rest of the University. The music, preferred by Othello, which 'cannot be heard' is not here in question, and due care must be taken to prevent the music students from interrupting the work of other departments, (2) a pianoforte, several black-boards ruled in staves, and a gramophone, (3) a department library consisting of a small number of selected books on the history, grammar, and aesthetics of music, and a large number of scores by the great composers. The choice of the former should be subjected to a rigorous scrutiny, for in no field of human knowledge is there so wide a difference, as in music, between the best criticisms and the worst: the latter should be in the first instance chosen for purposes of historical illustration and extended year by year until it includes all the compositions that can reasonably be wanted. To these resources should be added, as soon as may be, the cooperation of the University Choral Society, of the University Orchestra (a great deal can be done, as a start, with strings and piano) and of an adequate team for the performance of Chamber Music. The recent experience of Dr. Walford Davies in Wales would here be of great service.

The work of such a department is roughly twofold.

(I) The direct teaching which should find a place in the time-table and be tested by examination. This, as has already been suggested, is primarily for the use of students who want to attain some serious knowledge of music, but not necessarily to become professional musicians . . .*

(II) Indirect influence. Every University should have a flourishing Choral Society and the nucleus of an orchestra. . . .

The above sketch is no more than a bare outline, to be filled successively with varying detail as the course of music advances. For its effective realisation everything depends on the personal element, more than in any other form of University study because there is less good tradition, and the best advice that can be given is to choose the right man and give him, within necessary limits, complete freedom to settle his home and determine his syllabus. But the basis of it all is the firm conviction that music is not only a possible but a valuable element in general culture, and that the need of its more systematic study will be increasingly felt as the years go on.

The renewed musical creativity everywhere apparent after the war included the launching of several new musical journals. Probably the most characteristic of its period — and almost certainly the most short-lived, for it only lasted for seven issues — was Fanfare *which appeared under the editorship of the critic and composer Leigh Henry.*

---

*As printed here this letter is substantially cut. For a full transcript see SIMMONS: *So Deft a Builder*, op. cit.

(105)
LEIGH HENRY to EDWIN EVANS

Fanfare
edited by
Leigh Henry
for the Publishers
Goodwin & Tabb, Ltd.

London, 34, Percy Street, w.1
the 25th September 21

Dear Edwin Evans

Thank you very sincerely for your kindly attitude to *Fanfare*. I trust the future may find us, as the past has done, tilting in company against those gasbags which our enemies prefer to call windmills. Let me assure you now, once for all time, of my very real sympathy for your every effort, my unaltered admiration, after some fifteen years of not small vicissitude, for your mentality, & the courageous way in which you have used it to further the live efforts at all times, – often, I feel certain, at the risk of a certain sacrifice of material advantage & the popular kudos sought after, at all costs, by lesser people.

I would have written earlier, to ask your permission to include you in my list of contributors, (if only for an occasional article at some distant date, if you are too occupied at present), had I been able to get your address. But on my last enquiry at Curwen's I was informed that this pending your return, was unknown. Meanwhile the rush of preparations for commencing *Fanfare* intervened. But I ask you now; and hope very earnestly that you will consent, because no really contemporaneous effort in England can be really complete, to my mind, without the inclusion of your name.

You probably comprehend now – or have been told – why I so deliberately withheld my series of articles from M.N. & H? [*Musical News & Herald*] In case not, let me now reiterate that the sole reason was that I some time ago decided to contribute nothing whatsoever to any Curwen undertaking. (Not from animosity to the firm, or to Curwen, of whom I am fond), but simply because I refuse to allow Miss Greville's assumption of patronage towards Curwen collaborators, or to furnish a shadow of pretext to the implication that I was 'discovered' by her, or that she has any appreciable power to 'further', 'make', or 'aid' me, whose standing among first-class internationals, not to speak of my personal relationships, affords a not quite negligible opportunity for notoriety & 'advancement', (were these my objects in my art), – as witness the list of personal friends & acquaintances contributing to *Fanfare*. But, if you should still care to have my studies, I shall be only to[o] glad to send them to you now. I shall also be delighted if you care, as soon as you like, to send me a study on, say, *Modern French Music & Its Relation to Contemporary Development* (I leave title & choice to you, however)

Yours always cordially

LEIGH HENRY.

After World War I not only did British composers begin to regard themselves as distinctively 'British', or rather 'English', but commentators abroad began to do so too. Immediately after the war there was considerable antagonism in some academic musical circles to the new music, in particular the outspoken rejection of the classical masters which probably originated from Diaghilev and the composers who wrote for the Ballets Russes. In England probably the most outspoken in this respect, and certainly the widest in his sympathies for the new, was Arthur Bliss.

(106)
WALTER DAMROSCH to THE DAILY TELEGRAPH

Oct 4, 1921

SIR
—The *New York Herald* of Oct. 1 prints a cabled interview from London with Mr. Arthur Bliss regarding what purports to be an interview with me in 'Musical America,' in which I am made to express very harsh criticisms on the modern English trend in composition. It cannot be of any great importance to England what I or any other American musician may think of English composers, but, as I have many dear and valued friends among them, it is of great importance to me not to be misrepresented or misunderstood. Permit me to state, therefore, that in my interview I referred to a certain musical current which is now common to all Europe, and which manifests itself in France, Italy, and Germany just as much as it does in England. America does not largely figure in this as we cannot as yet lay claim to a national music, even though we already have a small handful of highly talented American composers.

At the banquet given by the British Music Society last summer I expressed myself very freely on this subject, but at the same time endeavoured to pay proper tribute to the marvellous results which Great Britain has achieved in music. I mentioned especially not only your great Edward Elgar and Vaughan Williams, but several of the younger men whose work we are watching over here with great interest, and I laid special stress on the fact that thirty years ago not only the conductors but a great part of the orchestras of London were foreigners, and that since the advent of Sir Henry Wood English conductors rank with the best in the musical world, and English orchestras, thanks to such schools of music as the Royal College of Music, are composed almost entirely of native-born players.

Mr. Arthur Bliss wonders why I still place Beethoven and Brahms on my symphony programmes. I have not yet lost my admiration for these masters and, to judge from the acclaim which your public still gives them, I fancy that there must be many in England who feel as I do. I have never heard any of the compositions of Mr. Bliss, and therefore do not know whether I should class him as a disciple of that 'ugliness in music' which some of the younger school seem to worship.—

The audience for opera, too, particularly opera in English, began to be developed largely owing to the activities of Sir Thomas Beecham. The demise of the Beecham Opera Company in 1920 was caused by financial misfortune rather than any lack of support or failure by the enterprise itself. Out of it was born the British National Opera Company which first appeared at Bradford with Verdi's Aida. *Percy Pitt, also musical adviser to the new BBC music department, was succeeded in 1924 by Frederic Austin, when Pitt became the BBC's first Director of Music. The Company lasted until 1929, but was subsequently re-formed as the Covent Garden English Company. It finally closed in 1932. (See also letter 120 referring to the Imperial League of Opera.)*

(107)
GRANT RICHARDS to PHILIP HESELTINE

GRANT RICHARDS LTD : PUBLISHERS
8 · St. Martin's Street Leicester Square London w.c. 2

June 27th, 1922.

Dear Sir,

Mr. C.W.Orr has permission to publish his musical settings of the four poems from 'A Shropshire Lad' which you mention. No fee need be paid for the use of these poems, but a statement must appear prominently that the poems are taken from 'A Shropshire Lad', by A.E. Housman, published by Grant Richards Limited, and two copies of each piece of music must be sent to us. Moreover Mr. Housman makes certain conditions: (1) the poems must not be printed in programmes or anywhere apart from the music; (2) if the poems are printed on the first page of the songs each one must be printed in its entirety even if the composer does not use the whole poem for his setting; (3) no titles must be given to the poems which are not given by the author. I draw your attention specially to this last condition in view of the fact that you use as titles 'Remembered Spring' and 'The Cherry Tree': it is Mr. Housman's wish that these should be given as titles the first words of the poems: 'Loveliest of trees, the cherry' and ' 'Tis time I think by Wenlock Town'.

Faithfully yours

GRANT RICHARDS

P.S. I am sorry for the delay in answering your letter.

A. E. Housman's A Shropshire Lad *was first published in 1896, and took several years to establish itself. It would appear that Sir Arthur Somervell's song cycle of the same name, published in 1904, was the first setting. By 1922 a very large number of settings had appeared but Housman, who was not musical, was very specific as to the conditions under which his work could be used. In particular his experience over Vaughan Williams's* On Wenlock Edge *he felt to be unfortunate, being irritated particularly because Vaughan Williams dropped lines from the poems.*

*

(108)
ROBERT RADFORD to THE DAILY TELEGRAPH

June 29, 1922

Sir—May I ask the courtesy of your columns in order to dispel the many rumours that are in circulation about 'Co-operative Opera' and, on behalf of my colleagues, state as briefly as I can what is being done with regard to the formation of a National Opera Co., to be run on co-operative lines? The liquidation of the Sir Thomas Beecham Opera Co. Ltd., and the consequent cessation of its activities is undoubtedly the most calamitous happening that has occurred in British music for many years. A splendidly-successful organisation, national in everything but its title, created by the genius and enthusiasm of one man, has ceased to exist. Everybody deplored it, but nobody seemed able to help it. From a national point of view the situation is the more distressing because the liquidation of the company was caused principally by the heavy losses sustained during the last grand season of foreign opera and Russian Ballet given at Covent Garden, in which the limited company were heavily interested.

In consequence of this liquidation the successful English performances (which were so finely supported not only in London, but in Manchester, Birmingham, Leeds, Bradford, Edinburgh, and Glasgow) have temporarily come to an end, and a company that was firmly established with a fine record of creditable work and a great following is no longer before the public. The circumstances which caused the break-up of the company were entirely beyond the control of the representative body of musicians concerned. These are unanimous in their determination to help forward the cause of English opera, and to place it on a solid foundation. The conductors, artists, musical staff, and chorus of the company allied with the Beecham Symphony Orchestra have therefore decided to form themselves into the British National Opera Co. Ltd., and to run the organisation on co-operative lines. It is obviously beyond the capacity of any one individual to undertake the financial responsibility entailed in running so big and representative a company. Co-operative effort, therefore, seems to be the only solution. It is the first time in the history of music in this country that well-known conductors, leading artists and a first-class orchestra have joined forces for the giving of opera in which all its active members will be shareholders.

At a representative meeting of the members of the company it was decided that the control of the organisation should be vested in a board of directors elected by ballot. Its constitution is as follows: Four representatives from the stage, Miss Agnes Nicholls, Mr. Norman Allin, Mr. Walter Hyde, and myself: three from the orchestra, Mr. Thomas Busby, Mr. Horace Halstead, and Mr. Van der Meerschen; and one from the musical staff, Mr Percy Pitt. The directors have power and intend to add to their number financial experts and members interested in the social side of opera giving, and a general manager will be appointed shortly. Mr. Thomas Busby (whose wide experience of the orchestral side of opera and whose successful management of the affairs of the London Symphony Orchestra are well known to music lovers) is managing director. The musical adviser is Mr. Percy Pitt, whose long association in the same capacity at Covent Garden gives him special qualifications for the post.

It is the intention of the company to give spring and autumn seasons of opera in London, joining them by a tour in the great provincial centres, and a continuous series of performances extending over a period of forty weeks per annum is their aim. It is their hope to provide not only a national asset, but what may eventually become a national property. The directors are most anxious to avoid clashing with other operatic interests, and they know from experience that there is a great public anxious to hear and eager to support performances of opera in English if given in the best possible manner and they are confident that the scheme can be made a sound commercial proposition. It is hardly necessary to draw attention to the great possibilities for musical benefit that are contained in the organisation, constituted as it is of so many leading native artists, and an orchestra that is so famous, all imbued with the highest artistic aims. The promoters will cordially welcome suggestions and advice towards the furtherance of their objects, and as the scheme is a co-operative one, and not subject to the control of any one individual, they are confident that they can count on the sympathy of all concerned in British music. . . .

Robert Radford (1874–1933), celebrated British bass, was a founder and director of the impoverished British National Opera Company from its inception in 1922. As a company it did much good and pioneering work in touring opera, in producing British works, and in fact the BNOC was responsible for the performance of Humperdinck's Hansel und Gretel *which on 6 January 1923 was the first opera ever broadcast from a theatre in Europe (on the BBC's station 2LO).*

*

(109)
BALFOUR GARDINER to PERCY GRAINGER

R.M.S.P. [Royal Mail Steam Packet Company] 'ORBITA'
Sept 29th 1922

Dear Percy

I am nearing the end of my journey: the chalk cliffs of Dover are in sight and in a few hours we shall be in Southampton. After all the rattling, jolting, swaying, pitching & tossing to which I have been subjected, I feel as if I should like to sit in my garden without moving for a month. . . .

I was so glad to be with you in Norway & to have the opportunity 'uns grindlich und zu sprechen', but all you told me about your dear mother saddened me unspeakably, and the revelation about Delius was a great blow. I find now I do not thoroughly get over these things: the memories of friends killed in the war, and of those who have suffered or are still suffering during their lifetime, leave their mark on me. But I will no longer speak of these things: one must carry on with a pretence of wearing a brave heart & with unapparent grief.

No more now, especially as every word I write has to be contested with the throb of the vessel & with the efforts of an amateur pianist in the adjoining room.

Ever yours

H. BALFOUR GARDINER

(110)
BRIDGMAN AND CO to THE DAILY TELEGRAPH

Oct 20, 1922

Sɪʀ—As solicitors for the British National Opera Company Ltd. we should be grateful for your publication of this letter. We trust it will dispel certain prejudicial opinions concerning this undertaking, which appear to have arisen out of the recent examination in bankruptcy of Sir Thomas Beecham. In one quarter it has actually been said that Grand Opera cannot be made to pay in this country.

Our answer to this contention (which we think is unfair to the music-loving public of England) may be briefly summed up as follows:

1. That it is the generally accepted opinion that the failure of the Sir Thomas

Beecham Opera Company Ltd. was due to the unfortunate change of policy made in the summer season of 1920 at Covent Garden.

2. That the British National Opera Company Ltd. starts in many respects where the Beecham Company left off. This may be illustrated by (a) The acquisition of an almost complete set of properties and costumes at an extremely low price. (b) The essentially important fact that Sir Thomas Beecham has by his splendid efforts created an opera-loving public such as never before existed in the country; and (c) that the present company has the advantage of profiting by experience concerning any errors of policy or otherwise that may have been made by the old company.

Again, it must be borne in mind that Sir Thomas Beecham was a lover of his art, and that higher considerations than commercial success may have often guided his policy. In the field of popularising opera he was a great pioneer: he sowed the seed, and the British National Opera Company should gather the harvest.

We have satisfied ourselves that the average takings of the late company for a period of nearly eighteen months were over £3,000 a week, and our clients find it difficult to see why the weekly expenditure should exceed £2,700 even in maintaining the high standard of production upon which Sir Thomas Beecham spent, as he stated in his examination, such large sums of money. On these facts, coupled with the many promises of support our clients have received both in London and the provinces, we are sanguine as to the success of the British National Opera Company Ltd., and look forward to the future of the undertaking with confidence.

Before the War quite a range of British orchestral music had been performed in Germany, in particular those scores published by German houses. Afterwards this momentum was never really regained, though, notable early successes included the appearance of British works at the ISCM Festivals which started in 1922. In the 1924 Festival in Prague, Arnold Bax's stormy First Symphony was heard under the baton of Fritz Reiner. Earlier, in the Winter of 1922–23, there occurred a little-reported concert of British music in Belgrade, where Thomas Dunhill's Symphony in A minor was given a notable performance with its composer conducting. This concert was probably arranged by two young Serbs, Bratza and Dushko Yovanovitch (violin and piano) who made their mark on the London season in the early 1920s and were friends of Dunhill through studying at the Royal College of Music.

(III)
THOMAS DUNHILL'S DIARY

December 23 [1922]
Very busy in morning making a simple version for strings of a little piece by Elgar, which Bratza is to play at the concert . . .

December 26
. . . . . . was up at 7 – and began rehearsing [the Royal Guard Orchestra] at the Barracks at 8.15. Dushko came with me. Had a frightful time with the Elgar, which is very hard for them – but did a lot of work with it. Also rehearsed [Balfour Gardiner's] "Shepherd Fennel". In afternoon. . . . did some of my symphony – but it got dusk and we couldn't go on as there were no lights in the room!

December 27
Up early again with Bratza to rehearse. Got there at 8 but no rehearsal till about 8.30
– so like them! Worked *hard* at symphony till 10. Short break, then [Vaughan
Williams'] Wasps, Shepherd Fennel and Elgar (all getting better – especially Elgar).
Another break (some food – brought by Molly [Dunhill's wife], and a cup of so-
called "tea"). Then again rehearsed bits of my symphony (1st movt) till 1.40. Then I
was told I must stop.

December 28
Up betimes for the third and last day's rehearsal. Got to the Opera House at 8, and
they were soon busy getting the stage prepared. It was an excellent arrangement –
with the automatic raising of the stage in sections brought into play. At about 9 I
commenced the rehearsal. Worked *frightfully* hard – and with two short intervals
continued till 2. Mostly at my symphony – but we did *everything* – including
Bratza's pieces. Then I had two hours rest on my bed – an early meal. Off to the
Concert at about 7.30. The house was sold out long before the doors opened – and
the posters we had printed were never circulated. A wonderful audience. Only one
disappointment. The King and Queen had expressed their intention of coming and
were expected. The concert delayed till 8.15 – but then I started. The Queen was not
well – and that was why they did not come. Prince Paul was in the Royal Box and
sent for me afterwards. He speaks fluent English and asked me about Eton and
Goodhart and others there (he was at school there).* He said he was delighted with
the music. I was quite a long time in the room but had to ask him (in the middle) to
excuse me to go on and bow again – as the audience refused to go – and kept
cheering and shouting!! (I was called about 6 times). Then went back to the Prince's
room and resumed the conversation. The music went amazingly well considering all
things. Bratza played *divinely*. A supper party at the Opera Buffet afterwards. I had a
prodigious thirst. Everybody seems delighted with the symphony. I had a large
laurel wreath from the *musicians* of Belgrade. Very gratifying.

(112)
JOSEPH HOLBROOKE to THE DAILY TELEGRAPH

Published in the issue for Saturday 21 April 1923 p. 17

Vienna, April

Sir
—It may be of interest to give some particulars of the several performances of my
drama, 'The Children of Don,' in this city at the Volksoper, under the masterly
direction of Felix Weingartner. I found the work well in hand on my arrival – some
few days before the first performance, on March 29. This delay since last November
is explained by the various difficulties of the work – scenic and dramatic, and the
orchestral complexities. A fine cast, consisting of M. Ernst Fisscher in the lead, as
Gwydion: M. Baumann, as Govannion; Mr. Fäbbe, as Gwion, the fanatic; and M.
Haas, as Arawn – excellent; M. List, as Math; Mr. Kaplan, as Nodeus; M. Hoders, as
the Sea King. A fine series of actors, well coupled with Fräulein Schimon as Grewin

*Dunhill had been on the music staff at Eton.

VOLKSOPER

Direktion: Felix Weingartner

Telephon 13060 (Direktion), Tageskassen und Billettbestellung: Telephon 13247 (Theatergebäude)
Telephon 3767 (Rotenturmstraße, Basar)

Anfang 7 Uhr　　**Donnerstag den 29. März 1923**　　Anfang 7 Uhr

Erstaufführung:

Unter Leitung des Herrn Direktor Felix Weingartner

KINDER DER DON

Ein Drama in drei Akten und einem Vorspiel von T. E. Ellis

Musik von Josef Holbrooke

In Szene gesetzt von Hrn. Oberregisseur Max Haas

Nodens, Gott der Unterwelt	Hr. Kaplan
Lyr, Gott des Meeres	Hr. Lazar
Math, König von Arvon	Hr. List
Arawn, König von Annwvijen	Hr. Haas
Gwyon, ein Druide	Hr. Fälbl
Gwydion, der Rächer von Arvon	
Govannion, Gwydions Bruder } Kinder der Don	Hr. Baumann
Elan, Gwydions Schwester	Frl. Salinger
Gwenin, eine Priesterin	Frl. Schimon
Erster Priester	Hr. Männling
Zweiter Priester	Hr. Dr. Lorenzi
Erster Dämon	Hr. Männling
Zweiter Dämon	Hr. Band

Priester, Druiden, Geister der Druiden und Wölfe

Vorspiel: Eine Höhle auf den nordischen Inseln — 1. Akt: Außerhalb des Tempels
von Cauldron — 2. Akt: Der Tempel von Cauldron — 3. Akt: 1. Szene wie in 1. Akt;
2. Szene am Meeresstrande

Dekorationen nach Entwürfen Prof. Schaffrans, ausgeführt im Atelier Prof. Hans
Kautsky & Franz Koltonara

* * * „Gwydion" Hr. Ernst Fischer a. G.

Nach dem zweiten Akt eine größere Pause

Während der Ouvertüre und der Akte bleiben die Türen des Zuschauerraumes geschlossen

Kassen-Eröffnung ½7 Uhr　　Anfang 7 Uhr　　Ende nach 10 Uhr

Freitag	den 30. März.	Geschlossen
Samstag	den 31. März. Anfang ½6 Uhr: Parsifal	
Sonntag	den 1. April. Nachmittags 2 Uhr: Der Wildschütz. „Bacculus" Hr. Rudolf Bandler als Gast (Ermäßigte Preise)	
	Abends 7 Uhr: Die Fledermaus	
Montag	den 2. April. Nachmittags ½3 Uhr: La Traviata. „Violetta" Fr. Marie Engel vom Nationaltheater in München a. G. (Einzigste Preise)	
	Abends ½8 Uhr: Kinder der Don. „Gwydion" Hr. Ernst Fischer c. G.	
Dienstag	den 3. April. Anfang ½8 Uhr: Rigoletto	
Mittwoch	den 4. April. Anfang 7 Uhr: Der Evangelimann	
Donnerstag	den 5. April. Anfang ½7 Uhr: Tannhäuser. „Tannhäuser" Hr. Anton Maria Topitz vom Stadttheater in Graz a. G.	

Druck der „Libersal", Wien II.

and Fräulein Salinger as Elan, all most difficult rôles. I can say no composer has put
up [with] more difficulties of diction and production, and these were all surmounted.
The orchestra played the score in very keen and warm fashion, but a better orchestra
all round would have pleased me, or more rehearsals for this department.

It is very pleasant to say Herr Weingartner gave a masterly reading of my score,
which was certainly increased at the second performance recently. I hope, however,
like all selfish composers, to get even better results at the ensuing performances on
the 11th, 20th, and 27th, under Herr Kraus, a most excellent conductor, who did all
the preparation of the work.

The system of star conductors in this country is most interesting to me. We have no such system in Old England, and I hope we never shall have unless the conductors all share the work in public. In this case it is absolutely necessary – as Herr Weingartner conducts in many cities – and, indeed, returned only from Bucharest a few days before the premiere of 'Don,' and now departs for Berlin.

The general effect here of a Celtic work and its idioms has been rather amusing and bewildering. No such work has ever been heard before here which does not give the 'reciprocation' feeling I like, and hope to bring about. The Press here is decidedly caustic, angry, and in cases abusive, and laudatory. But the public reception was excellent, and no one was more surprised than myself to find a warm welcome for a work which avoids love scenes as such, yet still delights the eye.

I have much enjoyed the work and the insight into the fine preparation of opera as it is here practised, such as sixteen orchestral rehearsals alone is found necessary. The invaluable assistance of Mr T. Fairburn in the preparation must be mentioned as he is fully familiar with the strange Celtic sagas here set to music.

Yours, &c

JOSEPH HOLBROOKE.

Musical Opinion *(May 1923) reported that the opera 'was very favourably received by the Viennese public although the press was fairly cold. Weingartner secured a magnificent performance, and said the score was the most difficult he had ever conducted. The cast was beyond praise.'*

(113)
SIR ARTHUR SOMERVELL to LESLIE BOOSEY

Terregles Banks
Dumfries.
29.5.23

Dear Mr Boosey,

I am *most anxious* that this new Cycle of mine [*The Broken Arc*, words by Browning] should have every chance given to it. I notice that whenever a new work is coming out, by one of the new young English school for example, there is always a paragraph about it in the papers a few days in advance.

The Cycle will be sung for the first time on Thursday aft[ernoon] June 14th at 3 o'clock in the Wigmore Hall by Mr Gilbert Bailey. *If time permits it will be repeated at the end of the programme for any who may wish to hear it again.* (?Publisher).

Could you send some such notice, or one embodying these points, to the papers? I expect you know how these things are done; for myself I am quite ignorant & should be most grateful for your help in this matter. I imagine that there is some News Agency where such paragraphs are sent & by them circulated to the papers.

Yours very truly

ARTHUR SOMERVELL

(114)
PHILIP HESELTINE to BERNARD VAN DIEREN

125 Cheyne Walk
s.w.10
September 20th 1923

My dear Bernard
I am very sorry we shall not be able to meet next week – and this week I fear is impossible. I shall be returning to Essex to-morrow or Sunday for about ten days and am then going to a folk-song hunt with Moeran and a phonograph in the eastern counties. However I'll be back in London early in October and we will then get hold of Mr Peacock and see what can be done about 'The Tailor'.

'Hassan' contains some very lovely music which you should hear. I saw the dress rehearsal last night. The play is wonderfully produced but I find it rather nauseously sadistic – everybody seems obsessed with a craving for blood and the spectacle of a whore caressing a nigger who has just performed an execution by slow torture and exclaiming

Whore: Ah – your black flesh smells of blood!
Nigger: And yours of roses.*

is rather unpleasant. But there are some very good scenes as well, and a ballet by Fokine in the approved manner.

Delius is at Cox's Hotel, Jermyn Street and may possibly stay till next week. He would be so pleased if you could contrive to visit him there. We have had to carry him in and out of the theatre in the Caliph's chair of state for the last day or two – but he has now got a proper contrivance on wheels and an attendant.

With love to you both –
Ever affectionately your
Φ.

I hope you will forgive me for printing your name over the enclosed but my justification is the command to 'Render unto Caesar . . . etc!'

Bernard van Dieren's opera The Tailor *had been sketched out by 1917, though a full score was not produced until 1930. Although the scene was conducted by John Barbirolli in 1925, it has never been produced and survives as a chaotic and problematic manuscript. James Elroy Flecker's play* Hassan *was to receive its first English production, by Basil Dean, eight years after its author's death, with incidental music composed by Delius. It opened at His Majesty's Theatre on 20th September 1923 and ran for 281 performances.*

Heseltine had enclosed 'Along the Stream' – the first song in the set he entitled Saudades – *which he had dedicated to van Dieren.*

---

*The published text of the play actually reads:

Yasmin: How you smell of blood!
Masrur: And you of roses

(115)
WILLIAM FENNEY to N. SAY

59 Regent Road, Handsworth
Birmingham
17.4.1925

Dear Sir,
I thank you for your letter of yesterday, duly received, in which you ask for a list of my works, at the request of Mr Edwin Evans. I am of course very pleased to have any enquiry about me, and to send the following dicta – trusting these will be of use.

Yours faithfully, WILLIAM FENNEY

I was born in Handsworth, Birmingham on the 23 May, 1891. I had an early preference for music and was self-taught in composition, until the time when I studied with Prof Bantock at the Midland Institute School of Music. From early years I studied the great masters, – Beethoven and Chopin were my first teachers; I liked Wagner only on the stage. I have never liked the 'modernist' school; my own style owes to Elgar.

I have always lived here, and produced the scores of my orchestral romances and the 'Vision of Ancient Empire', and two string quartets, here. The published piano trio I wrote in town; and a sonatina for violin and piano (MS) really admired by Mr Havergal Brian was purposely written there to give it a town atmosphere.

My orchestral works are the Avon Romance, Dawn, In Shadow and the Vision of Ancient Empire, – this last an incomplete performance, sufficiently striking, however, as I still think, in its fragmentary tone – picture of ancient Nineveh seen as in broken reflections in water. The score is in manuscript.

I think I succeeded with a string quartet (after the usual preliminary failures) though nobody has noticed it; and I have nothing better to show than my Ops. 20 and 26, – the latter – unpublished – consists of an Air for Violin and piano, a Romaint for Viola and piano and a Rhapsody for cello and piano, all of equal length.

I have lived like a streak of light!

WILLIAM FENNEY

The critic Edwin Evans dominated the inter-war period as a focus of sympathetic appreciation for both the rising generation of British composers and the new composers from abroad.

(116)
EUGENE GOOSSENS to EDWIN EVANS

The University of Rochester
Eastman School of Music
Rochester, New York
December 14, 1925

My dear Teddy:

You must forgive me this long silence but, frankly, I have been so very busy that letter-writing has been out of the question. This is just to wish you all the best for Christmas, and to hope that things are going as well for you at the moment as can be expected.

I have been working very hard of late, ramming your name down people's throats, and while all of them agree (and I have spoken to many) that it is a scandal that you are not in this country, they also realize the great difficulties of importing you at the present moment, owing to the fact that if you come over here at all, it must be for something good.

I have, however, still one or two cards up my sleeve, and going to New York as I am, to conduct the New York Symphony (and the Boston Symphony for three concerts) next month, I shall be more on the spot to give my real attention to the matter.

I am determined that in spite of all obstacles, the work you have done, not only for me, in the past, but also for the cause of contemporary music, shall not go unrewarded. Though you may wonder occasionally at my long silence, you know at heart my belief that practical help is worth a ton of sympathy.

I am still hankering after one of the big New York papers for you, not only in your capacity of visiting critic, but of a real *permanence*. The situation in this city at the moment presents rather an 'impasse' for many reasons which I cannot easily write here, though none of them is concerned with you, personally. But the situation, as a whole is still very undependable and I don't want to spoil the prospect of the future by being too eager at the start.

My own news is very scarce, but good. As you have doubtless read in the papers, I have been invited to conduct at Boston in January, immediately after my New York season, Mengelberg replacing me here. The concerts have been a great success in Rochester and the Orchestra is 300 percent improved.

I often think of you, and wish sometimes that we could be together again over a friendly glass of beer, and drowning the importunities of our adversaries in the delights of a gastronomic orgy.

Give our love to all our friends and a special greeting to Netta, and do write me soon with a synopsis of the situation as it stands for you at present.

Scholes passed through here recently, and expressed himself as delighted with everything.

It strikes me that a lecture tour organised for you on the same lines would be very beneficial and good propaganda, and I shall do all I can to start it.

Blessings on you and don't forget my health in your next Sunday morning's cocktail, (unless prohibition has been introduced since last I was in England . . .)

Much love from
Yours ever,

EUGENE

(117)
SIR EDWARD ELGAR to LESLIE BOOSEY

Napleton Grange
Kempsey
Worcester
July 25th 1927

My dear Leslie
Thank you for the cheque on acc[oun]t of the 'Land of Hope' film production; I had quite forgotten the proposal & am glad to learn that it is proceeding.

I shall be glad to consider Mr. Smith's suggestion as to conducting either the 'overture' or, possibly, the whole first 'show'. This w[oul]d be a matter of terms which had better be proposed by Mr Smith. I will gladly look through the arrangement of the music – I should think that the *whole* of the music sh[oul]d be mine as I feel 'Land of Hope' should not be used to advertise other authors: 'Cockaigne', for instance might furnish many themes & if I had a [   ] of free hand, w[oul]d be glad to suggest their use & w[oul]d go so far as to write some original music if this w[oul]d call attention to the film. I am anxious that Bristol Films sh[oul]d be put forward as much as possible.

Kind regards
Yours sincerely

EDWARD ELGAR
PS. I could make a rare pasticcio out of the four marches, the Coronation Ode, Cockaigne & if necessary for quiet effects the songs –

So far as is known the proposed film was never made.

(118)
RUTLAND BOUGHTON to STUART FLETCHER

Kilcote, Newent, Glos
3 July 1928

My dear Stuart,
Estelle tells me that you have the very kind idea of writing an article for the Sackbut shewing how my work arises in its own time rather than in my mere personality. It is very good that you should have thought of it, and I shall be glad to help providing you keep yourself clear of the personal interest that lies between us, and I think you can. I send you a copy of my Self-Advertisement belonging to the year 1909. Since then my chief works with their associations are as follows:

Arthurian cycle of Operas: THE BIRTH OF ARTHUR, THE ROUND TABLE (completed), THE LILY MAID OF ASTOLAT (not yet finished), THE QUEEN OF CORNWALL (Hardy), THE HOLY GRAIL and THE DEATH OF ARTHUR (not yet composed at all). The above are a mixture of personal experience and the will to public service. The best, because the least personal, is at present The

Round Table, performed many times and always successfully at Glastonbury, from the first production in 1916 (when the district military representative for the government press-gang walked out during King Arthur's anti-war speech) to its last performance at the Glastonbury Festival of 1924. It has not yet received an orchestral production.

BETHLEHEM you know all about; its last production in modern dress was its best and truest, though for the time being it has prejudiced the work itself and was the direct cause of bringing the Glastonbury Players and Festivals to an end.

ALKESTIS you know, and that also is too personal, though as a sheer work of art it is the best thing I have done except THE MOON MAIDEN, and that was written for impersonal ends, namely to express something of the emotions of virginal reserve when I was considering Ruby's education. AGINCOURT was a mistaken effort at public service at a time when I was actually in the army, and my mind much more confused regarding the rights and wrongs of the war than it was either before or since. THE IMMORTAL HOUR was really a religious expression at a moment when I was thrown back on natural paganism by the futility of the Christians. (The Holy Grail will be a much more definite and constructive work in the same direction while The Death of Arthur has a revolution for its central feature, but of that I would rather nothing were said at present.) The MAYDAY ballet you know, and can write about if you wish. About the same time was written a DEIRDRE ballet, very personal and romantic. THE EVER YOUNG follows on from The Immortal Hour, and is a kind of transitional work from private expression to public service. Of my smaller works the following have a broader interest than that of personal expression:

> Four Songs to poems by Edward Carpenter
> The Triumph of Civilisation
> In Prison (William Morris)
> The Love of Comrades (Whitman)

CHORAL VARIATIONS on Folk-songs alluded to in the Self-advertisement; the date of these shews what is a fact, that these pieces actually started the ball rolling in the direction of finding our English musical tongue by the help of folk-song. Vaughan-Williams who was present at their first performance at Leeds professed himself there converted to a sort of treatment which he had at first disapproved: since then he has done that sort of thing more frequently and conspicuously than I, for I was not out for final art-works, but only on a voyage of discovery, in search of my own natural musical language against the wind of an intense love for the work of Wagner. The silly fools of musicians who declare my music dramas to be derived from Wagner's have not realised that they are couched in another tongue & form CHORAL WORKS with a definitely Socialist quality are MIDNIGHT, A SONG OF LIBERTY, PIONEERS, THE CITY; and needless to say the same spirit informs much of my work. It is but little performed for that reason; as art it is beyond the possibilities of those who need it, while its ideas prevent its performance by the usual organisations. Someday when the workers have won their leisure I do not think it will be ignored. Of course you won't quote this letter. If you want to know anything else ask, and if you want me to play anything to you I shall be in town on the 15th.

Yours always

RUTLAND B.

The Cloud was just a song of great happiness & nature-worship, written during a holiday by Snowdon, where the clouds are even more wonderful than the earth.

Rutland Boughton had established an enormous following with the two London runs of his opera The Immortal Hour, *which between October 1922 and the spring of 1924 had notched up 376 performances, two further revivals in 1926 and 1932, taking the tally of London performances alone to over 500. When revived again in 1953 the magic appeared to have evaporated, but for those in tune with its unique world, its appearance on records has made it generally available in an idiomatic performance of high quality. Boughton's presentation of his works at Glastonbury started more or less with World War I, and continued until 1927. Very much a homespun affair, it still attracted considerable prestige and many of Boughton's works were performed there. In letter 118 Boughton is writing to Stuart Fletcher, his son-in-law, married to his daughter Estelle Boughton. Fletcher was a journalist. 'Ruby' mentioned in the context of* Alkestis *is another of Boughton's daughters.* The Lily Maid of Astolat *was completed in 1934 under the title of* The Lily Maid, *while* The Holy Grail *and* The Death of Arthur *were completed in 1944 and 1945 as* Galahad *and* Avalon. *Neither has been produced.* The Cloud *mentioned in Boughton's postscript is a cantata for women's voices. Boughton's 'Self-Advertisement' published in 1909, was a pamphlet promoting his own music.*

Various wealthy patrons of music, who had constituted the financial basis of musical life before World War I were still in evidence between the wars, though their influence was more limited. The major patron of chamber music at this time was the American Elizabeth Sprague Coolidge, who organised festivals of new music in the USA and instituted a celebrated composition competition. In 1922 she visited Europe and on 28 May, over tea with Mary Rogers, widow of the music publisher Winthrop Rogers, she met the composer Frank Bridge. Within a fortnight Bridge and his wife were invited to join the wealthy American on a motoring trip round France, and they became close friends. In 1923 Mrs Coolidge's Pittsfield Festival had a strong British orientation with a number of British performers there and Bliss, Goossens and Bridge present in person to hear their new works. The friendship with Frank Bridge blossomed and assumed a remarkable depth for the rest of his life; he wrote frequently and at considerable length to her about the musical scene.

(119)
FRANK BRIDGE to ELIZABETH SPRAGUE COOLIDGE

Friston Field
28 September 1928

My dearest Souzanne,
So nice of you to send me yet another wire. Ever so many thanks for it. Anyway I was *quite* sure that the actual playing of the Roth Quartet would be as lovely as when we heard them in Paris last year, and to judge by the leader's keenness on the purest intonation, at the rehearsals that I attended, I felt quite safe in my mind as to what they would do in the end. When I think of the queer obstacle to the first planned performance and that morning in Brussel's [sic] and the Paris 'Pro Arte' performance it seems a long, long story.

The Brosa Quartet, that played the work* at Siena, gave a perfectly magnificent show. The rehearsals in London during the Summer and then after their August

*i.e. Bridge's Third String Quartet.

holiday meeting them again, as well as a final rehearsal at Siena, allowed everything to sink in normally. There wasn't a hitch of any kind. I could *never be* more contented – except to have *another* work interpreted just as naturally. And now I can't see any difficulty in the thing at all – because there isn't any given the right sympathetic attitude. Of course I can never, never thank you enough for helping me to have these initial performances, dear Souzanne. We stayed a night in Paris and Florence to break the length of the journey to Siena. The heat of the trains, and the temperature in Italy was terrific! (O for that Cadillac of yours). There were mosquitos even at Sierra – 10cl up – and the whole time I was wishing the Festival were being held in Iceland! The generously arranged proceedings included an especially gorgeous Palio which you'd have loved to have seen, with all new costumes and no sagging 'tights' on any of the processionists!! It was just as interesting to see for the second time although I shouldn't have thought so. The concert at which a riot broke out – the Webern String Trio – was exciting while it lasted. I think it must have been anti-Viennese, although one sees that no Italian could hold himself in at a series of sounds that are entirely alien in their musical world, if indeed they are not equally alien to other nations. On the whole the popular successes of the Festival were the works that broke no new ground whatsoever, and on the principle that the audience likes to feel flattered at recognising rhythms and harmony that they consider should make music – in other words conventional music making them feel at home! – then, of course, one understands how it is.

One other incident occurred at the performance of 'Façade' by Walton – in the theatre. My own personal feelings happen to coincide with many of the foreigners in thinking this is concerned with a higher class cabaret and not much – if anything – to do with music itself. A great [   ] of poem recited through a megaphone with accompanying music. Listening one heard no words and so one concentrated on the small orch, which seemed to be performing stray items by the best jazz composers. All quite short. After ten of them – or thereabouts – subdued irritation began to show itself at the back of the stalls, and increased murmurs arose in the succeeding numbers. At the end of one number that ended rather abruptly, and before these murmurs of disapproval could begin, a voice called out 'Benino'! It was so ironical as to take the sting out of the antagonists who simply roared with laughter. On the whole a better way than that manifestation which followed on the Webern Trio. At the same time it doesn't follow that a large percentage of that audience knew much about anything, although if I had come a long way for this Festival I should have felt pretty much the same at being presented with that entertainment. I am told many of the Sitwell poems in 'Façade' are first rate, but as I couldn't hear them, or recognise more than half a dozen stray words, what could a foreigner get out of it? I got nothing, absolutely nothing.

But O the heat! the final impression that results is a kind of sandwich made up of hot trains, over-heated-Siena-with-musical-diversions and hot trains. I see that I am no bird for the semi-tropics, and if an International Festival is ever held in the Sahara Desert I shall not be present. Having said that, then I realize that that would be the very one which you would long to go to. . . . Well – alright – I shall promptly devise a species of vacuum flask into which I can creep so as to be there with you, although fears about next year's Festival are unnecessary as it is to be held at Geneva.

I expect you had a royal time at Pittsfield* – I hope so – and when you have the energy to tell me anything about it you know I'll be hugely interested.

*The Berkshire festivals of chamber music started at Pittsfield, Massachusetts.

A friend sent me one of the South Mountain Quartet concert programmes – the one on which appeared my Pft. 5^{tet}. It had been sent to him for some one who had been to the performances at the Temple. Scrawled across was:

'Where were you? missing this gorgeous concert!'

and against my Quintet:

'quite *sensating*!!!'

That is 1928 for something, I'm sure – but what?

With tons of love dear Souzanne,

Ever your devoted

2^{ZEE}. [two zee, Mrs Coolidge's pet name for Bridge]

(120)

SIR THOMAS BEECHAM to THE DAILY TELEGRAPH

Imperial League of Opera
161 New Bond St w.1.
OCT 27, 1928

IMPERIAL LEAGUE OF OPERA

SCOPE OF THE APPEAL

A REPLY TO CRITICISM

SIR—

It is almost too good to be true, and even now after reading them over and over again, I rub my eyes and ask myself, like the gentleman in Bret Harte's poem, 'Do I dream or is visions about?' I am referring of course to the three letters which appeared in your issue of Friday last on the subject of the Imperial League of Opera.

Your readers may possibly remember that, in the long communication of mine you were good enough to publish last Wednesday, I drew attention to the singular type of individual who takes the trouble to explain elaborately in the newspapers his reasons for disliking or refusing to support opera. As I pointed out, this superior person generally takes upon himself to speak in the name of the entire British public. May I, therefore, state as clearly as I can that the scheme of the Imperial League of Opera is designed especially for those who want opera and not for those who do not want it.

This is set forth in the original prospectus in words that do not admit the smallest misunderstanding. The appeal is not to the general public, nor is it to those who prefer other musical forms to opera. It is to that large selection of it which, during the past twenty years, has actually attended the performances I myself have given and which, I fully believe, will attend them again. Further, it was to reach this particular class that my letter was written.

Mr. Victor Marker styles himself a lover of grand opera. He must be a very young one, for apparently he has no knowledge of the dozens of opera seasons I gave between 1909 and 1920. Otherwise he might know that most of them were not given at Covent Garden, but in other London theatres just as well equipped for the purpose, and he would also know that on nine occasions out of ten it was possible to obtain a comfortable seat at a very moderate price.

If he had taken the trouble to peruse my scheme with the smallest care, he would have seen that the main object of it is to provide a first-rate opera at a moderate price of admission. Indeed, it is in a way the beginning and end of the whole project. Apparently, he wants an Opera House that will hold four to five times the number of persons that can be contained in Covent Garden. Does he really know what this means? It means an Opera House larger than the Albert Hall, a building which by reason of its size is considered by nearly every musical authority to be comparatively useless for serious musical purposes.

The letter of Mr. Stokes is equally pointless. I have not 'castigated Philistine England,' nor have I anywhere claimed that music and opera are one and the same thing. If Mr. Stokes had any acquaintance with current musical affairs he would have read that I am also concerned in the largest enterprise yet undertaken in this country for the establishment of a permanent orchestra which will have nothing to do with opera at all.

He is good enough to inform the readers of THE DAILY TELEGRAPH that Beethoven wrote but one opera! I envy him the large batch of correspondence he is likely to receive thanking him for this valuable piece of information. But would it not have been more pertinent to mention that an equally great composer, the mighty Handel, wrote fifty operas, that another equally great composer, Mozart, wrote over twenty operas, among them 'The Magic Flute,' 'Don Giovanni,' and 'The Marriage of Figaro' (three of the world's masterpieces), and that the whole output of Gluck, Verdi, and Wagner is operatic.

But these two monuments of irrelevancy are as nothing compared with the effort of your third correspondent who signs himself (or herself) 'M.E.' Here is the true self-appointed spokesman of the British public, which, as I have stated before, is non-operatic, for the one reason that it has never heard opera. But according to 'M.E.' it is anti-operatic because of its deeply serious and religious trend of mind, evidences of which are to be found in our festivals and community singing.

With festivals and choirs I have some acquaintance extending over thirty years, and I must say that if there is any such trend all signs of it have escaped me. And community singing! The last event I attended was one of the liveliest in my whole experience. Together with 10,000 other persons I joined in the uproarious bawling of such essentially profane selections as 'Cockles and Mussels,' 'There is a tavern in the town,' and 'Hullabaloobalay.' And we are asked to believe that to sit and listen in the theatre to the cathedral scene of 'Parsifal,' the ghost scene in 'Les Troyens,' or the last act of 'A Village Romeo and Juliet' would be something far too trivial for the public that participated in the exhilarating 'beano' to which I am alluding.

May I remind 'M.E.' that it is also the sober British temperament which has created such stupendously serious institutions as racing (of all kinds under the sun), music halls, musical comedies, ping-pong, and kiss-in-the-ring? And what of the cinema to which millions go weekly? Doubtless for these, too, the masterpieces of the great composers are not sufficiently solid and subdued in tone.

And now, in brief conclusion, I crave leave to be very serious myself. I utterly fail to understand how such letters as these ever come to be written. The Imperial League of Opera is the largest organisation of its kind in the world, and it grows in numbers daily. It might be a timely thing if a few only of its many thousands of supporters would come forward and tell your readers why they have become subscribers.—

THOMAS BEECHAM

(121)
FRED GAISBERG to SIR EDWARD ELGAR

2nd July, 1929.

My dear Sir Edward,
Many thanks for your letter of June 30th. I am delighted to hear you are well and are coming up to town next week. Do let me know which evening you will be free. We might dine and go to the Russian Ballet together if that will amuse you!

I am more than satisfied with our Opera Season this year. It was really a great success and I hope for even better things next Season.

As I told you some time ago, we are issuing the 'Wand of Youth' in an album, and I enclose the Album Synopsis and the proof of the Supplementary write-up. I hope this meets with your approval.

There is one other thing I have been wanting to ask you. I have seen in the press that you and Rudyard Kipling have collaborated in the production of a work entitled 'March of Praise' to celebrate the King's recovery. If there is any truth in this statement, I think it would be of interest to record this work at an early date, but no doubt you will tell me all about this when we meet.

Hoping to see you next week, and with best wishes,

Yours ever,

Elgar did not collaborate with Kipling on this occasion, but produced 'a simple carol for His Majesty's happy recovery' ('Goodmorrow'), a setting for SATB of the Tudor poet George Gascoigne which was performed at St George's Chapel Windsor on 9 December 1929.

(122)
ALBERT SAMMONS to GEORGE LLOYD

33 Craven Hill Gardens
Lancaster Gate
W.2.
Nov 8th 1929

Dear George
You are quite right about Elman.

He has a fine showy bow arm & big fine tone but his interpretations are erratic. A couple of years in a symphony orchestra & opera would have taught him something.

Could you come on 13th to my flat at 11a.m. instead of 4 as I have to leave at 4. for Barnstaple.

Yours sincerely

ALBERT SAMMONS

P.S. The new boy Yehudi Menuhin is wonderful. He is playing on Sunday at Albert Hall.

The sixteen-year-old George Lloyd was a violin student of the leading English violinist Albert Sammons. Mischa Elman (1891–1967) first appeared as a child prodigy, and enjoyed a very long career as a brilliant concert violinist.

(123)
SIR EDWARD ELGAR to THE EVENING STANDARD

Published in the issue dated 17 December 1929, p. 19

Brooks's
St. James's Square
SW

Sir

The most serious blow ever aimed at the unfortunate art of English music is proposed to be dealt by some of the very persons to whom creative artists might not unreasonably have looked for sympathy and assistance.

A situation such as that now existing could not have arisen in any artistically civilised community.

At this moment I do not enter into details concerning the monstrous proposals contained in the bill; I will only record my strong protest against it, adding that the passing of such a measure could mean the extinction of creative musical art in this country and the ruin of the majority of native composers.

EDWARD ELGAR

The bill, which had been introduced by the Labour Member Mr W. M. Adamson, had reached its second reading but proceeded no further. It would have reduced royalties by introducing a flat rate performing royalty of 2d. The incident was the subject of a well-known cartoon by Lowe in the Evening Standard. *The measure was finally defeated when Edward German pointed out how small his income from* Merry England *would have been under it.*

(124)
GUSTAV HOLST to ADRIAN BOULT

St. Paul's Girls' School
Brook Green, Hammersmith, w.6.
Oct 3 [1930]

Dear Adrian
You are too busy a man to be bothered unless the matter is urgent. The matter in point is my bewilderment as to how to bar my new thing now it is fully sketched. I want to collect conductors' opinions and am going to HJW [Henry J. Wood] on Sunday.

It isn't exactly urgent because I ought to decide it for myself. But I'd feel much happier if I could talk it over with you. I fear it would mean nearly or quite an hour. And I'd be quite miserable if you gave up that hour when you didn't oughter – when, for instance, you ought to be walking about a garden in Hampshire!

Would you kindly pass on the enclosed application for tickets?

Good luck to the concert.

Yr Ever

G

Are you continuing the Monday Chamber concerts of modern music? If so, may I come?

(125)
PHILIP HESELTINE to E. J. MOERAN

12A Tite Street
Chelsea, s.w.3
6.x.1930

Dear Jack,
The piano was delivered on Saturday morning. It was brought in without any difficulty and is safely housed in a room with a gas fire.

I carefully avoided hearing Bridge's composition. Walton's work improves at every hearing. He is the best musician this country has produced for a long while. Lambert is perhaps more talented, but I do not feel that music is his ultimate mode of expression. His keen observation, sensibility, wit, and critical intellect seem rather to point to literature as his medium, whereas Walton is specifically musical or nothing. Bax, as usual, drove me out of the hall after ten minutes. Ireland's concerto is very interesting but by no means a great or a particularly original work. My greatest musical experience has been Elgar's second symphony, of which the old gentleman gave a most moving performance.

The 'Severn suite' is all balls, of course. We contrived (Hughes, Greenbaum, E. Evans, Blunt and myself) to spend a very amusing half-day at the [Crystal] Palace; the promoter of the show [the annual brass band competition] was very pleased with the publicity given to it by the Telegraph and caused the booze to flow freely.

If you can get Midland Regional on Thursday, listen to Debussy's *Gigues* – his last orchestral work (1913) and most fascinating; originally called *Gigues tristes*, it is a kind of grisly-ghostly discourse on 'Weel may the keel row', which however is never stated in full but merely hinted at in sinister and distorted fragments. The orchestration is quite amazing, with quadruple wood-wind, including an hautbois d'amour.

I hope the leg is doing all that was expected of it since it has been let loose again.

All good wishes and many thanks again for the loan of the piano.

Yours ever

PETER W.

One Thiman (Thimple or otherwise) has infringed one of your copyrights. See this month's 'Monthly Musical Record'.

Heseltine committed suicide two months later, his body being found in a gas-filled room on 17 December. Heseltine's footnote refers to Eric Thiman (1900–1975) much later to become organist and director of music at London's City Temple.

(126)
STANFORD ROBINSON to ADRIAN BOULT

23/10/30

'*Morning Heroes*' *(Arthur Bliss)*.

I wish to thank you for the opportunity of going to Norwich to hear the first performance of 'Morning Heroes' by Arthur Bliss, conducted by the composer last night. The performance was a great success and was very adequately performed considering all things. I liked the work very much and am looking forward to rehearsing it with the National Chorus. The composer's estimate of the length was extremely accurate, as it took 59 mins. 3 secs. from the first notes to the last. The performance of Mr. Basil Maine as the Narrator was, I think, extremely good. He spoke his part without note and delivered it in an extremely satisfying manner. I do not think that we should improve upon him for our performance.

Item 126 is a BBC internal memorandum. In the remainder of this book a gradually increasing number of such documents have been reproduced, reflecting the BBC's growing involvement in British musical life. A further 19 examples may be seen as letters 138, 140, 147, 166, 168, 177, 179, 187, 189, 193, 203, 204, 244, 232, 238, 242, 244, 245, 247.

The BBC's performance of Morning Heroes, *first scheduled for 4 February, was subsequently postponed until 25 March 1931, when it was warmly received by the press. Basil Maine's performance of Wilfred Owen's words in 'The Spring Offensive' was recorded by Decca on one side of a 10 in 78 rpm record, but far from reminding us of a great performance, his accent now has a period quality underlining how styles change from one generation to the next.*

: NORFOLK AND NORWICH THIRTY-THIRD :

Triennial Musical Festival 1930

Wednesday Morning, October 22nd, at 11.30 a.m.

"GOD SAVE THE KING."
Audience, Chorus, Organ, and Orchestra.

1. **APOSTLES** ... ... *Elgar*

THE BLESSED VIRGIN }	
THE ANGEL } ...	MISS ELSIE SUDDABY
MARY MAGDALENE ...	MISS MURIEL BRUNSKILL
ST. JOHN ... :.. ,..	MR. FRANCIS RUSSELL
ST. PETER	MR. FREDERICK WOODHOUSE
JUDAS	MR. HORACE STEVENS
JESUS ... .,	MR. ARTHUR CRANMER

2. **SYMPHONY No. 3 in F** ... ... *Brahms*

(Conducted by DR. HEATHCOTE STATHAM)

Wednesday Evening, October 22nd, at 8 p.m.

1. **SYMPHONY FOR MIXED CHORUS, ORCHESTRA, AND ORATOR** *Arthur Bliss*

"Morning Heroes"

ORATOR ... ... MR. BASIL MAINE.

(WRITTEN FOR THIS FESTIVAL AND CONDUCTED
BY THE COMPOSER.)

2. **CONCERTO in A Minor** ... ... *Saint-Saens*

For Violoncello and Orchestra.

SIGNOR ARTURO BONUCCI.

3. **SEA DRIFT** ... ... *Delius*

For Baritone Solo, Chorus, and Orchestra.

SOLO BARITONE ... ... MR. ROY HENDERSON

4. **CONCERTO No. 2 in C Minor** ... *Rachmaninoff*

For Pianoforte and Orchestra.

MISS MYRA HESS.

5. **THREE SPANISH DANCES** ... *Granados*

(e) Norwich Festival programme for *Morning Heroes*

(127)
JELKA DELIUS to PHILIP HESELTINE

Grez-sur-Loing
29.10.30

Dear Phil,
Today the O.U. Press has sent Fred your new arrangement of 'On hearing' for piano duet. Fenby being in Scarborough there is no one who could play it properly to Fred. But Fred said, that if you thought it an improvement on the other one, you made before, he was sure it could go to the printing as it stands. I told him how you had put in the orch. instruments in red; he seemed very pleased. I am therefore returning it at once to H. Foss.

May Harrison with Bax is bringing out Fred's new [Third] Violin Sonata on Nov 6th at Wigmore Hall, and I hope you will go and hear it.

The other day we heard Beecham conducting in Leipsic at the Gewandhaus. He was in splendid form.* And really, Phil, when one hears him conduct after all those others it is quite wonderfully full of Life and I cannot help thinking that he will push thro' his affairs of the League finally too.

Your last letter made us so anxious about him, but you'll see: it will be alright. It seems quite wise to amalgamate with the C.G.S, and so absorb a rival. I can believe that Austin is unpractical in affairs, but I can hardly think that he could do anything not straight. So I hope in my heart that your views were too pessimistic. However, please let us hear any further developments, it will never go any further. We both love Beecham and admire him with all our hearts and we cannot bear to think of him having so much trouble always.

I was very sorry about your rich uncle being so mean to you in his will. If you could only get a little something out of the final Sale of Uncle Joe. As far as I can see his wife is too worn out and ill to do anything and all will remain as it is till after her death. Then, surely you might come in. He owned those houses, you know.

The O.U.P. have been most decent and bigminded about Fred's contracts. Excuse hasty scribble and please tear up.

Affly yrs

JELKA

*He gave Brigg Fair most poetically. The acoustic seemed glorious. There was such a peaceful calm, real mastery. It came thro' remarkably well, only fading away sometimes.

Jelka Delius is referring to Beecham's various operatic ventures, and in her footnote to broadcast reception of a concert including Delius's Brigg Fair.

(128)
E. J. MOERAN to PHILIP HESELTINE

11 Constitution Hill
Ipswich
Nov 5th 1930

Dear Philip
Thanks for your entertaining letter: I imagine that after a bout of mushrooms the resultant fluid would prove the ideal pick-me-up on which to sober down, and should as such be commended to publicans, who are frequently asked for something with a kick (Two double piss, miss, & a split baby). Seriously though, there might be money to be made by cultivating the amanita muscaria, providing it can be taken without dangerous results. All one need do would be to collect a company of good fellows, have a glorious blind on fungi, which I suppose could be pleasantly washed down with a barrel of Kenward & Court, afterwards carefully bottling the contents of the jerries & selling them as smuggled Turkish wine of a great and unusual type of potency. Or possibly to import the Lurgi into America: I wonder whether one would be up against the Prohibition act. In this case I think the reputable firm of Hitchcock, Philpot, Chambers & Chambers would give a sound legal opinion. I am returning some scores you lent me: I heard the B♭ quartet recently; the 3rd movement especially seems an amazing piece of work.

I have not heard much music of note lately, barring 'Tapiola' and Elgar's 2nd Symphony, also Reger's Variations & Fugue on a theme of Mozart, all of which were conducted by Heward. The Reger is a brilliant tour de force on a big scale & I hope soon it may be repeated. I have several times lately tried to listen to Mahler's music, but have never been able to feel anything but boredom at such futility on so large a scale. Boris Godounow was given from Warsaw opera house yesterday, but in the Rimsky-Korsakow version: I had quite expected to hear the original version from such a source. The Musical Times included a pleasant carol of yours which is new to me.

I wonder whether to send them some Church Music, rather than to the O.U.P. I have a fairly easy Te Deum all ready & copied out & am well on with an evening service into which I cannot resist inserting some luscious Stainerisms.

I spend a good deal of time writing music, but lack of privacy prevents me doing anything on a large scale, as I am still too helpless to be free of constant attendance. However, to-day has been a red-letter day in my drab existence. For the first time since May 16th, I have sat down on a civilised seat & enjoyed a good crap. I had no idea that there is such technique in wiping one's ars [sic], that one loses it after a prolonged period of the bedpan. It is really quite difficult for a beginner, but I look forward to making a cleaner job of it to-morrow morning.

I am thus gradually becoming more independent, and I hope soon to dispense with the Nurse.

I should be glad to hear any information you can give me about Novello's. Do they pay cash down?

I am afraid that my chancery affair will be a case of Jarndyce & Jarndyce*, & that I shall be hard up for some time to come. That is why I am writing this bilge for the

---

*In the case of Jarndyce and Jarndyce in Dickens's novel *Bleak House* the distribution of an estate is subject to the law's interminable delay until ultimately the costs absorb its entire value.

Church. It is very easy to do, & it is financially waste of time to write songs or piano pieces, although I am going to do another set of folk-song arrangements for Augeners.

Yours ever,

E.J.M.

(129)
*NINETTE DE VALOIS to GEOFFREY KEYNES

The Academy of Choreographic Arts
6a Roland Houses
Roland Park, South Kensington
[January 1931]

Dear Mr Keynes
Please forgive me . . . I got back from Dublin last Saturday week to be confronted with every imaginable sort of thing to cope with and haven't had much time to answer letters. Miss Baylis is distracted looking for eight thousand pounds. She can't even get out contracts because she doesn't know what theatre she will have by the autumn. An incomplete Sadler's Wells is much worse than no Sadler's Wells to worry about at all. Anyway the idea of putting this *Job* on now (a month before suggested production time) was only to be if there was no second theatre on the horizon at all. The point is if there were two theatres running it would be only a matter of weeks at any time and the two theatres must be running sooner or later. I know how wearing this must be for you and also for me although I am so used to it, even after this three year old scheme of a small ballet company at the Sadler's Wells — which must now be put off for another ten months or so, is an example of the present chaos.

Your ballet is one of the few things I mean to push down someone's throat. She [Lilian Baylis] is keen enough I know, but nothing but 'business first' at the moment and it would do no good worrying her. In the meanwhile I am sandwiched between theatres half built and not built at all, to a point of distraction I don't know whether I am going to die a pauper or a millionaire. Yes, in the meanwhile as far as I am concerned it is a matter of patience.

Yours sincerely.

NINETTE DE VALOIS

The first staged performance of Vaughan Williams's Job *was presented by the Carmargo Society at the Cambridge Theatre, London, on Sunday 5 July 1931 with Constant Lambert conducting. It was not seen by the Sadler's Wells Company until danced by them at the Old Vic on 22 September 1931.*

(130)
E. J. MOERAN to THE MUSICAL TIMES

Published in the issue dated March 1931, p. 254

11 Constitution Hill
IPSWICH

———

ELGAR AND THE PUBLIC

Sir,—

I was extremely interested by Mr. C. W. Orr's article in the January number of the *Musical Times* and while I am able whole-heartedly to share his enthusiasm for Elgar at his best, I feel bound to point out certain historical inaccuracies among his remarks.

The folk-song rage did not take place after the war, as Mr. Orr states, but before 1914, and it largely manifested itself in the excellent series of concerts given by Mr. H. Balfour Gardiner and the late F. B. Ellis, and with which were intimately associated at that time the activities of the Oriana Madrigal Society. The post-war period, in fact, had no bearing whatever on the revival of folk-song in this country and its application to symphonic art. Mr. Orr says that 'Parties of enthusiasts went back to the land', carefully noting down the effusions of rustics, 'to be worked up into English Suites, &c.' This is a statement which simply will not bear investigation. In the first place, practically the whole of English folk-song had been noted long before. (*Vide* the published journals of the Folk-Song Society.) The immediate outcome was such works as 'Brigg Fair' of Delius, Vaughan Williams's Norfolk Rhapsodies, and numerous works by Grainger, Holst, Butterworth, and others. Secondly, at the period of which Mr. Orr writes, new works by British composers, with one notable exception, were conspicuous by their absence from folk-song influence. Thirdly, by this time, save for rare and isolated instances, spontaneous folk-singing on the part of country people had died out. The idiom of folk-song in British music is for the moment submerged beneath a wave of unpopularity, possibly because, despite our national wealth of melodies, we have not yet produced a Haydn or a Moussorgsky. English folk-song, as is that of any nation, is apt to become exceedingly dull when it is handled by musicians, who, with the best intentions, possess more technical resource than inspiration, and who, by virtue of their surroundings, their sophistication and their respectability, have never experienced the feeling which gave birth to this kind of music. Even so, there exists already at least one really important achievement which owes its existence directly to the influence of folk-song, and that is the supremely beautiful 'Pastoral' Symphony of Vaughan Williams. I have an unbounded admiration for this work, and also for Elgar's second Symphony, which owes nothing whatever to primitive music. It is surely possible to wax enthusiastic over 'Tristan' and 'Parsifal,' without decrying the chamber music and concertos of Brahms, which are soaked in the good vintage of folk-song, and to appraise Tchaikovsky's Symphonies without detracting from those of Borodin and Balakirev. Mr. Orr, himself a composer of some distinguished songs, is of all people one of the very last who can afford to sneer at those musicians who have spent much time and money in searching out and noting down our tunes of the countryside, which on their own merits are surely worthy of preservation from the oblivion into which they must otherwise have fallen.

I, too, remember the first performance of Elgar's 'Falstaff,' as I was one of the few enthusiasts who was present at Queen's Hall, and I was shocked at the rows of empty seats on that occasion. It was difficult to square this with the public acclamation with which repeated performances of the First Symphony and the Violin Concerto had been hailed only a short while before.

In conclusion, let me express the hope that the recent report that Sir Edward Elgar is 'At it again,' after nine years of silence, and is writing a large work, may prove to be true, and that he may succeed in adding yet another masterpiece to an honourable series.—

(131)
ARNOLD BAX to RICHARD CHURCH

Orchard House,
Walton-on-Thames
Saturday
[April 1931]

Dear Church,
Harriet Cohen has shown me your note and Harvey Grace's stupid remarks about your article. I quite agree with you that it is very annoying, but I think it is best to ignore this kind of thing. It is my own experience that no useful purpose is served by stirring up mud with editors. I have done it once or twice, but they are in an unfairly Olympian position, and the only outcome has been that they have borne malice for years.

As a matter of fact there are a certain number of people who object to *any* kind of picturesque commentaries upon music. The other night before the performance of my two piano sonata – Rae Robertson made a short speech about the work, in which he let himself go to some extent, and there were objections afterwards from some members of the audience (privately expressed). I suppose it derives from the idiotic peculiarly English dread of the outward manifestation of enthusiasm bred in the mind at our glorious public schools.

Anyway I would like to tell you how sorry I am that this annoyance to you should have been caused in connection with a work of mine, and to assure you again that I am certain the article gave pleasure and help to thousands of readers of the Radio Times.

Yours with all good wishes

ARNOLD BAX

Particularly between the wars, strong passions were inflamed in many musical circles on the subject of programme music. The programmatic was somehow held to be less worthy of the highest consideration than the absolute. This was particularly unfortunate at a time when a whole generation were writing music which was more or less programmatic in its origin, but which most composers were unwilling to admit to in public. The writer Richard Church had recently written an enthusiastic programmatic article about Bax's symphonic poem Tintagel *(Radio Times, 24 April 1931, p.189) which had resulted in barbed ripostes from various academic quarters.*

When the second edition of Guido Adler's Handbuch der Musikgeschichte *appeared in February 1930 it contained an article on 'Modern English Music' by Edward J. Dent which was somewhat dismissive about Elgar, including the celebrated sentence 'Fur englische Ohren ist Elgar's Musik allzu gefuhlvoll und nicht frei von Vulgaritat': 'For English ears Elgar's music is much too emotional and not free from vulgarity'. Dent was Stanford's successor as Professor of Music at Cambridge, and had been his pupil. Possibly first noticed by Philip Heseltine who immediately organized a round robin about it which was issued as a press release to the main musical journals and newspapers of the day in both Great Britain and Germany. However, although Heseltine rounded up a good number of co-signatories, it is worth noting that Holst, Vaughan Williams and Bax failed to comply, among others. The appearance of the letter in* Musical Opinion *stimulated a letter of protest from the composer Havergal Brian who thought it a blunder, no matter who the signatories might be, concluding 'Elgar needs no such defence'.*

(132)
OPEN LETTER to THE PRESS

here from *Musical Times* April 1931 SIR EDWARD ELGAR
MUSICIANS' PROTEST AGAINST PROF. DENT'S
ALLEGED INJUSTICE
'G. B. S.' ON BELITTLING BRITAIN

The Press Association has received the following letter signed by representative musicians and music-lovers, and addressed to the editors of the leading newspapers of England and Germany:

SIR,—We, the undersigned, wish to record an emphatic protest against the unjust and inadequate treatment of Sir Edward Elgar by Prof. Dent in his article on 'Modern English Music' in Adler's monumental 'Handbuch der Musikgeschichte' (second enlarged edition, 1930) – a work that will be indispensable to all students of musical history for many years to come.

The fact that the learned professor devotes sixty-six lines to Parry, forty-one to Stanford, and only sixteen to Elgar is perhaps hardly a matter for criticism, but the statement that 'for English ears Elgar's music is much too emotional and not free from vulgarity,' the summary dismissal of all his orchestral works as 'lively in colour, but pompous in style and of a too deliberate nobility of expression,' and of his chamber music as 'dry and academic,' cannot be unchallenged.

At present time the works of Elgar, so far from being distasteful to English ears, are held in the highest honour by the majority of English musicians, and the musical public in general.

Prof. Dent's failure to appreciate Elgar's music is, no doubt, temperamental, but it does not justify him in grossly misrepresenting the position which Sir Edward Elgar and his music enjoy in the esteem of his fellow-countrymen.

(Signed) EMILE CAMMAERTS, JOHN GOSS, HARVEY GRACE, LESLIE HEWARD, BEATRICE HARRISON, HAMILTON HARTY, JOHN IRELAND, AUGUSTUS JOHN, ROBERT LORENZ, E. J. MOERAN, ANDRE MANGEOT, PHILIP PAGE, LANDON RONALD, ALBERT SAMMONS, G. BERNARD SHAW, RICHARD TERRY, WILLIAM WALTON, PETER WARLOCK.

Mr. Peter Warlock (Philip Heseltine) signed the letter not long before his death.

Mr Bernard Shaw, in attaching his signature, added the following postscript:

'I wish, however, to add that Prof. Dent's undervaluation is much more serious than our protest suggests. Elgar holds the same position in English music as Beethoven in German music. The 'vulgarity' of his more popular tunes is the vulgarity of Handel's 'See the Conquering Hero' or the Finale to Beethoven's fifth Symphony. 'The Kingdom' and 'The Apostles' are not oratorios in the Handelian sense: they are a new form of symphonic art involving a 'literarischen Bildung' of which Parry and Stanford never dreamt. Prof. Dent should not have made them ridiculous by such comparison, and should not have belittled his country by belittling the only great English composer who is not dwarfed by the German giants.'

*

(133)
LYDIA LOPOKOVA to SIR GEOFFREY KEYNES

7 August 1931
Tilton
Sussex

Dear Geoffrey
I went to Oxford to see Job and was much impressed, much more than on the wireless, when I thought the music was a noble, but a *dreary* way to spend an hour. But it had much more grandeur with scenes, costumes, and morning creatures. Job was truly a thing for the theatre, which I used to doubt. I congratulate you on your obstinate efforts without which Job would be never performed. I could see how your eyes gleamed when the curtain came down. My chief pleasure was that it differed from the Russian Ballet tradition – the most important merit of Job. Pat [Anton Dolin] surpassed himself – so perfectly devilish. Ninette had the most difficult task for, except for Satan, the music is not dancing – but her name, since Job, is quoted by managers. With more time and rehearsals it will stand up better.

[Ralph Vaughan] Williams bowed and looked a nice bear – all in all [the] Camargo [Society] is delighted with the work and so you must be very happy with such a great success. You must like to hear what was said at the Committee: 'With Job', Edwin Evans orated, 'Camargo stepped on to the map of Europe'. But, truly, we are grateful to you ...

(134)
RALPH VAUGHAN WILLIAMS to ADRIAN BOULT

The White Gates
Westcott Road
Dorking
September 20 [1931]

Dear Adrian
How very nice of you to write – I had no idea you were there – I wish I had seen you.

It would indeed give me great pleasure to hear you conduct 'Job' one day.

While I am writing I want to make a humble suggestion for what it is worth to the Control department. The Controllers seem in Concertos and songs to have the old fashioned idea of the soloists first and the rest nowhere – This is especially so at the Proms – for instance at the Bach concert last friday in 'Schlummert Ein'. When the soloist has long holding notes and the orchestra has a beautiful tune against it I heard nothing but the holding note – and similarly in the D minor Concerto in places where all the themes are in the orchestra & the pfte has only arpeggios I heard nothing but the arpeggios and I do not think this could have been my receiving set because presumably the *relative* values would be the same on any set.

Yrs

R VAUGHAN WILLIAMS

(135)
GUSTAV HOLST to ADRIAN BOULT

St. Paul's Girls' School,
Brook Green, Hammersmith, w.6.
Oct.19th,1931.

Dear Adrian,
Thanks for card. I hope to come to Studio 10 on November 16th at 9, but regret that the rehearsal is impossible. I presume it is the Ballet and not the complete opera? May I bring about a dozen people?

I hope to send *Hammersmith* on November 2nd, score and parts complete. Will you tell the programme writer that as far as the work owes anything to outside influences it is the result of living in Hammersmith for thirty-nine years on and off and wanting to express my feelings for the place in music; also it is the result of a B.B.C. invitation to write something for their military band; and, just as I was going to start on the work, I read A.P. Herbert's 'Water Gypsies'. There is no programme and no attempt to depict any person or incident. The only two things that I think were in my mind were 1) a district crowded with cockneys [*sic*], which would be overcrowded if it were not for the everlasting good humour of the people concerned and 2) the background of the river, that was there before the crowd and will be there presumably long after, and which goes on its way largely unnoticed and apparently unconcerned. Let me know rehearsal times as soon as you can.

Yours ever,

GUSTAV

(136)
JULIUS HARRISON to LESLIE BOOSEY

The Municipal Orchestra
White Rock Pavilion
Hastings
Oct. 29th 1931

Dear Mr Boosey,
I have had some long experience of lengthy unaccompanied Choral works such as Bantock's 'Atalanta in Calydon', 'Song of Songs' etc. From that experience I have made up my mind long ago that they inevitably sound extremely boring in performance for the reason that the pitch invariably sags so shockingly that it becomes impossible to listen with genuine pleasure. After a few initial performances these works seem to fade away. I have had an opportunity of looking through the Cyril Scott Cantata and admit that it contains some very nice moments, but there is the difficulty as I have stated it, and so leave the question of publication at that.
   I am returning the MS by registered post.

Yours sincerely,

JULIUS HARRISON

Bantock's unaccompanied choral symphonies were written for the crack choirs of the immediately pre-World War I festivals, and what is more were written for substantial numbers of performers. Their revival had to wait for the 1980s when the BBC promoted them using small all-professional forces, and under these circumstances they were certainly revealed to be worthwhile.

(137)
GUSTAV HOLST to ADRIAN BOULT

St. Paul's Girls' School,
Brook Green, Hammersmith, w.6.
Nov.2nd,1931.

Dear Adrian,
I had hoped to have sent Emma [i.e. *Hammersmith*] to you, but owing to a mistake in some of the parts I fear I cannot send it before tomorrow evening or Wednesday morning. I hope the delay will not bother you. I have been told to send the parcel to the Musical Librarian, B.B.C. I have promised to send one of the piano duet copies for use in the control. The copy will be in the wrong key and there are various differences, including bars added or omitted, as the piano version agrees with the military band score. I will send the piano part on Friday afternoon. I hope to come to all the rehearsals.
   With regard to pace, the Prelude should flow calmly and fairly slowly without

being impressive, and the Scherzo should be as quick as possible, as long as it sounds easy and good-tempered and not brilliant, hard or efficient. In short, it must sound like London and not Paris.

Yours ever,

GUSTAV

(138)
ADRIAN BOULT to OWEN MASE

'Belshazzar's Feast'
7th November, 1931.

I wonder if you think that the rehearsal on the night of the 24th would be a suitable opportunity for breaking our rule about inviting the Press to rehearsals. It is an important work, which many of them did not hear at Leeds, and I think they would like to hear it twice.

A.C.B.

Miss Wood: Please arrange for their invitation. I think a special letter.

O.M.

Asst. Music Director: The only expense will be 6/– for the Hall attendant.

D.W.

Music Director: Arranged.

O.M.

Walton's Belshazzar's Feast *had been first heard under the baton of Malcolm Sargent at the Leeds Festival on 8 October. The BBC's first London performance took place on 25 November with Boult conducting and received rave notices. The concert also included the first performance of the orchestral version of Holst's* Hammersmith *which was rather put in the shade by the flamboyance and impact of Walton's score.*

CHAPTER IV

1932–1939

Harvest and Seed-Time

Although Delius, Elgar and Holst were to die in 1934, the 1930s were a time of achievement so far as British composers were concerned, when British music tended to be centred on the orchestra. While chamber works of the quality of Bliss's *Clarinet Quintet* and Rubbra's *First String Quartet* were produced, their composers were so prolific of orchestral works (including symphonies, concerti, ballet music, and music for the new medium of the cinema) as well as for chorus and orchestra, that chamber music was rather overshadowed. Many operas were written too, but despite the fact that quite a number reached the stage, including Vaughan Williams's *Sir John in Love*, *The Poisoned Kiss* and *Riders to the Sea*; Holst's chamber opera *The Tale of the Wandering Scholar*; Goossens's *Don Juan de Manara* and two by a young newcomer up from Cornwall, George Lloyd (the magical, haunting Cornish folktale *Iernin* and the more conventional *The Serf*, written for the new British Music Drama Opera Company at Covent Garden, and subsequently toured) the time was not yet fully ripe for the British composer in the opera house. However, these works showed that many had what it takes to produce a major score for the operatic stage, and it is worth noting that Albert Coates's *Pickwick* as well as being produced at Covent Garden, was the first opera to be televised.

The thirties were a high point for the British symphony. This was a time that saw the production of Vaughan Williams's aggressive and dramatic *Fourth Symphony* which so surprised its first audience, and of the establishment of Bax in the public mind as a symphonist. (Bax's second and third symphonies were both heard in London in 1930, while the fourth, fifth and sixth appeared between December 1932 and November 1935.) Against this background, and the impact made by *Belshazzar's Feast* in 1931, the enormous public interest generated in the young William Walton's *Symphony in B♭ Minor* was perhaps not surprising (and not to be paralleled by another British work until the huge public demand for Britten's *War Requiem* nearly 30 years later). By 1934 Walton had managed to commit to paper only the first three movements of his symphony, and in despair Hubert Foss, Walton's editor at the Oxford University Press, proposed the performance of the incomplete score, which took place – to a tremendous reception – in the Queen's Hall in December 1934. Two more incomplete performances and another year had passed before the completed score could be heard.

E. J. Moeran was another composer of an 'impressionist-romantic' orientation and was one of those who, under the sway of varied influences, all of them more-or-less recognizable in his scores, welded a vital and distinctive personal idiom from disparate elements. Taking the harmonic languages of Ravel, John Ireland and Vaughan Williams, with a personal use of folksong, to which he later added elements from Sibelius and Bax, Moeran struggled with the bursting invention of his

Symphony in G minor for over a decade before it was first performed in January 1938. The influence of Sibelius in Moeran's symphony had earlier been felt in Walton's, and contributed to a clear change of direction in Bax. Even Vaughan Williams succumbed to the liberating influence, while another composer emerged who emerged on the scene with a succession of big-boned works in the 1930s, Edmund Rubbra, found his *Second Symphony* greeted by one journalist with the headline 'Sibelius's Eighth at last'.

In 1935, the British Council was host to Europe's music critics for a week of British music; in a publicity brochure Elgar's music was characterized by invoking the name of Richard Strauss. On coming to Vaughan Williams the copywriter despaired of parallels, and contented himself by saying 'Here is the authentic voice of England'. Vaughan Williams held the centre of the stage in the 1930s in England and was such a dominant voice that it was difficult for some of his contemporaries to imagine what direction his successors might take, although the example of Walton's *First Symphony* was to be seen as a liberating force by many young composers for the next quarter of a century.

Vaughan Williams influenced a host of imitators, but in the decade before World War II came he dramatically extended his range, not only in the *Fourth Symphony* but also with the ballet *Job*, and later two large-scale choral works. These were *Dona Nobis Pacem*, a warning against impending war in Europe in texts from Whitman, John Bright and the Bible; and *Five Tudor Portraits*, which perhaps hid a deeper message beneath a rowdy and sentimental surface in settings of poems by Skelton. In the latter work not only did Vaughan Williams demand virtuosity from his choir, making it a difficult work to sing, but also struck a curious parallel with another newcomer – like *Five Tudor Portraits*, first heard at the 1936 Norwich Festival. This was the young Benjamin Britten's *Our Hunting Fathers*. Vaughan Williams's score was received with warm applause, Britten's by puzzled antipathy, the composer Edmund Rubbra writing of 'its dry, cocktail cleverness, unrelieved by any real beauty of line'. Yet both composers draw on remarkably similar imagery for their most elusive movements. Vaughan Williams's fourth portrait presents the tale of Jane Scroop and her Lament for Philip Sparrow: a young schoolgirl at the convent at Carrow has had her pet sparrow killed by the cat. In his extended treatment of this domestic tragedy, Vaughan Williams generates such a heart-rending setting, the climax presaged by an accompaniment that reassembles the opening bars of his *Fourth Symphony*, that one is inclined to take it as a metaphor for wider sorrows of the mid 1930s, rather than as a delightful and superficial piece of sentiment. Similarly, in Britten's *Our Hunting Fathers*, the third movement *Messalina* is a tale of grief for a dying pet monkey, and both composers are patently drawing on a common tradition for their imagery which proclaims their common heritage and shared contemporary concerns – however much Britten would have rejected being bracketed with Vaughan Williams at that time.

The generation of composers beginning to emerge in the 1930s was, by and large, profoundly affected by the moral issues posed by the rise of fascism in Europe and especially by the Spanish Civil War. This tended to result, as the decade passed, in vocal rather than purely orchestral or chamber works – and possibly Britten's *A Ballad of Heroes* in 1939, with its contemporary texts ('It's farewell to the drawing-room's civilised cry . . . For the Devil has broken parole and arisen') by Auden and Swingler, was more immediately relevant than Ireland's idealistic sentiments in his more traditional choral setting of *These Things Shall Be* of a year or two earlier. Attendance at the ISCM festivals immediately before World War II (the 1936 festival was in Barcelona, the 1939 in Warsaw) resulted in a greater contact between young British composers and their continental contemporaries, and expanded technical and stylistic sympathies became evident in the music being written.

Viewed from the 1980s the inter-war period is also of note for the definition of what then was considered new music worth performing; and for the way in which this unspoken definition resulted in certain composers being rejected. Thus a BBC which was broadly Oxbridge-RCM-tonal in its sympathies rejected as unfit for broadcasting the music of John Foulds and Havergal Brian, as well as lesser figures such as Christian Darnton and Leighton Lucas, while still immediately recognizing Britten as the biggest rising talent. There was a tendency for any assessment, once made, to be irreversible, and because such assessments were anonymous they were resented by those who, bewildered by the system, did not find favour. Sir Adrian Boult was a Director of Music at the BBC of remarkably wide sympathies, whose placing of Vaughan Williams on a pedestal confirmed the latter's position in British music for the rest of his life.

(139)
Lt.-Col. BLOIS to F. A. SZARVASY

Royal Opera House
Covent Garden
18th February, 1932.

My dear Szarvasy,
I interviewed yesterday the secretary and two of the directors of the London Symphony Orchestra, with reference to their contract for the International Season.

The position is that, on the strength of their contract with us, the London Symphony Orchestra gave separate contracts for the International Season to each of their members who comprise the orchestra, and therefore these members can call upon the Board to carry out their contract. The Orchestra is evidently in financial straights partly owing to the death of Lionel Powell, and partly to the very bad attendance at their own Symphony Concerts. I think it would be almost impossible for most of their players to obtain other work to take the place of the International Season, and this fact will of course make the matter more difficult than ever for us to compromise.

I had hoped yesterday to get from them some informal basis from which we could start, but the attitude they took up was that, as the failure to carry out the contract was from our side, it was up to us to make suggestions for its compromise. From this attitude they declined to depart, and I told them that we would communicate with them shortly.

The meeting was perfectly friendly, but it is quite clear they know they stand on strong ground.

I think I told you in a letter last night that Cochran cannot come here with 'The Miracle', and my own personal opinion is that the Hoffmann suggestion would be extremely hazardous, even if it were possible to carry it out in this very short time.

If we were to give Symphony Concerts here, I am afraid they would share the same fate as the recent Concerts by the London Symphony Orchestra, the last of which, a great artistic success at the Queen's Hall under Hamilton Harty, took practically nothing in the seats, and the one at the Albert Hall last Sunday week under Beecham himself had much the same result.

Please do not think that all this is obstructive, as it is not meant to be so, and we are obliged to look round for any possible solution of the problem; but my own personal feeling is that an attempt to actually employ the Orchestra rather than compromise might lead into additional expenditure in these bad times.

I enclose a few alternative suggestions for compromise with the London Symphony Orchestra for your approval before putting them before them. Perhaps you would let me know whether I may deal on these lines.

Sir Hugh Allen, Principal of the Royal College of Music, who, you will remember, rang Reith up shortly before the last meeting, asked me to lunch with him on Tuesday last to talk over the matter of Beecham and the League of Opera. He told me that he had a long conversation with Beecham and that he was quite convinced of his, Beecham's, sincerity about the matter of the Covent Garden Opera Syndicate and the League of Opera joining in a scheme for National Opera. He said that when Beecham returned from America at the end of April he will be in a position exactly to know what funds will be available from the League of Opera, and that Beecham had asked him, as a person with no direct interest in the matter, to invite to a meeting the three parties concerned, that is, the C.G.O.Synd., the B.B.C., and the L.of O. At such a meeting it should be possible either to definitely agree upon a scheme of amalgamation or to rule it out finally as being impossible.

Allen is a very nice and clearheaded individual, and is very keen that all parties should be brought together and a real National scheme be evolved. Of course, in his position at the College, he carries a very considerable weight in musical circles.

Beecham is leaving for America tomorrow to conduct the New York Philharmonic. He has asked me to lunch with him tomorrow, and I shall endeavour to make some short memorandum of exactly what he says, and of Allen's remarks on the subject, and send it to you in as concise a form as possible.

Personally I am convinced that if the proposed meeting should lead to a combined National scheme, all these animosities and Press hostilities,etc., would automatically cease, that the public imagination would be fired, and we could then have a real permanent success. If, on the other hand, no such scheme can be decided, it would seem to me that all parties should wind up, as no one can go on separately.

I was so pleased and delighted that you took the attitude you did at the last meeting, because, if it had been decided to wind up the Covent Garden Opera Syndicate then and there and dispose of its assets and material, there would be no opera of any standard in this country in our time.

Yours very sincerely,

[Lt.-COL. BLOIS]

ALTERNATIVE PROPOSALS FOR COMPROMISE WITH LONDON SYMPHONY ORCHESTRA, re GRAND SEASON CONTRACT.

A: Payment of £2,500 at once in full settlement

or

B: Engagement of 50 players comprising usual instrumentalists for a Tour of eight weeks in Autumn of this year at an inclusive fee of £5,000. The engagement to include 56 performances, and a number of rehearsals to be agreed.

or

C: Payment of £1,000 now and £4,000 for Orchestra on Tour as indicated in B.

The above suggestions could only be adopted with the endorsement of the British Broadcasting Corporation.

The early 1930s found opera at the Royal Opera House in a parlous financial state, faced with commitments but having no immediate way to avoid a substantial deficit. Sir Thomas Beecham was invited to return to Covent Garden and reappeared in the pit on 8 May 1932 and remained in control until the War. Lt.-Col Blois (who died the following year) was Managing Director, and the Hungarian financier F. A. Szarvasy was Chairman of the Covent Garden Opera Syndicate.

The other side of opera in England can be seen in the activities of the long-standing touring companies, of which the best known was the Carl Rosa. Though encompassing a lower standard of performance than was the norm at Covent Garden, they provided a regular repertoire of operatic performances in the provinces where the visiting international big names never reached. The BBC found itself becoming involved with both ends of the operatic spectrum.

(140)
ROGER ECKERSLEY to SIR JOHN REITH*

CARL ROSA OPERA COMPANY
5th July, 1932

I met Mrs. Phillips, Mr. A. Van Noorden and another representative of the Carl Rosa Opera Company on Friday last and had a good three quarters of an hour with them. Mrs. Phillips did most of the talking. The first part of the interview consisted in my listening to a general complaint of injustices in the past. It was pointed out by them that the Carl Rosa Company was 60 years old, has had a vast experience of opera giving, and only works on the most economical lines. For these reasons they said they felt that it was very unjust that a subsidy given by the Government should have been concentrated on a new body which had little or no experience and which was, according to them, wasteful in its business methods. This was their main argument, as they felt that with even a little of the subsidy given to them, their standard could be enormously improved and their performances made fit for broadcasting.

I then induced them to talk of the immediate future, and asked what their plans were. I attach a letter from Mrs. Phillips which details their autumn and winter tour, which, however, cannot apparently be considered as definite until they are certain of the necessary funds. They said that a reasonable amount of broadcasting would be of great value to them. I pointed out that even if we took as many as ten broadcasts in the provinces at, say, £50 a time, it would not mean very much in their pockets. They seemed to think that the odd £300 or so profit to them would be a great help.

I feel sorry for them and think they have a certain case. I do not want to broadcast them Nationally as their standard is not very high at present, but as they attract very good audiences in the provinces it may be that they would be popular from a broadcasting point of view with provincial listeners. I would suggest, therefore, we

* BBC Director of Programmes to the Director General.

might try and give them the maximum of ten broadcasts between September and March from our Regional transmitters, and this irrespective of any amalgamation schemes which may come into being.

I spoke to them in regard to the general scheme. They seemed very uncertain as to whether such a scheme would ever come into operation and doubted its value even if it did. I said, however, that I thought they would make a great mistake if they did not take advantage of such a scheme if it became practicable. Personally, I think they would have no option but to co-operate if a definite sum of money were set aside to help them with their work in the provinces.

(141)
BERNARD VAN DIEREN to E. J. MOERAN

68 Clifton Hill
St. John's Wood, N.W.8
2 November 1932

My dear Moeran

Thank you very much for your letter; I am really grateful to know that my tribute to Philip's memory has reached some sympathetic hearts. After the concert, John Ireland spoke to me about the work in such a sincere and touching way. And now your own words again make me feel that I fulfilled part of the purpose that brought the work into being. I loved Philip with all my heart and am moved to think that others remember him with lasting affection. All too frequently I have found that many people's friendships did not remain long after he had gone, but made place for a vague feeling of just remembered comradeship which fades in the light of today's events. "O yes, poor old chap!" is as much as I hear from many a man who has reason to pretend even better! Still, as long as there are some like yourself who realise where and which he was and who feel the lasting gift his being brought to us it is well enough.

I planned work on a larger scale written in memory of him, for which the present was a kind of sketch and I am hoping and waiting for Bruce Blunt to produce something that can be used for it.

You speak of Philip's kindness of heart. I have reason to know something of it and of his perfectly beautiful devotion. For years he was a friend a brother and a son to me, and always gave me the most lovable signs of his friendship and thoughtfulness.

I am still trying hard to collect as much material as possible for the biography Gray and I have been planning. It has taken a great deal of energy to overcome the laxity or the halfheartedness I have been meeting in too many quarters alas. You however will not, I am sure, let us down. The reason why I particularly appealed to you over again is that you yourself wrote to me last year that you had a number of interesting letters.

Philip used, lately, especially when I was away here, and ill (there were about your words) to write to me often, giving his opinions of people and on works. Now that, apart from personal matters, is of course exactly what I am looking for, and you may be certain that intimate things will be disguised with all friends.

I have been even handed most intimate communications from woman friends and am getting quite trained in the difficult ways of selecting the right material and yet respect all susceptibilities.

Well, anyhow, I shall await your promised message.

Once more, thank you very much my dear Moeran, for your appreciation of my musical In Memoriam.

I very greatly value it.

BERNARD VAN DIEREN.

The night before Philip Heseltine died from gas poisoning, Bernard van Dieren and his wife Frieda had visited him and they were thus the last people to see him alive. There were two memorial concerts for Peter Warlock. Van Dieren's major contribution to the second was collectively entitled Hommages, *and as performed consisted of 'three main items with specially composed introduction and linking material. The accompaniment was scored for flute (doubling alto flute), oboe (doubling cor anglais), piano and string quartet. Two items were Philip Heseltine's compositions:* Along the Stream *from* Saudades, *and* Christmas Hommage to BVD. *The third was Bernard van Dieren's setting of Bruce Blunt's 'In Memoriam' poem,* The Long Barrow. *(See: Tomlinson, F:* Warlock and van Dieren. *Thames Publishing, 1978 p. 38). No music has been traced which may have been part of the hoped for larger project. Cecil Gray's biography* Peter Warlock: a memoir of Philip Heseltine *was published in 1934.*

(142)
ADRIAN BOULT to WILLIAM WALTON

11th November, 1932

Many thanks for your letter. I certainly think that we gave a better show of 'Belshazzar' than last time, in particular I think we solved the problem of 'The Kings of the Earth', expensive though that solution is, for as you know the Wireless Chorus is entirely professional. I expect you were able to hear the rather slower tempo and determine whether you found it too slow. Personally I thought it worked out just right though we reduced the Double Basses to two and had a good deal of trouble with the bass line altogether, Bass Clarinet and Bassoons and so on had to be very much damped down. This with rather an exaggeration of the portamento between the high crotchet and quaver of the accompanying figure I think gave the passage its right value and meaning, and the unaccompanied passage finished dead in tune.

One other point; there still seem to be a great many discrepancies between the score and parts in regard to dynamic sounds, in particular a good many of the fps and quiet marks generally in the Feast Scene are missing from the parts. This is very important. It gave us a lot of trouble to scale this time to something that would still leave power in reserve for the final F major.

However, we all enjoyed ourselves very much.

A.C.B.

(143)
DONALD FRANCIS TOVEY to the MEMBERS OF
THE REID ORCHESTRA

November 22 [1932]

Dear Colleagues

It is the greatest possible comfort to me in my absence to have continual evidence of your artistic progress, both by report and by actual experience. Though it is difficult to pick up an Edinburgh broadcast in the south, I have now heard your performances three times, and quite enough has reached me and other listeners to assure me that our work – the work that you and I stand for – cannot fail to convince the world at large that the Reid Symphony Orchestra is an institution that must go on.

Your performance of Elgar's *Falstaff* [on Thursday 17 November conducted by Stewart Deas] was very brilliant: the wireless revealed great clarity in every complexity of counterpoint: the strings produced the most rapid passages with crystalline clearness and – a point which I did not know broadcasting could make, – the beautiful tone and style of the leader [Mr Watt Jupp] – as shewn in solo passages – was not more clearly that of an individual player than the tone of tutti strings in rapid as in sustained passages was that of a chorus. In other words, even the wireless made it manifest that we are an orchestra throughout, to every desk. Broadcasting usually favours the wind; but the beauty of our string-tuttis has come through very well indeed.

You will not believe for a moment that I can wish to stay away from Edinburgh at this or any time of our existence. It cannot be supposed that I would make more of my illness than the best medical opinion I can get. There would not be much sense in my disregarding the doctors and coming back to conduct, say, two rehearsals and a concert, in order to be useless or dead for ever afterwards. I have every reason to believe that the doctors think I am recovering a great deal faster than they expected. To me it seems very slow: but I consult your interests better by ensuring my recovery than by forestalling it. In the meantime I recognise with gratitude, what I have always known but have not needed to put so extensively to the test, that I have left you in excellent hands; and I am sure that you will continue to do everything in your power to lessen the great labour and difficulty of their task. It is a delightful artistic experience to conduct the Reid Orchestra, and if that were all that had to be done to keep it in being our anxieties would be negligible.

One word I wish to say in regard to the programme of December 1st. Strictly speaking I ought to leave this to the conductor: but it happens to be a matter in which the support of my own opinion must be explicit, lest I should be supposed to think otherwise. Let me remind you of the well-deserved success of Mr Moonie's *Riders of the Sidhe* [conducted by Tovey on 23 October 1930, and to be repeated after Tovey's illness on 23 November 1933.] From that work we learned that Mr Moonie has a copious invention of themes in a strong and dignified style, besides technical and formal mastery of a very high order. The work which you are now producing, *Springtime on Tweed* [described by the composer as a 'Rondeau for orchestra', and conducted by him on Thursday 1 December 1932 – in a concert otherwise conducted by Adrian Boult, which featured Lionel Tertis in Walton's Viola

Concerto], is on very different material, but no less masterly in form and style. I have taken great pains to make its purpose clear in my programme-notes, and I want us all to understand that these are not intended to conceal or in any way allegorize my real opinion. Nobody in Great Britain would be in any danger of misunderstanding this work if we played more Mahler and Strauss, and so became ready for the Barry-ish spirit of this admirable piece. So Dr Grierson and Dr Boult will forgive me for taking the initiative in pointing out to you that the style of *Springtime on Tweed* is neither to be criticised as if it represented the composer's mature ideas of music, nor to be treated as caricature. I trust that both it and the Walton will be included in the broadcast, though I also greatly covet the Haydn [symphony no. 95].

Yours as present as doctors permit

DONALD FRANCIS TOVEY

The Scottish composer W. B. Moonie (1883–1961) was another who like Grainger, Cyril Scott and Roger Quilter, had studied at the Hoch'sche Konservatorium in Frankfurt am Main. He was probably best-known for his Scottish picturesque opera The Weird of Colbar. *Tovey returned to conduct in 1933, and died in 1940 shortly before his 65th birthday.*

(144)
ARNOLD BAX to HERBERT HOWELLS

153 Fellows Road. N.W.3. Feb 3rd [1933]

My dear Herbert

I am always grateful to you for your delightfully generous appreciations. If any among my friends take the trouble to write to me about my work it means a very great deal, and you and 'R.V.W.' are particularly nice about this.

It was a very fine performance of Fand – *nearly* as good as Tommy Beecham's (to me) never-to-be-forgotten effort a little while ago.

Personally, I love that work of Ralph's and like it indeed better than anything else of his that I know. I don't think it is right formally at the end, for that last cadenza confuses the issue, but in my view that dynamo-like toccata is splendid, and the stretto of the fugue one of the most stimulating bits of primitive violence in all music. Perhaps the Valse wants some re-phrasing to get more kick out of it, but that is good too. I believe you will come to delight in this work if you have a chance to get to know it well, as I did at rehearsals.

Ever yours with kindest wishes

ARNOLD

Vaughan Williams's Piano Concerto *had received its first performance at Queen's Hall on 1 February 1933 during a BBC Symphony Concert, with Harriet Cohen as soloist and*

Adrian Boult conducting. The programme had also included Bax's tone poem The Garden of
Fand *and Delius's* Sea Drift. *The earlier performance of* Fand *to which Bax refers,
conducted by Sir Thomas Beecham, had taken place in the same hall on 23 November 1931.*

(145)
GRACE WILLIAMS to BENJAMIN BRITTEN*

[Feb 1933]

51, Warwick Road
s.w.5.

Dear Benjamin,
Now that is a truly remarkable work [Britten's *A Boy Was Born*] in many ways. I
like best the IIIrd ['Jesu, as Thou art our Saviour'], and the 'bleak mid-winter'
[variation 5] i.e. as music; it's <u>older</u> than the rest. Of course all that <u>skill</u> bowls one
over right through – but I can't <u>help</u> feeling that some of it – (about a third of it) –
<u>again solely as music</u> – isn't up to the standard of the rest. But hang it all what youth
of 19 ever wrote a work that was completely a masterpiece? ('Mid-summer Night's
Dream' said she in a whisper – but then the poor chap never surpassed this supreme
feat of his 17 years – tragic, I think, to have written one's best work at 17.)
    I was disappointed in the way they did the 'Herod' [variation 2] – it seemed to me
to want lots more fire – and they <u>could</u> have done it; – the 1st ['Lullay, Jesu'], apart
from the rather hazy performance, I feel is a bit too reactionary; I know I liked it
when I first heard it but now I feel it's too typically English and this same criticism I
apply to a part of the Finale – can't remember the tune, but I believe it's got the rise
of a 7th in it and is a bit stodgy – it's towards the end; I think most of the Finale quite
<u>thrilling</u>but it seems to me too long and this particular tune I feel is rather an
anticlimax.
    I <u>was</u> sorry the Herod wasn't done better, because from what I remember of it,
from last year, it is tremendously good and I think I might be inclined to raise it to
the standard of III and V. And I was quite heartbroken at the dreadful singing of the
boys – rubbish! – and why on <u>earth</u> were they engaged when there are <u>surely</u>, <u>dozens</u>
of choirboys in London who <u>can</u> at least sing. A terrible shame, – but <u>never mind</u>,
when it's done at Q.H. [? Queen's Hall], you'll have to see that you get really angelic
choirboys – and put them in the gallery; I do feel that the boys ought to be away
from the big choir (which of course is impossible at Broadcasting House).
    Now Benjamin aren't you getting angrier and angrier and have you taken up
your pen already and dashed off a letter to me 'Grace you are talking through your
hat and are quite wrong about everything –' which I know is true and God knows
why I bother to write – oh yes He does, and I do too, because I've just remembered
I've two questions to ask, and I should be v. grateful for an immediate reply.

*It was a condition of the Britten Estate permission to reproduce the Britten letters that they faithfully
reflect the originals, including underlinings rather than italics, even though this made them inconsistent in
treatment with the rest of the book.

(a) Please what does a cymbal tr ~ with fingertips sound like? I've got one in my Overture.

You see I want a sort of cymbal shimmer and Forsyth says you can get a very rapid diminuendo w. fingertips. Is it all right?

2) The whole thing finishes thus:

In that final quip will the oboe give the sort of 'twang' I want, or will it sound like an accident? Wd. it be wise to have the clar. alone?

If you could <u>possibly</u> see your way to letting me have a reply by the first post on Tuesday I should be more than grateful – the thing has to be sent off on Tuesday; quite a few people have sent their blessing but it's no good it hasn't got an earthly – I'm rather sorry I didn't make you come and hear it because I think it's quite good in it's way – and I know that when it comes back I'll fling it on the shelf and will never have the courage to show it to anyone. [. . .]

Yours

GRACE

P.S. [written at the head of the letter] You <u>must</u> go to Italy – and then dash all over Europe – see everything. Then you'll write.

P.P.S. I've just written a very dramatic song (one of Byron's Hebrew melodies) for Parry Jones. Full of it at the moment.

Britten's A Boy Was Born *is his Op 3. It anticipates his later choral music, not only in the actual writing, but also in the use of a sympathetically chosen anthology of texts. The majority are anonymous fifteenth-century verses, but it also encompasses texts by Thomas Tusser and Francis Quarles and, notably, the fifth variation is a setting of Christina Rossetti's 'In the bleak mid-winter'. There are seven sections – the theme and six variations – and the music is laid out for unaccompanied mixed chorus with boys' voices. The 'Herod' variation presents an account of the massacre of the innocents in what at the time must have seemed very difficult writing for the men, not only quick but also using an irregular rhythm and awkward intervals (largely fourths). Over 50 years after the first performance it is instructive to find that Grace Williams was unhappy at passages being 'too typically English', when now the work is surely regarded as quintessentially English, underlining the truism that what constitutes a national character in musical language is continually re-defined from generation to generation, and is an intuitive quality which expresses the composer's roots.*

Grace Williams's piece for Parry Jones was her setting of Byron's 'Oh! weep for those that wept by Babel's stream' for tenor and orchestra (or piano). It has remained unpublished.

(146)
HAVERGAL BRIAN to HAMILTON HARTY

1, Jasper Road,
Upper Norwood,
London S.E.19
1933 May 9

Dear Sir Hamilton Harty
I was astonished and delighted when Michaud rang me up on Saturday & told me
that you were with him. I have *not* sought any performances of the Gothic – neither
have I ever any anticipated in England, but if I had my choice I should plump for
you because of your race and perfect Berliozian instincts to lead it. I can imagine you
making a fine sensation with it if you had your way. But I *am* glad you have got it. I
can imagine that you may grow to love it even if you never perform it. I suppose
you read or may not read my notes in 'Musical Opinion' on your 'Fantastique' – I
have always tried to put you on the top with regard to him – for the obviously
perfect way you interpret him.
    Well good luck to you & my blessing on your saintly head with the Gothic.

Yours Sincerely

HAVERGAL BRIAN

I did not know until today you were still in Manchester or this note would have
reached you three days ago.

*Michaud was the British representative of the publisher Cranz, the firm who had published
Havergal Brian's* Gothic Symphony *in 1932. Although there were several expressions of
admiration from conductors of the standing of Harty and Goossens before World War II, the
symphony, although becoming something of an unheard (and therefore to many suspect)
legend for its extravagant instrumental and choral requirements, was not performed until
presented by Bryan Fairfax in June 1961.*

(147)
*   ## VICTOR HELY-HUTCHINSON

BBC internal circulating memo

19th June 1933

I do whole-heartedly subscribe to the general opinion that Mr Britten is the most
interesting new arrival since Walton, and I feel we should watch his work very
carefully.

Britten's Phantasy Quintet *for strings had been performed in London the previous
December, and broadcast on 17 February while the* Sinfonietta *had been heard on 31
January. Britten himself was still a student at the RCM and was not destined to take his
ARCM examination until the end of the year.*

(148)
RALPH VAUGHAN WILLIAMS to LESLIE BOOSEY

The White Gates,
Westcott Road,
DORKING.
August 6 [1933]

Dear Mr Boosey
These youthful indiscretions were a great shock to me. I think they were printed in proof by the 'Vocalist' company but never published & that you must have taken them over when you took Linden Lea etc..

Of course they belong to you and it is for you to settle whether to issue them or not – but I am not very proud of them – If you do decide to issue them I must insist that the date of composition must be printed on the copy – I have corrected the proofs and return them – if you decide to go further please let me see a revise. As regards the copyright of the words I have never made any arrangements with the authors or publishers. So will leave that to you –

Yours sincerely

R. VAUGHAN WILLIAMS

The Two Old Airs, 'Adieu' and 'Think of Me' were German folksong arrangements for soprano and baritone and piano. First performed in 1903 and 1904 respectively, they both actually appeared in The Vocalist for October 1903 and were subsequently issued as separate items. Boosey went ahead and reissued them later in 1933.

*

(149)
BENJAMIN BRITTEN to EDWARD CLARK

21 Kirkley Cliff Road,
Lowestoft.
Aug 13th 1933

Dear Mr Clark,
I have received a letter from the B.B.C. asking for scores and parts of my Sinfonietta for performance on Sept. 15th. Since Mrs Waterman has erroneously asked for 3 First Violin pts. 2 second, etc., I presume that it is intended to be placed in an orchestral concert. I wonder if there is any possible chance of this being altered. I should so much prefer it being put in a chamber concert, when the listeners are tuned up to chamber music, and have not been listening to full orchestral sounds. . . . I happen to know that the Brosa string quartet are keen to do the string parts, & if you could get the leaders of the woodwind section, I am sure there would be a more satisfactory result. I believe that it would be financially not so easy, but I am sure it is worth the change. Also I should think that rehearsing would be easier. They wouldn't be tied down to one or two hours, which is not nearly enough, as you must feel yourself. . . .

consider these points as I do feel it essential that a chamber work be played in a chamber concert. . . .

I do hope you were able to listen in to Leon Goossens beautiful performance of my oboe Phantasy. . . .

(150)
JOHN FOULDS to ADRIAN BOULT

43 St James' Place
SW I
16th August, 1933

Dear Dr Boult

In accordance with your letter of 23rd June I herewith forward you the score of my 'April – England'. I hope you will excuse me if I take the opportunity to make a few remarks about my serious works in general.

Dr Hans Richter considered my early works good enough for performance, and himself gave several performances of them with the Halle orchestra, including one at his farewell concert. He actually promised me a Festival performance of my concert opera 'The Vision of Dance', Opus 7 (completed 1905), concerning which Sir Edward Elgar wrote me, after reading the score: 'It will be most impressive in performance'. (There was some hitch, however, which caused this Festival performance to fall through, as a result of which this work has never been heard).*

With regard to my choral work, 'A World Requiem', Opus 60, Professor Donald Tovey studied the score and tried out the work with his Edinburgh orchestra subsequently writing me a long letter concerning it, of which an extract reads: '. . . . . work of such calibre. It must and shall make its mark. I question whether any work of this calibre has been more practically devised'. Mr. Arthur Fagge, after giving me great assistance in training the chorus for the first performance, wrote to me: 'It is a great achievement in the realm of serious composition, and of outstanding merit', adding that he found that the better people knew the work, the greater their appreciation of its merits. The British Legion sponsored the work through the mediation of Sir Hugh Allen, after he had read the score, and I would remind you that the Selection of Music Committee of the British Music Society put on record (through the Society's Secretary, Dr. Eaglefield Hull), the statement that they were very much impressed with the work and considered it worthy of performance on a national occasion.

*[pencil footnote] Sir Henry Wood included two of my early works in the Promenade Concerts: 'Epithalamium', Opus 10, in (?) 1903, and 'Music-Pictures Opus 33, in (?) 1909. [pencil note continues in left-hand margin] The latter, incidentally, was probably the first occasion on which quarter tones were heard in a London concert hall.

With regard to my latest works: 'Dynamic Triptych for Pianoforte and Orchestra' Opus 88, has been approved by and performed under Professor Donald Tovey, Mr. Leslie Heward and Sir Dan Godfrey. I think I may fairly claim that the latter's recent performance with the B.B.C. orchestra on August 4th seemed to be a complete success in every way. My most recent work, a String Quartet, Opus 89, has been approved by Mr. Arthur Catterall, and will be performed by him when opportunity permits.

Within the last two years I have submitted four works to the B.B.C. These in my opinion, contained some of my most valuable work. In each case they were rejected by your Selection Committee. The position, therefore, is that while my principal serious works have received the approval of some of the greatest names in the musical world, and also of practical conductors it would appear, judging from past experience, that any serious work of mine has a poor chance of winning approval of the B.B.C Selection Committee.

In the meantime my light works are continually broadcast. These light works number a dozen or so, as compared with the total of 50 of my serious works. This state of affairs, I think you will agree, is rather a galling one for a serious artist.

Yours Sincerely

JOHN FOULDS

(151)
ARTHUR BLISS to LESLIE HEWARD

East Heath Lodge
One East Heath Road
Hampstead N W 3
Sept 29th [1933?]

My dear Leslie

Your letter *terrified* me – the concerto* is not going at all well – I have had so many things apart from music to attend to this Summer that I could not concentrate on it. I fear a postponement to the next season is almost inevitable. I am going to give it till Christmas, & then if it is not well on the way, I shall write to you & Smeterlin putting it off till the season 1934/35 – I want a stunning work, & it takes time for the right mood – Don't think too harshly of me. I am trying! – but that's no good – It has not yet taken me by the throat – Do conduct my Introduction & Allegro. I made a new score you know (totally new) at the same time as I revised the Colour Symphony. Curwen's have it in MS (the printed one being destroyed) It takes twelve minutes & sounds very brilliant – I am coming up for Cunningham's† performance of Morning Heroes on Nov 8th & shall hope to see you. I will give you more definite news of the Concerto then.

Yours totally lacking in inspiration (meaning exactly WHAT?)

ARTHUR BLISS

Where were you in Norfolk? I had a bottle of good brandy open ready for you.

---

*Bliss started work on a piano concerto which was announced for performance on 22 March 1934 with the Polish-born pianist Jan Smeterlin as soloist. It was to be almost six years before Bliss's Piano Concerto was first heard at the New York World's Fair, in June 1939.
†George Cunningham, conductor of the City of Birmingham Orchestra.

(152)
ALAN RAWSTHORNE to ANNE MACNAGHTEN

The Macnaghten concerts founded by Anne Macnaghten, Iris Lemare and Elizabeth Lutyens, were influential in the 1930s in bringing forward a new generation of young composers, especially women composers.

Dartington Hall,
Totnes,
S. Devon
23 January 34

Dear Anne –
Just as I am about to write to you, lo! your letter comes popping through the letter-box, and I can cut out the 'Miss Macnaghten' without appearing forward! Thank you so much for writing; I'm awfully interested in the comments on the quartet. Someone showed me the Telegraph; I too was amazed at the remarks about May and Gow. I thought the Gow songs were beautiful and I wish I knew more by her. They seem entirely free from that woolliness which characterizes most English modern music. It was nice of you to play my quartet to Blom; I feel there is a connection in style between the 1st and 3rd movements, but I rather think he's right that the middle one is out of the picture. In fact I believe it isn't a stylistic unity in itself; I tinkered at it for a bit, but there comes a time when one says 'Hell!' and the only one thing to do is to write another quartet.

What I was about to say when your letter interrupted me! – was how deeply and sincerely grateful I am for your work. You do understand modern music; your playing always has an authentic ring. I do hope you're feeling better; it was good of you to do the concert anyway, and to do it so successfully was grander still. I've always believed in a close intimacy between liquor and art; I was feeling a bit drunk too, but only with the excitement of the occasion, which lasted until I arrived in Devonshire at 6.30 a.m. on Tuesday morning. It's a shame about the B.B.C. dates, but bed or Brighton, or both, are better than B.B.C.'s which is at least highly alliterative and even Tennysonian. I hope you really didn't do yourself any harm on Monday, beyond exhausting yourself and your nerves – I'm not a Jeremiah but concerts like that are no joke.

I shall hope to see you at Easter if not before, unless you've gone off to Russia or Southend or somewhere. Don't bother about the score and parts. And thank you most sincerely for your performance.

Please give my love to the other three, and to yourself

With best wishes

ALAN

(153)
E. J. MOERAN to THE DAILY TELEGRAPH

Published in the issue dated 27 January 1934

It is easy to criticise, and after all, the B.B.C. deserves praise for what it has done. But I heartily agree that we ought to get back the old system at the 'Proms.' Works that prove their merit at the 'Proms' should be repeated at the winter symphony concerts – but not segregated.

With one line of argument I distinctly do not agree, and that is the suggestion that the fact of a man's being a professor at the R.A.M. or R.C.M. entitles his works to a hearing at Queen's Hall. In the dreadful old days the Philharmonic used automatically to produce whatever orchestral stuff the bigwigs of the Academy and the College turned out. We don't want the B.B.C. to land us back into that.

It was a pity an opportunity was not found to include something by Jacob, and I should have liked to hear something by Finzi, Rubbra and Elizabeth Maconchy, who seem to claim attention more than anyone else of that generation. It is high time Miss Maconchy's fine work, 'The Land,' was heard again.

A serious omission from the programmes was the name of Edward German. He is interesting historically, apart from the value of his music. In the 1890s, when others were purveying second-hand Brahms, German was producing symphonies and suites with a distinctly English flavour and original character.

Peter Warlock should have been given a place. He was our outstanding song-writer since the Tudors. I should have represented Cyril Scott by his piano concerto; it is Scott at his high-water mark, and is not widely enough known.

(154)
SIR HAMILTON HARTY to JOSEPH HOLBROOKE

1, Norfolk Road,
St John's Wood,
London N W 8
Feb. 21 1934

My dear Holbrooke

I was on the point of writing to you when your letter arrived. The success of the 'Raven' the other night gave me much satisfaction and pleasure – because, in studying the work, I came to like and admire it immensely. There is beautiful and impressive music in that work, and, as I told the orchestra it is so infinitely superior to the foreign *muck* with which we are deluged nowadays. You know, without undertaking more than I may be able to perform, I felt rather guilty at not knowing more of your works – and had resolved to study others as closely as I did the 'Raven' – and to produce them as opportunity offers. Will you tell me which, in your opinion, are the most successful and suitable of your orchestral works, and tell me where I can obtain the scores? I know you like honesty, my dear Holbrooke, and I will not behave in any other way but honestly to you. I will do my best to understand and appreciate your other music. If I fail in this – put it down to my limitations if you like – but I can't conduct music I don't understand. On the other hand I will be equally keen in doing everything I possibly can for your works – as I expect I find things as good and warm and touching as the 'Raven'. Is it a bargain?

Do not think conductors are all stupid and selfish and careless of the composers intentions. Some of us are only anxious to interpret music with reverence and without thinking of our own glory and notoriety.

Finally, let me again congratulate you on the 'Raven'. It gave me (and the orchestra) the greatest pleasure in doing our best to interpret what we considered lovely and important music.

Yours ever

HAMILTON HARTY

By the 1930s Holbrooke had been passed by as a composer whose orchestral works were barely on the fringe of regular repertoires, so this performance of the work which had been his first orchestral success is of special note. First heard at the Crystal Palace in March 1900, The Raven had most recently been performed at Queen's Hall under the baton of Weingartner on 31 May 1923.

(155)
SAMUEL COURTAULD to EDWIN EVANS

12 North Audley Street
w.1
5/3/34

Dear Mr Evans

My commitments in connection with music are already heavier than I care for, but I agree so fully with all you say in your letter that I am ready to guarantee the £60 which you appear to need for the International Festival in April.

I rely on you however to collect what you can from Messrs Nettlefold & Harmsworth – when they come back. As we are constantly being told that we are a musical nation it seems strange that there is no public backing for an enterprise of this sort. I have a shrewd suspicion – alas! – that financial support by the government would *not* be endorsed by the electorate!

I do not mind your committee knowing about my offer, but please see that my name *is not made public*.

Let me know whether – or when – to send you a cheque.

Yours sincerely

SAMUEL COURTAULD

(156)
RUTLAND BOUGHTON to HERBERT THOMPSON

Kilcote
Newent
Glos
16 April 1934

Dear Mr Thompson
Very many thanks –
   So far I've £170 in guarantees, most of it from professional musicians, some of them believing that I am being penalised today for my political opinions, even though my political activities ceased in 1929 – *Is* this a free country? But I decline to grow into a man with a grievance – There are too many beautiful things to enjoy in *any* Circumstances; and this Spring I've had an amazing attack of composition – a fever inducing a thoroughly optimistic tendency

Yours sincerely

RUTLAND BOUGHTON

(157)
WALTER LEGGE to C. W. ORR

Nineteen
Carew Road
W.13
[1934]

My dear Orr.
First of all congratulations on the songs. They are really superb. Usually it is an embarrassing business to write to a friend about music he has written – the composers I know usually or rather habitually write 'platitudes'. But your songs place me in a different dilemma for, frankly I know no other songs in our language to compare with them – an opinion with which Bax agrees. We discussed them for an hour & a half and parted having placed you among the immortals.
   The songs I like best are Bax's and mine. Bax's is a lovely song, a remarkably penetrating moving song: mine by Tristan out of Isolde with the big bad Wolf looking on, is exquisite. I'll discuss them in detail when I see you. I have only two complaints – the difficulty of the pianoforte parts – and the other is a purely personal one – a preference for other poets than Housman.
   Onegin [Sigrid Onegin (1889–1943), German mezzo-soprano] I know too well. She sings sharp with monotonous regularity: the voice is lovely the brain is not too bad – but Oh her intonation. But I'll make a test.
   I'll make a point of visiting Painswick in the not far distant future. How are you for Sundays on which you may be called upon? I get occasional Saturdays free now and I'd dearly like to see you both again.
   Kindest regards to you both.

Yours always

W.L.

The songs under discussion are C. W. Orr's cycle A Shropshire Lad, *which had recently been published by J. & W. Chester, in a subscription edition of 300 copies. The cycle comprises seven songs, of which the second 'When I watch the living meet' was dedicated to Walter Legge and the fourth 'Farewell to barn and stack and tree' to Bax.*

(158)
EDWARD J. DENT to HERBERT THOMPSON

Hotel Helvetia
Florence
4 April 1934

Dear Thompson,

Many thanks for your kind letter. I hope you were pleased with *Orpheus* at Leeds; Mary Jarred sings it very well, I think. I am sorry I did not see you at *Jephtha*; I went to several performances, but always in the gallery, and so I dare say I missed various friends. Our 'foyer' at the Guildhall is very inadequate!

I went up to Glasgow for the last performance of *Idomeneo*; I thought it was a wonderful achievement to put it on, and in spite of amateur singers and very scanty scenery. I thought it gave a very good impression of the work.

I am at Florence for the International Festival [of Contemporary Music]. We have had endless worry over it, and have been obliged to change things at the last moment; but it is going very well, and so far we have had excellent audiences and good programmes. The weather is pleasant and Florence always makes everyone feel happy. I created much amusement at the opening ceremony by making a speech (in answer to the Prefect of Florence, who made the usual oration all about Mussolini) in which I emphasized the dangers of nationalism and the necessity of free thought and speech for the artist. It was the sort of thing no Italian would dare to say now, but I gathered that they were all enormously pleased to hear someone else say it! I carried it off by paying all sorts of compliments to Italy and Florence as the homes of music, and watched my audience getting nervous as I brought out all sorts of dangerous words like 'revolution' and then qualified them with the adjective 'musical'. The Germans all liked it very much, but I expect it would have been more risky to make such a speech in Germany itself. Our German section is in a state of suspended animation and we don't yet know what will happen to it. For the moment it is standing aloof and sending no representatives; but Dr Holl of the Frankfurter Zeitung is here. Otherwise the Germans are all Jews and alleged Communists; Scherchen is conducting and will have a great reception to-night, I expect – he is popular in Italy. But of course the orthodox Nazis will be furious at that.

We have had some amusing incidents over the programme: yesterday a work was played by a young Jew from Breslau who is living at Strasbourg. I put him down as belonging to 'Germany'; but Casella objected, as *he* doesn't want to risk any rows with the Nazis himself, for fear his own music should be boycotted there. Casella therefore put the young man down as coming from 'Paris' – to which *he* objected; so finally he was ascribed to 'Germania Indipendente', which I thought a very amusing alternative name for Alsace!!

The persecution of the Jews has upset our finances; the German section refuses to pay for anything at all, and the other sections seem to object to paying for the

22 Langham Place before the BBC. The Queen's Hall is to the right of All Souls Church

23 George Butterworth

24 Edwin Evans

25 John Goss

above **26** Ivor Gurney
top right **27** Herbert Howells

28 Philip Heseltine ('Peter Warlock')

35 E. J. Moeran

36 Sir William Henry Hadow

above **37** Constant Lambert

38 Arnold Bax

39 Edward J. Dent, by Kapp

40 Sir Henry Wood

refugees – and we have several on the programme. However, we shall settle things somehow, I hope. Hindemith was to have played in a trio of his, but refused to come, for fear of trouble with the Nazis. The Galimir Quartet from Vienna was to have played a work by Leopold Spinner, but telegraphed 3 days ago to say they could not come – no explanation given. We have 4 other quartets on the spot – Kolisch, Poltronieri, Griller (London) and a Jugoslav quartet, but I don't think any of them can get the work up in the time.

The most enjoyable thing is the number of young musicians from different countries, many of them here for the first time in their lives, like Benjamin Britten. They make friends with each other as far as languages permit, and all seem very happy together.

The next Festival will probably be at Carlsbad in September 1935, though Carlsbad is a very Nazi place; however, the Czech section thinks it will be all right, and the Carlsbad authorities are tremendously keen to have us, which is gratifying. As to the Germans, I think they are hedging. The patriot mediocrities who are now running music in Germany hate modern music, and therefore hate our Society, because we don't perform their works, but I gather that in higher quarters there is a strong desire to keep in with us, because they are afraid of Germany being musically boycotted and considered as 'das Land ohne Musik'.

I am going on to Rome and Naples next week; it is nearly 30 years since I was at Naples, and I want to see old friends there, as far as they are alive. I come back to England at the end of April.

Yours Sincerely

EDWARD DENT

(159)
LESLIE BOOSEY to JULIUS HARRISON

24th May 1934

Dear Harrison,
I am enclosing two part-songs by Benjamin Britten. No 2 is very difficult and I don't really consider it possible for publication, but I thought you might be interested to see it. No 1 is much more suitable for the Festival Series and I should like to have your opinion on it.

You may remember that the composer had a work performed at the Florence Festival this year. Also a choral work of his entitled 'A Babe is Born' was performed at the B.B.C. Festival of British Music in January.

The part songs are presumably 'I Lov'd a Lass' (words by George Wither), and 'Lift Boy' (words by Robert Graves), which had received their first performance in London the previous December. Boosey published them later in 1934.

(160)
SIR THOMAS BEECHAM to GEOFFREY TOYE

16 Abbey Lodge
Park Road
London N.W.8
May 14th/34.

Dear Mr. Toye,

I quite understand the line taken by Mr. Colles in his letter to you; perhaps it would be better if I put into writing what I had in mind to say to him.

For several years there has been a feeling among many musicians and amateurs that The Times is unduly critical of nearly everything with which I am connected and equally uncritical of many things done by other organizations and artists. This opinion is not limited to this country; I have encountered it everywhere on the Continent as well as in America – particularly in the latter place. On several occasions I have had to complain of actual inaccuracies of statement, some of them most flagrant, and there have been many more of which I have taken no notice.

I am the last person to object to honest criticism; I like it. But it is the view of hundreds of intelligent musical people that much of the criticism in The Times is either unfair or unenlightened where I am concerned. This sort of thing, contrasted with the lenity displayed towards others, is the subject of very unfavourable comment.

For instance, two performances of the works of a famous living composer were given early in the year at Queen's Hall by an organization other than my own and found to be beautiful and satisfying by the critic of The Times for that occasion. A week later I received a letter from the composer describing them as 'murderous and heartrending' (which in truth they were) and enquiring if it were possible to prevent this organization giving any more performances of his music in the future. This is but one instance out of dozens which I have observed and noted.

But I am not so much concerned at the moment with this aspect of the matter as with one that is far more serious – namely, the attitude taken by The Times towards my co-operation with foreign singers. Everyone who knows the Continent well is aware of the alarming decline in the efficiency of the opera-houses both in Germany and Italy. The most conspicuous feature is the inaccuracy and faulty tradition of the singers. I do not mean their vocal deficiencies, which are of course deplorable, so much as their musical slovenliness. This has been the same wherever I have conducted, and of course I, as a visitor, have been powerless to remedy it. But I made up my mind when I re-associated myself with Covent Garden two years ago that I would not stand it here.

Remembering the magnificent and flawless ensemble I was able to secure with the English company I ran years ago, I resolved that the foreign singers should no longer be allowed to disturb and even ruin the intentions of the composer as they have been allowed for so long to do. One can imagine my chagrin when I found that so far from backing me up in this essential purpose several London journals, including The Times, truckled to the foreign visitors and cast the blame on me for such faults of ensemble as are always evident when first the conductor determines that the composer rather than the singers must be respected.

Last year in 'Aida' I had the poorest cast of singers that ever sang this opera under my direction; they were so panic-stricken and inefficient at the first performance that I had literally to drive them on in order to preserve any line at all in the work. (Incidentally, I have conducted this piece over two hundred times). I was criticized by The Times for not 'accompanying' the singers, although the more conspicuous inaccuracies occurred in ensemble movements! This year, in the first performance of Fidelio the soprano had an attack of nerves during her song and proceeded without warning to indulge in a quick acceleration of the time which made two bars almost into one; and this was just when the accompaniment given to the horns was particularly trying for these dangerous instruments. For me to have followed the singer at this point would have resulted in chaos in the horn department, so I waited a bar until the strings entered and then picked up the time. But there was no criticism of the singer for distorting the line of melody, for imperfect control of breath or for playing tricks with Beethoven, only fault-finding with the orchestra for not accompanying adequately.

The Times also appears to imagine that there are differences of view between the foreign singers who came here and myself in respect of tempi, which is a source of embarrassment to them. I have conducted opera in seven or eight German theatres and no one there has ever yet suggested anything like this. Would a German conductor have any advantage over me at Covent Garden? Here it is not a question of a company which has sung these works together abroad; the singers at Covent Garden are drawn from every theatre in Germany – some of them have never met until they arrive in London. Further, does The Times think there are no piano rehearsals at which the conductor is able fairly successfully to establish an understanding between his heterogeneous units? Also, is it unaware that at least one prominent member of the cast in 'The Ring' is no longer engaged at Bayreuth because of his ensemble inaccuracy? In London, however, these truly terrible deficiencies are always glossed over by the Press as differences between the singers and conductor!!

Frankly, this is is nonsense, and it is deplorable nonsense, for it encourages the singers in their downward course and weakens the authority of the conductor. Some of these so-called artists have now been so flattered and defended that they do not scruple here to take liberties with the music they would not dare to do in their own theatres. In other words, the musical Press of London is not taken seriously.

It was my privilege, when very young, to obtain my operatic knowledge from the conductors of the day, such as Seidl, Fiedler, Richter, Nikisch, Mancinelli – all of them absolute disciplinarians who would have been driven frantic with rage by the inexactitudes I have to endure. The business of a conductor is to conduct and to insist upon the intentions of the composer – singer or no singer. In the case of Wagner, I claim to know what these intentions are; I claim that my interpretations of Wagner are far nearer to the letter and spirit of the period 1880–1900 in Bayreuth than those of modern German conductors. The German Press has repeatedly emphasized my true Bayreuthian orthodoxy. It can be supported by an appeal to facts. Let The Times or any other journal examine the time I take to play each act of a Wagner opera as compared with my contemporaries. In the case of The Ring and Meistersinger my tempi are (save in one scene) identical to the very minute with those of Seidl and Richter, whereas in the various cases of my German colleagues there are enormous variations and discrepancies. All these records are at Bayreuth and Covent Garden and are open for the inspection of anyone who desires to see them.

I shall continue to impose this correct tradition on the inefficient second-raters (there are no stars nowadays) who come to Covent Garden until I have restored it completely. But I shall be seriously hampered in this honourable task if the Press here continues to praise and defend the singers in their iniquities at my expense.

This is not a personal matter; it is one of principle, and the principle involved is of the highest seriousness for the future of opera in London. I charge The Times as being not only the utterer of prejudice and inaccuracy but as the defender of reaction and incompetence. This is a grave business, and if it continues there is going to be open war between us.

I am
Yours sincerely,

THOMAS BEECHAM

(161)
BENJAMIN BRITTEN to GRACE WILLIAMS

25 September 1934

My dear Grace,
What a good show! I have never known the West Regional behave better. Except for a slight wobble at the end of the 'Service', it was perfect althrough. Parry Jones was miles better than I expected, and except for one high B♭ (B♮) (in the 1st, I think),* aquitted himself with credit. I should never have thought that such a 'Tristan' could have done it. // I like the first song the least of the three, though the climax thrilled me. I am not sure whether the opening bars are strongly enough scored; the effect was tame compared to what you obviously intend it to be. Perhaps the players hadn't got hold of it by then. If I remember rightly, I felt also that P.J.'s first phrase in that song didn't hit me enough. It didn't carry conviction. Perhaps it's too low for him – anyhow, you will get few tenors with a reasonable high B♭ to do it satisfactorily. // N°·2 was to me by far the best of the three. The middle section is beautiful & touching – really. // I love the opening bars of the 'Service', but do you want it as fast as that? It didn't sound nearly spacious or solemn enough – only just uncomfortable. The end puzzles me. It seemed too long and indefinite. The wireless behaved rather badly here, consequently it is hard to judge. But from what I remember from looking at the score, the end isn't as satisfactorily managed as I feel it might be.

I was thrilled with the folk-song arrangements – they are by far the best arrangement of any folk-songs I know. We <u>must</u> get someone to print them. Until you get them translated, though, I am afraid that few publishers will look at them. Why not have a shot yourself? I marked off Brecon as being the one that was most immediately attractive; and the last Ogmore has a query against it, for I think that St. Athan would make the most satisfactory concluding one if you issued them as a group. (Of course a high and loud ending revolts you [. . .] but an audience would love it!!) Mari lwyd is a lovely song, and I will die in the effort to see it in print somewhere. What does Parry J. say? Can he suggest a likely publisher whom he might influence? Perhaps if he was asked nicely he might go and sing them for you at

*In the extant copies the highest note of the first song (and of the whole group) is a'.

Booseys [Britten's own publishers]. Write and say if you are willing for me to communicate with them.

Finally, the composer at the piano lent distinction to the evening (((But the end of the last song sounded as if the train to Wales had been late!!!)))

Excuse the awful scribble but I'm writing against time. // Many thanks for telling Fred. May to write to me. // The weather has been lovely today; I thought of you basking in Wales.

Once again – hearty congrats.,

Yours,

BENJAMIN

(162)
BENJAMIN BRITTEN to GRACE WILLIAMS

Hotel Regina,
Vienna.
Nov. 8th 1934

Meine liebe Grace,

This won't be a very long letter I'm afraid, as I haven't got too much time for writing – can one ever find time in this place? Well, we are here, & I hope you arn't too jealous – after all you've been here an awful lot, & this is my first visit.

I am probably not living the life here that you would enjoy very much – but I am loving every moment now – and hate the idea of leaving. The friends we stayed with in Basel were such dears & treated us so well – I've never had such a time – everyone seems to be wealthy there – wonderful houses, marvellous food, & they took us everywhere in glorious cars. Musically too – very good. There is an excellent opera – I heard four operas very well done, a simply lovely show of Zauberflöte. One of the people I stayed with knew Weingartner (who lives there) & I had a very long talk with him & found him nice & helpful, tho' not interested in modern music at all – in fact I went to a rehearsal & show of a concert of Strauss he conducted and it was VERY BAD – but the orchestra was first-rate, and oh – Elizabeth [*sic*] Schumann was a dream. But I am all E.S. mad now – I heard her here on Sunday – but more of that later. – We stayed in Basel – (talking plenty of German as they speak very little English) – just a fortnight, & then spent 3 days in lovely Salzburg on the way here. Of course, after Zauberflöte I was thrilled with the Mozart relics, & there are many of those there.

You will laugh when you know that we are going to stay on here for the rest of our stay in Wien – we went round & looked at pensions, & found out terms – and this Hotel took us for the same amount as the pensions would – & it is a lovely place, just off the Ring [in the Maximilian-Platz, now the Roosevelt-Platz] as you said. Food excellent, and nice quite room to work in, (& I am working alot) & awfully nice people.

Music: – 3 times to the opera so far – Fledermaus on Saturday, 'Cav. & Pag' (this was substituted for something else at the last moment), & Falstaff last night. Vienna went mad over this last – it was a new production & the applause lasted for nearly a quarter of an hour – Prohaska (from Berlin) & Krauss coming back time after time.*

Grace – you must admit that this is great stuff – I don't expect you to accept early Verdi – but the Requiem, Otello, & this, you must like – especially when done as it was last night – it was thrilling. Of course the orchestra – it was the full number last night – is unsurpassable. I went to a show at the Konzerthaus on Sunday, & sat next to an awfully nice young Viennese, who told me lots about everything. Mengelberg, who wasn't too good – his Pastoral was BAD – conducted. Oh – but the orchestra, it nearly drove me potty!! Never such tone, & precision, & spirit – the first horn – well, all the horns – the orchestra played as if it wanted to play – I felt sorry for you with those London orchestras! Much as I want to like them, & do admire a lot of their playing – it's nothing like this. However you know it already.

I met a very nice man from the Universal Edition – introduction from [Hubert] Foss – one Dr. Heinsheimer. I had a long talk with him, in broken English & German, and he has kept some of my stuff to show to Erwin Stein whom I am to meet on Saturday.†

Of course the Viennese themselves are lovely people. I love going into shops just to talk to them – to ask how much things cost. I think they are the kindest, cheerfulest, people I've ever met. And they are going through pretty dreadful times too, but it doesn't seems so by their expressions.

And the tragedy now is that we have to leave in less than a fortnight. Betty Humby is playing those piano pieces of mine at the Wigmore [Hall] on Nov. 30th, & though I don't want to hear the show particularly I must see that she plays them as I want them.‡ So I've got to be back on Nov. 29th or before – and, having especially got some travellers' marks for Germany we have got to go there – to Munich – for at least a week. If we don't use these marks we have to sell them at a great loss. However, I shall either go by self to Paris for about 10 days before Xmas, to see a young composer I met in Florence – or save what money I've got left, & come here again next year – travelling 3rd, and living on nothing when I get here.

Adieu, Grace, I hope everything's going well. Are those Welsh translations done yet? I hope you're well, and working alot.

Herzliche Grüsse

BENJAMIN

P.S. [written at the head of the letter] I didn't say that the concert on Sunday included the Mahler 4th of which I bought the score. It really is a most lovely work – & was beautifully played – Elizabeth [*sic*] Schumann singing the last lovely solo like a dream. I am longing for chances to hear more Mahler

---

*The Viennese baritone Jaro Prohaska (1891–1965) joined the Berlin State Opera in 1931. He sang the title role in *Falstaff*: Clemens Krauss (1893–1954) conducted.

†Hans Walter Heinsheimer (*b* 1900) worked for Universal Edition from 1933 to 1938, and then (until 1947) for Boosey and Hawkes in New York. Erwin Stein (1885–1958) was, at the time Britten wrote this letter, an artistic consultant for Universal Edition. In 1938 he took up a similar post with Boosey and Hawkes in London, and was further associated with Britten from 1947 as director of the English Opera Group.

‡*Four Holiday Tales* (first performance). They were later published by Boosey and Hawkes as *Holiday Diary*, op. 5.

(163)
BENJAMIN BRITTEN to GRACE WILLIAMS

Kirkley Cliff Road,
Lowestoft.
Jan 16th 1935

Meine liebe Grace,
Es tut mir sehr leid, dass ich nicht vorher geschrieben habe.* But I have really been very busy – and so have you, by Jove! I am really getting quite tired of the name G.W. in the Radio Times. I heard your first show – stayed in especially to hear it – and also the Suite from the W. Regional, in sections; but really the thing came over so badly that I can't attempt to judge it – all I seem to remember, between grunts and whistles and shrieks is the diminished fifth B–F – But I remember some exciting wind passages in the last movement. It is going to be done at Iris Lemare's show? When? I must definitely come along to hear it.†

Re- the first concern‡ R.V.W. [Ralph Vaughan Williams] I know is a very nice man, but he shouldn't conduct. It was <u>hopeless</u>. The concert came over quite well; it wasn't the wireless's fault. But, oh, the ragged entries, the half-hearted & doubtful playing – and the beastly tone. I know I have heard the Vienna Phil; but I was also listening to the Basel Symphony to-night – under some quite unknown man – and it was <u>streets</u> ahead of that show. [. . .] your two Psalms were a great relief. I know they arn't your best work, but they (no 1. especially) contain some good stuff. I must borrow the orch. score when I come to town. There are things I want to know. After you of course the music in the programme was finished. I struggled for about three or four minutes with R. O. Morris and then switched off. I tried to be politely interested in Robin Milford, but failed utterly. The fifteen biblical songs of R.V.W. finished me entirely; that 'pi' and artificial mysticism combined with, what seems to me, technical incompetence, sends me crazy. I have never felt more depressed for English music than after that programme – putting your effort aside – especially when I felt that that is what the public – no, <u>not</u> the public, the critics love and praise.

I was terribly sorry to have to miss the Overture last night.¶ I always have to go to an orchestra in Bungay near here on Wednesday evenings, and at that time we were actually stranded in a car without any water, and in a thick fog. How did it go? Charles W. is at least a musician whether he can conduct or not.

And now – when is your next show? What kind of a Christmas did you have? Ours was pretty quiet, rather naturally. Now I am waiting for Adrian Boult to

---

*'I'm very sorry not to have written earlier.'

†Grace Williams's Suite for Chamber Orchestra was broadcast on 14 January 1935 in a performance by the Western Studio Orchestra conducted by Reginald Redman. Iris Lemare conducted the first public performance on February 4. The work was later withdrawn, but the score survives.

‡Broadcast 28 December 1934: BBC Orchestra and Wireless Chorus (Section C), conducted by Ralph Vaughan Williams, with Megan Thomas (soprano) and Roy Henderson (baritone). The programme included Grace Williams's *Two Psalms*, orchestral works by Elizabeth Maeonchy, R. O. Morris and Robin Milford, and Vaughan Williams's *Five Mystical Songs*.

¶The first performance of Grace Williams's *Concert Overture*, played by the BBC Orchestra (Section D), conducted by Charles Woodhouse. The broadcast was on 16 January 1935, so Britten must have interrupted this letter at some point and continued it the following day.

return so I can be examined to see if I can be any use on the B.B.C. Until then I seem to be spending my whole time correcting proofs – and what a job! I am dead sick of it – after four long works to be done. And much more of it in sight, too.

You'll have to excuse this letter. I am writing on my knee, and the wireless is making a distracting noise in my ear. But it is warm in here, and the other rooms in the house are draughty to say the least of it, in this wind.

O for Wien! But I have a lovely record of Elizabeth [sic] Schumann in some Fledermaus solos.

How goes life with you?

BENJAMIN B

(164)
GRACE WILLIAMS to BENJAMIN BRITTEN

[Jan 1935]

Dear Benjamin

Well, well, there's no accounting for people's tastes, is there? [...] Now don't malign poor old Uncle Ralph and call his mysticism artificial. There's nothing artificial about the man: I swear it; and I happen to know him pretty well. Those songs are absolutely sincere and well scored. (I wish all his works came off as well – but that's another matter.) He can't conduct – he knows it – but then, who on the B.B.C. can? He knew that if he accepted their offer he'd be able to choose his own programme. See?

I thought anything might happen to my Psalms (a) because he kept making slips during the rehearsal – and then apologising and calling himself an idiot (b) because Megan lost her nerve at the last rehearsal (mostly because of him). However the show wasn't too bad, except that I did feel the orchestra were unduly cautious and didn't get the feeling of the music at all. But I thought Megan's voice thrilling – she can't be dramatic enough in the first – it's not in her – but she can sing – I think you must have heard more of the Suite from Cardiff than you care to admit. You say all you can remember of the 1st mvt is the dim. 5th B–F. Isn't it awful, that's about all there is in that mvt. So you have hit the nail on the head with full force this time! – Nevertheless I find the whole thing more satisfying than anything else I've done and I felt very sort of exhilarated during the rehearsals (they gave me three hours!) and felt perhaps it was worth while after all.

Iris [Lemare] is doing it on Feb. 4th, but I'm not particularly looking forward to her performance because it will be awful having Anne [Macnaghten] & Co. instead of my Cardiffians (who are dears – and professionals) – and if the thing isn't played with conviction (it sounded v. firm and wholesome at Cardiff) it will sound stupid. Also I shan't be able to go to the first rehearsal. Teaching.

I am very relieved, in a way, that you didn't hear my Overture; but, in another way, I wish you'd listened, because I'd have got the truth from you about how it came off over the air. All the people I know – Iris [Lemare], Dolly [Dorothy Gow], Betty [Maconchy] – who listened-in are very polite and say the scoring was allright – but I can't conceive that it could have been allright. The awful thing was that in the studio (Maida Vale) it was terribly hard to judge. They had the orchestra arranged thus

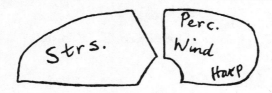

There is a terribly hollow sound about everything in that studio and – honestly – if you stand on the conductor's left you hear nothing but strs. – but if you get over on the other side, it's all wind! And if you stand at the back away from the orchestra everything has a sort of hollow jangled sound. And the timps. drown everything. So God knows what my poor Overture was really like – but I do know this; I'd given the wind some quite uncrackable nuts: and they were very sniffy about it. I'll never look Mr. A. Whittaker in the face again. There was one rather swift run that he just spluttered over. The wind scoring on the whole seemed much too thick and even smudgy, so I felt very sick about it. In fact I have never felt so miserable as at that rehearsal, and lonely – and intimidated. C. Woodhouse was nice in a way – but he must have been annoyed at having been inveigled into conducting such a work, and I kept seeing his point of view, which made things more and more embarrassing.

Now that orchestra had been v. nice to us all at Uncle Ralph's show – because they all adore uncle R. But on Wed. there was no Uncle R. to break the ice and the orchestra were horribly aloof. (The only one who seemed to take any interest in my thing was a rather shy double bass player who crept up afterwards and asked me what idea I had had at the back of my mind when I wrote it – what did those seconds represent – and was it anything to do with the sea?!!!) – Oh – and Sidonie [Goossens] told Uncle Ralph (who came to the evening performance) that it was a brilliant work and much better than any of the 3 prizewinning works – ! But, as I said before, there's no accounting for tastes. My difficulty at the moment is that I can't make up my mind whether it is worth the bother of rescoring. In a way it's bright, and has some go in it (The strings made a good sound, though they were dissatisfied with my bowing, and Woodhouse gave me a sound lecture about this in the middle of everything, with all the strs. looking on.) Please, when you come back to London to begin work at the B.B.C. would you look at the score and decide for me? Look here Benjamin, I'll strike a bargain with you. If you promise to tell me the truth, the whole truth etc. – about my things I'll do the same to you about yours (not that my comments about your things will be of any use, but it might make it easier for you to slash out about me). I'm dead sick of having tactful things said to me.

I went to a Viennese film this afternoon – Maskerade* – the usual stuff; but I took it all in and loved it. I must go back again this Easter – only about 10 weeks to go.

So, mon vieux, don't bother to come to Iris's show on Feb. 4th: I don't think you'd enjoy any of it v. much.

Yours,

GRACE

*Willy Forst's film (1934), starring Paula Wesseley. It was being shown at the Academy Cinema, Oxford Street.

(165)

EUGENE GOOSSENS to C. W. ORR

Cincinnati Symphony Orchestra
Office of the Conductor
January 23, 1935

My dear Orr:
Thanks for your nice letter of the 6th and the songs which in spite of so-called bad reviews have given me intense joy. There is so much in them which at first glance is lost to the reader, musically speaking I mean, of course. In other words, there are many subtleties which are not immediately apparent.

Before I say anything further about them, I want you to do one thing for me, or rather not for *me* but for the sake of giving singers something worthy to sing with orchestra. Please orchestrate numbers 1, 2, 6, and 7, or, if you prefer, numbers 1, 2, 4, and 6. On second thought, 7 is a little too pianistic and the others are certainly much too pianistic for orchestral garb. By the others I mean 3 and 5. Or if you think four are too many for an orchestral cycle, take only three of the ones I have suggested, but for the love of Heaven, do *do* them. Numbers 1 and 6, in particular, would sound entrancing.

As you probably guess, I am a terrific lover of the Shropshire Lad poems. The particular psychology they express is something which belongs only to Englishmen and it is idle to expect an American (as I know from experience) to try and understand the underlying idiom of these poems. Nobody who hasn't lived somewhere near the Wrekin or Bredon Hill or, to go a little farther afield, the Cotswold country, as I have, could ever hope to relish these works and their peculiar 'aura'. I remember well the first performances of Vaughan Williams' cycle for tenor, string quartet and piano (in which I took part) and the incredible beauty of his setting of, shall we say, Bredon Hill. I must confess that for a long time I have considered it impossible for any other composer to realize the peculiar color of Housman until your songs came along, for I consider all other settings of these poems by other composers are tawdry and unmeaning.

Only one criticism would I make of your songs. It is that the piano writing is terribly involved for the average, even though passably good, accompanist. I don't know what the critics have said about them, but I imagine that the difficulties offered by the piano accompaniments of the songs were, by some, severely criticised. As you know, I do not approve of reducing things to the essence of simplicity and there is no early reason why an accompaniment should not be as complicated and involved as you have made yours in certain of these songs. But I am afraid you must resign yourself to many bad criticisms of performance lacking the brio and accuracy called for in the accompaniments of the seven songs you sent me. Anyway, thank God for some more good music. How beautifully you have 'timed' the words – a none too easy job to accomplish in these particular poems. I found the same difficulty in my settings of Joyce (Chamber Music), published by Curwens. Well, write me again when you feel like it and, in the meantime, here's good luck to you and your future work.

As always sincerely,

EUGENE GOOSSENS

(166)
AYLMER BUESST to ROGER ECKERSLEY

MUSIC PROGRAMME ADVISORY PANEL
25th January, 1935.

According to the memorandum from M.D. to you dated November 20th, 1933, concerning the formation of the above, the general idea then reached with and agreed by Sir Hugh Allen and Sir John McEwen was that the Panel should consist of two members only, namely, Waddington and Dale, Waddington as the senior to retire at the end of the first year and becoming again eligible a year later, when Dale would retire. It is also mentioned at this point that the substitution of Dale would have to be considered, as before, to be an Academy matter. In the same memorandum Dr. Boult urges that Bliss be added to the Panel as a third member, and this was subsequently agreed by the Director-General on a following memorandum, although there is, so far as I can see, no specific confirmation of his election.

The whole matter has been discussed with M.D. [i.e. Adrian Boult], and he feels very strongly that, as agreed, at least one member of the Panel should retire at the end of each year. This will not only bring in new blood and fresh ideas, but it means that every man who has served on the Panel becomes in the outside world of professional music an ideal witness of our methods of work and the principles for which we stand. He also knows better than any outside musician can possibly do, the peculiar problems with which we have to cope; thus we should be accumulating and strengthening the confidence of the professional world in our own organisation.

Whatever method may be adopted to determine who should be the retiring member or members, Dr. Boult is whole-heartedly in favour of retaining Bliss for a further year as he is undoubtedly the most stimulating and constructively helpful member.

The Panel is, I think, entirely ignorant as to the procedure in regard to retirement, and I would suggest that a definite one be laid down. In order that the matter be put on a totally impersonal basis, I would propose that

(a) for the first three years members should retire in order of seniority of years – i.e. Waddington, followed by Dale, followed by Bliss;

(b) thereafter retirements should be based on seniority of service on the Panel and irrespective of the age of the member.

I presume that you would discuss it all with the members of the Panel in a private interview?

AYLMER BUESST

The Music Programme Advisory Panel was instituted with Bliss, Dale and Waddington as its members, and lasted in that form until Dale's death in 1943. Effectively it was only an advisory body which had no power to push through far-reaching programming initiatives, much to the annoyance of Bliss. S. P. Waddington (1869–1953) was the elder statesman of music and effectively represented the RCM interest, Benjamin Dale (1885–1943) the RAM; neither were in sympathy with new trends even in the 1930s.

(167)
RALPH VAUGHAN WILLIAMS to E. J. MOERAN

The White Gates
Westcott Road
Dorking
February 8 [1935]

Dear Moeran

Many thanks for the copy of the Nocturne – I thought it beautiful – I think the references to Delius in the Press are absurd. Doubtless if Delius had not existed it might not have been written. Just as Delius would not have been written without Grieg or Grieg without Schumann and so on back to Tubal Cain.

I find in your work a distinction of style that I fail to find usually in Delius with the notable exception of the Wedding Procession (*not* the Paradise Garden) in [A Village] Romeo & Juliet.

Yrs

R VAUGHAN WILLIAMS

Moeran's quarter-hour choral setting of words from Robert Nichols's play Don Juan Tenorio the Great *was written in 1934 for the Norwich Philharmonic Society, and is inscribed 'To the Memory of Frederick Delius', who had died on 10 June 1934. If Vaughan Williams wrote on the publication of the vocal score, the date should be as given. If, however, he wrote after the first London performance, it could be a year later.*

(168)
ADRIAN BOULT to M. H. GORHAM

4 March 1935

I hope you will forgive my interference, but I am a little disturbed at the paragraph concerning the Bax Symphony, which appeared in yesterday's Regional programme in the current Radio Times, page 22.

There are quite as many critics *con* and *pro* the statement that Bax and Sibelius are the greatest living symphonists, and in any case I do not feel that a statement of that kind should ever be allowed to appear unsigned in the programme page of The Radio Times. It surely represents in the minds of most people the corporate opinion of the BBC, and I think there are plenty of people inside the BBC also who would consider that Vaughan Williams is a far greater symphonist than either Bax or Sibelius. I feel some communication should go to Vaughan Williams, though personally he does not care in the least about these things, and I am not sure what you would like to do in the matter. I could easily write a short private note if you think fit.

A C BOULT

I think it would be best for you to write. Sorry for causing trouble – I quite see your point. We will be very careful in future.

M H GORHAM

The concert on 3 March had seen Boult conducting the BBC Orchestra (Section B) in a programme consisting of Elgar's Froissart, *Holst's* Scherzo *for orchestra, May Harrison and Lionel Tertis in the first performance of Delius's* Double Concerto *in Tertis's arrangement for violin, viola and orchestra. The second half was taken up with Bax's* Fifth Symphony, *of which an unsigned annotator had written: 'Arnold Bax is one of the few contemporary composers who is still working along the lines of the romantic symphony and turning out works of vital interest and importance. Five big symphonies stand to his credit, all of which show a melodic invention and mastery of construction and orchestral resource that bear comparison with the great symphonies of the great masters of the nineteenth century. Certainly as a symphonist Bax has only one rival today and that is Sibelius to whom his Fifth Symphony is dedicated . . .'*

(169)
GEORGE DYSON to G. N. POCOCK

26 S. Swithen St
WINCHESTER
April 18 1935

Dear Pocock

Forgive the delay in answering your letter of the 10th.

I have been away and did not want to write in a hurry. The autumn is not possible. That is certain. But I might be able to undertake a series of talks in 1936, providing the subject, the times and the fees could be made mutually suitable.

Please don't tie me in any way yet, but if I may tell you my view frankly, you can consider and reply in due time.

If I am able to tackle the subject of modern idioms for the B.B.C. public, it would have to be along the following lines:

1) a few introductory talks on the subject in general, followed by

2) Individual talks on a selected group of modern *British* composers. These are, to my mind, incomparably the ablest group in the world of our time.

The point of this scheme is that I must talk about something I really believe in, and be at liberty to say also what I *don't* believe in.

The second main consideration is that of fee. Will you tell me what is the *maximum* fee you are authorised to offer? I am quite candid about this because if I am to clear my calendar to give time for the study and preparation of complicated items, I should want to feel that it was in every respect worth the sacrifice.

If you prefer, we could have a talk about the whole matter sometime. There is no hurry.

With best thanks and all good wishes,

Yours sincerely

G. DYSON

The rise of the broadcast talk about music – and of musical appreciation generally – on the
BBC during the 1930s, was initially in the hands of three popularizers, of whom Walford
Davies became by far the best known. Yet the viewpoint of two other significant speakers is
also of importance, both of whom believed British music to be at the centre of things musical.
They were George Dyson and Herbert Howells. Dyson was then Musical Director at
Winchester College, and soon to become the Director of the RCM, while Howells was
already teaching composition at the RCM. Howells was the more outward-looking of the two
(see letter 180/180A). Pocock championed the concept of the broadcast talk about music in the
BBC at that time, and hence was a notable pioneer.

(170)
SIR HAMILTON HARTY to E. J. MOERAN

1, Norfolk Road,
St John's Wood,
London N.W.8
April 19 1935

My dear Moeran
    Excuse my delay – Concerts and such like have kept me busy. Thanks so much for
the gift of those two pieces for small orchestra. I am glad to possess some autograph
music of yours, and will place the scores with the few pieces which I keep in a special
place, and regard as particularly my own.
    I am going away for a few weeks in the sun. Some years of continuous work have
left me tired and unfresh in my mind and I feel about me a good many longuers of
fatigue through which I must swim up to the fresh air and blue sea again.
    I saw your letter in the 'Telegraph' – Poor old Cowen – it is impossible that he
should feel otherwise than he does, considering his musical history and his own facile
and melodious works. I also admired the strength and vitality of the V. Williams
Symphony, it is hugely powerful and I think, a very important work. I don't know
that it struck me as a work that will live, and it is rather hard to explain why. Perhaps
it is that its brutal strength and blind vitality seems to be balanced only by moods of
philosophic musing – not quite completely human. But, it is a big effort and I have
plenty of sincere admiration for it. I thought it seemed a first class performance and
that Boult did the composer proud.
    I will not worry you by enquiries about your symphony – for I know quite well
that you are at least equally anxious for its completion. I don't know if you hear
much gossip – there is a little stir here over H.J.W.'s latest appearance as

[In fact from Richard Strauss: *Don Juan*]

and over Kreisler's successful forging exploits and his spirited defence of the same.
But very little else. I hope to see you on my return. In the meantime the best of luck.

Yours ever

HAMILTON HARTY

The veteran composer Sir Frederick Cowen (1852–1935) had been famous in his day both as composer and conductor. His six symphonies (1869–97) were notwithstanding the works of Cipriani Potter, Macfarren and Sterndale Bennett, perhaps the first British symphonies to be widely played. However, he found Vaughan Williams's Fourth unbearable and in an outburst to the press wrote that it was not music! The musical quotation is from Richard Strauss's Don Juan and refers to the scandal and gossip occasioned by Sir Henry Wood's parting from his second wife and the arrival of Jessie Linton who later became Lady Jessie Wood. The violinist Fritz Kreisler had composed and performed many concert encores in a pastiche style, ascribing them to actual eighteenth-century composers. When he admitted the ruse many critics were scornful.

(171)
JOHN IRELAND to WILLIAM LLOYD

The Studio
14A Gunter Grove
Chelsea, s.w.10
July 4th 1935

Dear Mr Lloyd

I must felicitate you on the pluck & enterprize which led to the production of 'Iernin' in London: It is due entirely to the enthusiasm of Mr A.W.Ganz that I was induced to come to hear it, in the first instance. I am not primarily interested in Opera, & as a rule, I rather dislike it; & I cannot listen intensively to music for very long in the ordinary way, & as a rule, the addition of stage action to good music (even in Ballet) reduces for me the reaction I gain from it. But in the case of 'Iernin' it seems different. I am very glad I was able to come on the last night, as it confirmed the strong impression made previously.

Apart from the excellence of the work as a whole, I was particularly stirred by the points when there is a tentative return to the thoughts of pre-Christian religion & beliefs. I wondered, in listening, if you & your son could produce an opera entirely on that subject? for it is so evident that you both feel it strongly.

As you mentioned, I have written 'The Forgotten Rite' – also the Rhapsody 'Mai-Dun' wh[ich] is based on my impressions of the hill-fortress of that name – so, naturally, I would feel some hopes you two could produce, in opera, some real characterisation of that subject, which, tho' now hidden & overlaid, is after all, really present in the minds & hearts of all really sensitive people – however much hidden.

I think I have already said to yourselves, & to others, what I felt about 'Iernin' – so I need not labour that point. As was said some 2000 years ago, there are two kinds of people – the children of this world, & the children of Light – the work of your son and yourself shows very clearly where you stand – & the criticisms of 'Iernin' wh[ich] I have heard assist me in placing the mentality of a good many otherwise cultured people.

When convenient, I will be only too honoured if your son will come & spend an evening with me.
[Regards] to him & yourself & his mother

Yrs. always

JOHN IRELAND

George Lloyd first appeared as a composer at the age of 19, when his First Symphony was produced in 1932. Second and third symphonies followed in 1934 and 1935, the Third was performed by the BBC at the end of November 1935, recommended by John Ireland. Lloyd's first opera Iernin, to a libretto by his father William Lloyd, was first produced in Penzance in November 1934. Frank Howes (the music critic of The Times) was amazed to find 'out of the blue, a full length opera in which the balance of interest is fairly held between the voices, the stage situations, and the orchestra'. In June 1935 it ran for a short season at the Lyceum Theatre, London, but was then not heard again until extracts were broadcast by the BBC West of England Service in 1954, when Maurice Johnstone voiced an influential BBC view 'after 20 years the music seems to be as naive and trite as the libretto'. It was not heard again complete until Chris de Souza's atmospheric radio production conducted by the composer was broadcast in July 1986, when opinions were more favourable. It is certainly a remarkable piece for so young and inexperienced a composer.

(172)
JOHN IRELAND to A. W. GANZ

THE STUDIO,
14A Gunter Grove,
Chelsea, s.w.10.
July 10th 1935.

My dear Ganz,
As I understand there is now some question of the publication of the opera 'IERNIN' by George Lloyd, I should like to have the privilege of putting on record some of my views about the work.

Having heard the opera twice, I have no hesitation in saying that it is quite the most remarkable work produced by a British composer during the last 20 years, whether in the form of opera or other musical forms. As a composition teacher of long experience, it is at once evident to me that the composer of this work has a unique talent, which one may well suppose to be genius, sparing as one must be in one's use of that word. I would go so far as to say that 'IERNIN' is the only British work in this form which shows a complete sense of stage requirements, with all the technique which this implies. As for the music itself, it is entirely fresh and original in inspiration, and shows clearly not only great power but also an intense sense of beauty, and a deep emotional and imaginative sense.

It is built on musical material which is bound to appeal to a very wide public, and I feel certain that it will command a permanent musical interest, and obtain a foremost place in the English operatic repertoire.

If there is a prospect of the Carnegie United Kingdom Trust, which has done such inestimable work for native music, undertaking the publication of 'IERNIN' I, as a composer, feel that a great and vital step would have been taken towards the vindication of British music, not only here, but in other countries – for, to my mind, there is no doubt at all that this truly remarkable work will be accepted, wherever it is heard, for what it actually is – a great opera, and a splendid piece of music.

Yours always sincerely

JOHN IRELAND

After the success of Belshazzar's Feast *in 1931 William Walton's First Symphony was eagerly awaited, and indeed the first three movements were given three performances before the fourth movement was completed and the whole work could be performed. Within a few weeks of its first complete performance the Decca Record Company were planning to record it.*

*

(173)
WALTER YEOMANS to ADRIAN BOULT

(personal)

17/11/35

... Although the records (if made) will be published by Decca, the money for the recording (about £650) will be found by the very enterprising & generous Mr E R Lewis who virtually owns the Decca Company. It is *his* enthusiasm & private cash that made 'Dido' a fact & will make the Walton Symphony a fact.

On 20th November 1935 it was announced that the recording of the Walton Symphony would be on December 10 and 11. This in fact took place in a freezing deserted London warehouse, with the London Symphony orchestra conducted by Sir Hamilton Harty.

Purcell's Dido and Aeneas *previously generally known by Dido's celebrated lament 'When I am laid in earth', was introduced to a wider public by the Decca recording on 7 × 12 in records (X 101/7) of Edward J. Dent's edition, with Nancy Evans as Dido and Roy Henderson as Aeneas and the Boyd Neel String Orchestra conducted by Clarence Raybould. The* Gramophone *(Dec. 1935 p. 285) judged it 'a truly fine set of records embodying some of the loveliest music of all time'.*

(174)
WALTER YEOMANS to ADRIAN BOULT

The Decca Record Co Ltd
1–3 Brixton Road
LONDON s w 9
8 Feb 1936

Dear Boult

Willy Walton informs me that you are playing his Symphony in Zurich during the tour of your orchestra. Would you kindly let me know the date of this performance and the dates of any other performances you are to give of Walton's Symphony, as I would like to tie up your performances with an announcement of the Decca records.

I think you will be interested to know that the records are selling splendidly, about four hundred sets have been sold since 20th December, and the sales are becoming more rapid. In the seven working days between December the 20th and 31st we disposed of eighty seven sets – a remarkable happening.

We recorded Vaughan Williams' 'Tallis Fantasia' on 28th of January with Boyd Neel and his Orchestra enlarged to thirty players. Vaughan Williams attended the recording session and supervised the performance. We have secured fine records. Boyd Neel is a most intelligent fellow.

with *very very* cordial greetings
Yours ever

WALTER YEOMANS

In reply, Kenneth A. Wright was only able to note two performances of the Walton, on 1 March at the BBC Maida Vale Studios (Sunday Symphony Concerts), and on 21 April in the Tonhalle Series, Zurich. In the event only the Walton Viola Concerto was given in Zurich.

(175)
BENJAMIN BRITTEN to GRACE WILLIAMS

Barcelona
pm: 26 April 1936

Thank you for your card. I was going to send you a card but Wellesz, who is here, was going to sign this as well & I can't find him; so I won't wait any longer. This is really a lovely spot, and the festival has been beautifully organised – not too much music, good excursions (Montserrat is uncanny) – & great dancing – the whole town turns out to dance Sardanas on the slightest provocation! Oh – this native music! The new Berg concerto [1st performed on 19 April 1936] is great – Best of the festival. Back by air on Thursday.

BENJ

Grace Williams had been a pupil of the Austrian composer Egon Wellesz some five or six years before. Wellesz would soon leave Austria and settle in England.

(176)
KENNETH WRIGHT to WILLIAM WALTON

27th May, 1936.

Dear Walton,
Julian [Herbage] has told me of his conversation with you, during which you suggest re-casting the Promenade Concert so as to include 'Portsmouth Point', the Viola Concerto, 'Facade' Suite and the Symphony. First of all, I should like to tell you how

much we sympathise with you and agree that from the purely musical point of view this programme is better than the other. We have to consider the concert as a Promenade event, and we are anxious for your sake and for that of the concerts generally to get as many people into the house as possible. The outstanding fact that Promenade experience has always taught us is the superiority and popularity of the Piano Concerto over all forms of concerto music, and Solomon in particular is one of the most popular Promenade figures. Our intention, therefore, was to pack the house for you, which makes for a good concert, great enthusiasm and the general impression to the listeners outside of 'a successful evening'. The Viola Concerto is the least attractive from the point of view of the Promenade public and in view of this I do hope you can agree to forgo purely aesthetic considerations and agree to the programme comprising the 'Facade' Suite, the Sinfonia Concertante with Solomon, some songs and the Symphony. I would add in conclusion that Sir Henry, while very keen on the idea of a Walton evening and anxious to do all in his power to help it from the point of view of rehearsal and preparation is very anxious that the original programme should be done, as he knows from his long experience that it is the most likely one to bring you a real success.

Yours sincerely,

KAW

(177)
KENNETH WRIGHT to JULIAN HERBAGE

Symphony Concert Draft, 1936/7.

7/7/36

I would like to begin these notes by recording that Mr. Graves told Dr. Boult and me at lunch to-day how very pleased he was with this set of concerts, and how he felt that every possible requirement was met in them.

The Panel spent a long time discussing them in in a friendly and constructive way to-day, and here are important notes from this discussion, which I should like you to talk over with Mr. Arthur Bliss and myself Thursday, the 9th, at 2.30 p.m., before we all go down with them to M.A.C. In the meantime I think it would be better to have copies done for the whole committee on the present lines and any important alterations can be announced at the meeting.

November 4th: Two points. Myra Hess not considered good in either Beethoven 3 or 5 and her No. 4, which is much better, has been overdone. Cesar Franck Variations suggested as alternative. [In fact Brahms's Second Piano Concerto was performed.]

Vivaldi [Concerto Grosso in A min, op 3 No. 8] strongly queried as dull, but it was understood that Mengelberg is particularly interested in this work and strongly wants to do it.

November 25th: This was considered a good programme for Heward's first appearance in our major series, but why not ask him to suggest a good opening British work instead of Weber? Is the Sibelius Symphony 5 or 7? [In the end the programme started with Berlioz's *Les Francs Juges* overture.]

December 2nd: No comment, except that Clifford Curzon was not felt to be quite the pianist that he promised some years back, although it was admitted that he plays this work very well. [It is not known what Curzon was intended to play as Boult actually gave *The Dream of Gerontius* on this date.]

December 9th: Busoni – 'Dr. Faust', no comment, but I wondered whether anything has been done with Professor Dent about the translation which ought to be going ahead with all speed. [Krasner actually gave the Berg Violin Concerto on this date, the Busoni XXX broadcast on 17 March 1937.]

January 20th: No comment.

January 27th: Is Hindemith being invited in a near-by Sunday Concert to play the Schwanendreher Viola Concerto?

Have we considered the alternative of inviting William Primrose to produce Walton's new version of his Viola Concerto instead of repeating Tertis in the old one.

February 3rd: Gieseking was felt to be so fine a pianist can we not ask him to do something bigger, like Beethoven No. 4, with all due respect to his beautiful Mozart playing?

February 10th: Is not this concert too long? Why not do a Liszt second half, since the second Liszt Concerto is a work not typical of the composer, and something like 'Mazeppa' or the 'Rakoczy' March would make a good finish.

February 17th: No comment.

February 24th: Again strong feeling against Ansermet's Mozart and the question since it is probably doubtful whether the substitution of a new work for this would affect the house, it might not be a good idea to ask Ansermet to do a suitable British work to open the concert, e.g. Dirge for Cuthullin (C. T. Davies*), which involves chorus and is a sincere, effective and affecting work:

A further point. Krasner apparently can do nothing after December. Shall we leave the Berg out altogether, or put ourselves out to include it earlier with him, and even so, when?

Waddington and Dale repeated their opinions that Ansermet is a second rate conductor, but Bliss strongly defended him on the grounds of specialist who gives certain modern music in quite an individual and what may be described as an inspired style. Other proposals for opening item were Unaccompanied Motets by Rubbra and Van Dieren, the latter rather in an In Memoriam sense, and 'The Trees so High' (Hadley).

The violinist Louis Krasner gave all the early performances of the Berg Violin Concerto, and had given the work its second performance with the BBC Symphony Orchestra with Webern as guest conductor in the BBC's Berg Memorial Concert on 1 May 1936. Krasner's re-engagement to play the work took place on 9 December 1936, this time with Sir Henry Wood conducting.

*Cedric Thorpe Davie, born in 1913, the same year as Benjamin Britten.

(178)
ALBERT COATES to LESLIE HEWARD

4 Queen's Gate Terrace,
London, s.w.7.
25th July, 1936.

My dear Leslie
I should be so happy if you could find time to listen in on the Regional at about 8.50 p.m. on Friday, July 31st. My Piano Concerto is being broadcast then from the B.B.C. Maida Vale studios, with Frank Laffitte at the piano and myself conducting. If you happen to be in London, do come to the studio. Anyway, I should be most interested to know what you think of it.

The whole programme starts at 8.30 p.m., with a symphony by Kavalewsky [i.e. Kabalevsky], a modern Russian, whom you may like.

With best wishes,

Everyrs

ALBERT

(179)
LESLIE WOODGATE to ADRIAN BOULT

THREE CHOIRS FESTIVAL (HEREFORD), SEPTEMBER, 1936

16.9.36

The first work I heard was Elgar's 'Apostles'. The performance under Dr. Percy Hull was, on the whole, very good. The Choir is the best I have heard at the last three festivals, and sang with life and vigour.

Two Preludes (on 'Eventide', Monk, and 'Dominus Regit Me', Dykes) by Vaughan Williams concluded the morning oratorio. These pieces are written in the usual Vaughan Williams manner, and do not throw any new light on his great mind. They were beautifully written, and I think will sound better in a concert hall, as many of the subtleties were lost in the acoustics of the Cathedral.

The evening performance began with a splendid Motet by Charles Wood 'Glory and honour and laud'. This is finely conceived, and spaciously written music, full of dignity, and well written for voices. The new piece by Dyson* proved to be a very unsatisfactory work to my hearing. It began with a Prelude, which sounded as though it were going to be of vast importance, but this soon petered out to a feeble dialogue between 'Cello Solo and short sections for Wood-Wind. There was no particularly striking theme anywhere in it. The second movement (Fantasy) lived up to its name, and owes a great deal to the Enigma 'Dorabella' variation, besides a little Brahms here and there. It had a certain charm, but how much of Dyson's I know not. The final section (Chaconne) was quite odd. In the programme note, Dyson

---

Prelude, Fantasy and Chaconne.

says, 'The Chaconne derives from Buxtehude and Purcell'. The derivation was not too obvious, unless he means that both were fond of ground-bass. The actual working of the theme owed nothing to anyone important. It just went on weaving patterns that were pleasant to listen to, but not to enthuse about.

It may sound as though I am being rather cynical about this work, but it seems to me that Dr. Dyson is being set up as one of the great new English composers, and I do not understand why. He certainly has technique and ability, but that, to me, is all.

Mendelssohn's 'Hymn of Praise' was sung after the Dyson work, and the clarity of thought, technique and sound was quite refreshing.

LESLIE WOODGATE

(180)
HERBERT HOWELLS to GEORGE BARNES

Redmarley,
Station Road,
Barnes Common, s.w.13

29 Oct 1936

My dear Barnes,
I have it in my mind, in the general course of my talks, so to examine the complexities and diversities of so-called 'modern music' as to discover and trace what I may call a 'compromise-in-Sanity' running through the apparent chaos. I believe in the existence, in any given epoch, of that element which ultimately will represent sane progress; and it may often be recognised, in its own day, for what it is.

I shall examine the 'extremities' of modernity but chiefly to induce listeners to conserve their powers for what lies well on this side of *ultra*-modernity. Most contemporary manifestation, in any Art, is falsely coloured in the mind of the many by its imputed threat against proved and established creeds. That was as true of 1836 as it is of 1936. But listening in Europe a hundred years ago was comparatively simple. The environment of the listener was limited in space, if not in time. The chances of aural comfort and intellectual satisfaction were enormously greater then than now, because there was time for 'assimilation' on the part of audiences. But now, in an age in which all our physical, nervous, and mental resources are much more on the stretch, there is the further strain that the ear itself is subjected to the worst of temptations – to practically constant promiscuous attention to music of all sorts and kinds. The power of assimilation is being perilously reduced. Aural and mental discomfort are – in most of us – acutely increased. So is the sense of rebellion. A feeling of being 'rushed' through a world of sound increases a disposition hostile to novelty.

There is, therefore, an over-riding need that the ordinary listener shall come to his listening with as little as may be of active hostility towards the 'new' trend of things in music. He owes it to himself – as much as to the contemporary composer – to be actively sympathetic. All listening sh^d be (as I believe) in the first place an act of submission, in the second, a quest for understanding. But in these days of facile communication there is the further need that every listener must, after submission and search for understanding, select and renounce from the mass of aural experiences.

I shall invite listeners to consider with me, some of the universal difficulties besetting us. Such as

a) inherited harmonic notions – which begin to play havoc with our receptive powers before we've left our late teens.

b) the immemorial habit of 'top-part' listening, which makes all contrapuntal texture of these days a sort of 'dark continent'.

c) Our dubious assessment of pace-in-music, and our divorcing it from harmonic thought.

d) Our disposition to search for rhythmic excitements that are merely metric.

e) Our inborn sense of Tonality – an inherited thing of 3 centuries.

f) The habit of 'pianistic' listening to orchestral texture

g) The incubus of cut-and-dried notions of Form.

I could add to these: but won't at the moment. I am not proposing to discuss all this in gloomy terms: on the contrary I shall make copious use of key board and gramophone. These notes, here, are only as it were a means of shewing which way the illustrational wind will blow. And they are not to be taken as more than a general indication of some of the ground I hope to cover.

Anyhow; I've gone past the hundred words you asked for – and you must forgive me for that!

Yours very sincerely

HERBERT HOWELLS

(180A)
HERBERT HOWELLS

Music and the ordinary listener: the modern problem

I: A review of the complex state of affairs in present-day music. Contributory causes – and immediate antecedents of the 'new' music. So-called 'Modernity': Can we define it?

Polytonality. Is it new? – and is it necessarily difficult for the listener?

Note. Under this heading I can – and shall – link my arguments with those of Mr. Newman.

Atonality. This is the real threat to continued sympathy and contact as between listener and composer. The ordinary listeners extreme difficulties in the presence of a language whose structures, symbols and syntax are foreign to him.

The listener's concern for and attitude towards these will be examined. Ordeal-by-sound: and the Judgment-of-the-Ear.

Note. It is here
chiefly that I shall
discuss the
difficulties inherent
in listeners them-
selves – as indicated
in my earlier notes
to you on these
talks.

II: The three fundamentals – Melody, Harmony, Rhythm.
Their 'new' appearances: their quarrel with inherited
conception of their nature, quality, and function. The
struggle we are put to with every break-away from the
'known' aspect of these within the limit of our experience. In this connection it will be shown that the
inherent difficulty in Melody is that it has moved so far
from the conception of this element as being imme-
morially rooted in 'singable' tunes. The origin of music
in song is a thing 'modern' music seems bent on deny-
ing. Harmony-by-ellipsis – difficult enough in small
'doses' in the past – is now, under the terms of polytonality and atonality, a bewildering enigma to most
people. Rhythm in abstract as against Rhythm-with-
melody, or structural rhythm. (Here the atavistic tendencies of 'modern' rhythm make a readier appeal than
the new melody or harmony can claim to do.)

III: Tonality – the crux of it all, the complete divorce of
listening and aural experience: the focal point of all the
most extensive radical change in the aspect of music.
Here one considers the later work of Schonberg (the
extreme) and Berg (the compromise), and seeks for
'formal' features to which the atonal composers still
cling in much of their music. Schonberg's counterpoint. . does it, as such, offer us a chance of 'meeting'
with the composer? The case of 'Wozzeck' – where
known formal devices are a potent sign of friendship
with traditional causes. Our readiness to accept any
helpful aid must be cultivated to the utmost limit of
our sympathy. The whole extreme nature of atonality
seems to make us seek for compromise. Is such possible?
Is there a 'line-of-sanity' this side of extremity?

IV: It ought to be possible for the listener to advance
confidentially to a point of understanding with the less
extreme modernity. There is a chance of co-operation
between composer and audience if we can by selective
listening make approach – through the smaller and less
uncompromising utterance of representative 'advanced'
composers. Here I shall use illustrations from Bartok,
Hindemith, Prokofiev, Walton, Holst, and Stravinsky.
Here too will be discussed the innumerable points of
contact made between the 'new' and the 'old' by the
persistent employment today of accepted technical devices – and by extra-musical features.
Of the former devices, illustrations will be drawn from
Holst's vocal canons: from Walton's Symphony (for
pedal points): from Scriabin (to show his close relation-
ship to the Victori [anismus]* of Barnby): from Hindemith (in comparison with the Bach inventions), and

from others to show rhythmic complexities which are fundamentally identical with the madrigal. Of the extra-musical features – pictorialism a) of the direct sort – as in Honegger ('Pacific 231') – Mosolov – Stravinsky ('Fireworks' and 'Petrushka'): b) of the more musical sort, Honegger's 'King David' Alleluias (cf. with Handel and with Bach's Sanctus): Walton's 'Facade' etc.

V: The search for repose and beauty in contemporary music can yield further 'reconciliation' if made with an open mind. It is paradoxically true that, though the strongly contrapuntal bias of modern music has often put a limit upon our receptive powers (allied so much, as it has been, to polytonality and atonality), it is in the new counterpoint that an unexpected beauty can be found. It is through counterpoint, and simple contrapuntal texture, that the quieter voice of modernity is best heard and most appealing. Walton is a master of this type of appeal – (slow movement of 'Symphony Concertante'). Stravinsky too, (second movement of 'Symphony des Psaumes'), Hindemith (in Third String Quartet), Berg (where, in the Violin Concerto, he quotes and works upon the Bach Chorale), Vaughan Williams (in the 'Pastoral Symphony' and the slow movement of the F minor Symphony), and Lambert (in the ballet 'Pomona').

VI: The bigger view of things . . . and the question of Form, with special reference to Sibelius.

In November 1936 the newly established BBC Television Service made the first attempt in the U.K. to broadcast opera. The opera chosen was Albert Coates's new opera Pickwick, *from which four extracts were chosen for televising. The performance, which was described as 'a rehearsal' took place on a specially constructed set in the BBC Television Studios at Alexandra Palace. The television transmission was on Friday 13 November at 3.35 in the afternoon. The stage premiere took place a week later at Covent Garden, the four performances being given on 20, 25, 28 and 30 November, when Act I was, in fact, broadcast in the usual way. This was the first season of The British Music Drama Opera Company, which under the artistic direction of Albert Coates (conductor) and Vladimir Rosing (producer), with Arthur Hammond as Assistant Music Director produced all British casts in* Boris Godounov, Sorochintsy Fair, Madame Butterfly, Pagliacci *and, as well as Coates's opera, an operetta by Roger Quilter, first announced under the title of* The Wild Boar *but later given under its more familiar name of* Julia. *In the theatre the London Symphony Orchestra was in the pit, but on television credits were given to the 'BBC Television Orchestra'.*

*The original is torn at this point. It might conceivably read 'Victorian harmony'.

*

(181)
F. BUCKLEY HARGREAVES to E. C. THOMSON

32 Great Queen St
Kingsway
W C 2
9th November 1936

Dear Mr Thomson

I am sending you herewith a copy of the notes about 'PICKWICK' which I issued to the Press the other day and hope that these may be of some interest to you in preparing your Press release for Wednesday about the television broadcast of 'PICKWICK'.

I am also sending you herewith a photograph of Coates and Pickwick taken at a rehearsal on Saturday. I propose to release this for Thursday morning's dailies with a caption about the television broadcast on Friday . . .

The extracts from Pickwick *that were actually televised were:* Overture *(under the announcements);* 'Inn Scene' *Act I sc 4;* 'Pickwick's Rooms' *Act II sc 1* 'The Debtor's Prison' *Act III sc 1a; and* 'The Seven-Bedded Room' *Act III sc 1b. F. Buckley Hargreaves handled the publicity for the British Music Drama Opera Company Ltd. E. C. Thomson was the Press Representative for the BBC Television Service.*

(182)
THOMAS DUNHILL to FRAU MIMI MERCK

27 Platt's Lane
Hampstead N. W. 3
12 Nov 193[6]

Dear Frau Merck

Thank you very much for your very kind letter. Of course I should be delighted to have a Ballet produced at Hamburg.

I have written 2 Ballets recently. The first is rather a long one, & as it is founded on a particularly English story 'Dick Whittington' I very much doubt if it would be suitable, or would appeal to the public in Hamburg, or the performers.

The second is shorter & would be more suitable. It takes about 25 to 30 minutes. It is called 'Gallimaufry' (which means a 'Medley') & can be danced in any way that the choreographer wished to devise, as it is a succession of dances, & is a 'Divertissement' with no story attached. There are 8 numbers in it – including a Valse, a Galop, a Polka, a 'Pas de Fascination', & it ends with a 'Romp' for the whole company! I am, however, going to play it to Dolin on Sunday, & if he wishes to do it in London you will understand that it would not be free for performance in Hamburg just yet. I should have to have other copies made – as it is still in manuscript. I do not know Dolin's plans as yet. May I write to you again, & if the work is available for performance in Hamburg perhaps I could have a copy of the *pianoforte score* sent out to you. It is scored for ordinary full orchestra, which would I presume be available for a performance in Hamburg, if they cared to perform it. It is essentially *orchestral* music.

I appreciate your kindness very much indeed. Mrs Kerr mentioned the admirable way in which Ballets were performed in Hamburg, & I should be very proud to have my work produced there if it is possible.

I will write again. Meanwhile please accept my sincere thanks & believe me

Very truly yours

THOMAS F. DUNHILL

(183)
MEMORANDUM FOR MR. ROUCHÉ,
from SIR THOMAS BEECHAM.

December 9, 1936.

It was with great pleasure that I received Mr. Rouché's letter favouring my proposition that he should participate in next Summer's Coronation Season here, and his agreement, in principle, as to the three Operas to be produced. I also appreciate Mr. Rouché's courtesy in holding himself in readiness to discuss more closely the details of such productions.

It may be difficult, and indeed, after much experience, I know that it is difficult, for even the most knowledgeable persons on the Continent to comprehend exactly the English point of view about Opera. The fact is that, to the audiences of Covent Garden, and this has been so for about 200 years, Opera has meant singing, singing, and again singing, and not only singing, but singing of a very definite character. It is the commonest occurrence for artists who are a great success in their own country and the idols of large audiences, to come to London and to meet with no success. This is more frequently the case with French and Italian singers than German for, in the case of German Opera, which is infinitely more popular in London at the moment than anything else, the public minds less, putting up with a good deal of that which they consider to be indifferent singing for the sake of the music which they like. But this is not the case with French and Italian Opera, which today is rather under a cloud in England, and if the singers in it are not to the liking of the public, nothing else, be it beautiful orchestral playing or magnificent production, avails for five minutes.

I am permitting myself the reflection, because I am forced to remember that, during the past ten years, hardly any French or Italian singer has succeeded in winning the affection of the Covent Garden public.

It may have been that we have been unable to secure just those persons who might have been more fortunate, but Mr. Rouché will understand that hitherto we have been largely dependent in the matter of singers' engagements upon the advice of agents, and, judging by the result of such advice, it would appear that either we get the wrong singers in London or the good singers are not to be found in France today – which is, as Euclid might say, absurd – but I am raising these questions not only that Mr. Rouché, whose knowledge and experience of them is even greater than my own, may realise before we come to the discussion of just how these Operas are to be presented at Covent Garden, but to enable him to have plenty of time to consider this particular side of our casts, as it is by far the most important.

Undoubtedly, in this as well as in other directions, a great deal of time would be saved if Mr. Rouché could find it convenient to send to London a representative who, on the spot, would see the theatre and the stage.

I feel that, to correspond frequently and at length about the intricate technical things of stage work is always unsatisfactory. Perhaps Mr. Rouché would consider this suggestion and, undoubtedly the best time for a representative to come would be during the forthcoming Winter Opera season and, if possible, round about the new year.

> (Of course, I have written the above upon the assumption that nothing happens in the present constitutional crisis of the country to change or modify the scope and character of the extensive plans arranged as part of the Coronation proceedings of next Summer. At the moment, the position would seem more hopeful, but I am bound to bear in mind that the Coronation of a King other than Edward VIII would be a highly different affair to the sort of thing we have been looking forward to and planning for the past eight months.)

I have received a letter from Miss Lisa Perli in which she asks for my advice. Firstly, I may say that it was at my suggestion that Miss Perli abandoned a highly successful career as Concert singer in this country for the Opera stage. What led me to advise this change-over was not so much that Miss Perli was a good singer and had also the right kind of appearance for the stage, but that she was an actress of a singular and remarkable ability. Miss Perli has received an offer from Mr. Chauvet, of Vichy and Bordeaux, to sing for him the role of Melisande about the beginning of February in Bordeaux. I am advising Miss Perli to accept this offer. Together with all those who are acquainted with the work of this artist, for a long time I have held the view that Miss Perli is capable of being the Melisande of our time. Having this conviction, I have engaged her definitely for Covent Garden next Summer. But this role is something that is unique in music for complexity and delicacy, and requires far more than any other in the world a most extensive preparation. My own experiences are that the best preparation for an artist singing a role in one of the great theatres of the world is to have sung it in advance somewhere else, as no other form of study can replace this practical experience. In other words, Miss Perli has got to sing this role somewhere before she goes to Covent Garden. I understand that there is some slight possibility of Mr. Rouché considering this lady for his own production of PELLEAS ET MELISANDE at the Opera Comique, but I have no information about the possible dates of this production, and, anyway, it is only natural that Mr. Rouché must be considering the important question of finding singers for it with care and deliberation. And, in connection with this, I should not like Mr. Rouché for one moment to think that, because Miss Perli is singing Melisande at Covent Garden in a French Season which would be largely his affair, that I am in any way hinting or designing that she should take part in Mr. Rouché's very own representation at the Opera Comique. I always, in my own musical affairs, avoid as far as possible these international courtesies which involve the exchange of artists as, in nine cases out of ten, they never work well nor are they happy for anyone. At the same time, so far as Miss Perli is concerned, it would undoubtedly be a high compliment to her and to what might be generally called English singing, if she were for some time to sing this role at a French theatre. Without wishing to do more in this than express what would appear to me the commonsense of it, I think that the appearances of Miss Perli at Bordeaux are not only of the greatest value to her but might be of some service to Mr. Rouché's own artistic advisers.

I have indicated above the principal reason which led me to advise Miss Perli to take a theatre career, namely, her very remarkable power of stage imagination, quite rare in every kind of dramatic work. In my view, it is impossible for any Impresario or music expert to form an opinion of Miss Perli unless she can be seen as well as heard actually upon the boards of the stage. We all know that this lady can sing, but so can many other people. That which is the distinguishing note of her representations is that singing, acting and everything else form a complete synthesis, to be observed at the present moment in the operatic world in the case of two other artists only.

If Mr. Rouché has any interest in this matter, as I am casually informed, I think that the Bordeaux performances would provide an occasion for him to make up his mind in what is always a difficult and trying problem – the choice of a Melisande.

Miss Perli has also asked my opinion about the advisability of singing the role of Mimi in 'BOHEME' in French, and I have declared myself against this suggestion.

If I were a singer, I would never sing this opera in its original language if it were a question of my debut somewhere. In other words, it is a handicap which none making his first appearance in a foreign country should burden himself with.

This is all I have to observe on this subject.

Lisa Perli was the name used for operatic work by Dora Labbette. Under her real name she had sung in Beecham's 1927 recording of Handel's Messiah *and had frequently sung with him afterwards. It is said that her operatic name was arrived at because she came from Purley, Surrey.*

(184)
THOMAS DUNHILL to FRAU MIMI MERCK

27 Platt's Lane
Hampstead N.W.3.
14 March 1937

Dear Frau Merck
Very many thanks for your kind letter. It is very good of you to give me so much information. I shall be very happy if the Opera-danse authorities will pay my expenses to come over for the first performance. I know it is not possible for one to take any money out of the country, & I should not, in any case, expect to do so.

I hope they will arrange to have the orchestra-parts copied in Hamburg.

I do not think it is much use arranging for an agency for my works in Germany until I know that they are to be done in other places – or until the music of 'Gallimaufry' has been printed. And I thought I might write to Schott's house in London & ask if they would consider publishing the work – & I could tell them it was to be done at Hamburg & suggest that it might be performed in other places in Germany. Schott's already publish some of my violin solo pieces. I used to know one of the Strecker's very well – the one who was manager for Schott's & Augener's in London before the war. He was a very nice man. I think he must be in Germany now – probably at Mainz, which is their headquarters.

I am much interested that you have met Jean Francaix – I heard a Symphonietta [sic] of his on the Radio recently & thought it a very delightful work. He must be a very clever young man.

I have written *two* violin & piano sonatas – & both of them are published. I am getting copies of them which I will send to you. I think they are amongst my best chamber music. I should be so pleased if you were to play them – & I hope you will accept the copies with my very kind regards.

I am so grateful to you for so much continued help & kindness.

I am still confined to the house with sciatica – but I am getting slowly a little better, I am glad to say.

Yours very sincerely

THOMAS F DUNHILL

Dunhill's ballet Gallimaufry *was first produced in Hamburg at the Staatsoper on 11 December 1937 under the title* Die Eiskönigin *to a scenario after Hans Christian Andersen (see illustration 20). Dunhill subsequently went to Hamburg, arriving on Friday 31 December 1937.*

(185)
THOMAS DUNHILL'S DIARY

Saturday 1 January, 1938

"Eiskönigin".

At 1 o'clock I went to the Mercks to lunch. Afterwards, I drove with Dr M and the elder daughter to the Opera House. We had excellent seats in a box facing the stage. The performance began with my ballet. It was conducted by Theo Ziegler (?). Orchestra fine! It all came off most splendidly. The staging and dancing all *delightful*. Then they did "Maria im Walde" (a lovely episode) and Strewelpeter by Norbert Schultze – a modern who has the courage to be simple! My work was quite *modern* in style by comparison! But Schultze's music is most delicate and charming – especially the Maria ballet – *lovely* on the stage, too. Afterwards there was a tea-party at the Mercks', to which Helga Swedlund (?), Schmidt-Isserstedt and Schultze all came.

(186)
FRANK BRIDGE to BENJAMIN BRITTEN

F[riston] F[ield]
May 3 1937

My dear Benjy,
I intended sending you a line before this. It is an odd thing that music has to have really the right approach in order to make its own mark. I felt rather a lot of sympathy for you about Friday night's performance. Beyond 'Our Hunting Fathers' I heard almost no other words and this left everyone wondering precisely what it

was all about. Even Marg. 'Over the air' didn't hear the words. But, both Ethel and I got much more of your work at Norwich with all its shortcomings and bad conditions of rehearsal etc. The quintessence of disappointment on your face was so marked that had I had a few minutes alone with you, I might have consoled you with the fact that many a good work has begun its public life much in the same indifferent way. It is extremely hard to bear, but one *must* and I suppose *does* anyway. Of course, a real blot on the programme having a further display of xylophone* colour immediately, was perfectly sickening for us, and surely for you too?

You'll have to reconcile yourself about even the smaller public getting to know your work. Opportunities are not likely to be many. When we get together again remind me of this, there are a few things I should like to say sometime.

In the meantime try to get on with something important and forget the temporary nuisances of a composer. On occasions like Friday, it is a mistake not to be ready to put in an appearance. Even if audiences don't enthuse after a performance, they *may* like the *composer* when he appears.

But do cheer up,
love from us both,
Ever,

FB

P.S. Show me what the press did say. I noticed and thought a section of the Observer's notice had been cut out by the editor for want of space. If it were so then such manners are deplorable.

(187)
KENNETH WRIGHT to JULIAN HERBAGE

8/7/37

Since we heard the news from Alan Bush that his Pianoforte Concerto is going to run from 45–50 minutes, rather on the Busoni style, with Male Voice Chorus in the last movement, I have had two independent remarks from musicians who have heard the first three movements, and consider it Bush's best work and one of the few significant pieces of strong modern music available for concerts such as ours. Obviously Bush would have difficulty in finding anyone else who could produce it.

It cannot go in on March 18th with Maconchy and Darnton, because of timing. We might consider a work like Milford's Concerto Grosso as the last work here, as it deserves a public hearing, without perhaps being strong enough for a Symphony Concert, and would be rather a good foil to the uncompromising austerity of the Maconchy and the presumed gloom of the Darnton.

I suggest we revert to seven Contemporary Concerts, making No. 5 February 18th, (when the Wednesday Symphony Concert will contain a high proportion of

*The BBC performance of *Our Hunting Fathers* shared the programme with two premières – Leighton Lucas's *Sinfonia Brevis* for horn and eleven instruments and Rubbra's *First Symphony*. The Rubbra attracted much critical attention and was very favourably received. The Leighton Lucas, while sounding very mild to present day ears, incorporating Javanese Gamelan effects which included a lot of xylophone tone, which as it preceded the Britten, must have taken away some of the brilliance of Britten's score!

standard music) and make Bush's Piano Concerto with either Petri or Steuermann the main work. This is provisional upon some of us hearing the completed three movements at an early date and being convinced it deserves this inclusion. I have asked Bush if he will play it to us.

The last movement of Alan Bush's Piano Concerto *features a setting of words by Randall Swingler for baritone, and male-voice chorus, the movement altogether lasting about 20 minutes. This extract from the poem will give the flavour:*

> Bar: Yet in our day the influence of thought is caged and bonded
> like a bird whose wings beat in a vacuum.
> Music itself must fret like a pent flood
> that cannot reach the thirsting fields.
> The utterance of the human spirit is something that can be
> bought and sold as a mental luxury,
> while the poor hunger and their minds are warped and stunned
> by years of slavery and a servile education.
> And those few in whose hands the reins of power are gripped,
> hold the lives of millions harnessed, jealously guarding
> their wealth and privilege.
> And fear the liberating impulse & the uniting spell,
> the revealing beams of knowledge that all art begets.
> Choir: These are they who propagate subtle falsehoods daily,
> like poisonous gas, to corrupt opinion . . .*

(188)
PATRICK HADLEY to CECIL GRAY

Cozens Hotel,
King's Lynn
27 Aug 1937

Dear Cecil,
Something clearly must be done about that young man! It is noble of you to suggest financing the venture, but if I *could* manage to take him on I'd give him the time though deeply appreciative of your offer (how often one is expected as a musician to give something for nothing – but a case like this is quite different). The trouble will be fixing a time, for you say that being a medical student he is free only in the evening. I am normally in London only on Weds & Thurs. A considerable number of which evenings are taken up by Queen's Hall concerts, frequently both those evenings for several weeks running. So if, as seems only too probable, I shall not be able to help, we must think of others. There is Alan Rawsthorne, who would have to be paid definitely, and who doesn't like Delius, but who otherwise is fresh & keen, familiar & sympathetic with 'modern' continental (rather than English) effort, and who has at his command (I think) a fine 'modern' 'international' technique himself (I mean that in a good sense), and who moreover has been through the academic mill, be that an advantage or not as it may. I recommend him in the blue of course,

*See also: letter 193.

because I know at present neither the young man's work, nor the kind of study you think he should pursue; but if he were requiring a judicious mixture of purely technical work in the traditional but not too academic vein and free composition in his own style (with incidentally an ever watchful eye being kept over the harmful workings of that Delius influence) why then, I would (very tentatively of course for the present) be distinctly inclined to ask you to consider this Rawsthorne, whose composing talent I rather think will shortly be recognised by at any rate a few. He is easy to get on with, broadminded & the reverse of pedagogic and intolerant (I think H.H. may have begun to address a public meeting on the occasion of that contact).

If you would be inclined to consider this, what would be the next step, I wonder? I shall not be being in London for some weeks, but Rawsthorne is, and I am sure would come round and see you if you were to say the word. If you think it would help at all, I would of course be delighted to see his work, and to see the kind of words (if any) he likes to set, and so on, because all that naturally influences one's recommendations about a teacher, and the above is, as I said, only in the blue, and I am well aware of a certain danger, namely that such tendencies as he has in common with Delius whether the good ones or the bad may receive under the guidance I recommend a certain, though I am sure not merciless, discouragement. On the other hand this very thing might prove salutary if as seems clear the young man has character.

By the way, I've meant for ages to say how pleased I've always been that you put that young Chapman on to me. For years we've gone steadily on at a diverse variety of things – he always with the handicap of being overworked, underpaid & under leisured by Boosey & Hawkes. Now at last he's got a leg up, and I'm particularly glad because I always recommended him to stick to them on the chance of their one day recognizing & using his musicianship & now they have, but it means I shall only see him at rare intervals. He goes round to conductors, managers etc recommending scores & talking to them about them, and so far he has done very well. It is a new post created especially for him. He has, of course, inferior stuff to deal with as well, but he says he's had success with lots of serious modern & fairly modern, music for which B & H are agents.

Will you write another few lines to Heacham [Hadley's home]? I go back on Sunday having been turned out just temporarily on account of chimney sweepers. I was sorry I was just too short of time to get round to see you & Constant [Lambert] in Piccadilly that day, but I saw him the other day while passing thro' London.

Love to Marie

Yrs PADDY

(189)
LESLIE WOODGATE to SIR ADRIAN BOULT

THREE CHOIRS FESTIVAL – September, 1937
(GLOUCESTER)
26th October, 1937.

A great many interesting details emerged from this year's festival. Firstly that Herbert Sumsion is a very good musician and has improved enormously in his direction of the Choirs and Orchestra, secondly that the music of the Gloucester meeting is always a little better choice than the other meetings. It a great pity, however, that their ambition does not rise to greater heights. The most modern works in the programme were by Kodaly, and he was represented by two Choral pieces which are not to my mind, in the greatest style.

The Sunday service was not distinguished by any good performances, but it showed that the Choir was as good as usual. Lee Williams's Magnificat and Nunc Dimittis were sung 'In memoriam', and they are in good style, but rather imitative of Stanford. On Tuesday the main work was 'Elijah' and what a fine work it is. The first part is brilliant for its dramatic effects and splendid orchestration. The second part rather lags, I feel, in inspiration. The Soloists (Suddaby, Jarred, Trevor Jones and Henderson) sang well. Henderson acted dramatically, but did not quite 'get over'.

Wednesday's performances were excellent. The great work by Vaughan Williams 'Dona nobis pacem' took on an especial significance, and I think this is one of the greatest of all his fine works. The text is chosen with an insight belonging to genius. The bi-annual performance of St. Paul's Voyage to Melita by Dr. George Dyson was well done. In the evening the orchestral concert opened auspiciously with a light hearted overture by Arthur Benjamin 'Overture to an Italian Comedy'. This is an excellent bit of fooling, and I am surprised it is not seen in some of our lighter orchestral programmes. It is certainly worth performing. Myra Hess played beautifully in the Beethoven C minor. What a superb artist she is. Kodaly conducted his Dances of Galanta in a rather uninspired fashion – but they are lovely pieces.

The great work on Thursday was the Bach Mass. Dr. Percy Hull did extremely well with this, although I did not care a great deal for his nuances and dynamics. It was one of the best bits of Chorus singing during the week. In the evening Kodaly's 'Te Deum' was performed under the composer's direction. It was fairly well done, but I do not think Kodaly's conducting is at all helpful. A pleasant string piece by Herbert Howells, 'Elegy' came next, and the final item was Verdi's 'Requiem'. This was sung with great fire and zeal, and sounded grand. It is a fine piece, but to English ears a little over sentimental. I love it.

The final performance included 'Jesus and the Traders' (Kodaly). The choirs were woefully unprepared, and it was rather a fiasco. Kodaly conducted this too. I was most anxious to hear the scenes from Parry's 'Judith' (conducted by Sir Ivor Atkins) but I was terribly disappointed. It seems to me to be a rather manufactured piece, with only a little real Parry inspiration. Most of the tunes are four-square and the harmonisation calculated and not felt. The libretto is so bloodthirsty that I had hoped for some full-blooded music, but alas, nothing happened to make me shiver.

These Three Choir Festivals are a splendid mental tonic, and they are helpful to me so far as the training of Chorus is concerned. It is extremely useful to hear where the singers go wrong, and why, also to know why they sing so well, and why so badly. On the whole, the Gloucester Music meeting this year was one of the best ensembles I have heard.

LESLIE WOODGATE

Ivor Gurney, mentally unstable at the end of World War I, was little known before his forty best songs were published in four volumes starting in 1938, under the auspices of his friends Marion Scott, Howells, Finzi and Howard Ferguson. Gurney remained in the City of London Mental Hospital at Dartford, Kent, from 1922 until his death in 1937.

His later letters to his friends are incoherent as may be seen in this example, the text established from Gurney's manuscript by Dr R. K. R. Thornton.

(190)
IVOR GURNEY to MARION SCOTT

n.d. [ca 1937] letter from City of London Mental Hospital, Dartford

Dear Miss Scott.
Thank you so much – I return the W W. with the same acknowledgement as the
Shelley –
but perhaps the Football score. (Sunday)
   Hamilton Acads. 5. Dundee. 1. is as useful
However, there has been much music / and some yesterday. (I hope tea and
shortbread came after . . .), and much triumph over the survival of Carlsruhe. (x
London. a victor.)
if the present philosophy of Weimar is hard (to accept x) at least the terrible
memories of collapse (of the music-world) are forgotten.
Hampstead looks down on a tranquil and (determined) world, it seems.
   The thoughts on Kent are harder and fiercer – I leave them with F. W. Hebbel.
and with Gowans and Gray –
Today Langesulm may only be read. (instead of its divine music heard.) but I hope
the Dickens Inn has content and courage (.romance). it seems/England under
Richard III has pretty well all the same thoughts. As if Weimar could no more do
without Charles Dickens than we can – But perhaps this is that Kent County for a
while has to endure on Richmond ethics – (I call them glorious; as pain calls them
terrible). Its grand aspects forgotten until the spring. (x)
   But Gloucester City. and Gravesend (Rochester) are well remembered;
   And Richard Plantagenet. Earl of Gloucester. is a noble figure – that has won Paris
Province favour. (I mean all Prague praises . . .)
   Perhaps it was inevitable Hertford must have followed Richard of Gloucester.
   But I write under permission of Richmond or Brentford – or their secondary
councils.
   And there it is, this morning, later than the shadows of war.
(Strange that what R.L.S. prizes is as noble as victory itself.
   That W S is as noble and desired as war-victory.) Certainly W E Henley could not
avoid the honour of Rochester (x) as on January 25.

(I wonder truly   at the victory).

/ / I wish to write for some more money if I may. (Uncertain as to what there is,
perhaps 4/6^d)
There is so much torture/unforgivable).
And so therefore here to write for more money.

          —————

(I am sorry both the tales of P. B. Shelley & of Wordsworth
have had to be left-aside.
But remember Half Moon St. and remember Oxford
City's honours.)
It is true there is Thackeray. and there are Robert
Bridges books. (his Shelves. Methuen. etc)

And so. for David of Israel's sake may England receive
the honour of Robert Schumann's letters.

(x   Dusseldorf. 2. Weimar.   5)   f-s

With best wishes

IVOR GURNEY.

Last night was wonderful. (Barnet and Blackheath.) Richard III
as lord of all shelter and all night-freedom. (guilds.)

(191)
SIR ADRIAN BOULT to LESLIE BOOSEY

THE BRITISH BROADCASTING CORPORATION
Broadcasting House, London, w.1
December 2nd 1937

Dear Leslie

I have delayed some time replying to your letter of November 5th, I am very sorry. I
will send a small subscription to the League of Audiences, as you have asked. One is a
bit doubtful about the large number of societies that come and go, but it certainly
looks as if the League of Audiences was going to do valuable work.

I used yesterday, as you know, for the second time the full score of John Ireland's
'These Things Shall Be'. You have probably seen it; it is a very beautiful score in his
own handwriting, I think. I cannot help feeling that the work has in it the germ of
real popularity and importance at the present time, though whether that would ever
warrant the reduplication of that score is not for me to say. Personally, if I cannot get
the composer's own manuscript I very much enjoy studying and working from a
facsimile. I believe these photographic processes are becoming more reasonable now
and if I have the pleasure of conducting that work again I shall always ask for that
score. I can do this, I think, with some confidence because, with the exception of one
or two marks in light red pencil, I have left it absolutely untouched.

Six years ago Walton's manuscript of 'Belshazzar's Feast' was in the same
condition. This has, I believe, had one manuscript copy made of it, but I asked for
the old score for my own use on this occasion, and it is not too much to say that it has
been so covered with marks it is sometimes quite hard to see what the composer's
manuscript is underneath it all. It is highly probable that the next conductor who
gets hold of that Ireland score will start making the same infernal mess of it.

It is not for me to tell you your business, but you will probably forgive me for
calling your attention to what is, I fear, imminent!

Yours very sincerely

ADRIAN C. BOULT

(192)
ROBIN MILFORD to EDWIN EVANS

The Way House
Hermitage
Newbury
Berks.
26. XII.37.

Dear Sir,
The Oxford Press tell me that you are kindly writing programme notes for the Courtauld-Sargent performance of my Concerto Grosso, & would like to see the score.

I have got terribly behind owing to an appaling [*sic*] term of teaching, in which I had hoped, amongst other things, to find time to look through my parts for this performance, but couldn't do so.

So I am afraid I *must* keep the score a bit longer, as I must have everything as correct for Dr. Sargent as I can, but will let you have it as soon as possible (I do not know when Dr. Sargent will want it).

As to 'biographical material', I was born in 1903, and studied music under Peppin (at Rugby), & Holst, Vaughan Williams & R. O. Morris (at the R.C.M.).

My chief performances, previous to the present one, were of 'A Prophet in the Land' under Sumsion (Three Choirs Festival 1931), & of my Violin Concerto, my most recent work, with Brosa as soloist, conducted by Raybould (B.B.C. Studio Concert Jan. 29th 1938).* The Concerto Grosso was first performed at a Patron's Fund Concert in Jan. 1937, & again in June at a B.B.C. Studio Concert, both times under Dr. Sargent.

Please let me know if I can give you any further help; & I will send the score as soon as possible.

Yours truly

ROBIN MILFORD

(*This is a bit previous, I'm afraid – but I must hope that the fates will be kind & that this performance will actually take place on Jan. 29!) [It did.]

(193)
BBC PUBLIC RELATIONS EXECUTIVE to SIR STEPHEN TALLENTS

CONCERTO BY ALAN BUSH: Friday, March 4th.

2nd March 1938

D.D.M. [i.e. R. S. Thatcher] has brought this poem along as he is not sure whether it ought to be printed in the programme of the Contemporary Music Concert. He thinks it might possibly be picked on as an expression of opinion supported by the BBC. On the other hand, if it is not included the composer will doubtless feel that his work is not being justly treated. It will be sung by a male chorus. Do you see any harm in its being printed in the programme?*

Sir Stephen Tallents, the BBC Controller (Public Relations), noted 'Better print'. At the concert very considerable applause is reported after Bush's work had been played; Boult cut it short by launching the orchestra into the National Anthem.

(194)
KENNETH WRIGHT to ARTHUR BLISS

9th May, 1938

Dear Arthur,

Would you have first read of this report and hand it back to me at Panel tomorrow, if you have time to peruse it by then?

You will realise that this is purely my personal report: as unprejudiced as I could make it, and less enthusiastic than I would have honestly have liked it to be, especially as regards Lessing. I have never been to Germany before, whether for music or anything else, so I have had to rely on others for information concerning pre-war conditions and also last year's Baden-Baden Festival. Had I realised you were there in 1937 I should have consulted you before writing the report.

At least, I hope I may be privileged to renew my acquaintance with it next year in your company. It would be a nice gesture if you could find an opportunity to write something for Lessing. Ireland is working out something for Sacher. I feel it very important that there should be occasional first performances of British works in such festivals or series alongside Bartok, Honegger, Malipiero and the others. It all helps to line us up – as we can so easily be lined up – with music creation elsewhere. If you can't manage anything for Baden-Baden for 1939 I shall try Vaughan Williams or Britten, but I think you are a much more suitable composer for 'young Germany' in your present form.

By the way there wasn't a single critic from England at the Festival.

Looking forward to your visit on Thursday,

Yours ever,

KAW

*See letter 187.

(195)
BENJAMIN DALE to PATRICK PIGGOTT

17c Abbey Road
St John's Wood
London N W 8
22.7.38

Dear Patrick

I was glad to hear from you and to have news of your doings. It is disappointing for you that Casadesus is away – I suppose Fontainebleau is too far out for you to get along to him. Concerning Mlle. Boulanger, I am hoping you will be able to settle down and to do some good work with her: she is a remarkable person, and you can learn much from her, even though you do not share her taste for Poulenc and Stravinsky! Sometimes it is the other way round: my old teacher Frederick Corder, used to execrate Strauss and pooh-pooh Debussy (both of whom I secretly admired!) – but we understood each other quite well, all the same. Her understanding of *old* music goes very deep, and will help to point the way to useful things for you. Personal tastes are queer things in these days – you can find quite intelligent people belauding Donizetti and belittling Wagner! – and I don't mind much about [what] a person's views may be so long as he/she does not pretend an affection for the music of Schoenberg! Does Mlle B. give you any *technical* work to do – the writing of variations, or fugal work, etc?

I wouldn't worry about absolute pitch – I have had one or two *very* unmusical pupils who *had* it: and I believe Wagner had *not* got it! I am glad you have found a second theme for the Concerto. I thought the work began really well: remember it must be *idea & line* first: once you get these, *manner* and *texture* look after themselves: the last thing to worry about are the rhetorical flourishes! When the Concerto doesn't go, try some smaller pieces. If you could bring yourself to write within certain limits of difficulty, I feel sure the Associated Board would be glad to consider your pieces.

We are off tomorrow: address until about Aug. 20:

> GASTHOF SCHAUER,
> POSSENHOFEN
> STARNBERGER SEE,
> BAVARIA
> GERMANY

Let me have a line there.

All good wishes, and kind regards to your mother.

Yours

B. J. DALE

Patrick Piggott was one of the few British pre-War students of Nadia Boulanger in Paris, of whom possibly the best known is Lennox Berkeley, though he had completed his studies by this date. Patrick Piggott notes 'Nadia and I were certainly at one on the subject of Fauré, whose work we rated among the "great" music of the 20th century. Where Nadia and BJD were totally of one mind was in their hatred (extreme in Nadia's case – she compared him to a drug-peddler, deliberately perverting the young!) of poor Schoenberg!' Piggott's early uncertain reaction to such of Stravinsky's music as he had heard soon changed to a warm admiration of the greater part of the Russian's oeuvre, *and he several times joined Dale in a four-handed version of part of* The Rite of Spring, *to illustrate the latter's lecture 'Some Aspects of Modern Harmony'.*

(196)
CHRISTIAN DARNTON to KENNETH WRIGHT

Café-Restaurant du Théâtre
Neuchâtel
Thursday (whatever the date is) [October 1938]

Dear Wright,
I want to write to thank you for having put me in the way of Scherchen, as you so kindly did. He gave a lovely performance of my 'Suite Concertante' at the Lausanne Radio on Monday.

Although I have known Scherchen slightly for some years, I have never made close contact with him until the Festival, when we became very friendly & he invited me to stay with him in Neuchâtel. What a thousand pities that he has not a regular orchestra now! – I feel that his particular qualities place him very high among musicians. I can certainly say with regard to my own work that I had so many years given up expecting to hear a *true* realisation of my ideas that it came really as a terrific shock to find that at the *first rehearsal* of my work the effect was really moving. . . .

He is giving a series of 12 concerts in Paris this winter; he has done me the signal honour of asking me to write a special work for one of them. But I can't write music now. Unfortunately. I wish I could, for music is my life; although since I translated myself into engineering I have been living pretty satisfactorily.

(Please excuse the cafe pen – it's too hot to wear a jacket, so I haven't got my own on me.)

With regard to the rest of the broadcast, although I know Betty Maconchy's Suite, it was like hearing it for the first time. And the Purcell was absolute magic. I can but hope that when next Scherchen comes to our little island he will do something of mine.

Kind regards,

Yrs sincerely,

CHRISTIAN DARNTON

The pioneering conductor Hermann Scherchen, who appeared regularly in London between the wars, was to conduct a Contemporary Concert for the BBC on 10 March 1939. But in spite of lobbying by Darnton, Kenneth Wright was unable to include a British work. He wrote to Darnton on 6th January 1939: 'The programme is therefore to consist, in all probability, of the Schoenberg Kammersymphonie *in its original orchestration, and a work of Stravinsky. The latter would be ideally "Renard", but the Cimbalon part is so difficult that I am afraid we will never find a player sufficiently reliable to withstand the nerves and excitement of the performance . . .'*

(197)
OWEN MASE to SIR ADRIAN BOULT

LONDON MUSIC FESTIVAL
50 New Bond Street London W1
29-8-38

Dear Adrian

I'm a littled puzzled about Rubbra's Second Symphony. He does not seem to know anything at all yet about whether the BBC are going to put it on or not, & knowing how soon the Symphony Concert prospectus must be out, it seems strange.

He will, I understand, have the master ink score ready for you fairly soon. It strikes me there are possibly some weaknesses in the work (in what work are there not!) but that it is incomparably greater than say Britten's [Piano] Concerto performed at the Proms is surely unquestionable. What do you think is going to be done about it?

Hope you are getting some rest in this horrible climate.

Yours
OWEN

Owen Mase was director of the London Music Festival. Rubbra, writing on 10 November 1937 to thank Boult for a performance of his First Symphony, had indicated then that he had prepared a fair copy piano score of the Second Symphony, and played it through to him on 24 January 1938. On 16 August Kenneth Wright had written to Rubbra indicating that 'there are no plans for its inclusion in our programmes, although there will surely be some opportunity here or elsewhere next season'. Rubbra wrote again on 27 August and in the light of that letter and the one above, Boult felt that he must write to Rubbra with some hard information asking his staff 'what is our excuse for not giving the Rubbra symphony this season'. It had apparently already been proposed by Arthur Bliss as a replacement for a scheduled performance of the Walton Symphony in B♭ minor, but the Walton had been confirmed. In the end the Rubbra Second Symphony received its first performance on 16 December 1938, in a Special Concert. It is interesting to note that those admitted to the rehearsal included the composers Gerald Finzi, William Busch and Howard Ferguson.

(198)
WILLIAM WALTON to LESLIE HEWARD

Ashby St. Ledgers, Rugby
March 28th 1939

Dear Leslie

I'm sorry not to have answered your letter but what with having to give an unexpected performance of my symphony and all this bother with the British Council, I've had rather a chaotic and distracted ten days.

As you may have seen I've withdrawn my Concerto from the World's Fair not as is stated because it's unfinished but because Heifetz can't play on the date fixed (the B.C. only let him know about ten days ago!) Heifetz wants the concerto for two years and I would rather stick to him. But actually I'm afraid there is little to be said for either the British Council or myself, so keep this 'under your hat'.

So I'm out of the World's Fair altogether. I understand that all the music programmes barring those of the B.C. have been cancelled and that nothing is happening at all.

Unfortunately I know very little about American conditions, but I am going over sometime soon to look with Heifetz on the concerto probably the same time as you, and I most certainly will scout around and unreservedly reccommend [*sic*] you, which for once I can do with a clear conscience.

I couldn't sympathise with you more about Brum & opportunities here generally I must say are not too bright. But as I've said I will do everything possible when & if I ever get there.

Hoping to see you sometime soon.

Yours ever

WILLIE WALTON

(199)
E. J. MOERAN to MAY HARRISON

The Lodge
Kenmare
Co. Kerry
Whit Sunday 1939

Dear May

First of all, I must tell you I have had a series of misfortunes. (1) 'flu, when I rang you up. (2) I went to the Bournemouth Festival, stayed at Poole & was in a motor car collision, resulting in a dislocated elbow. (3) When I was fit to return here about early April, I was awfully run down. However, this was only natural, but apart from that I developed strange symptoms in my tummy, dyspepsia, little appetite etc: Arnold [Bax] may have told you if you saw him. This thing came to a head nearly 3 weeks ago: I should have gone to a doctor before. However, for a few days I was very ill indeed with fever & intense & sudden spasms of acute pain in what a certain very Victorian parishioner of my father's (she called legs 'limbs') once described as 'the lower chest'. It seems gallstone was the trouble – very unpleasant but, as you probably know there is now a treatment by means of diet & tablets that disperses any cause of future trouble i.e. if taken in the early stage. However, it cured my father, & he frail at the age of 75. He was very bad: he had had it coming on for years & had done nothing about it. I have a splendid Dr who, incidentally, is an old friend of my Valencia days: his home used to be there: he used to stay at the house where I lodged for week-ends, but he practises in Kenmare.

As a result of his treatment, I now feel better in health & more vigorous mentally than I have done for years. I have been working on some piano music, but it is too hot to try out fireworks at the keyboard. I am at the moment enthusiastic to get on with the vln concerto. Will you please as soon as possible get the 1st movement copied & sent to me with the bill, keeping the original for yr own use; I want to do the orchestration, & I made a number of alterations in your copy, so it differs from mine. I am going out to farm kitchens and out-of-doors Celiollies [*sic*] (they have dancing platforms on the Xroads here outside every parish – Irish Dancing only of course) & soaking myself in traditional fiddling with its queer but natural embellishments & ornamentations. This time of year the whole countryside is on the dance round here. In the 2nd movement I am planning to work some of this idiom into concerto form. I may tell you some of these people have a terrific technique in their own queer way. My landlord is motoring me out 16 miles this morning to hear one Murty Larry. He, I am assured on all sides, is the most brilliant fiddler in Kerry & Cork.

I am not actually doing much indoor composing this fine weather: it won't hold through the summer. My other musical activity consists of going up the mountain & filling pages of notebooks with ideas I am working out for another symphony. I might actually commence the actual composition thereof in the winter when the concerto & also the short pfte & orchestra work are, I hope, finished. It will be entirely different to No.1. I may say I think I have hit on a winner for my opening subject, thanks to the view from Moll's Gap looking across to the Reeks & Killarney Lakes 1000 ft below on a brilliant spring morning. There will be no gloom or Atlantic in winter in No.2. Please keep all this to yourself: I don't like being talked about, nor my activities either, as sometimes I go off at a tangent, e.g. the case of 'Phyllida & Corydon', which will be published any day now. I will, of course, send you a copy.

I think the Phil: are going to do it next season. The BBC would have liked it for the Prom: the night they have the chorus for the ninth symphony, but it is too long, 29 minutes.

As for the Vln: concerto, I see that next year it is proposed to extend the Bournemouth Festival to 2 weeks. How about my proposing to Dick Austin the production of it there? As you know it is a very important occasion, with the full battery of London & provincial press. I am too late to fix anything for London until the season 1940–41. If you agree, I shall go down & see Dick next time I am over to discuss it with him. I am all in favour of it: this last Festival the house was sold out every night. I expect to be in England from about June 23rd to July 10th. First of all, I want to see some cricket. As I prefer Kent to London in June, I shall go to the Tunbridge Wells cricket festival the last week in June, or part of it. Your sister Beatrice has often asked me to spend a day at Limpsfield (or is it Oxted?), but I can't find the address. Please let me have it, as I should like to avail myself of the invitation then. If you should be going down there, we could discuss the concerts: I may have more to show you, but I want to be in London at that time of year *as little as possible*.

Yours,

JACK MOERAN

The first performance of the Violin Concerto did not take place until the summer of 1942, when the soloist was Arthur Catterall. The Second Symphony was never completed.

(200)
HAVERGAL BRIAN to WALTER ALLUM

Ravens Field.
35 South Croxted Rd
West Dulwich. s.e.21.
1939,
May 10

Dear Walter Allum
I found your parcel readdressed from Lunham Rd when I arrived today. I thought
you knew all about this address. We came here eighteen months ago. I often thought
of you and wondered what you were doing: but letter writing has become a bore & I
never write unless compelled.

Those months we spent together under the same roof 22 years ago are vividly
recalled in this book.* You were very young then & I remember suggesting to Mrs
Valentine that you had abundance of brains & imagination. She agreed. Now where
are we? I think the book is a fine piece of writing – it gives the impression of having
been even slowly written – yet it has a light hand and plenty of poetry. I have no
criticisms to offer – but I have no influence with publishers. A man in Australia
requisitioned a book from me some five/six years ago. It was written & sent there –
but never claimed or paid for. I never heard again from him. Having the mss on my
hands – I sent it or took it round to various publishers, but had no luck. They all have
a routine of reading mss but there are certain publishers who are disposed to musical
books – Gollancz, Dent, Oxford Press, Kegan Paul, Macmillan, Constable, Arnold,
Putnam, Jonathan Cape for instance. Take care to register it when sending. I should
think that from a speech made by J.B. Priestley at Dent's Jubilee celebration dinner
that mss get fair treatment from readers. Priestley did say that as an author he loathed
the name of publishers and distrusted them. *This was said at a gathering of publishers* in
Stationers Hall a year ago!! I've no wish to alter anything you have said about me–I
think it 'just' as it should be. I will look up what Matcham Lee did write and send
you a marked copy – did you miss the publication of my Blake songs by Augener. I
will try & find a set. You never ought to have missed these for they were the two last
things written by me at Erdington and the climax of a phase I lived in during my
stay at Erdington when my opera [*The Tigers*] was written. Do you know that the
opera was *published* seven years ago? Not performed yet! I have often wondered
what my development would have been had not Mrs Brian been so urgent to pack
up soon as the war closed. Or if I *should* have continued to develop that way. One is
not conscious of such things and only recognises them years after they have taken
place. It is a fact that I have not written any music like the Blake in the years since I
left Erdington. I shall put these copies in your mss case when I return it on Friday. Of
course I shall be delighted to write an introduction and do all I can for it after
publication. I am so delighted that you have continued to employ your imagination
– you know I urged you to continue to practise continuously at composition &
poetry *every* day if only a little.

The most revealing thing is that *you* have tackled Shelley's 'Prometheus
Unbound'. Will you believe I started it a few months before we came here. I finished
the *pencil* sketches of the *first* act last Xmas Eve. It took me 3 months (spare time) to

* Walter Allum's unpublished autobiography.

ink them in and I started Act 2 on March 31. This has a long orchestral Prelude which runs direct into Asia's big song. Now I am just where Panthea is describing Prometheus' transfiguration. I agree with your criticism of it as being static & I remember that after I had got away from the great opening Prologue of Prometheus – I felt it collapse. I picked up Shakespeare & lost myself in the speed of the finale of 'Romeo & Juliet' – that I thought is the dramatic urge of which I am now full but which is not in Shelley. Perhaps I've made Prometheus bigger than it is. Anyhow I swore when a youth that I would do it – so I shall have to finish it to be loyal to myself.*

After I had commenced it – I tried to get into touch with the young parson with whom I used to discuss Shelley 34 years ago. He became vicar of Radley. Eventually I heard from him. He is now Chaplain at the English Church School of Music (Dr C S Phillips) & is a great authority on hymnology. But we haven't met. As he says – he is no longer young. When he was he had the Puccini fever – now he hasn't. But he tells me I taught him all he knows about modern music – I was very pleased at that: he says he looks out continuously for my name either as writer or composer & has listened to broadcasts of my things. I was very fond of him. I was listening to a young genius lecturing in the open air today on the birth and development of mother Earth. He was expounding things as I believe in them – yet there is one unsolvable riddle – even if we trace beginnings (physically) to protoplasm. We are still left guessing where mind came from – or how it originated. Our knowledge of such things is infinitesimal – the mind of a Shakespeare, Euripides, Aristophanes, Bach, Beethoven, Wagner – stands out apart from millions of others that the pity of its ceasing to function after death disputes such a claim as some make of its continuity.

I remember many years ago as a young man who had served his time to the English & foreign timber trade – going with my governor one Whit monday into Pelwall near Market Drayton to look at an enormous English Oak which had been felled & which he bought as it lay on the ground for £70. It was the talk of the county of Shropshire & he got it so cheap because – teams of horses had smashed up their harness in trying to move it & a traction engine had also come to grief. So the man who sold it thought my governor was cracked for buying it. When asked how *he* intended to move it in the face of what had already happened to the horses & the traction engine – he said in his broad Staffordshire – 'I *shan't* move it – I shall have a saw pit dug under where it lies and quarter it on the spot'.

It was my job to see to this and also to engage the hand sawyers for it – which I got in the Potteries. When the governor had completed the purchase – he said – 'Now lets have another look at it'. So he counted the rings and we agreed that the tree was standing there at the time of the Norman Conquest (1066). It had stood in a hedgerow between two meadows. When I went down there later I met the man who had sold it & I told him the age of the tree. He said 'I don't know anything about that – but the spread of the branches was so great – that both those meadows were kept in perpetual shadow'. So for hundreds of years, those two meadows never saw the summer sunlight until the great oak was down. The end of it was Bass's Brewery. Is not this an epitome of so many other natures[?] entanglements?

All my best wishes & good luck

Yours Ever

HAVERGAL BRIAN

*Brian completed his setting, of the first two acts only, of Shelley's *Prometheus Unbound* in 1944. It has never been performed, and the orchestral score is at present lost.

(201)
JULIUS HARRISON to LESLIE BOOSEY

6 Lyndhurst Avenue
Hastings
June 29th 1939

Dear Leslie
I return herewith the Five Madrigals by Edmund Rubbra after going through them
very carefully.

They are, of course, the work of a first-rate musician who knows how to write
splendid contrapuntal parts for each voice. Yet I ask myself the continual question –
can their many modern dissonant effects endear them to the public? I think not. The
Elizabethan madrigal composers managed to illustrate the changing moods of words
without recourse to such extreme dissonances, and nothing that a composer of today
can do will equal the felicity of expression found in the old works.

As an example of these dissonances turn to the last bar of Madrigal IV and two
similar places where a D Major chord has a superimposed F in the top part. While
admitting that these effects are less objectionable on voices than on the piano, yet I
find that my ear (used as it is to modern sounds) cannot endure such effects as this.

Nor will choirs like them any the more than I do. (I know Rubbra is trying to
illustrate 'beauty' as a 'painted hell' – yet that could have been done otherwise).

Then again – why that chord at the start of Madrigal II on 'I'?

Reducing my criticism to practical politics, I cannot see a definite market for the
madrigals.

I give you my frank opinion on them. I agree with you that they are indeed
interesting but I think many a musician will be frightened off by their dissonant
style.

Yours sincerely

JULIUS HARRISON

(202)
BERNARD HERRMANN to CECIL GRAY

Columbia Broadcasting System Inc
485 Madison Avenue
New York
Aug 1/39

Dear Mr Gray

Please forgive the lateness of this note. Your score and parts have arrived safely. I really do not understand your shyness in regard to your music; and why you should use a nom de plume. I think that your score is a fine, grand and exciting work. Tremendously original and very effective. The orchestration has many new and striking passages in instrumentation and I'll bet that the first orchestral entrance after the cellos in the very opening must throw one out of their chairs. The only influences I can find in the score, and only in a slight degree, are those of van Dieren (the II movement) and an echo of Busoni. Altogether you are to be congratulated on a really fine work. I am looking with a great deal of pleasure to hearing it. As I wrote to you, the orchestral apparatus is larger than what I have at my disposal at the present time so I have pass[ed] the score and parts to Howard Barlow (here at C.B.S.) and I know that at the first opportunity he will do it. Could you let us have score and parts for another four months? Perhaps I will still have the chance to do it yet. I really think you should change the title. The present one is much to[o] mystify[ing] for the general public, and I am afraid will scare them off. Why not simply call it 'Symphony'. You know it really is one, if not perhaps in the modern sense, certainly in the Greek sense of the word. Please use your own name on it, you really ought to be proud of the composition. I would love to see your St. Anthony, if only for my own pleasure. Could you send it over to me?

I am leaving next month for Hollywood to write a score for Orson Welles's movie 'The Heart of Darkness' of J. Conrad and I expect it will be a lot of fun. I will be back in N.Y. about Nov. 1/39 and then I hope I will be able to conduct your score, if I can't get the orchestra here at the station and if Barlow hasn't gotten around to it, I'll look around for an orchestral engagement and do it then. May I have the parts until then?

What are you doing now? Let me hear from you, won't you.

BERNARD HERRMANN

Cecil Gray used the pseudonym of 'Marcus Lestrange' when writing his 'Syllogism: or Thesis, Antithesis and Synthesis'. One deduces the work played to be Syllogism. *Gray's opera* The Temptation of St Anthony *was published in vocal score by Chappell in 1954, but remains unperformed. Gray remains the most enigmatic unknown quantity of British musical composition during the second quarter of the twentieth century. The Welles film* Heart of Darkness *was never made, and was cancelled in December 1939.*

(203)
J. W. LAWRENCE* to C. A. L. CLIFFE

THE THREE CHOIRS FESTIVAL AT HEREFORD,
SEPTEMBER 3rd–8th, 1939
18th August, 1939

The Three Choirs Festival at Hereford, September 3rd–8th, is a sufficiently interesting and important event to be worth broadcasting to Germany. Home programmes are not taking anything live but I should like, if money were available, to make a sixty minute sound picture for broadcasting to Germany, making use of extracts from the rehearsals and Even-song, Bach's *Mass in B Minor*, Vaughan Williams' *Pastoral Symphony*, Parry's *Job*, Elgar's *Gerontius* and finally Vaughan Williams' *Dona Nobis Pacem*. It might be possible to introduce some goodish material about the festival itself – how in Handel's time one meeting was given up entirely to his works, how Elgar was encouraged by the reception given in Germany to the first performance of *Gerontius*. We might be able to have a few words from Elgar's daughter and from Vaughan Williams.

The cost of the recording, I am told, would be about £25; we could probably get round the question of fees for artists by making a contribution to the festival funds and the total cost would probably not be more than £40 to £50.

I understand that German News talks are spending an average of only £20 a week and that reserves are already sufficient to pay for the News Sub-Editor until Christmas. There will therefore be enough surplus to cover this broadcast. May I have your consent for approaching O.N.E. with the idea of stealing some of his money?

War was declared on the day the Festival was due to commence, and it was cancelled.

*BBC European Programmes Organizer.

CHAPTER V

1939–1945

'Unless the War comes to an unexpected end...'

The initial reaction of musical entrepreneurs to the declaration of war in 1939 was much as it had been in 1914: cancellations of contracts and arrangements. In the case of the BBC it encompassed the wholesale evacuation of the organisation out of London (initially to Evesham and later to Bedford). For the musical profession the outlook was as bleak as that facing it 25 years earlier, with a dramatic decline in available work, and with many performing artists joining the forces.

Gradually a degree of normality returned, and indeed over a period of years an unprecedented demand for serious music arose in the public at large. This avid audience resulted in many initiatives to tour music and stage performances (ballet in particular demonstrating remarkable growth) and allowed many conductors and performers to develop careers that led to post-war celebrity. The BBC's role in the country's music making was reinforced, and many significant composers worked in various administrative capacities – including Bliss as Director of Music, and Berkeley, Searle, and others in various subordinate but important roles. The BBC's role in developing a national music policy was substantial, and its bureaucratic procedures provided important precedents for another institution which arose from the war, the Arts Council (originally CEMA).

As in the case of World War I there was some reaction against foreigners, though perhaps not so blatantly practised as 25 years earlier. However, it did result in many of those refugees who had fled to Britain from Nazi Germany and Austria being interned on the Isle of Man. Understandably, too, there was a rise of narrow musical nationalism and an official opposition to pacifist organisations and individuals. Those who managed to find themselves the wrong side of officialdom in these matters included such celebrated names as Alan Bush and Michael Tippett, and their predicament is touched on at appropriate points in the correspondence.

As far as established composers were concerned, one or two, notably Vaughan Williams, reinforced their stature in the eyes of the musical public during the war. Later the composition of specially commissioned scores for wartime films brought a wide popularity to several composers, and most of the serious composers of the period were involved in the cinema to some extent. At the climax of this trend came Walton's hugely popular score to Laurence Olivier's film of Shakespeare's *Henry V*. The BBC too commissioned many scores for use in dramatic productions and radio features, the most extended being Britten's for Edward Sackville-West's *The Rescue* and Walton's for Louis MacNeice's *Christopher Columbus*, both scores of considerable stature.

Possibly the most far-reaching influence on post-war music came from a group of musicians who were centred on Morley College in South London, and included Michael Tippett, Walter Goehr, Walter Bergmann and Matyas Seiber. Certainly Victorian and Edwardian composers were increasingly unfashionable, and, although a few orchestral works by composers such as Stanford were still played, most of the music of the earlier period was more and more neglected.

Of more far-reaching consequence was the emphasis on mainstream British music of the time, and the virtual disappearance of knowledge of or sympathy with avant garde trends, though towards the end of the war there were the very beginnings of an interest in such matters and a few isolated figures who had some appreciation of them obtained positions of influence.

It took some time for a style to emerge in musical affairs which would carry through the war, in the same way that in 1939 it was impossible to see how attitudes would develop and what positive might emerge from it all.

(204)
R. F. J. HOWGILL* to ROGER ECKERSLEY

27-9-39

Subsidies

I shall be glad if you will let me have a general statement regarding our position vis-a-vis bodies subsidised up to the outbreak of war. You have already dealt with the case of the Hallé Society and this and the circumstances applicable to all other bodies, should be enumerated.

For your guidance the decision taken by Control Board and the Board of Governors concerning Sadlers Wells was that no subsidy payment should be made during war time both on financial grounds and on the grounds of not using outside bodies of artists at the expense of B.B.C. employees but that we would pay for any programmes used on ad valorem basis. . . . This decision should, I think, apply to the other two opera ventures we subsidise, i.e. Covent Garden Grand Season and Carl Rosa. I think that you will have to study the contract letters and contracts in all cases to ensure that we are not liable despite the emergency. You may have to refer to B.M. for interpretation and to Programme Finance for any particulars not available for you.

I should like this statement by Tuesday next, 3rd October, as it has to be dealt with at Control Board on the following day.

*The BBC's then Assistant Controller (Administration).

F.C.Ex.
through
B.P.A.

Copy to
E.M.

(205)
HERBERT HOWELLS to MARION SCOTT

Redmarley
Barnes Common
s.w.13
25 Oct 1939

My dear Marion

I was glad of the post-card postscript that came with your letter: and I hope that by now H. Ferg[uso]n has received the proofs [of songs by Ivor Gurney] and looked through them. If there remains any further reading necessary, don't hesitate to send them to me: I have more than enough time to look them through these days.

I was glad to know that you were all in the quiet safety of Bridgwater – The quiet here is – as we all believe – only a preparation for the barbarities that will soon come – I marvel at the calm of mind in the population here – and pray it won't suffer too great a break when the raids come.

RCM goes on: and its being open at all is a sort of savings from the economic ruin that stares most of us in the face. Something of the initial economic fright is disappearing from the faces that were so long-drawn with anxiety in those early days of September: and I think Dr Dyson has shewn a very real courage – some have called it sheer stubbornness!

The sight of the young men going out of College and into War is depressing: but re-assuring too, because of the completely unfussed transfer they make between work they love and work they must hate.

I've been writing to young Eric Harrison*. Do you know him at College. He's a Halifax Scholar: pianist and composer – of quite outstanding gifts – but now a member of the 58th Anti-tank Regiment. He has been training for a month, but is already told he is to go to France in a few days time!

I hear Manning and Showan and the Commissionaire are all there.

Give our best love to Mrs Scott. And we hope you will find quiet and refreshing hours in Bridgwater.

Yours affcy

HERBERT

(206)
SIR ADRIAN BOULT to RALPH VAUGHAN WILLIAMS

October 26th 1939
Private

Thanks for your second letter. I return your B.B.C. reply. I did not write sooner because I have been moving about and I wanted to think over your letter a little more carefully.

I think you will realize that in a post mortem of this period I do not intend to be

---

*Eric Harrison survived the war. In 1945 he was the pianist in the first performance of Howell's Clarinet Sonata.

unvocal, and I think you will guess how I feel about the whole matter. I have perhaps been too easy-going in the past and only occasionally put forward the plea that I am the only broadcasting Director of Music in any broadcasting organisation who is not absolute master of his own programme policy. Between these four walls I can tell you that I am saying it pretty forcibly at the moment, but I do not think resignation would be any use or threats of that kind because I have reason to believe, though I have not been officially told, that a certain amount of the instructions that came to us in regard to these emergency programmes both at the present time and when they were planned some time before the crisis, had emanated from Whitehall, and I do not think Whitehall, or that part of it that is capable of giving instructions that the public is to be amused at all costs even when they have just been told that a battleship has been sunk, cares whether A.C.B. or X.Y.Z. is Director of Music of the B.B.C.

I do not want to make any excuses, but it is a fact that between September 2nd and 11th nine symphonies were performed by the following composers, Haydn, Beethoven, Dvorak, Mendelssohn, Mozart, Schubert, i.e. one a day. Did you realise this? I admit that many of them were at impossible times to listen, but, rightly or wrongly, we have assumed (no doubt here again under instructions) that most of Britain had gone on to a shift system and would be listening at all times of the day. Did you see that delightful letter from Manchester in last week's Radio Times about the eight o'clock Concerts? It made me want to do one every day.

In regard to the enclosure, which I return, I have taken steps to see that the Director-General personally sees your letter. He has been travelling a good deal, and it may have been passed on in his absence.

(207)

E. J. MOERAN to MAY HARRISON

The Lodge Kenmare Co. Kerry
Nov. 4th 1939

Dear May
Many thanks for your letter. This war is a crazy business and by to-day's papers looks horribly like spreading. I do not think the B.B.C. come out well. Having half-ruined the L.S.O. & other organizations by competing as public givers of concerts, they sack about half or more of their players in London & the provinces & retire to the country. The L.S.O., Phil: and others stick to Queens Hall and carry on. The[y] have completely let down Bournemouth for no reason that I can see. Why on earth should the war prevent that weekly outside broadcast, the contract of which enabled Dick Austin to maintain a fine orchestra [the Bournemouth Municipal Orchestra], & now he is reduced to 24 players!

I found I could do no work at all when the war started for some weeks. I have now steeled myself to the task and am pegging away. I was at the Violin Concerto yesterday I saw Ken Wright just before I left England last time. He made a definite offer for you to do it next Proms. By the way, with regard to the Phil: I had already more or less promised it for the B.B.C. I never spoke to the Phil. about it, but you seem to have done so. However, unless the war comes to an unexpected end, it is no good discussing these things.

I imagine the B.B.C. orchestra is at Evesham, for I heard from Wright from there the other day c/o P.O. Evesham Box 6. If I am in London I will ring you up. It is very unlikely that I shall be, although I hope to go to Kington for Christmas. It is rather complicated getting out of Eire. One has to have a permit and this takes time to get. I hope London will continue to be safe for you!

Yours sincerely

JACK MOERAN

P.S. If the war continues & there are no Proms, if the Phil: continues to function it might be worth sounding them but the work is by no means finished, as I have re-composed the middle movement from the beginning.

Moeran refers to the Royal Philharmonic Society. The work he is preparing is his Violin Concerto, *ultimately dedicated to, and first performed by, Arthur Catterall.*

(208)
SIR H. WALFORD DAVIES to RALPH VAUGHAN WILLIAMS

The Deanery
Bristol
9th November, 1939

Dear Ralph
The various efforts to promote music-making through every part of the country are clarifying, and Adrian, Thatcher and I met Barnes of the B.B.C. yesterday and got approval for instituting a weekly broadcast to give, by word of mouth and by examples sung and/or played there and then, all possible practical help to amateur music-making.

The scheme is meant, and will be conceived throughout, as an attempted national service to music-makers everywhere and not as a broadcast 'turn', more or less entertaining to listeners generally.

It will be necessary to ask those who have done things to come and suggest to listening amateurs how things are done. And I'm afraid you are the first we are obliged to trouble about it.

We have been offered to begin with an introductory set of six talks at a *Sunday* time when everybody is likely to be listening, 8.45 to 9.0 pm, just before the 9 o'clock News. I am to introduce these on November 26th, and on the four succeeding dates – December 3rd, 10th, 17th, 24th – four orders of music-making in all districts throughout the black-out of winter are to be dealt with. I promised Adrian I would write and beg you to take the first of these on December 3rd. I was afraid it would mean going to London to do it that Sunday evening, unless indeed you felt able and inclined to come on the Saturday to Bristol and do it from here with Adrian to arrange any illustrating of your points (solo or ensemble) which would be much better.

Yours

HWD

*

(209)
SIR HENRY WOOD to JULIUS HARRISON

The Old Ship Hotel
Brighton
January 26th 1940

. . . I quite appreciate your difficulties with regard to programme making, for obviously there is only one thing to do these days, and that is to give the public what you know it wants, and not perhaps just what *we* should *like* them to hear; but sufficient be it, if the flag of the Symphony Orchestras can be kept flying – even with the depleted numbers which are at present the rule. Such work as you and your colleagues of the watering places round England are doing, is worthy of great support, for well I know you must suffer musically, and yet peg away as you are doing.

. . . if I can but bring the subject of subsidy for music to the notice of the public, and later on the Government. If only every musician would pull the same way for this cause, I honestly believe the time is ripe, in spite of the War, as people realize more than ever what a tremendously important part fine music plays in our National well being, now that it is missing so much. Can't we think of something?

*

(210)
GRACE WILLIAMS to THE BBC

9 Old Village Road
Barry
Glamorgan
26–2–1940

Dear Sir
I should be grateful if you would submit the enclosed M.S.S. to the Reading Committee

1. Five Pieces for Orchestra } Daniel Jones
2. The Sorrows of Bronwen

3. Fantasia on Welsh Nursery Rhymes
4. Gogonedawg Arglwydd } Grace Williams
   (Praise the Lord Eternal)

Last year I had my Magnificat for Soprano & Orchestra accepted by the Reading Committee, but on the outbreak of war it was returned to me as there was little prospect then of any new works being performed. May I ask whether by any chance you wish to recall all those works which had already passed the readers & were ready for the Programme Division? ...

(211)
CHRISTIAN DARNTON to KENNETH WRIGHT

22 Fitzroy Street
w.1
10 March, 1940

Dear Kenneth Wright,
... A long, long time ago; such a long time ago that it is now almost 'once upon a time'; we had a grand time in Poland* ... At intervals since then I have frequently been on the point of writing to you; have even reached the stage of formulating the opening sentences of my projected letter. But it is for me a herculean act to nerve myself actually to write a letter. When I do, however, I am not easily stopped.

... Now believe this or not; but I hope you will believe it: on Monday last, a week ago today, that is, as I lay preparatory to getting up in the morning; once more I said to myself 'I must write to Kenneth and ask whether the B.B.C, who always used, until for the first time my name (such as it is) became briefly quasi-internationally known through the Festival, always to do quite handsomely by me, have not now quite forgotten my existence. Because', I reflected, 'I used to get about 3, 4 or even 5 broadcasts a year until 1939, the year in which, after all, those pieces of mine did have some success; and in that year the BBC took not the slightest notice of me. And so', I went on in my mind (continuing my draft letter to you) 'it really is about time that something was done – if not something new, then something not so new'. I was, you see, definitely going to write to you last Monday, saying something of this to you, and telling you also that I am now engaged on a Symphony, which has been keeping me busy since the beginning of December. I am now half way through the 2nd of the three movements.

... I went downstairs for the post – and I recognised the BBC typewriter, that envelope which defies all normal methods of opening, and which only my solicitors use apart from your goodselves, and finally the Bristol postmark. Ah, I thought, is it possible at last that some one has remembered me?

... Consequently, you may imagine that I was surprised to read your letter – for I knew nothing whatever of OUP having sent the score of my 6 Pieces to you. I can but bow to the judgement of your Programme Committee, and leave it at that. For it is never for such as I to reason why; mine but to do and, alas, die. It is true, of course, that a passing thought comes into my head: are we not, I ask myself, supposed to be fighting someone in the name of the preservation of Civilisation? Yes, I answer myself, indeed we are. For our own Prime Minister has said as much. He also threw in Liberty as an additional cause for good measure. The stumbling

---

*The ISCM Festival in 1939 was in Warsaw and was attended by several British composers. It was the occasion of the first performance of Rawsthorne's *Symphonic Studies*.

block here in the argument is the definition of Civilisation. It is there, probably, that the Prime Minister and, perhaps, the BBC, differ from me. (I am not abashed: I am not afraid of differing from the Prime Minister). For he, I feel, had in mind the Sanctity of International Treaties, the Freedom of Expanding Trade (British Trade), and a Liberty whose nebulosity is so finely embodied in our glorious Constitution which has made England what it is. I concede readily that all these things are most important. But for myself, speaking as one of the Oppressed Minorities, I hold also that a little word, culture, which the Germans spell with such a large K, is also an integral part of Civilisation; and that always the status of a people depends not so much on its relative advancement of technology and sanitary services as on its place in the World of Ideas. I conclude, therefore, that at this particular moment in time, more possibly than at most others, when this World of Ideas, this precious thing, is (as the Prime Minister admits) in danger of occlusion if not eclipse, it is of the greatest importance to foster and encourage its exponents and representatives in the *avant-garde* of the Cultural Front. An occasional glance at the Radio Times, however, shows me that in this view I am at variance with the BBC – or with someone. For I can but beg you to believe that it is not only for my own sweet advancement's sake that I take so earnestly to this problem. I look in vain for any music by significant composers who are not actually dead. I see no sign of Stravinsky's new symphony, of Hindemith's latest 7 sonatas, of Webern's latest work, or, indeed, of any of their important works of any period . . . And they are only three names of many.

. . . Well well . . . I retire and go on patiently writing my Symphony. It must be written, because I have a kink that way. And it's going well. But the outlook is, on the whole, not very encouraging, is it?

. . . This letter must cease. Apologies for its exorbitant length. If ever you come to the metropolis, can we meet for a drink? I'm not on the phone here at a studio I've taken for working while my family is rusticating.

– Kind regards, Yours sincerely,

CHRISTIAN DARNTON

To see the way the war affected the practical business of everyday musical life, one needs to look at how one of the leading music publishers coped. The following letters are from a continuing correspondence between Ernest Chapman and Erwin Stein, both of Boosey & Hawkes. First Chapman was called up, and then Stein, a refugee from Austria, was interned to the Isle of Man. Chapman attempted to keep Stein, his boss, up to date about the progress of business.

(212)
ERNEST CHAPMAN to ERWIN STEIN

Guards Depot
Caterham
Surrey
30th May 1940

Dear Mr. Stein,
Numberless apologies for the long delay in replying to your interesting letters and
enclosure of the 16th. Since I came out of hospital (just over a week ago) I have been
very busy indeed and, indeed, have not written a letter to anyone during the last few
days. Owing to the length of time I was in hospital (10 days) I had to start my
training all over again when I came out – curse my luck! Despite the strictness of the
discipline, I'm beginning to take rather a liking to this place – there is a huge number
of recruits here, of the most varying types – most of them labourers, factory
workers, drivers and suchlike, and I've made friends with quite a number of them.
Three in particular, with whom I keep close company, are, respectively, a taxi
driver, a footman, & a meat salesman! It's a highly interesting experience; a lesson in
human nature, & I'm glad to have had the opportunity of making contact with so
many kinds of people one does not usually run up against in everyday life. 'Out of
evil' . . .
    Dealing with your letters: (1) the 'Concertino Pastorale' records sent to Hein-
sheimer were paid for by B & H. If he is willing to pay for them, so much the better.
(2) *Engravers*. It's obvious that we are getting seriously behind with our publications
schedule, and I certainly think we ought to have some more men working at the
engravers. I dare say that not much business is being done in England or Europe at
the moment, but on the other hand, we must keep U.S.A. supplied with new items
if we are to build up our reputation there, and also there is everything to be said for
having a good list of new works in readiness for when the war finishes. At any rate,
either the new scores should be brought out at once, or not at all. It's not much use
publishing the things in the autumn when the concert-seasons in all parts of the
world are already in full swing & the programmes all compiled.
    (3) *Szell, Perpetuum Mobile*. I note H.H. says in his letter of May 3rd that *they* are
publishing this in New York! To hell with 'em! Everytime they get something (such
as the 'Chestnut Tree', or this) which might prove really popular, they print it over
there, but when it's something doubtful or bad – Copland 'Music for Radio' or the
Bach-Vivaldi Concerto – they send it over to us, to spend *our* money on it! Surely
this ought to be put right, or at least pointed out? Otherwise Dr. H will appear in the
light of an infallible chooser of 'Winners' and make us appear responsible for the
'duds'. Impertinence!
    (4) *Veress.** *Verbunkas*. I'm awfully glad Mr. R.H. has agreed to publish this. No
doubt you have already written to Sandor to tell him. Do, please, start engraving it
soon. The piece has distinct possibilities, and it's certainly time we did something for
our young Hungarian friend. Don't forget it is also available in an orchestral version.
We shld. have the score & parts for hire (in MSS), & a note to this effect shld. appear
in the printed V. & Pfte. version. Perhaps also a short note explaining the title? If you
write to Veress during the next few days, tell him I'll write him a letter during the
next week or so.

*Sandor Veress (b. 1907–   ), Hungarian-born composer

(5) *Ferguson. Piano Sonata.* I was v. interested to read Mr. R.H.'s remarks about this. Is it to be published, and if so by whom? I honestly cannot see the point of it being published by U.E. London. Hawkes have always published F's works, and to skip about from one edition to another makes the whole idea of keeping the various editions separate a farce. Why not a new firm and name for every new work? Even although I do not think any money will be made out of the work, I still think that, if it is to be published Hawkes shld. issue it, for the sake of uniformity.

(6) *John Field Suite.* I'm glad to see that this is making such a favourable impression in U.S.A. Personally I *am* in favour of selling it outright. I think that had it been issued in the Concert Edition (with score, of course), it might have sold & been played v. widely indeed. As it is, I think that many amateur orchestras, who could easily play the work, will not pay a hiring fee. However, perhaps it wld. be better to keep for hire only during the war, as so many of the less important orchestras will obviously not be carrying on.

(7) *Bartok.* Very glad to hear that Kolisch is going to do the 6th Quartet, but do you really think he will pay us $10.00 each for thirty performances? Publishing the miniature score in November will be alright, but a note will have to be included saying that K. has the rights for 1 year, and that printed *parts* will be available after that date. Otherwise other quartet players will be liable to forget its existence by the time K.'s period is up. What a splendid article Glock wrote in the 'Observer' about 'Mikrokosmos'! I presume of course that you sent one or more copies immediately to R.H.? By the way, there are some important pianists in England who should receive free copies of the 6 Books. They are: *Harriet Cohen, Louis Kentner, Clifford Curzon & Kathleen Long.* Would you ask Mr. Schwalbe whether copies have been sent to any of them or not. I suggest it wld. be very good propaganda to do so.

Would you please send me scores of the Bartok Divertimento and Copland's 'Music for Radio'. I don't know either work very well yet and can look at them during odd moments.

Any news from John Ireland? The Downland Suite?

Many thanks for mentioning the fact that I am keeping contact with you in your letter to Mr. Ralph. I hope it won't be many more weeks before I am able to spend part of each day in the office!

You may be horrified to hear it, but I don't mind confessing that I've taken quite a liking to hot dance music since I've been down here! Actually, there is so much of it on the radio (which is installed in every barracks) that it sinks in the subconsciousness like a pleasant and harmless drug. I can whistle nearly all the latest dance tunes – the slow ones are the best – and am beginning to wonder whether I shall appreciate serious music at all when I return to the world of music again.

Yours ever
ERNEST CHAPMAN

P.S. I am returning the letters from New York in a separate envelope as they will not fit into this one.

*

(213)
ERWIN STEIN to ERNEST CHAPMAN

Boosey & Hawkes Ltd
London w.1
6th June 1940

Dear Chappie,

This time I must apologize for not having written to you before, but of course the delay was caused by my fellow workers as well! ...

Now about business: The main trouble is that we are well behind in our publication schedule. . . . However, you may be sure that I shall try to push things on as much as I can.

VERESS – I wrote to him immediately and will write again as soon as the assignment is sent. Please let me know whether you have also written to him.

FERGUSON – I understand that this question has not yet been decided and indeed such decisions are not likely to be taken at present. At all events, I expect the work will be Hawkes when it is published.

BARTOK – The 'Divertimento' was not performed in Basle owing to Swiss mobilisation which also affected Sacher. However, he hopes to be able to do the work during the next few weeks, but he cannot make any plans for next season. I'm afraid the same will happen with all European societies. Schwalbe sent copies of 'Mikrokosmos' to the people you mentioned and to the press. He did the same with Bartok's 'Divertimento' and Britten's 'Illuminations'. Copies of the Copland and Delius will be sent out later on.

DELIUS – 'HASSAN SERENADE' – I have sent out scores for inspection to conductors in England and free copies to Wood, Harty, Boult, Cameron, Warrack, etc. When 'Walk to the Paradise Garden' is ready, I am going to send out a circular letter.

I have had no news from John Ireland. Do you think I should get in touch with him? As far as I know, he is still at an hotel in Guernsey – Birnam Court Hotel, Queen's Road, St. Peter Port. I was very amused (Miss Reid too!) to hear about your predilection for 'Swing'! I should be very glad to hear your views on this.

'KERMESSE CANADIENNE' – I was not able to go to Bristol as there are further restrictions now for aliens and I should have had to get a Permit from the Police. Honestly I was not very keen to do this. I wonder whether you will be able to hear it this evening. I quite agree with your idea of sending out a press communique about Britten. Thank you for your offer. I will send you a draft shortly. The only trouble is that the boy writes so many new things at the same time. (See the enclosed articles from the 'New York Sun').

PROMS – I wrote to Sammons and asked him whether he had been in touch with Keith Douglas about the Bloch Concerto. So far I have received no reply from him. I think it might be a good idea if you wrote to Keith Douglas yourself, though of course nobody really knows whether the Proms are definitely going to take place! ...

NEW PUBLICATIONS – I quite agree with you about the prints. The Bartok and Britten scores are much admired everywhere (even in America, as you will see from Mr. Ralph's and Heinsheimer's letters). . . .

The L.C.M.C. concert was very interesting. I went to one rehearsal of the Berg and they all tried very hard with it. They are all good musicians, but to master a piece of this kind, they really need another fortnight's rehearsal. Nevertheless, it seemed to impress the public.

DELIUS – COMPLETE EDITION – We have taken up this matter and are meeting Mr. Philip Emanuel, the Estate lawyer, very soon. I have been in touch with Dr. Geissmar about this, and she thinks that some of the scores in Beecham's Library are suitable for printer's copies. This is, of course, a matter about which we should have to communicate with Beecham himself, before actually starting on the engraving. I will let you know all that happens in this connection.

(214)
SIR ADRIAN BOULT to RALPH VAUGHAN WILLIAMS

September 9th 1940

I am delighted that you even 'consider' the possibility of accepting the commission.

You ask for more details. I had better quote the terms of reference in the document dealing with this commissioning.

'The commission will be for a song or lay hymn, with orchestral accompaniment, the *theme* patriotic but not necessarily warlike; an *air* theme especially welcome; caveat – the word "England" to be avoided as a synonym for Britain. For the *lyric*, the composer can take his choice of existing lyrics, or, if preferred, he can await the result of the commissioning of the poets; the *length* to be two or three short stanzas totalling, say, not less than six and not more than eighteen lines'.

The B.B.C. would be glad to be able to know the poem you propose to set before you actually embark on the setting of it.

To answer specifically the question you put in your letter: it is certainly the 'Jerusalem' brand that we want. If you can find your inspiration from the old masters, so much the better; but anyway I will ask Miss Somerville (who is the medium for commissioning on the literary side) to let me have appropriate modern poems to send you. Finance I am not in a position to tackle, but I will get the detailed proposals sent to you straight away.

Presumably this resulted in Vaughan Williams's England, My England, *for baritone, chorus and orchestra, first performed on 16 November 1941.*

(215)
FRANK BRIDGE to BENJAMIN BRITTEN

Friston Field
[undated]

My dear Benjamin (as Sophie Wyss would have it)
You never pointed out to me that Benjamin was the signature of the tribe! I imagine you have had your permit to stay in the USA seen to long ago, unless you are

buzzing back to Canada. Ralph said he would invite me to hear a run through of the Concerto by Paul and Henry Boys, but it never came off, although I was in London on the very day that it did happen, by chance. That's all I know about it. There are rumours of a Piano Quartet with Orchestra for Toronto and a Revue for New York. I wish I felt happier about this last (with the New Statesman writing of the two recruiting sergeants . . . being away in America).

As you probably know, there was a complete breakdown of programmes and entertainments generally on the B.B.C. when hostilities began. Quite apart from the removal to 'somewhere in England', no one seems to know precisely what upset the organisation. But upset or upside down it assuredly was. Everything was cancelled. For the first five or six weeks, except for news, it was quite difficult to understand what was being aimed at! However, there is recently some improvement. They managed to get Gracie Fields to broadcast sometime before she entertained the troops in France. And Sir A.B. 'did' the *Eroica* just before midnight, and people give piano recitals at 7.10 am and so the art of giving the crowd what they want is now thoroughly understood.

You can say nothing appreciative about America and the Americans that is not endorsed by me. That is, all those that I know are a part of one's own small world. They add to it rather an important section. One where queries and question marks are taboo, a kind of buffer between inevitable old age and the last remnant of youth and any other fantastic expression which includes rest, sympathy and personal interest. In other terms, I never knew how much I had been without until I found myself in possession of it, and since 1923 too!

Upon looking closely at your address, I see it is not Coney Island Home. No connection with our own Colney Hatch. Oh dear, dear no !! I never could make out that American enthusiasm for Ville. I always thought they felt it rather 'chic' . . . a touch of French, say. Now – Amitystadt – what about it?

Some years ago, driving on Long Island, I remember getting out of the car, the road having ceased abruptly on a sandy shore, bending down and swishing my hands in the sea sending a few ripples straight over to Cornwall. Just a sentimental moment, of course.

We have had some of the most fiendishly bad weather ever in our Friston history.

At long last, the billetting officer foisted two evacuated children upon us, they are Croydon kids.

All this is a nasty socialist move – make the blighters that have six inches more cubic space than they need, than they positively need etc. All very well, then, but to force one to look after evacuees is the limit. One's personal attention is demanded, and enforced. Think of it! To be caught, because one has a cottage, to take kids, see that they have baths, cure their colds – poor Bill – and me, and her not able to leave Friston because of . . . Defence of the Realm Regulations.

And you've no idea what you miss . . . ! All good wishes for Xmas, my dear Benjie.

Understand this if you can, Tosc. [anini] gave one in London with NY orch, a super performance of *Eroica*, of which you have heard before now. But Bill and I heard a really poor show of Tsch. *Romeo and Juliet* in N.Y. only last year, and other things too. But, dear Benjie, – hold tight – only those capable of criticism understand the truth of criticism, very few, I fear, do not attribute base or false motives to serious criticism, in fact – as you and I know – the entire world of music is out of step . . . with our Johnny! Isn't that so?

*

(216)
ERNEST CHAPMAN to ERWIN STEIN

6th September, 1940

Dear Mr. Stein,

Many thanks for your letter of August 9th. I must apologize for not having answered before, but it has been very difficult during the last fortnight as Thompson has been away on holiday and of course I am only able to come here for a few hours each afternoon. There are numerous air raids nowadays and we have to keep stopping our work to go down into the basement, all of which means even less time to get through the various jobs which have to be done. So I hope you will not think I have been wilfully neglecting you.

Mr. Leslie tells me that he is still making every effort to procure your release, and I sincerely hope it will not be long before you are back here. Having been three months in barracks, I have a good idea of what it is like, although of course none of us can hope to carry on our lives just as though the war never existed. Mrs. Stein was here the other day and we had a very nice talk together.

Life in London is very exciting nowadays. We have several air raids each day and night, but for all the planes the Germans send over and all the bombs they drop, it seems to make very little difference to the populace. . . .

I quite understand about the exchange of materials between New York and Canada and South Africa and Australia. I will see that this is done wherever expedient.

Regarding Continental business in general, do you think it is worth my while trying to do business in the few remaining free countries? (Portugal, Switzerland, Turkey, Sweden, etc.) I have such a lot of work on my hands that I honestly do not feel inclined to make any efforts. However, I should like to know your opinion as to whether it would really be worth while.

BARTOK – The performance of Bartok's 'Divertimento' did take place incidentally and press reviews came through from Basle the other day. They have not been translated yet, but Miss Reid says they are very good. Bartok and his wife are going back to America in November and are going to do a big tour both performing and lecturing. B.H.B. have arranged quite a number of performances of the 'Divertimento', notably under Barbirolli and Vladimir Golschmann. The composer will probably be present at some of them.

As you request, I am sending the MS of the String Quartet No.6 so that you can look this over before we commence engraving. We have, however, just received a letter from Mr. Ralph saying that he would like to have the score printed as soon as possible, and I should, therefore, be glad if you could deal with this as quickly as you conveniently can.

BENJAMIN BRITTEN – I am sending you a piano reduction of the Violin Concerto. I sent the work to the Royal Philharmonic Society but they turned it down and Keith Douglas said that Britten was 'unpopular' with them because of his domicile abroad! I am afraid there have been similar hints from other quarters about Britten recently and it seems as though it may become difficult to keep up his performances. I have also contacted the B.B.C. and the Courtauld-Sargent Concerts about the work, but there is no definite news yet. Did you know that Britten has been commissioned by Paul Wittgenstein, the one-armed pianist to write him a Piano Concerto for the left hand, and that he suggests paying him $1000 for it?

Weis ordered the parts of 'Les Illuminations' at the same time as 'Music for Radio'.

KODALY – Mr. Ralph in his last letter from New York, says that he is in touch with Kodaly and that big things are in the offing. But . . . I refuse any longer to take any notice of such vague promises. Only when a Kodaly contract is sealed and signed shall I expect to see the score of a new Kodaly work!

THE FAITHFUL SHEPHERD – Thank you very much for sending back the proofs of the Handel-Beecham Suite. Mr. Leslie passed on to me your letter of August 17th with the detailed instructions about this. Although it will mean an extremely long delay before we can publish it, I shall certainly send the proofs to Sir Thomas in Australia together with a list of queries concerning points which we cannot decide for ourselves.

CHRISTIAN SCIENCE MONITOR – I gladly fall in with your suggestion. It is very nice indeed to suggest that I write the Bloch article for this paper until such time as you yourself can contribute to it. I wrote to Miss Rintoul about this and I am glad to say that she has agreed. I intend to start on the article this week-end and look forward to writing it very much. Since I last wrote to you, your Bartok article has appeared in the 'Christian Science Monitor' and I am enclosing a copy with this letter.

There are some other points which I am sure you will be interested to hear about. Mr. Ralph has started a concert agency in America in conjunction with Schulhoff and Heinsheimer. It will, of course, deal primarily with our composers such as Bartok and Britten and will also arrange conducting and solo engagements, lectures and teaching appointments.

There was quite a minor Ferguson festival on the wireless a couple of weeks back. His Violin Sonata was played on the Sunday by Isolde Menges and on the following Thursday Defauw* conducted his 'Partita'. (Cheers!) Defauw is now a refugee from Belgium and was in England for a short time before leaving for America. . . .

The Promenade Concerts are going ahead very satisfactorily in spite of the war. I do not know whether you ever saw the prospectus so I am sending you one with the music. I will not comment on the programmes, beyond saying that the choice of modern works is somewhat painful and not many of our publications are included in them!! The new work by Hamilton Harty†, announced for 3rd September was not completed in time, and therefore they did a second performance of the 'Children of Lir' instead. We all felt like doing a victory march to Queen's Hall to celebrate the occasion! Mr. Leslie went to the performance and came away with the conviction that it was a great work. Berkeley's 'Introduction and Allegro' for two pianos will be given to-day and I will let you know the reaction.

---

*Desiré Defauw (1885–1960), Belgian violinist who subsequently became a conductor and settled in the USA. He was in London during World War I as a refugee, and in the second he went to Canada, taking a conducting post in Montreal.

†A John Field suite.

*
(217)
ERNEST CHAPMAN to ERWIN STEIN

Boosey & Hawkes
18th September, 1940

My dear Mr. Stein,

Air raids have of necessity been the main thing in all our lives since I wrote you last, but as you see the papers now, I will not mention anything beyond the fact that all of us are safe and are carrying on as best we can. As you know, we have to take shelter in the basement when 'that horrid banshee wailing' commences, and it has happened so frequently during the past week that more permanent arrangements are now being made whereby we can carry on our work down below – where I am dictating at this moment!

I am afraid the Promenade Concerts had to come to an end a fortnight ago on Saturday – not because of small audiences, but because of the danger of having such a huge audience in so small a place during air raids. As far as it went the season was a great success and the audiences on some nights were of a record size. Berkeley's 'Introduction and Allegro' was done on September 6th, but it proved rather disappointing. The Introduction is by far the best part of the work. It has a subtle and beautiful Adagio with scoring of a very individual character. Unfortunately the Allegro fails to keep up the same standard, and as this is by far the larger section of the work, it spoils the effect of the whole. The main fault here seems to be weak construction. The movement is carried on by a number of short episodes, none of which, as far as I can discover, has any relation to the others. This creates a rather unsatisfactory effect, which is made worse by the fact that the ending is very abrupt and unexpected. The two pianos are not very successfully balanced against the orchestra, and it was sometimes impossible to hear them when they had an important part to play. I have advised Mr. Leslie to reject the work, and feel sure you would have agreed with me if you could have heard it.

On the following day, there was a performance of 'Three Short Pieces' by Elisabeth Lutyens, daughter of the famous architect who designed the Cenotaph and many other important English monuments. As there was a comparatively bad air raid that night, I did not go, and was all the more sorry when I found out from the press reviews that the work was in the 12-tone system! So we have an English 12-tone composer at last! Surprisingly enough the critics were quite kind to it, but how far this was connected with her distinguished father I should not like to say. I gather that all the pieces were very brief and that the main point was in the scoring, which I understood had a late-Webern luminosity. I rather hope that I shall be able to hear this work on another occasion, although I have not been much impressed with earlier examples of Lutyens works which were rather sickly chromatic. . . .

I sent a number of scores to the Royal Philharmonic Society including the Britten Violin Concerto and Bartók's 'Divertimento'. Keith Douglas replied saying that the works would be considered, but that he could not hold out much hope for any of them. . . .

We had a very nice piece of publicity in the 'Observer' last Sunday. As it is now some weeks since the 'Times' gave us their Saturday morning column, I felt it was only our due! William Glock, the 'Observer' critic was reviewing the musical year since war began and the only two works he mentioned are both ours . . . 'Les Illuminations' and 'Mikrokosmos'. I quote from his article:– 'Of the many

41 May Harrison

42 Benjamin Britten

43 Grace Williams

44 Ralph Vaughan
Williams

45 Cecil Gray

46 Bernard Herrmann

47 Leslie Woodgate

48 Thomas Dunhill

49 Sir George Dyson

HERBERT THOMPSON · ANNO DOMINI · MCMXXXVI ·
ÆTATIS SVÆ · LXXX ·

50 Herbert Thompson

51 Leslie Heward

52 William Walton

v.s.

53 The BBC Symphony Orchestra

54 Victor Hely-Hutchinson

55 Adrian Boult

contemporary works heard under various auspices the most notable was Benjamin Britten's "Illuminations", a song-cycle to words by Rimbaud. ... Britten has matched the poet's thought with a brightness and excitement of his own. He does not approach to Rimbaud, but the task has keyed him up as a setting of the Mass might have done in another age; no musician will fail to admire a work that is so vividly written and so full of ideas. Bartók's "Mikrokosmos" should also be mentioned, but cannot conceivably be discussed in a few words. It was published by Boosey & Hawkes in April; it consists of 153 pianoforte pieces, beginning with five-finger exercises and ending with studies which mark the furthest point in Bartók's development; and it is, incidentally, one of the most vital and far-reaching works of this century.' I think this is very gratifying, don't you. All business has been pretty poor since my last letter.

(218)
SIR ADRIAN BOULT to THE AUTHOR

Published in the Autumn 1940 issue.

THE B.B.C. AND BRITISH COMPOSERS.

DEAR SIR,

—You published in your summer number a letter signed by ten representative British musicians containing criticisms of recent B.B.C. programmes. These criticisms cover a wide field. Some merely refer to the inevitable restrictions and rationing of war time. Others are not justified by facts. It is impossible within small compass to take the points raised seriatim. I will deal with the two most important.

'The proportion of good-class music provided in these days is, indeed, so small that it is causing listeners to tune in regularly to foreign broadcasts.'

An analytical comparison of programmes being broadcast at the present time with those broadcast during corresponding periods in 1938 and 1939 will show that an equally substantial proportion of broadcasting time is at present devoted to 'good-class' music. This fact emerges despite the additional competition of especial war features—news in various languages, propaganda programmes and so forth. If anything, the 1940 balance is favourable; if it is admitted that the amount of time devoted to music-programmes in pre-war days was adequate, then the complaint that 'music of real merit, both serious and light, occupies a secondary position' is obviously unjustified.

It is admitted that a certain amount of music is broadcast at times inconvenient to many listeners—thus many fine chamber works have been played after 10.30 p.m., and chamber concerts and recitals have been given between 7.0 and 9.0 a.m., but our listener research figures reflect the changing social habits of our people in an unmistakeable way and justify our confidence in the existence of a considerable listening public at times which might appear to be unsuitable. In fact during the period 7.0 to 9.0 a.m. the figures are quite remarkable.

The musician can be certain of a good deal of music to his taste at generally convenient times—*i.e.*, between 6.30 and 10.0 p.m. on most weekdays, and throughout the day on Sundays. Music programmes broadcast at these times are designed with a majority appeal; present depleted programme space inevitably means that the listener on the lookout for unfamiliar music must be catered for during much less convenient periods. For all that, specialised interests have never been left out of consideration.

But the main complaint of the letter has referred to the share of broadcasting time allotted to British composers. Throughout the first six months of this year there has been an average of ten performances of British works of a serious character (excluding works of smaller genre, songs, etc.) each week and it should be pointed out that this represents a proportion of 18 per cent. of the total output of serious music. In other words, out of every 22 hours devoted to serious music, four have been given up to those British composers whom we are charged with neglecting. Furthermore, all this music has been presented 'in a satisfactory way,' that is by the type of orchestra for which it was written.

There has certainly been only one performance of a choral work of the largest scale—the severance of the orchestra from the B.B.C. Choral Society is, of course, the explanation of this; of choral works demanding a smaller number of voices there have been many performances—Vaughan Williams' Mass in G minor, many motets, favourite cantatas like 'The Revenge' and 'The Pied Piper' while, week by week, the B.B.C. Singers have sung many programmes of madrigals and part-songs, exploring the published output of nearly every modern British composer, as well as the Elizabethans.

One word about light music, as it has been mentioned in the letter. An average over two months, taken at random, one early in the war and one recent, shows that in the programmes of the Salon Orchestra and its groups the percentage of copyright British music to its whole output of copyright light music is 43 per cent. This omits many arrangements of old folk tunes, etc., most of which are British. Considering the enormous amount of American and Continental music of long established popularity here, it is submitted that this percentage is remarkably high. Various distinguished British composers have been invited to contribute to the repertoire by writing new pieces, or arranging old ones, and as a result an attractive new repertoire is being made which should have lasting value.

The proportion of British music in the programmes of the outside light orchestras naturally varies with the type of the orchestra; those of Continental style, which is widely popular among listeners, have to draw on the numbers which are mostly published, or originate, abroad, although British publications of that style are used whenever feasible.

The signatories of the letter seem to have overlooked chamber music. The list of British chamber works broadcast during the first nine months of the war comprises twenty-two sonatas or works of similar calibre, of which eight were given twice; five trios (one twice) twelve quartets or quintets (two twice). Incidentally of the considerable amount of chamber music written by our most prolific composer in this field, all but one work—a sonata—happen to have been broadcast since the outbreak of war. In addition, countless piano pieces and songs by British composers, serious and ballad, are broadcast every week.

In reviewing the above facts and figures which, it should be pointed out, the *Radio Times* makes readily and constantly available to all, it is difficult to see what real cause the British composer can have for complaint of non-recognition in broadcast programmes. Nor does it appear that the Corporation is unaware of 'the real need of our people today for healthy, inspiring music, adequately and regularly performed.' The Corporation will continue, as in the past, to make every effort to serve the great repertoire of all that is best in music of all types and of all ages.

Yours faithfully,

ADRIAN C. BOULT.

Ten composers had written to the editor of The Author *(Frederic Austin, Sir Granville Bantock, Thomas Dunhill, Theodore Holland, John Ireland, Sidney Jones, Constant Lambert, Martin Shaw, Dame Ethel Smyth, Vaughan Williams) complaining about the 'secondary position occupied by music of real merit, both serious and light', and that 'British composers should be allotted a far bigger share of broadcasting time than it [sic] enjoys at present'. Sir Adrian's response was followed by further comment signed by six of the original signatories: '. . . of every twenty-two hours of serious music provided today eighteen are given over to the foreigner! It is inconceivable that any fair-minded listener will consider this to be an adequate recognition of native music at such time as the present'.*

Sir Adrian was allowed a final rejoinder in the issue for Christmas 1940.

(219)
HAYDN WOOD to THE RADIO TIMES

Issue dated 15 November 1940 p. 10

Enemy Composers

I was interested to read in the RADIO TIMES Ralph Hill's article about the complete banning in this country of the music of enemy composers. Though I agree with him that, to quote his own words, it would be 'childish, totalitarian, and anti-musical' not to perform any works at all of enemy origin, I am strongly of the opinion that the *copyright* music of these composers should be entirely eliminated from broadcasts and public performances. I know we should be depriving ourselves of a great amount of enjoyment, but there are sterner things to be considered these days.

For instance, why should the Performing Right Society be put to the immense trouble of carefully and conscientiously collecting fees to be handed over to our enemies after the conclusion of hostilities? Possibly the general public does not realise that every time it hears a copyright work by these composers *hard cash* is put on one side as a nest-egg for their future benefit, and Heaven knows our own composers could do with this supplement to their incomes. I often wonder how much British music, copyright or otherwise, is played on the Continent these days.
—*Haydn Wood, Westward Ho.*

(220)
ALAN BUSH to PICTURE POST

From One of the Victims

Last week, the two Governors of the B.B.C. drove that institution one more step along the totalitarian path. I had a meeting with two B.B.C. officials from whom I learned that it is proposed to ban not only the microphone appearance of all People's Convention signatories, but their compositions also. I asked why the B.B.C. proposed to ban my works and yet broadcast those of Richard Strauss, who occupies a leading official position in Nazi Germany (though I agree Strauss's works should not be banned). The B.B.C's answer was that Strauss does not derive financial benefit! Further, they declared that if I stated in writing that I no longer supported the People's Convention, now or at any time in the future, I should be readmitted to broadcasting. This sounded to me like a palpable attempt to threaten or bribe me to change my political opinions. But the B.B.C. denied this was their intention. 'Democracy is fighting for its life,' said Mr. Ogilvie in last week's PICTURE POST. I wonder what he means by democracy.

ALAN BUSH, B.MUS., F.R.A.M.

The more politically active composers of the pre-war period achieved some notoriety, and caused views to be sharply polarized among music lovers as a result of their political stand. The BBC was involved with two who received wide publicity. Firstly Hugh Roberton, the conductor of the Glasgow Orpheus Choir, was banned from broadcasting owing to his pacifist views and his refusal to perform the National Anthem. Those who subscribed to the People's Convention also ran up against the BBC, and the banning of Alan Bush from the air led to Vaughan Williams's much publicized support of him. Although the BBC rescinded the ban, the bureaucracy involved in treating him fairly – and resulting in reluctance to come to a decision – meant that though the ban may have been officially lifted, exposure of his music on the air suffered, and never really recovered until many years afterwards.

The new British music that tended to be projected to the overseas listener often had overtones of a rural England that may well have appealed more to expatriate Britons abroad in wartime than to more intellectual music lovers in Europe. A typical example is the treatment accorded Julius Harrison's soaring pastoral evocation Bredon Hill *– very much in the mould of Vaughan Williams's* The Lark Ascending *of a quarter-century earlier.*

(221)
SPOKEN BY JULIUS HARRISON AND ELIZABETH POSTON

Broadcast in the North American Transmission, 29 September 1941

E.P.   Do you remember, Julius, when we were fixing up a meeting earlier this summer, how you wrote and apologised for the delay in writing, because you said you had been very busy with a brand new work for Violin and Orchestra, which you were going to call 'Bredon Hill'?

J.H.   Yes. That was in May of this year – and it took me four days to get it finished. I remember showing you the score in manuscript and I played it over to you on the piano rather lumpily, I'm afraid!

E.P.   Not so lumpily as you think! It was when I was staying with you in Worcestershire . . .

J.H.   And we drove on a perfect summer afternoon high up in that lovely countryside of mine and had a picnic tea in sight of Bredon Hill.

E.P.   Yes – and I felt how really you had caught the essence of that English scene and put it into your music, and that you had written a real Rhapsody.

J.H.   Yes, I think so – because it grew out of itself in my mind from all those scenes I have known all my life. After all, we mustn't forget that this part of Worcestershire speaks of England at its oldest. It is the heart of Mercia, the country of Piers Plowman, and it is the spirit of Elgar's music too. If I've been able to catch something of all this then I'm indeed glad.

E.P.   What was it your friend Gordon Bottomley wrote about this new work of yours? I thought he put it so beautifully.

J.H.   Oh, I remember . . . He was speaking of the harmonies and he said some very kind things. Something about

> 'The dew was so fresh and undimmed by
> footsteps. Some of the harmonies came from
> farther off than Bredon: perhaps there had been
> footsteps on them that didn't show on the dew'.

E.P.   Yes, he's right. It's all in your music.

Bredon Hill was well received. Among those who wrote appreciatively of it, E. J. Moeran, Dunhill and John Ireland were particularly warm – Ireland noting it was a 'most poetic and deeply-felt piece of writing . . . lovely in colour, thought and construction – & most heartening to hear in these days of dissonance, & ugliness for its own sake.'

(222)
BBC OVERSEAS SERVICE

PACIFIC TRANSMISSION, OCTOBER 3rd, 0545 GMT
AFRICAN TRANSMISSION OCTOBER 2nd 2030 GMT
NORTH AMERICAN TRANSMISSION, SEPTEMBER 29/30, 0400 GMT.

OVERSEAS ANNOUNCER: This is London Calling. 'The Music of Britain'. We have this now-famous series to thank for the fact that one of the loveliest works of the year – indeed, I would go so far as to say – of our own time, was completed by the composer with a view to its special appearance in the Music of Britain. You will now hear its first world performance. 'Bredon Hill', by Julius Harrison, a Rhapsody for Violin and Orchestra, played by Thomas Matthews, solo violin, and the B.B.C. Northern Orchestra, concert master Laurance Turner, conducted by the composer.

It is a fact remarkable in itself that such music as this comes out of the present time. That it does, is perhaps the best witness to the eternal spirit of England. Julius Harrison, Worcestershire born of generations of countrymen, lives in sight of Bredon Hill.

He has the love of our English countryside in his veins – a sense of it that you will hear in this lovely music, which springs and grows and rises soaring – a true rhapsody – in expression of the words of Housman's poem:

> Here of a Sunday morning
> My love and I would lie,
> And see the coloured counties,
> And hear the larks so high,
> Above us in the sky.

The issue of individual conscience, of British musicians who moved abroad at the outset of war, and who should be excused service in the armed forces, polarised views strongly in the first part of war. Later Michael Tippett would go to prison (see letter 237) rather than compromise his view. This polarity was underlined in the autumn of 1941 by a correspondence in The Musical Times, *initially attacking Benjamin Britten, then still in the USA but soon to return. Under the heading 'English composer goes west', E. J. Moeran summed up what we may now see as the voice of sanity.*

(223)
E. J. MOERAN to THE MUSICAL TIMES

Published in the issue dated October 1941

Kington
Herefordshire

It seems to be assumed that Mr. Britten went to America at the beginning of the war. The very title of this unfortunate correspondence implies it.

In fairness to Mr. Britten I would point out that he left this country many weeks earlier, and that at the time of the outbreak he was already fulfilling engagements in the U.S.A.

Provided that he keeps valid his artistic integrity, I consider that he is doing his duty in remaining where he is.

The death of Butterworth in 1915 [ie. 1916] was a tragedy, the nature of which no country with any pretensions to the preservation of culture and a respect for art can afford a recurrence. Are all composers to be exempt from service? Heaven forbid! There is far more contemporary music than can get itself performed, and always has been, but a young artist of the established creative ability of Britten is too rare a bird to be lumped together with the general run of practising musicians. Their services are essential to the cultured life of the country, but there is always a plentiful supply.

Whether or no one likes his work, the very existence of a musician of Mr. Britten's unique natural gifts is exceptional. No contemporary British composer ever did more in his early twenties towards placing the country's music on the map of Europe. Such concert organizations and selection committees responsible for this incorporate members who are musicians of international repute.

Surely that in itself is an answer to any tribunal which might be called upon to settle rival claims of possible exemptions.

E. J. MOERAN.

Even as this correspondence was going on Britten was making his decision to return to England, though there was to be a six months wait until, with his friend Peter Pears, he could find a passage in a cargo ship. On his arrival home his conscientious objection required that he soon appear before a tribunal, for which the BBC provided the following testimonial: 'This is to bring to the notice of the Tribunal considering the case of Mr Benjamin Britten that Mr Britten has been commissioned by us to write music for a series of important broadcast programmes designed to explain this country to listeners in America, and we hope to be able to use Mr Britten's services for musical composition in connection with a large number of similar programmes in the immediate future.'

During the War that perculiarly vivid radio form which the BC referred to as a 'feature' was developed to a high degree, and came of age. Not only did the soon to be powerful Features Department produce wartime documentaries, but substantial works of the imagination; including radio dramas such as Louis MacNaice's Christopher Columbus *and Edward Sackville-West's* The Rescue. *One of the most considerable achievements of BBC producers in this area was their reliance on specially commissioned music, and this influence was felt in all BBC departments, including those preparing features for broadcast overseas on short wave.*

(224)

(a)

KENNETH WRIGHT to ARTHUR BLISS and R. S. THATCHER

BBC Internal Circulating Memo

From:
 Overseas Music
  Director
To:

 Mr. A. Bliss

Subject: CHRISTIAN DARNTON.
14th November, 1941.

Darnton might be tried for music of the peculiarly pungent sort if it is needed, but I am not certain that it would be suitable for short wave. I would rather try people like Rawsthorne and Berkeley first, as I feel that they are inherently more musical. Do you agree?

K. A. WRIGHT

[Added in ms]
1. Walter Leigh
2. Arnold Cooke   in order of
3. Lennox Berkeley   practicality
4. Alan Rawsthorne
5. Christian Darnton   AB

(b)
KENNETH WRIGHT to R. S. THATCHER

BBC Internal Circulating Memo

From:
  Overseas Music
    Director
To:

  D. D. M.
  (Bedford)

Subject: CHRISTIAN DARNTON.
18th November, 1941;

I would be grateful if you could discuss this with the Music Department and let me have your views on Mr. Bliss's suggested order of preference. It should be borne in mind that Lennox Berkeley is now in the Corporation and that if he succeeds in finding his right place soon (which is unlikely to be in Overseas Music Department) it would be preferable to put any commissions outside the Corporation, in which case Rawsthorne moves up to No. 3.

Arnold Cooke had great success in writing Incidental Music in Cambridge and adapting himself to slender resources, which Dent and others have assured me he handled very efficiently – hence his appearance so high up on the list. I feel that Darnton's contribution might be suitable for background to a flash of modern battle in its starkest form, or scenes of abject desolation and poverty, but I fancy they might not be effective on short wave!

K. A. WRIGHT

(c)
R. S. THATCHER to KENNETH WRIGHT

BBC Internal Circulating Memo

From:
  Deputy
    Director of
    of Music
    (Bedford)
To:

  O.M.D.

Subject: CHRISTIAN DARNTON.
21st November, 1941

Your 'batting order' of composers for Feature Music is generally agreed.

Haven't you forgotten one of the most successful – Richard Addinsell? I personally should put him in first, or at any rate first wicket.

R. S. THATCHER

(d)
KENNETH WRIGHT to R. S. THATCHER

BBC Internal Circulating Memo

Subject: CHRISTIAN DARNTON and LIST OF "INCI-
DENTAL" COMPOSERS.
25th November, 1941.

From:
    Overseas Music
      Director
To:

    D. D. M.
      (Bedford)

    Copy to:
    A.O.M.D.
    Eur. M.S.
      (Bush H)

<u>Incidental Music</u>

Thanks for yours of the 21st November. I am sorry I did
not mention that Addinsell was in the forefront of our
minds too; but we did not include him in this present list,
because we found, on asking for his collaboration in our
"Composer at the Piano" series, that he is so busy on
Ministry of Information films he cannot spare the time
ever to run up to Evesham (or even London) for a broadcast or recording. We therefore assumed that a commission for incidental music, with its concomitant consul-
tations with producer etc., attendance at rehearsal and so
forth, would be out of the question. We should much like
to have him on almost all kinds of feature.

    If and when John Greenwood* is appointed to assist
Isaacs, it may be desirable to let him have a shot at some
'incidental effects-music' (as distinct from 'full-blooded'
music per se) for one or two European features, if only to
begin weaning producers away from the eternal commercial recordings of Elgar, Sibelius, Strauss etc. On the spot,
he could handle the job expertly, in the way that he has
for years been doing film music. I think that later on there
would be plenty of commissions of all kinds to available
outsiders.

K. A. WRIGHT

---

*John Greenwood (1889–?) is perhaps best known for his film score for Basil Dearden's film *Friede*. His
serious compositions include a symphony and a violin concerto.

Of the composers named, the only one who was to produce a number of scores for BBC features was Rawsthorne. Walter Leigh (1905–1942) was killed at Tobruk on 12 June 1942, while Arnold Cooke (b. 1906), who like Leigh was a pupil of Hindemith, was a serving naval officer during the War, and thus not available. Lennox Berkeley produced music for one wartime radio feature Yesterday and Today in 1943 (as well as much later, in 1952, music for Wall of Troy). Darnton does not appear to have been asked to write for radio at all, while Addinsell, the composer of the very popular mock-Rachmaninov Warsaw Concerto, in the film Dangerous Moonlight, appears to have written on a number of occasions for wartime radio features, but is much better known for his films which also include Blithe Spirit (1945).

After the War, Louis MacNeice's two 75-minute dramatisations of the Icelandic Njal saga, The Death of Gunnar and The Burning of Njal, were both broadcast in March 1947, but had been commissioned the previous year with music composed by Arnold Cooke and conducted by his friend Alan Rawsthorne, who had by then considerable experience of writing for BBC Radio features. In fact, Benjamin Britten at this period was the pre-eminently successful British composer in this genre, with his substantial score for The Rescue (1943), and for Pericles (1943). He crowned this period of unique development, in 1946, with one of the most celebrated of all Radio Features' achievements, MacNeice's The Dark Tower. However Rawsthorne* composed the largest number of scores. His first wartime task in this vein had been to arrange various eighteenth-century pieces for Douglas Cleverdon's version of Max Beerbohm's The Happy Hypocrite, in 1940. In December 1941 came music for Francis Dillon's reworking of Pushkin's The Golden Cockerel), and later music for Radio Newsreel, for which he was granted two weeks special leave from the Army. In 1943 there followed an extended score for Louis MacNeice's 45-minute play The Story of My Death, the true story of a young Italian poet whose death in 1931 had been a personal protest against Fascism. Evoked in poetry and music, it rehearsed techniques that MacNeice would use more dramatically in later, better-known, programmes. In 1944 Rawsthorne produced two short scores for radio: Sitting on the Fence, light music for a BBC series, and an arrangement of the traditional tune 'Rock a-bye baby' for use in MacNeice's extended commemoration of his friend Graham Shepard who had died on the Atlantic convoys, called He Had a Date. Rawsthorne produced another seven scores in the three years following the war, and was clearly highly thought of by MacNeice and the staff of Features Department, even if these scores are now remembered by only a few.

John Greenwood (1889–?) is perhaps best known for his music for Basil Dearden's film Frieda. His serious compositions include a Symphony and a Violin Concerto.

*For full details of Rawsthorne's incidental music see Alan Rawsthorne: a catalogue of his music, compiled and edited by Alan Poulton; Kidderminster, Bravura Publications 1984 pp 58–73.

*
(225)
HERBERT HOWELLS to JULIUS HARRISON

Royal College of Music
Prince Consort Road,
South Kensington,
London s.w.7
Tues: 9 Dec 1941

My dear Julius,
It was good to get your letter – and a saintly act on your part to send an ancient friend red-hot news . . . all about your return to organ-playing. I can cap that news! For you're not the only musical Methuselah crawling up organ-loft steps these days, or persuading leg-muscles to recall their pedalling acts of 20 or 30 years ago, or making the seat of his trousers 50% more shiny than they were before war interfered with the decencies of our careers. The fact is, I myself have been doing all these things since early October – at St. John's College, Cambridge: Rootham's old place. Latterly their man has been Robin Orr (who was at Leeds for a time) – and he's in the RAF now. I'm still 'rubbing my eyes' about it: seems absurd for me to be 'in church' again after being out of organ-lofts for 24 years. (Salisbury was the last – 1917!)

I've been given the status and privileges of a Fellow of St. John's: and a suite of rooms: and free dinners in Hall etc. etc. in addition to my pay. I go down to Cambridge on Thursday evening and return to London on early Monday morning, each week.

Our house was blitzed and bashed and ruined one awful night in Sept. of 1940. Ursula was mercifully in Scotland (and has been there ever since as a busy and acting member of the highly-competent Dundee Repertory Company). D. and I were visiting a brother-in-law that night in Sanderstead – and only by that lucky chance escaped pretty certain death. Our part of Barnes was simply devastated – for no military cause whatsoever.

Homeless, we sought refuge in Cheltenham for sometime, (I going to and fro' London where Dyson gave me a "bedroom" in the basement of the RCM – with himself and Sammons and Topliss Green for occasional companions).

Now D. and I have taken a small furnished house – again on Barnes Common. Perhaps that'll bring on a new London Blitz! It has been a divided and desultory year . . . but many of one's friends have been worse hit – no use grumbling therefore! . . .

I have to bring my mind down to the minima of existence to get any comfort. And the fact of your doing and liking the Hymn Tune 'Michael' is one such . . . and I'd be grateful for that, anyhow, since it gave you the immediate cause of my hearing from you, my dear Julius. I've a great affection of you always – and always shall be glad of direct news of you and yours.

Bless you,

HERBERT

I'm writing this in a Harrogate Hotel – ass-boarding [acting as examiner for the Associated Board] for a week.

Howells's hymn tune Michael *is named after his young son Michael who had died, aged 10, in 1935.*

(226)
CHRISTIAN DARNTON to W. W. THOMPSON

12 Fitzroy Street W.1.
18:3:42:

Dear Tommy –

. . . I am writing to you at the suggestion of Parry Jones. For the past 5 months I have been writing a choral work called Ballad of Freedom, for Tenor Solo, Chorus, Brass, Percussion and Strings – 46 players in all, excluding chorus. Parry has sung through half the work with me; and, although a man of few words on such occasions, appeared to like it very well; although I am not in a position to say that he will definitely sing it, since he has said no such thing. But he has given the strong impression that he will do so.

. . . Now it is an odd thing that even after 15 active years in the musical profession, I still do not really know how to set about securing a performance! – It is true that up to the spring of 1939 I was accustomed to 4 or 5 broadcasts every year. But then, in 1939, something which I've never properly understood, seems to have happened; and the BBC shut down on me completely. To do the situation justice, however, I must add that I have only very occasionally made the most casual and desultory attempts in a quite informal way to have anything done about it. Now, however, comes this work. All I propose to say about it is that the music is designed to make a *direct* appeal. There is in it no 'private language' which can be understood by only the privileged few. The Workers' Music Association (of which you will surely have heard) is intending to publish a short score of the work, and to stage some kind of a run-through as soon as the copies can be prepared. This was arranged yesterday.

. . . Parry is at the moment ill in Glasgow. He sweetly took the trouble to write to me from his sick-bed, making the suggestion that I should get in touch with you. If I may permit myself to make the comment, I very much doubt whether any representations to the executive music department (or whatever the latest title may be) will be likely to have any effect, the mere mention of my name being probably sufficient to damn the music from the start. Yet I (and one or two others who have heard me run through it very inadequately on the piano) feel that it is of great importance that it should be performed as soon as possible – if only for political reasons; it being a call to people to fight fascism *now* – and a very stirring appeal it is. Could we make an appointment the next time you're in town, so that you could come along to my place and hear it?

I hope you dont consider it a liberty that I approach you in this matter. I am not very good at 'Sales talk', as you see. And this work is the first of its kind – it plays, by the way, for 36 minutes.

– Yours very sincerely,

CHRISTIAN DARNTON

During the war there were various occasions on which serving members of the armed forces who were also composers wished to obtain leave for the purpose of completing or performing a latest composition. Channels through which such applications could be routed were very ill-defined, and although the forces took as much public relations advantage as they could from the sight of a composer conducting in uniform, many applications fell on deaf ears, while those that were successful were only so because of extensive string-pulling.

(f) Darnton: *Ballad of Freedom:* page of vocal score

(227)
EDMUND RUBBRA to ARTHUR BLISS

No. 11259304.
Gunner E. Rubbra.
Admin. Battery, Watson Unit.
133rd O.C.T. Group, R.A.(A.A.)
Shrivenham, Wilts. May 8. [1942]

My Dear Bliss,
Many thanks for your letter which my wife forwarded to me here. I shall be
delighted and honoured to write something for V.W's 70th birthday. (Will there be
some co-ordination to see that we don't all write Variations on Themes by V.W.!)
The only question – a big one – is the lack of leisure and facilities given for such
work in the Army. Curiously enough a propos of my conducting the first
performance of my 4th Symphony at the Proms. on August 14th next, I wrote to Sir
Henry only yesterday to see if he, through the B.B.C. (I understand it will be the
B.B.C. Orchestra that will be playing on that date) would be willing to write to the
C.O. here to see if I could get an extension to my week's leave (due in the middle of
June) so that I could have time to prepare the score, correct parts, rehearse etc. If I
could have a 3-weeks' extension, no doubt I should also be able to write the work for
V.W's birthday. Do you think such a letter could be written? They are very
considerate here, and you may remember that Alan Rawsthorne, who is also here,
had six week's leave granted to him for some special music wanted by the B.B.C. . . .

I do hope something can be done.

With all best wishes,
Yours sincerely,

EDMUND RUBBRA

(228)
CONSTANT LAMBERT to LESLIE HEWARD

42 Peel St. w.8
May 22nd [1942]

My dear Leslie
So glad to hear from Cecil this morning that your operation has passed off all right. I
do hope it hasn't been too painful. I've had 7 myself & know what bastards they can
be.
    I'm afraid that I must prepare you for a slight shock which is that I am forced to let
you down about June 18th. As you may remember I asked you to pencil in the date
& not fix it absolutely as I couldn't be certain about deputy etc. I now find alas, that
not only can I get no deputy for that night but the parts of Sleeping Princess are
unavailable also. I'm frightfully sorry to let you down like this but you do know
how difficult my situation is in this respect. Only this morning I have had to turn
down 3 gramophone sessions which is rather a bore. I suggest that you keep the 1st

part of the programme as it stands, put in a new second part & get Wa-wick* to do it as he seems fairly free at present.

Incidentally Cecil told me this morning that you were particularly keen to get hold of Obata's translations of Li-Po (incidentally by far the best translation of Chinese poetry I know). We went to Bumpus but found it was difficult to get. My own copy (as you know I have set 8 of them) is with my wife which presents a slight difficulty but fortunately I have found one belonging to my brother which I am sending off to you to-day. No hurry at all about returning it.

Please forgive me about the 18th & don't let it stand as a black mark! All the best

CONSTANT

(229)
EDMUND RUBBRA to THE HON. JAMES SMITH

Gunner E. Rubbra
No.11259304,
Admin. Battery, H.A.A. Unit,
133rd O.C.T.Group, R.A.(A.A.)
Belford Barracks, Shrivenham, Wilts.
June 2.

Dear Capt. Smith,
I have been asked by the B.B.C. to write an orchestral work for a programme in honour of Vaughan Williams' 70th birthday, and also to conduct the first performance of my 4th Symphony at the Proms. on August 14th. In order to do the work connected with these two events my C.O. here is perfectly willing to extend my privilege leave, due on June 15th, for three weeks, making a month in all, but as he cannot grant such leave himself the B.B.C. approached the Director of Public Relations for the necessary sanction, but apparently this has been refused: for what reason I do not know. What is stranger, I understand that a request on behalf of Alan Rawsthorne *has* been granted. My C.O. cannot understand the reason for the refusal, and thinks that perhaps the request did not reach the Director of Public Relations at the War Office, but got vetoed in a routine office. Could you kindly help me at all in the matter, or suggest what could be done. The two events for which I am asking leave are, I feel, rather important ones in my life, and I should be very sorry to lose the opportunities they afford. So if it is not worrying you too much I should be most grateful for your advice as soon as it is possible for you to give it to me.

I am very happy down here, and am running a small orchestra. We give a concert next week with Wilfred Parry (who is now assistant Adjutant here) and Arthur Fear, who is here as a cadet.

With all best wishes,
Yours sincerely,
EDMUND RUBBRA

P.S. Those Sonnets of mine that you liked are being published, and I will send you a copy as soon as they are issued.

*i.e. Warwick Braithwaite.

(230)
THE HON. JAMES SMITH to SIR ADRIAN BOULT

Headquarters,
Home Forces
8th June 1942

Dear Sir Adrian

I received the attached letter from Rubbra a few days ago, and sent it straight on to A.W.2 at the War Office for their comments and advice. I have now had a reply from Army Welfare & am passing the following extract from it to you as I thought it might interest you apropo of Rubbra's request. They say—

'Our experience is that the only way to get a thing like this through is to get the backing of the Minister concerned; in this case the Minister of Information. It is possible that the B.B.C. failed to play their best card when they went straight to the D.P.R. War Office, and our suggestion is that they should enlist Mr. Brendan Bracken's support; if they do, it is not likely that his (Rubbra's) request would be refused by the Secretary of State'.

I just thought I would let you know this in case you were still anxious to get Rubbra. I do think that it is a case that ought to be given careful consideration, but the trouble one is always up against is that the individual who dealt with this application was probably someone who had never heard of a Prom Concert & much less of Vaughan Williams.

It makes me very angry sometimes that soldiers should be released for making so called propaganda films, while an application in respect of something of real cultural value is turned down.

Forgive me please for bothering you. I hope you flourish and that all is well with you. I am now at the above address – exceedingly interesting work but long hours. I rarely leave before 8 P.M. so have little chance of hearing any music.

Yr sincerely

JAMES SMITH

Rubbra duly obtained permission to conduct, the performance taking place on 14 August 1942 in the Royal Albert Hall. A record is preserved in the BBC Sound Archives.

(231)
JOHN IRELAND to GEOFFREY BUSH

Feast of St Michael & All Angels, 1942
Little Sampford
Saffron Walden
Essex

My dear Geoffrey

Many thanks for your letter dated 'Saturday' – I notice you never give the actual date – why?

Yes, I am also sorry we did not meet this time. I got let in for the incidental music for 'Julius Ceasar' [*sic*] and had to get it done in a very short time – about a fortnight – which meant I had to put everything on one side and just stick at it all day & every day and a good part of the night as well. In case you heard it the 'Battle' music was not by me – they used bits of Honegger's music to 'The Tempest', on record.

I also had to practise a bit, in order to play the piano part of my 2nd violin sonata at the Boosey & Hawkes concert on September 23rd – the novelties of this concert being new works by Bartok and Britten – the latter, settings of 7 Sonnets (in Italian) by Michelangelo, sung by Mr Pears and the Composer – very effective. Britten's detractors, while admitting the effectiveness, said – 'a pastiche of Verdi, Bellini & Donizetti'. I feel hardly competent to judge. In some ways the music seemed very Italian, also the treatment of the voice part – but some current English harmonies were not entirely avoided. If I can find it, I will enclose the programme so that you can form some opinion of the motif of these songs – but please return it ...

There are *too many* composers whose names begin with B. Bach, Beethoven, Brahms – Bax, Bliss, BRITTEN, Bantock, Bartok, Bush, Busch – and others I don't at this moment recall.

So you feel the time devoted to writing is a pleasant holiday. Well, well. Compared with writing the music for 'Julius Caesar', penal servitude would have been a recreation. The only number I enjoyed was a setting of 'Come live with me and be my love' written for a boy, impersonating Lucius. And it was sung by a boy, too, with an execrably played *lute* accompaniment – (not *flute*). I was told I shld have the B.B.C. orchestra, or else the L.P.O. or the L.S.O. and planned accordingly. But in the end they had to get a scratch lot of *bandsmen* from the R.A. – & the stuff was far too difficult for them, of course – though they did their best. I used 8w.w. 11 brass, percussion & 3 contrabasses – no other strings. A nice, clear-cut sound.

You did tell me about the musical evening you treated the young delinquents to – if they were pleased, I have not lived in vain! I'm glad they recognised themselves in 'Ragamuffin' – grubby but beautiful. (I don't mean *they* are grubby!)

I wonder if you have seen my Three Pastels for piano (Augener) 'A Grecian Lad' 'The Boy Bishop' and 'Puck's Birthday'. Your young charges would like Puck, I think. The other two are perhaps a little serious for them.

It is nice of you to say you appreciate my letter – I appreciate yours, certainly. I have been overworked lately – and am very behind with things I am expected to do – (but never accomplish) – a work for viola and orchestra for Tertis to play in Portugal on a Tour he is making for the British Council – and orchestral work for some concerts Boosey & Hawkes are arranging – and Moiseiwitsch has asked me to write a piano concerto for him – having ignored my music all his life, he now wants a nice, big, *new* piece, all to himself – and doesn't understand why I don't display much enthusiasm for the idea.*

My days of teaching at the R.C.M. seem a long way off – I haven't given a lesson since June, 1939 – 3 years and 3 months.

In some ways I like being here – it is unspoilt, attractive country, and this is a big, rambling house, with a large garden – one becomes accustomed to the absence of electricity & gas. Getting up to town is a bit of a trial, as the coach, which used to deposit one at King's Cross, now only goes as far as Bishop's Stortford – whence one has to proceed by train, to Liverpool Street. In the Spring you might come here for 2 or 3 days.

My host, the parson, is a very old friend of early days – he is 69, but is cultured & a

---

*Ireland never composed the viola concerto or a second piano concerto.

good scholar. His wife, who is about 38, runs the place, now, practically single-handed. I have 2 good-sized rooms, overlooking the garden – & now I have got 2 pianos – an old but very fine Broadwood grand, which I bought in 1914(!), and in my bedroom a Chappell upright. I can play all night if I want to. I do not have to go to Church, & everything is very easy-going. In a way, one misses the amenities of a small town, but there are compensations.

Have you heard from Father Thompson? I have had 2 airgraph letters from him – he has been ill, & had an operation. I gather that his ship is, or was, in tropical waters. I miss him quite a lot & hope he will come back on leave soon. He suggests a possibility of this.

By the way, has anything happened to that piece of music for clarinet & strings which you wrote? You might send it up to the BBC . . . I have been appointed Chairman of an Advisory Panel to report on scores sent in. Of course, we are not responsible for the programmes, 'can only make recommendations' – which may not be acted upon.

Write again when the spirit moves you. Convey as best you can, my affectionate regard to the budding Ragamuffins – tell them if Tredegar were nearer here I would come and play to them myself.

Yours as always

JOHN IRELAND

P.S. I did not hear Rubbra's 4th Symphony. I heard the 3rd. It has some striking features, if a bit dull in places – but consistent in style, & free from cheap showmanship – a great merit in these days.

(232)
ELIZABETH POSTON to JULIAN HERBAGE

29 March, 1943

SONGS BY WILLIAM BUSCH

May I ask for sympathetic consideration of the William Busch songs? They are some of the most interesting settings I have come across within the past eighteen months: finely-written, arresting and in each case of sensitive literary perception (Blake, Herrick, James Stephens, A.E., W. H. Davies). I have broadcast them myself (European), they have received other most successful performances in both European and Latin/American services, and as they undoubtedly represent a fine contemporary talent, I feel that they would certainly be of interest in Home Service. The songs were written for Henry Cummings, and, as they make such an interesting group, I feel they would be most successful on their own as a fifteen-minute recital.

ELIZABETH POSTON

Miss Elizabeth Poston
DDM agrees with me that we ought either to see these songs, or hear a recording, if

one was made, before including on Home Service, even though they have been included overseas. Could you therefore please get copies or records?

J Herbage 1/4/43

The composer William Busch (1901–1945), although beginning to make a reputation during the war, with his Cello Concerto well received at the Proms in 1943, never became well-known to a wide public.

(233)
MICHAEL TIPPETT to ALEC ROBERTSON

Whitegates Cottage
Oxted
Surrey
4 Dec 1942

Dear Alec,
Thanks for your letter of the 27th last. The 31st of Jan is alright, providing I am at large then. I'll keep you informed immediately of anything untoward if it were to happen.

I've been thinking–over lots of ideas, but rather come back to 'Stravinsky & the Dance' or some other such title. I would like to show how deep-seated is his feeling for dance & movement & rhythm – then exemplify his unconscious, perhaps, attitude by playing a few moments from a Bali gong orchestra & then Stravinsky himself a few moments, playing his own Piano Rag music. And so to lead thro (or to) Petrushka & the Russian dance towards some final piece to be played complete: Either a portion of the Symphony of Psalms, or Les Noces (the final scene) – or a (living) 2 pf. version of the Dumbarton Oaks Concerto, 1st movement. The great point about Stravinsky is that the initial musical experience for him, & for his likeness therefore, is abruptly physical & immediate. Played properly it is gay & unsentimental, Exhilarating.

By the way, I'm using the week end to look at his new Symphony* before the score goes to the BBC. Stravinsky's publisher is mine too! [Schott & Co.] All by accident. So what with my natural interest, I have good opportunity to get hold of all I want.

Will you let me know sometime soon if this strikes you as the right idea & then I'd like to get a script out & to you complete as soon as possible.

I had been to supper with Ben & Peter last Saturday. Showed them my magnum opus, an oratorio, called 'A Child of Our Time'. The text is my own, with advice from T S Eliot, & the whole work is modern & contemporary, but religious without being in the cult. Sometime I want to show it you. Ben has just written me a p.c. 'What a grand work the Oratorio is & A performance *must* be arranged soon.' Easier said than done! But meanwhile Schotts are going to bring out a piano–vocal score as

*Stravinsky's Symphony in C was completed in 1940, but was not published until 1948. Its first BBC performance was broadcast on Wednesday 17 November 1943 in a BBC Symphony Orchestra concert conducted by Sir Adrian Boult.

the first move. If you're interested I must try to get hold of a text for you. There were some prints made, but I'm short of them. One, by the way, went to [Clarence] Raybould [BBC staff conductor] & must be buried in the Corporation – wish you could recover it.

I've still no word from [the BBC at] Bedford as to the Fantasia [on a Theme of Handel] for Pf & orchestra & a date. But I suppose it'll come one day.

The new Stravinsky score has the same dedication as the Psalm Symphony 'Composée à la gloire de Dieu & dediée au Boston Symphony Orchestra'. Is he a crozant?

Excuse the rigmarole. I'm feeling v gay as I've finished the new 4tet [the second] & it looks like a performance at Wigmore in Feb.

Please let me have a word on the Stravinsky thing – & shall I try my hand at a script?

Yours

MICHAEL TIPPETT

Tippett's Stravinsky programme was broadcast on Sunday 31 January 1943. A Child of Our Time with soloists including Peter Pears and Joan Cross was first heard under the baton of Walter Goehr at the Adelphi Theatre London on 19 March 1944. Its first BBC performance at the Royal Albert Hall on 28 February 1945 in a concert in aid of the children of Poland was preceded by a radio talk on the BBC's 'Music Magazine' programme which included live musical examples sung by Peter Pears and Joan Cross.

(234)
CONSTANT LAMBERT to EDWIN EVANS

42 Peel St. w.8
Jan. 9th '43

My dear Edwin
    A very belated note to apologize for not helping you over the Soviet music. I tried to telephone you several times but one of our telephones must be out of order. My life is chaotically busy with far more concerts than any conductor should have to do in the time & has been additionally complicated by illness & family affairs so please excuse me. Best wishes to you & your wife for 1943.

Yours

CONSTANT

(235)
BRUCE BLUNT to GERALD COCKSHOTT

Breach Plain Cottage,
Bramdean,
Nr. Alresford,
Hants.
May 20th / 1943

Dear Gerald Cockshott,
Thank you for your letter.

I know nothing about music, but, apart from this failing, I will give you what information I can about the songs which Philip [Heseltine] and I did together.

The first one was a carol called 'The First Mercy', which was printed as a poem to 'London Mercury' and was published as a song by (I think) Hawkes & Co.

In December, 1927, we were both extremely hard up, and, in the hope of being able to get suitably drunk at Christmas, conceived the idea of collaborating on another carol which should be published in a daily paper.

So, walking on a moonlit night between the 'Plough' at Bishop's Sutton and the 'Anchor' at Ropley, I thought of the words of 'Bethlehem Down'. I sent them off next morning to Philip in London & the carol was completed in a few days, and was published (words & music) in 'The Daily Telegraph' on Christmas Eve. We had an immortal carouse on the proceeds, and decided to call ourselves 'Carols Consolidated'.

In 1929 we did another carol, 'The Frostbound Wood', which was published in the Christmas number of the 'Radio Times'.

Of Philip's methods of composing the music for these two carols I can tell you nothing, because I was not with him at the time.

I can, however, tell you the whole story of 'The Fox'.

He was staying with me in Bramdean in the summer of 1930, and we had spent a long evening in 'The Fox', which is the local pub.

When we got back home, Philip went almost straight to bed, but I stayed up and opened a bottle of Chablis (what an inadvisable addition to a lot of beer) and wrote the words of 'The Fox'.

As I did not go upstairs till about 3.0, I thought that Philip would probably be down before me, so I left the poem on the table with a note to the effect that I thought it was unsuitable for setting to music on account of the shortness of the lines.

When I got down at about noon next day, I found Philip sitting at the table with music MS paper in front of him, and he was working at the song. He said 'On the contrary, my dear sir, I think that this is admirably suited for setting to music'.

We were going to Salisbury that afternoon and, when we got there, Philip hired a room with a piano at some music shop, played and whistled the thing over, and finished the song on the spot. So 'The Fox', words and music, was conceived and completed within about eighteen hours, which may, or may not, be a record.

Van Dieren added some accompaniment to it later, and others of our songs seem to have been changed from their original form, but these comprise technicalities of which I have no knowledge.

And it is quite obvious that this letter can give you very little knowledge of Philip.

If you would like to have more (and I feel that you will use it rightly) I shall be delighted to make an appointment with you at any time in London. I am there nearly every week, usually on Tuesday or Wednesday.

Yours sincerely,

BRUCE BLUNT

P.S. I have probably not answered clearly one of the questions which you asked.

Except for 'The First Mercy', the verses of the songs were written for Philip to set to music.

It is interesting that you should comment on their suitability to his style of composition, because he used to say that my verses were the only ones which he could set with perfect ease.

I only wish that I could have thought of another carol for Christmas 1930, because he would then have had something to interest him, and the end might have been postponed, but not, I think, indefinitely.

(236)
PATRICK HADLEY to SIR ADRIAN BOULT

Angel & Royal Hotel
GRANTHAM
Lincs

P A S Hadley
as from:
Borrowdale Hotel
near Keswick
Cumberland
22 June '43

My dear Adrian, thanks for your note of last week in answer to mine about S. Kutcher.

There's another thing I'd like to bother you about now, which I'm sure you would feel sympathetic about, namely the case of A. Rawsthorne.

I've been trying to see ways and means of securing him 3 months leave to complete his violin concerto. I quite thought that Keynes could succeed in this but it seems that CEMA is primarily concerned with performers. They can get film stars off, and possibly even a saxophonist, but composers never. In the correspondence about it Miss Glasgow said she thought by far the best chance was through the BBC. Hence this letter.

This work was within quite a short time of materialization when it got totally exterminated by bombs at Bristol, and the composer sucked into the military machine (unlike others less unfortunate, notably B. Britten).

My hope is that the 1st perf should take place in Camb. in one of those concerts under the combined auspices of the BBC and us, the Arts Theatre Trust.

Should you feel sympathetic, a word from you would surely go very far and might just do the trick. It is just a bit of *leave* that's required, nothing more.

I've been here just for the night on my way to the Lakes & Fells. To the Borrowdale Hotel, near Keswick, Cumberland for a week. I was up there last year and got up Gable. [ie. Great Gable, a remarkable achievement for someone with a wooden leg!]

With all good wishes

yrs

PADDY

(237)
MICHAEL TIPPETT to EVELYN MAUDE

5/7/[1943]

In replying to this letter, please write on the envelope:–

Number 5834   Name M.Tippett
                        H.M.PRISON WORMWOOD SCRUBS, W.12

The following regulations as to communications, by Visit or Letter, between prisoners and their friends are notified for the information of their correspondents.

The permission to write and receive letters is given to prisoners for the purpose of enabling them to keep up a connection with their respectable friends.

All letters are read by the Prison Authorities. They must be legibly written and not crossed. Any which are of an objectionable tendency, either to or from prisoners, will be suppressed.

Prisoners are permitted to receive and to write a letter at intervals, which depend on the rules of the stage they attain by industry and good conduct; but matters of special importance to a prisoner may be communicated at any time by letter (prepaid) to the Governor, who will inform the prisoner thereof, if expedient.

In case of misconduct, the privilege of receiving and writing a letter may be forfeited for a time.

Money, Postage Stamps, Food, Tobacco, Clothes, etc., should not be sent to prisoners for their use in Prison, as nothing is allowed to be received at the Prison for that purpose.

Persons attempting to communicate with prisoners contrary to the rules, or to introduce any article to or for prisoners, are liable to fine or imprisonment, and any prisoner concerned in such practices is liable to be severely punished.

Prisoners' friends are sometimes applied to by unauthorised persons, to give or send money, under pretence that it will be for the benefit of the prisoners. The people who make these requests are trying to get money for themselves by fraudulent pretences. If the friends of a prisoner are asked for money, either verbally or by letter, they should at once inform the Governor of the Prison about the matter, and send him any letter they have received.

Prisoners are allowed to receive visits from their friends, according to rules, at intervals which depend on their stage.

When visits are due to prisoners, notification will be sent to the friends whom they desire to visit them.

Evelyn dear

Yr letter was a great pleasure to get. I will reply to its contents first. Books – I got the 2 Devotional books, but haven't yet read them. In fact I read little. Cell task occupies a lot of time & there is a baby prisoners orchestra here wh I conduct & try to improve – & that takes 2 hours out of possible reading time. It's a sort of light café orchestra, & with instruments all of different pitch – in fact throw-outs. But we manage – & I hope to get in better music. On Sunday we are to play in chapel, in the middle of a recital by Peter Pears & Ben Britten – all v. amusing. So don't worry to chase after books. But there is a text-book I'd like (I've got the Bach) – will you ring Alec Robertson & ask him from me if he cld spare me a copy of his book: The Problem of Plainsong – on the art of wh he is an authority. If & when you get it, take it to Friends House as you did the Bach. I shdn't send the Cornford just yet.

Tell Mother if you're writing any time, not to wonder at the letters about me to her – I'm sort of a general favourite. As to getting down there, I might manage after the proper holiday on way back from Cornwall if it's to be there – otherwise I think to write the long delayed 1st movement of the old 4tet. & then take another break away, at Exmouth p'raps, & then start the Symphony – wh will be a big thing.

I agree with you completely abt press hoo-ha – no interested party shld write at all.

Holiday – I'm quite as ready to go with David first. The point is anyhow that I come out Sat. 21st Aug. & will make the 4tet. performance at Wigmore the public meeting ground for all & sundry. Rhse choirs etc – then come home & get things together etc Sunday.

The question of my getting something from people like books is difficult. I don't know for instance how much I really get from David – sometimes I'm rather repressed by him. I get a great deal from you – but that is a more subtle business, & in this case must wait till I'm properly home & at work again.

Keep the Hölderlin, Maritain etc. they're for my library & the autumn.

Haven't read any Paul yet. It hasn't worked out quite as I expected. One gets not only fallow but sluggish. We're all the same. You can't manufacture the proper conditions & there's a lot of interval & strain – a great deal of dreaming & inner adjustment – & the weeks inside seem monstrously lengthy & disproportionate, so that you fail to realise how easily they pass to those outside or how little one might oneself get done outside.

As far as I know there is nothing against length in letters in. Write on thin paper perhaps. You might send some 18 or 20 stave score – a few sheets – with the Robertson book. I shall probably get permission to use it. But 12 stave will do, if the other is too big.

And now messages, a special one this time to Ben & Miriam, who use after all my home & my own. Tell Miriam to use the tin of sugar in the larder wh Den gave me, for jam. I shall have forgotten the taste by the time I come out. I have already. Is anyone in the cottage yet?

A message of greeting to the choirs p.o. Tolworth (book under T.): hope they're managing. Write if you will to the deputy Tanner & say he must choose music to suit himself & that I shall probably take at least September clear away for my own work – (if not give the choir up altogether). Ask to pay for those times he deputised for wh I signed the register – & generally to try & solve the payments, claims problems of that choir, via the Sec. of the W.E.A. It is done terminally, & so quite soon. p.o. Tooting (under T.) Just send them greetings, either via Tony or the Sec. Will see them again next term of course.

Morley. Give them best wishes for the concert on the 17th, & hope they do well. Will be thinking of them. You can let them know sometime that I shall make my first reappearance on 21st Aug at Wigmore.

Fresca: Give her my love – tell her I'm managing fine – that I came across a typical Irish ABBA tune in Songs of Praise masquerading as English Traditional Melody. If she thinks to come to the 4tet. on the 21st, would like to lunch with her beforehand, & go with.

If this gets you in time ring Peter & Ben, Primrose 5826 & wish Ben well for his Prom on Sat evening – & tell them not to be distressed by the 'orchestra' in Handel's 'Largo' & Bach's Chorale on Sunday. It's for the sake of social progressiveness not to rival their artistry. If they're still at home on the 21st would like to breakfast with them & bath!

John Amis: Not to forget 6 tickets for Tooting choir via Tony for 17th – & if to spare send a couple to Wilf Franks, c/o 45 Holmesdale Rd, N.6. To send my love to the two Walters: to Goehr, not to worry abt the 17th, but that he'll probably gain by all the publicity – & good luck to him & it To [Walter] Bergmann my love – & could he possibly begin to look at the printed church music of Weelkes for Morley next season. I think 'Absalom, my son', or some such title a v. fine one. To Schotts in general, Cheminant & Steffens my regards & good wishes. John can do all that. As to visit, the order is due on Mon 19th, but it probably wont reach John till 21st or 22nd. It will have 3 names on it: his, Tony's & Britten's (?) – is that O.K? Otherwise we must invent. All the 3 come together – 2.30 at the prison is a good time. You take a no 7 bus from Oxford Circus to the door ($\frac{1}{2}$ an hour) or Central London to Wood Lane, $1\frac{1}{2}$d. Trolley Bus a minute or two to Du Cane Avenue & Walk down 2 or 300 yds. Quite quick. Ring the bell & ask to see me & show the order. Shld like to see read to me any press notices etc.

As to the new 4tet. movement (please keep these notes): I think the 2nd subject needs a longish bit (B) & the repeat of A to lead straight to the constricted portion; probably using some of the old material of [   ] to reach the same chord before cello up-going cadenza as before – then a possibly contrapuntal development of wh the reprise of the opening themes will form the climax – & a recapitulation as varied as the material allows & leading by the same coda material to the down-going cello cadenza.

So far I've only had this one 'thought' about my music, as above; I don't think its any good trying to make things move when the circumstances forbid any real output or creation. Prison is not a creative experience at any point – except perhaps in human contacts. I dare say it will seem less wasteful when one looks back – p'raps it may be a real holiday mentally. It's difficult inside not to give exaggerated importance to its actual length of days – & to brood on them so that they go slower. In fact I am pretty active & the time passes somehow.

Razor blades we are allowed to change the permitted one each week. I have 4 only in 'properly' if you post some more to me, they'll just be put with the rest & I can either use them or bring them home. I like to keep shaven & as clean as maybe. Its better for one's self-respect. Any blades that fit a Gillette 3 hole type – or slots.

I've experienced a lucky chance with eye exercises that may be helpful afterwards. Its v.hard on the eyes here. Sewing etc. & bad light in the cell & little time to exercise at all. I shall just about manage to keep them no worse than they are.

One has moments of nostalgia, but not too many. I shall come through. Its boring of course. It *is* good to know things happen outside. Much love to all friends & especially to you.

MICHAEL

I dreamed of a green flowering olive tree in spring last night. Good.

(238)
KENNETH WRIGHT to J.G. ROBERTS

It is generally agreed in principle by C(P) and others that the BBC should commission Vaughan Williams to write a 10-minute anthem, to be used when

Germany is defeated. Bax, as Master of the King's Music, has expressed his complete approval of the idea, and it is probable that the Anthem, when written, would be regarded as the country's official victory anthem and be done at Westminster Abbey etc.

Vaughan Williams has agreed to write it and is now choosing a suitable text, probably from the Bible, although he might perhaps draw on Walt Whitman. He expresses his intention not to draw from a modern poet and would prefer not to be asked to collaborate with a present-day writer.

Now comes the question of commissioning and the provision of the necessary finance: before we discuss the matter with Copyright Director, may we have the assurance that the necessary finance is available? It is difficult to guess how much. The work will not last longer than 10 minutes, but is to be a fine and probably complex anthem for large choral resources, may be with soloist(s) and the commission should include the symphonic score which would probably be reduced later for organ, but this point seems to me a matter rather for the publisher.

D.M. says that the composer is a little touchy about the question of terms and, of course, his recent commissions by the Strand Film Unit on the Ministry of Information's behalf have been generous ones – good round sums like £200 or £300 and no haggling. D.M. thinks that when you give us the all clear we should approach him and find out his own ideas on the subject rather than risk damaging relations by what he would consider an inadequate offer.

I take it that we would only purchase the broadcasting rights of the first performance or something of that kind, and leave all other rights to him, but I think we should have the right to record it for transcription purposes as it is the sort of thing we could send all over the world. The sum I had in mind is £100.

As we would be the first to produce it, should we stand the cost of copying all the material in the hope of recouping this from the publisher, or should the commission be worked conjointly with the Oxford University Press who would, no doubt, wish to publish it including vocal scores in readiness for victory.

K.A.WRIGHT

(239)
RALPH VAUGHAN WILLIAMS to MISS C. N. NEWBERY

The White Gates,
Westcott Road,
Dorking
Aug 1st 1943

Dear Miss Newbery

I do not know how to thank all you singers for your beautiful gift. – You evidently are not afraid of the formidable amount of music which that music case suggests!

But after all the best present you have given me is your splendid singing & enthusiastic devotion to hard work, which sometimes almost overwhelms me with a sense of my responsibility to you.

Yrs sincerely

R. VAUGHAN WILLIAMS

(240)
GRACE WILLIAMS to KENNETH WRIGHT

30 Willow Road
London NW3
[Receipt stamp: 20 Dec. 1943]

Dear Mr Wright
I am glad to hear that the Fantasia [*Fantasia on Welsh Nursery Tunes*] recording is O.K. & hope it may prove useful to you.

I am afraid that the list you enclose [of the tunes used] is rather inaccurate – so I have scribbled out the tunes on a grubby piece of music paper (sorry – I just can't spare a decent sheet because I am literally down to my last page & don't know where to turn for fresh supplies & shall have to start rubbing out old pencil sketches & re-using the paper – I have a little scoring paper left but no 12-stave – if you know of any shop where they still have some for sale do please let me know) – well, to conclude this sentence – I have scribbled them down in the order in which they appear. They don't always appear in full – & in one instance (Deryn y Bwn) I have used only the first half of the tune & finished it off with the second half of another tune (Gee ceffyl bach!) – & then have brought in the *real* second half of Deryn y Bwn just before Yr Eneth Ffein ddu – all of which is in the nature of a Fantasia. The rest of the material is, I suppose, original – though very reminiscent of lots of things.

With the season's greetings
Yours Sincerely

GRACE WILLIAMS

[The tunes were transcribed on an enclosed sheet of manuscript paper]

    I Jim Cro (Jim Crow)
   II Deryn y Bwn o'r Banna (The Bitten of the Beacons)
  III Migildi Magildi (Miggledee Maggledee)
  IV Si lwli'mabi (Lullaby, my baby)
   V Gee, geffyl bach (Gee up, little horse!)
  VI Cysga di fy mhlentyn tlws (Sleep, pretty child)
 VII Yr eneth ffein ddu (The lovely dark maid – or – Where are you going to, my pretty maid?)
VIII Cadi ha! (Caddy ha! – A Morris Dance Song)

Grace Williams's most popular work, the Fantasia on Welsh Nursery Tunes *had been completed in 1940, though it was not to be published until 1956. It was the subject of a fairly negative series of assessments within the BBC, most of the readers themselves being composers. No one appears to have foreseen the work's popularity. Maurice Johnstone the Northern Region Music Director at Manchester had the work under consideration. Herbert Murrill wrote to him from Belfast on 7 October 1941, noting that the work appeared to have 'scraped through [the Reading Panel] but without any great enthusiasm'. He went on to quote the assessments as follows:*

'Only really suitable for a children's programme – it is well done, but the musical interest is very slight.' B. J. Dale and S. P. Waddington

'Agree with S.P.W. and B.J.D. that this, though well-done, is not suitable for present orchestral programme.' C[larence] Raybould

'May I appeal for a performance now on the grounds that (1) we do wish to encourage the creation of Welsh orchestral music (2) this is the first thing of its kind (I believe) in Welsh musical literature (3) it is competently done, not brilliantly, but worth a hearing (4) could it not be put into a little Welsh programme to be conducted by Idris Lewis in Bristol as a gesture to his position and recognition of the temporary suspension of the Welsh Orchestra?' K. A. Wright

'Good workmanship. Material slight. Its justification no doubt would be in A.D.M.'s [ie K. A. Wright's] suggestion.' Reginald Redman

'Very slight in interest. Fairly dull but might be done if a Welsh choral work were essential.' H. Murrill

Maurice Johnstone in Manchester, complaining about the way it was being done, and of Murrill's mention of a non-existent chorus, agreed:

'Thank you. On the evidence of her letter I assume she received an acceptance notice from somewhere, which has got to be honoured by someone, so why not the long-suffering us! I admire the competence of the work, but I failed to notice a choral part! M. Johnstone

The work had been first performed by the BBC Northern Orchestra on 29 October 1941, conducted by Eric Fogg.

The recording that Grace Williams refers to in her letter was made by the London Symphony orchestra, conducted by Mansel Thomas for the Welsh Recorded Music Society and issued by Decca in 1943 (AK1999/2000). With his reply Kenneth Wright enclosed some packets of manuscript paper.

(241)
ERIK CHISHOLM to STUART DEAS

3 Carment Drive
GLASGOW S I
10/4/44

My dear Stewart Deas
I hear you are back in Scotland again & working on The 'Scotsman' so another good native has come home! As for me I've been on tour now for about 3 years, & have been conducting the Anglo-Polish Ballet for 18 months. I was with the Carl Rosa Opera Co. for a year but didn't like it much: ballet dancers are much easier to work with than (conceited!) singers. This week I am out but go to Grimsby tomorrow & so on tour for 2–3 months. You once very kindly promised to write an article on my ballets & if you are still of the same mind I can start sending you through some scores. I start off with the 2 pft-version of the [Forsaken] 'Mermaid' ballet & can send you the full score later.
   I have also written in ballets

   (1) 'The Pied Piper of Hamelin'
       (Scottish Ballet Society)
   (2) [The] 'Earth-Shapers' (symphonic ballet) (Celtic Ballet)
   (3) The Hoodie (to be performed here in November)

(4) Pigs in Clover (1 act)
(5) *Piobaireachd* in 4 acts.

Scottish Arts & Letters will publish your article if you will write it & possibly also Eric Blom in 'Music & Letters'. Let me know if you are still interested.

What other activities have you in Edinburgh? Take you half-way round the globe since I saw you last.

All good wishes

ERIK CHISHOLM

Erik Chisholm was a Scottish composer, pianist, organist, conductor and teacher, who, like Stewart Deas, was a pupil of Tovey. Of enormously wide musical interests and energy, he was strongly interested in the latest musical trends and was the soloist, for example, in Bartók's First Piano Concerto *at an early date. Part of his* Forsaken Mermaid *had been heard in Edinburgh and Glasgow (Scottish Orchestra) in 1938, and his First Symphony was broadcast in 1939. Some readers may remember his own* Second Piano Concerto, The Indian *(1949) on Hindustani themes, which the BBC broadcast in the 1950s with Agnes Walker as soloist. In 1957 the same work achieved a wider reputation when it was included in two concerts that Chisholm conducted in the Soviet Union. His interest in ballets was a practical one dictated by his direction of the Celtic Ballet from 1935 to 1940, and conductor of the Anglo-Polish Ballet from 1941 to 1944.*

He is probably chiefly remembered as the champion of Berlioz's operas, particularly The Trojans. *In 1945 he became Professor of Music in Cape Town, where he died twenty years later, and like W. H. Bell in an earlier generation, was subsequently forgotten in the UK.*

(242)
KENNETH WRIGHT to STANFORD ROBINSON

11th July 1944

TRANSSYLVANIAN RHAPSODY – Seiber

This was looked at by the Panel and turned down in a rather highfalutin sort of way on the grounds, I think, that it did not do justice to Seiber as a symphonic rhapsody.

It does not pretend to be a symphonic rhapsody. It is an effective, popular rhapsody on Transsylvanian tunes, and done with a good deal more skill and musicianship than most such popular rhapsodies. I cannot help comparing it, for instance, with 'Waltzing through Czechoslovakia' which although a piece of real hack work by Mr. Tausky, nevertheless finds favour, and rightly so, with light orchestras, including even your own. So I wonder if you would be good enough to glance at this and see whether you agree with me from the point of view of light music by a competent international musician, and based on authentic tunes. He got these by the way from Bartók and Kodaly, with whom he studied.

If you are willing to add it to the T.[heatre]O.[rchestra] repertoire, I am sure we can find a useful occasion for it. It has already been broadcast in the European Service by Goehr and the Orchestre Raymonde. If you can manage to do it, it is cued down for an orchestra like the M.L.O., but I feel it deserves the fuller sound of the T.O.

Mátyás Seiber had been born in Budapest. Composer, conductor and cellist, he had been a respected teacher at the Hoch'sche Konservatorium in Frankfurt. He settled in England in 1935 and earned his living by freelancing, and in 1942 was invited to teach at Morley College by Michael Tippett. He became one of the most influential teachers of composition in Great Britain in the immediate post-war period. In 1944 Seiber was preoccupied with the problems of becoming a naturalized British citizen.

(243)
REV. J. W. WELCH to RALPH VAUGHAN WILLIAMS

Please reply to:
Kingsley Hotel, Bushmead Avenue, Bedford.
12th September, 1944.

Dear Dr. Vaughan Williams,
Many thanks for your letter of September 8th. We are all very excited about the Victory Anthem and much looking forward to assembling our musical resources for rehearsal and to making a record. We thought it best to make a record, in case victory came suddenly and we were unable to collect the children, the chorus and the orchestra at the same time – besides there may be occasions when we wish to broadcast the Anthem by itself if necessary. Our present intention is to have the first broadcast of the Victory Anthem in the Sunday morning service following Victory Day. I believe the Oxford Press has now printed copies, and I am looking forward to seeing one this week.

Thank you for your suggestions for the music in the rest of our services; we shall almost certainly have the *Old Hundredth* to 'All people that on earth do dwell' or to 'Before Jehovah's awful throne', and Thalben Ball or Leslie Woodgate will certainly have it sung to its proper version with the long notes at the end of each line. We shall have 'O God, our help' to *St. Anne*.

If, however, we meet I should very much like to have your mind on the whole question of our using German music in broadcast religious services. We do not, e.g. ever broadcast Haydn's *Austria*, because listeners in occupied Europe, not knowing the English language, would be conscious only that we were broadcasting the old German national anthem; so my colleague [Cyril V.] Taylor has written a very good alternative tune called *Abbot's Leigh*. But I must confess that *Ein Feste Burg* seems rather different: it is essentially in Church history the hymn of believers in freedom struggling against tyranny, and when the Nazis dismissed the leading Norwegian pastor and put a quizling [*sic*] in charge of the Church, the congregation assembled outside the Cathedral with the dismissed pastor, and sang to the Nazis' dismay and anger *Ein Feste Burg* in Norwegian. What would you think, e.g., of our singing 'Now thank we all our God' on victory day? That comes from the same tradition of Church history, the Lutheran proclamation of freedom against what was thought to be the tyranny of the Roman Catholic Church. The B.B.C. in its broadcasts of orchestral music has not allowed the German origin of great music to weigh against our broadcasting it, and I am just wondering whether you think that in a religious service people's feelings are more sensitive and that we ought to feel 'all things are lawful, but all things are not expedient'. Our general impression is that the average listener doesn't know where tunes like *Ein Feste Burg* and *Nun Danket* come from, and the people who do know feel that great Church music is the possession of the whole Church and not of any one nation. Still, I must confess that I am puzzled about all this, and when next we meet I should be grateful for your views.

We have just finished a three-day meeting going through the B.B.C. hymn book, and I hope our suggestion of tunes will be ready to send to you in the early spring.

Yours sincerely,

J. W. WELCH

Vaughan Williams's Thanksgiving for Victory *was recorded in a BBC studio on 5 November 1944, and was broadcast on Sunday 13 May 1945, in a special radio Thanksgiving Service.*

(244)
VICTOR HELY-HUTCHINSON to H. VOWLES*

WORKS ACCEPTED FOR BROADCASTING

Herewith a short report of the meeting held in my office on Thursday, September 28th, at which you, Mr. Herbage, M.P.O., and Mr. Berkeley were present.

The existing list of seventy three works outstanding was gone through and reduced to thirty six, which we felt ourselves absolutely committed to do. Of these it was decided that some ten could be done either by the Theatre Orchestra or Northern or Scottish Orchestras. Mr. Berkeley undertook to notify these Orchestras of the works suggested for them, and M.P.O. agreed to fit the other works into Symphony Orchestra programmes as convenient. It was agreed that we should meet again in about three months' time, to see to what extent the 'swelling' has been reduced.

With regard to Panel recommendations, it was agreed that I should ask the Panel at their next meeting to grade accepted works in three categories:

> *Category A* to be of very high standard – i.e. works which are so striking that we cannot afford to omit them from our programmes. The placing of a work in Category A would constitute a *positive* and *urgent* recommendation to broadcast.

> *Category B*: Good, well-written works which it would be well to have in our programmes, but whose presence is not actually essential.

> *Category C*: A somewhat paler version of Category B – that is, works which are not bad enough to warrant turning down definitely, but of which we need make no effort to secure a broadcast.

In the cases of Category B and C and it should be understood by the Panel that these

* BBC Senior Administrative Assistant (Music).

works are merely declared 'suitable'; the placing of a work in one of these two categories does not constitute a positive recommendation.

It was also agreed that S.A.A. and I should scrutinise and if necessary re-draft the stock letters to composers whose works had been accepted, making it clear that our acceptance of their works as being up to the standard we require does not in itself constitute a commitment to broadcast.

V. HELY-HUTCHINSON

Hely-Hutchinson had succeeded Bliss as Director of Music on 1st September 1944.

(245)
VICTOR HELY-HUTCHINSON
POLICY IN MUSIC AND PROGRAMME BUILDING

12th March, 1945

Further to our recent discussions of this matter, I think there can be no doubt that our broad policy should be to represent adequately over a period the whole range of established classics, and at the same time to introduce into programmes a reasonable number of interesting new works, both by established and by coming composers. As regards works of not quite the first importance, *we should have a bias in favour of British composers*, on the principle that we want to give our own products a proper hearing, and we also want to learn from, and compare them with, the best that is being performed abroad; but except for unusual considerations of programme-building there is no reason to introduce foreign works that are not the best of their kind.

I say above 'to represent adequately'; this does not necessarily mean to represent completely; in fact, it cannot, because there are too many established works. But it is a reasonable aim to ensure that over a period a listener should have an opportunity of hearing a representative corpus of classical and romantic works, plus the best of the moderns.

The length of the period over which this is to be done needs defining. I feel that the period should consist of the six winter months – October to March, inclusive. The Proms, which when the war is over will probably cover the months August and September, should be regarded as an independent entity, which gives a comprehensive but less detailed picture of the orchestral repertoire. There will probably also be some sort of Summer Festival during June, which again is a specialised venture though in a different way to the Proms, and may again be regarded on its own; and during the remaining three months, when listening is not on the whole so concentrated or so regular, music programmes need not be built so systematically on a large scale, but might well be used for more miscellaneous and specialised programmes. Thus we have three main periods:

1. The Proms.
2. October to March
3. April to July, including a Summer Festival.

The way to get a properly representative series of programmes is, undoubtedly, to plan each of the periods mentioned above as a complete entity as regards the major concerts, and then to use the less important studio concerts both with the Symphony and Regional Orchestras to fill in the holes. But until the Symphony Orchestra is back in London, and also until international affairs are much more settled than they are, I do not see the possibility of making reasonably complete plans sufficiently in advance. Ideally, the Proms should be planned by about the middle of April (as in fact they are); the Winter Season should be completed during July; and the remaining part of the year at some period during the winter months. Until conditions are so settled that we can plan the Winter Season completely in advance to this extent, I do not feel that our object can be obtained. The best we can do is to keep it in view and get as near to it as we can. . . .

V. HELY-HUTCHINSON

(246)
HUBERT CLIFFORD to MÁTYÁS SEIBER

35 Marylebone High Street
6th June 1945

Dear Matyas,
Ben Frankel spoke to me very enthusiastically about the work of yours for horn and string orchestra. Would it be possible for you to let me see the score, as I am looking out for works suitable for performance in the Eastern Service. Perhaps at the same time you would be good enough to let me know the duration.

By the way, I heard the recording of your cello work and think that it is very remarkable for the tragic intensity which it conveyed – in spite of it conforming to tone row!

With kind regards,
Yours sincerely,

HUBERT CLIFFORD

(247)
VICTOR HELY-HUTCHINSON to R. J. F. HOWGILL

10 March 1946   PRIVATE AND CONFIDENTIAL

During the present week I have met both Constant Lambert and David Webster, and have acquired some information as to the policy and commitments of Covent Garden as at present envisaged. Although I set some of this down some months ago as the result of a meeting Mr Herbage and I had with Lord Keynes and Mr Webster in the Treasury, it may be worth while for me to make a further interim report, as when my previous memo was written their plans were entirely in embryo.

Webster's ultimate aim is to have a permanent season of opera and ballet in Covent Garden for about eight months in the year; the remainder of the year will be occupied by touring and holidays. He is, however, faced with the situation that whereas we have native ballet resources of adequate standard, the same cannot be said of opera, and the cast will need building up. He hoped to have an opera company functioning this autumn, but he may reinforce it from abroad in the case of rôles which cannot be efficiently undertaken by any singer at present in this country (eg the title rôle in "Carmen"). Ultimately he hopes to make the opera company an entirely native concern. The possibility of bringing over foreign artists, either singly or in companies, when the opera company is established, is not exluded for short seasons during the time when the Covent Garden opera company is occupied elsewhere.

Until the autumn Webster plans to fill the time with ballet and visits of foreign opera companies; the ballet, of course, is going on at the moment. He has been in negotiation with the Opera Comique and the Stockholm Opera for visits of their companies, but the former – whose visit was planned to take place about now – have fallen through, at least temporarily, for financial reasons. There is a remote chance that they may come in September. The Stockholm Opera Company is expected to come in July; but this, I take it, is not absolutely definite.

My object in meeting Webster, together with OB and OB Manager, was to see if any basis of contribution could be agreed on for future relays; but when Webster told me that he and Lord Keynes were in consultation with the DG and SO on the broader aspects of our relations with Covent Garden (a fact of which I was not previously aware), I felt it would be inappropriate for me to proceed further at this stage. I did, however, say to Webster that I was concerned with the matter from the supplying end and my immediate interest at an appropriate moment would be the question of ways and means. Webster put forward his statements of policy, as indicated above, entirely voluntarily, and indeed seemed glad to discuss them.

Two other points emerged, respectively from Lambert and Webster. The first was a statement by Lambert (this was at a separate meeting and not with Webster) that he was trying to make Covent Garden orchestra into a thoroughly efficient and coherent entity, and with that in view he hoped to get them concert and recording work in due course apart from their work in the pit at Covent Garden. I did not pursue this subject with Lambert; nor – for the reasons above stated – did I bring it up with Webster; nor do I even know whether Webster knows or approves of Lambert's idea in connection with the orchestra. But it has since occurred to me that we might in due course find this orchestra useful for periodical studio bookings, if suitable terms can be arranged.

The other question, raised by Webster, was whether we would care to envisage holding the Proms in Covent Garden (he envisages the possibility of letting Covent Garden for some part of the year). I could not, of course, give any indication as to the possibility of our doing this in the future, but gave Webster an idea of our present policy as regards the Proms. The future of other available concert halls is so indefinite that it will be impossible for some time to come to any conclusions on Webster's suggestion; but it might be worth carrying in the back of our minds for the future. At present, to my mind, the size of the audience which can be accommodated at the Albert Hall, and the consequential financial considerations, far outweigh the consideration that the Albert Hall acoustics are incurable. So for the time being, at any rate, I certainly do not propose any change. But there is no doubt that the sound would be better in Covent Garden; the season could be run with a smaller orchestra; and the building has traditional associations with pre-war Henry Wood Promenade Concerts.

In conclusion, I would say that both Webster's and Lambert's ideas, as put to me, struck me as being absolutely on the right lines and calculated to produce ultimately results of an excellent standard, and I told them so. I also said that we should certainly want to relay from Covent Garden, as I felt that this was a venture of national importance which we ought to reflect. The difficult part of the negotiations will come when we get down to finance. My own experience with Webster as General Manager of the Liverpool Philharmonic Orchestra and as associate of Thomas Russell (in connection with the NYSO) has given me the impression that finance is a subject on which he is fairly tough – and he will, of course, be handling something like a monopoly. On the other hand, I have previously come across him only in the capacity of "supplier" and consequently the receiver of money, and now that he is an 'impresario' on his own and has to look at things from the opposite point of view, it is conceivable that the experience may do something to soften him in this matter.

(248)
DAVID WEBSTER to BENJAMIN BRITTEN

Royal Opera House

15th November, 1946

My dear Ben,

This is just a note on our conversation and not in any way a formal letter, although immediately after our next conversation I will write to you formally at least on the points of our desire to have you do an Opera for us in the 1947/48 season.

Karl and I said that we very much wanted a new work on a large scale from you for the 1947/48 season, and in that matter we spoke on behalf of our Trustees as well as ourselves.

I confirm that all the details of the casting, designing and production would be in the hands of Karl and myself in consultation with you.

We also touched on our very strong desire to produce "Peter Grimes" in our first season and I cannot sufficiently underline how sad it would be if this project were not possible. We have done our best to try and fit in the dates we have already had from Peter, but we have found this utterly impossible. The time we have scheduled for your Opera is June 3rd and we have put down seven performances in three weeks. We would also like to take the work on tour in the early autumn.

So far as the Opera House production is concerned, we would very naturally like Peter to be able to sing there and also Joan.

We further said that we would like another cast, and while we have an immediate possibility of another Ellen, we have yet to find a Tenor, but that ought not to be insuperable.

Clearly, however, if your own projected Opera Season takes place at the time it was originally planned for Glyndebourne, then we cannot have Peter and Joan.

Further I am very much afraid that we would not be able to release Goodall for you until some time in June.

So far as these overlappings are concerned, I am quite certain that in planning ahead for 1947 they can be avoided and we would at all times be very glad to try and help to fit in with whatever plans you had of your own.

So far as the possibility of your Company finding a home at Covent Garden is concerned neither of us can see anything against this, indeed we would be delighted to welcome you here and to pursue enquiries to make that possible if you, on reflection, say so.

We would like to assure you that no one connected with us would feel anything but the strongest desire to help and to co-operate with you in any plans you have for your own Company.

We realise from all that you said how intent you are in maintaining the freedom and independence that you feel you need for yourself and the people immediately collaborating with you. We completely understand your desire and both of us feel you are absolutely right.

You will remember that my own immediate reaction was that while we will collaborate with you in every way we can, I felt that this organisation should be completely distinct from us and reflection has not changed that point of view.

Both Karl and myself, however, would very much appreciate being taken into your councils and your discussions, completely unofficially, and we will willingly arrange as I have said as far as is possible for you having the use of any of our artists, or anyone you want.

Further, we have here a production unit and we would be very happy before it is over-loaded with our work, as you can well imagine, to put that facility or any others we may possess at your disposal as you might require.

You need, I am sure, no assurance that both Karl and I feel most warmly to you personally and to your very great talents, and if there is anything that we can do at all to help you to realise your own ambitions for your Company, you have only to ask us.

I would suggest that Karl and I might meet you again and may be some of your colleagues, to talk the whole position over still further, and to see how best we can collaborate to a practical solution.

In the meantime, I do so hope personally that you will see your way to do an Opera for us and if you make the necessary indication then I will write you immediately formally on the subject.

Yours ever,

[DAVID WEBSTER]

'Karl' is Karl Rankl who was Musical Director at Covent Garden from 1946 to 1951, having settled in England in 1939. He conducted at the Royal Opera House during the 1940s. Britten's opera Peter Grimes *had been first performed at Sadler's Wells Theatre on 7 June 1945 to an ecstatic reception. The work was soon produced abroad (Hans Werner Henze has noted that it was one of the first pieces of 'modern music' that he heard, in Mannheim in 1946), but was not to be seen at Covent Garden until 6 November 1947 when it was conducted by Rankl. A British Council subsidy was quickly proposed to record the opera, but this initiative did not come to fruition. The first opera specially written for the Royal Opera House by Britten was* Billy Budd, *which Britten himself conducted there on 1 December 1951.*

BBC Statements of Policy About Music
1942–1946: four assessments

Board Paper G28/42 was prepared before 1 April 1942, the date Sir Adrian Boult relinquished the post of DM to Arthur Bliss while remaining Chief Conductor. Hely-Hutchinson became DM on 1 September 1944.

I
DRAFT BY C(P) AMENDED IN ACCORDANCE WITH SUGGESTIONS MADE BY D.M., D.D.M. AND ARTHUR BLISS

BBC MUSIC POLICY

Creative Principle: *Music is an ennobling spiritual force, which should influence the life of every listener.*

Practical Interpretation

Inexorably to continue and expand the principle of great music as an ultimate value, indeed a justification of life.

Faithfully to enrich leisure hours with entertaining music.

Physically and mentally to stimulate, cheer, and soothe tired bodies and worn nerves.

Statement of Policy

1.   (a) The BBC exists to further the cause and develop the art of music *through broadcasting*, i.e. through the transmission of programmes of music or about music. It follows that musical programmes that don't make good broadcasting (sec 2. below), are intrinsically a hindrance. This is an important principle which often conflicts with non-broadcasting musical activities and considerations.

(b) The BBC believes that the recognition of the above principle, and adherence to it in practice, will prove to be in the best interests of music as a whole, even when at times loyalty to the requirements of broadcasting seems to conflict with non-broadcasting musical and professional considerations. A strong broadcasting policy in music is likely in the long run to operate in favour of the interests it may seem to be temporarily opposing.

(c) Music is an international 'language', which through the medium of broadcasting is heard and understood all over the world. This impact involves immediate competitive and prestige considerations of great consequence to broadcasting, with ultimate implications in the sphere of international goodwill of the very highest importance.

(d) In spite of this recognition of the international factor, the BBC regards it as a matter of first importance to develop a strong sense of pride in British music in order to exorcise the long-standing national sense of inferiority in music and rid music of its status as a foreign art.

2.   Good broadcasting of music means:

I.   The observance of the artistic and technical limitations of the medium, in order to achieve –

II.   The best possible broadcast performance of all worthy music.

III.   Securing by all worthy means the maximum appreciation of such broadcasts by winning the largest possible audience, thereby continually raising public taste.

Note   'Political' considerations may sometimes conflict with II and III: e.g. restrictions on the use of foreign artists, the necessity for encouraging British music, relations with outside musical organisations, etc.; but, within commonsense limits, I.(b) above applies and they should be discounted where necessary. For instance, the relay of first-class opera from Milan may, in the long run, be a better way of fostering opera in Britain then setting false standards by undue encouragement of, say, provincial touring opera.

The objectives set out in I., II., and III., above are interlocked and inseparable, but, for convenience, various musical activities will be considered here in an arbitrary classification under the above three headings.

I.   Limitations

It must be recognised that the microphone has certain technical limitations, which result in artistic limitations in the performance of music. These fall into two classes:

(i)   The absence of vision. In music this mainly affects opera, where fundamental adaptation to the absence of vision is necessary, even though it conflicts with tradition and ordinarily important considerations of the music.

(ii)   Limitations of timbre, texture, and dynamic range, which involve a continual adjustment of the technique of performance. Certain limitations are obvious, such as the difficulty of reproducing large choruses, and the unsuitability of some forms of scoring; but others are matters of detail requiring continual awareness of the medium by the performer.

Note   (i)   With the continual progress of radio science, the technical limitations are steadily disappearing.

(ii)   There are also certain 'political' artistic limitations. These, however, are more apparent than real, and can usually be overcome by a constructive BBC policy. Examples of these are the use of English translations of foreign songs and opera, English titles, and so on.

Performances that do not observe the limitations of the medium cannot be good broadcasting.

II.   The Best Possible Performance

This must be primarily conditioned by the foregoing limitations, although in music which is suited in texture to the medium and can be adapted in range for successful reproduction, there may be a point at which the limitations are not felt, and a first-class concert performance and a first-class broadcast performance make an equal impression on the listener. In certain circumstances the broadcast may even provide a better result than the 'live' performance. For example, microphones may be so placed for a broadcast performance of an aria from a Wagner opera as to make the solo part more audible than it would be in the concert hall.

There are certain factors which directly and indirectly contribute to a high standard of performance:

1.   Regular public concert-giving in London and the provinces by the BBC orchestras is necessary to keep up the standard of performance as well as to attract the notice of the public and thus secure new adherents and further the spread of music. The listening public is entitled to regular opportunities of seeing the orchestra it pays for. The concerts should not contain works unsuitable for the microphone, and the performance in the hall should be subordinated to the requirements of broadcasting. Foreign tours are justified for prestige and political reasons.

2.   It is in the interests of the BBC to foster the work of outside musical societies on the ground that any well-found activity in the cause of music will prove to be in the interests of the BBC, will help to spread the appreciation of music, and by inducing comparisons will have a salutary effect on the BBC's own standards of performance.

3.   Amateur music-making must be encouraged, partly in order to foster a general interest in music, and partly to ensure a supply of material for professional recruitment.

4.   British composers must be encouraged within competitive limits, as a flourishing condition of British music must react favourably on the BBC and its aims.

5.   British artists must also be encouraged in order to safeguard the supply of performers and retain their goodwill. Encouragement should always be subject to acceptable minimum standards of performance.

6.   Foreign artists. The inclusion in programmes of foreign artists of international repute is desirable in the interests of programme quality. Such representation should be reasonably controlled, having regard to the adequate representation of the best native artists. Foreign artists who fall short of international standards are included in programmes only if they have something distinctive to offer in repertoire or style which could not be supplied by British artists. (The international complications of wartime inevitably affect the spirit and practice of this ruling. The scarcity of artists of international standing and the desirability of special compliments to our allies are two factors out of many which modify the normal peacetime policy.)

III.   *The Audience*

If the Creative Principle is accepted, there follows the responsibility for broadcasting the maximum amount of fine music to all who need it. This maximum must in practice be determined by the competing claims of other types of programme; but the Creative Principle carries its own justification of programme time and expenditure.

There follows from it also the responsibility for spreading the appreciation of music as widely as possible. The B.B.C., in addition to its obligation as guardian of cultural values, must accept the duty of educating the public. It must therefore plan continually to add by worthy means to the number of those capable of enjoying fine music.

1.   These two objectives should always be before the planners of programmes of music. The use of the English language and of English titles, the attraction of audiences by special forms of presentation, the acclimatising of listeners by planned repetition, are important expedients.

2. In broadcasting it is not possible to secure a particular type of audience of listeners and exclude all others, but in any programme the planners, producers, and performers, should have a clear idea of the type of audience at which the programme is primarily directed. In music, it may be said that the performers normally play for the musical expert, the producer presents the programme for the maximum audience, and the planner builds for both.

3. Certain forms of persuasive presentation of music require dialogue, narration, and dramatisation, of various kinds. It is vital here:

    (i) to determine the intellectual level of the audience primarily aimed at;

    (ii) to attain a professional standard of acting, writing, and production, equivalent at least to the standard of the performance of the music.

4. The cult of the maximum audience conflicts with purely musical considerations in various ways, particularly in the matter of transferring good music to a less appropriate medium in order ultimately to gain adherents to it. The BBC's policy is to accept what purists would regard as unwarranted transcriptions of the classics in order to further the ultimate objectives. There are limits however to this acceptance which must usually be set by arbitrary decisions in individual cases.

    (i) The playing of appropriate lesser classics on cinema or theatre organs must be accepted within limits as defined in (a), (b) and (c) below. In view of the great popularity of the theatre organ, occasional programmes of popular classics, given by the best players, should be encouraged as ready opportunities of bringing such music to the attention of a vast number of people. Three stipulations should be strictly observed:–

    (a) Complete faithfulness to the original text;

    (b) Good taste in registration (in so far as the genius of the instrument allows)

    (c) High technical standard of performance.

    (ii) The playing by brass and military bands of works written for orchestra: e.g. a regimental band playing the Overture to 'Figaro', or the BBC Military Band playing an accompaniment to the Grieg piano concerto. Both are acceptable in principle subject to (a) and (c) above; the former probably disallowed in practice, the latter licence not extended to all concertos or bands.

    (iii) The playing of music normally involving big orchestras – e.g. the Overture to 'Tannhauser' – by octets, etc. The limits here would again be set by arbitrary decision, and would necessarily be extremely narrow on the grounds of absurdity.

    (iv) The jazzing by dance bands of classical tunes or the borrowing and adaptation of them. This is normally quite unacceptable. On the most favourable estimate, music so transcribed can only be considered to have 'entertainment' value and many of the transcriptions are definitely offensive and musically harmful. Each example must be reviewed and arbitrary decisions taken regarding inclusion or exclusion, recognizing that there are degrees of adaptation ranging from the innocuous to the obscene. The more serious experiments in this genre which obviously arise from a sincere artistic impulse should, if acceptable, be broadcast with special presentation.

    Note A small Standing Committee (interdepartmental) with a catholic attitude to this problem, would probably provide the best machinery for taking the arbitrary decisions indicated above.

5.   General considerations of programme operation necessitate accurate timing of all broadcast programmes. For programmes which have a minority appeal, like serious music, this necessity is strongly reinforced by considerations of securing or losing the goodwill of the majority, who form the great reserve of potential listeners to good music. The prestige of the art is secured and conserved by good timing as by good performance, and much genuine antagonism is caused by bad.

B. E. NICOLLS

1st April 1942

II

DRAFT BOARD PAPER

On September 14th, 1946, Dr. Whitfield wrote to the Chairman in the following terms:—

"I have come to the conclusion, as a result of my attendance at Promenade Concerts, listening to musical broadcasts, and conversations with Sir Adrian Boult and other colleagues, that a reconsideration of our policy on Music is essential. I am not clear as to what our aims are in providing music. Is our object to give rough and ready entertainment; are we trying to familiarise our public with the largest possible number of musical works; do we want to give the highest attainable aesthetic satisfaction; do we wish to place Britain in the front rank of musical nations? I fail to find any definite direction.

"A satisfactory enquiry, as I see it, would involve us in quite a lot of work. We should have to decide whether we are anxious to provide music at the highest level; we are falling far short of this. None of the concerts that I have attended has been properly rehearsed. At the same time some of the orchestral performers seem to be tired, possibly due to the strain of having to play with inadequate preparation. I should like to consider whether we are wise to run a Promenade Season on traditional lines, several fundamental alterations seem desirable. It will also be necessary to find out why some of our best players, e.g. key men in the wood wind section, have left us. It may be that changes would involve heavier financial commitments or alternatively, either a change in the amount of music presented or in the type of music broadcast".

The Board at its meeting on September 19th referred the matter to the Director-General for report.

A.   *The B.B.C.'s Aims In Providing Music*

These were set out in Board Paper No. G.28 of 1942, which was approved by the Board at its meeting of 9 April 1942. This document was written for the particular purpose of elucidating our Music policy as a preliminary to the war-time appointment of Arthur Bliss as Director of Music. The draft was approved with various modifications by the then Director of Music, Sir Adrian Boult; the then Deputy D.M., Dr. R. S. Thatcher, and by Arthur Bliss, the D.M. designate. The departmental document carried two appendices dealing with matters of an ephemeral nature, and these were therefore not included in the Board Paper.

The answers to Dr. Whitfield's questions are as follows:—

Our object *is* 'to give the highest attainable aesthetic satisfaction' consistent with the circumstances of each programme and the resources of the B.B.C. generally. We do seek 'to place Britain in the front rank of musical nations', and the B.B.C. might well claim to have done, at least before the war, a great deal towards achieving this.

Our object *is not* to give 'rough and ready entertainment' although this may in fact be the result in some cases (notoriously the Proms.) of a compromise between aesthetic standards and practical considerations of finance and resources.

We are *not* positively 'trying to familiarise our public with the largest possible number of music works', although we do seek to extend and vary the accepted repertoire in view, firstly, of the enormous sustained output of music, which will become monotonous otherwise and, secondly, of the generally accepted obligation to perform works which do not get performed under the Box Office conditions of commercial concert giving.

To sum up: the B.B.C.'s output has always involved compromise between ideals and practical considerations. We cannot avoid *quantity* in our output (although we can vary or reduce it from time to time, but not beyond the point where there are no substitute programmes available), but we strive all the time for *quality*.

Three rather obvious examples of quality being compromised by other considerations are the 'Proms', the economical use of the B.B.C. Symphony Orchestra, and the use of artists and orchestras which are not first-rate in order to encourage British music and tap the reserves of amateur talent.

III

REPORT ON PROMENADE CONCERTS, 1946 BY SIR ADRIAN BOULT

September 21st 1946

1. *Future of the Orchestra*

Before reporting to you in detail on the recent Prom Season, I would ask you to give consideration to the status and future work of our Orchestra. Perhaps I may be forgiven for repeating the judgments of a few people. In 1939 Toscanini told a number of people that he had never conducted a finer orchestra. Monteux told a member of the New York N.B.C. Orchestra only recently that his last stay with us in London (1937 I think) was the high spot of his life in music. Menuhin told me last year that his performance of the Bartok with us was better than any recent performance he had had in America (these included Boston and New York).

The Orchestra has since 1939 suffered a 60% change in personnel and its work in the recent Promenade Season, though promising enough, was nowhere near the 1939 Festival level. On the present personnel (with perhaps one exception) I see no reason why the old level should not be recovered, provided that working conditions are right, and it is on this that I would ask for a prompt reply from a high level. Put bluntly, does the Corporation wish me to try and bring the Orchestra up to its 1939 standard or would it prefer to have a useful and efficient working body that will accede to all the demands of the various Services? There is naturally in planning circles a strong bias in the latter direction, and the Corporation's apparent agreement to the assumption both at home and abroad by various British orchestras of the premier position in this country, makes me feel that it might perhaps be simpler to yield to all planning demands, work our schedule on a minimum of rehearsal, and a minimum of public appearance, and give up inviting our Toscaninis and Menuhins, or at any rate acquiesce in their refusal to visit us when they discover what is happening.

This is the decision I would ask immediately from those in charge of Corporation policy. There is no compromise, and if the old reputation is to be regained the Corporation must expect to be asked for some (not I hope unreasonable) sacrifices to the needs of rehearsal. In the past our Orchestra has always had to do a great deal of Studio routine work. It has been a very considerable effort on many occasions to get them back to Symphony Concert form, and it has often only been possible to achieve it by means of extra rehearsals and special concessions from Programme Planning. I submit that this is unsatisfactory.

To return to the Proms: I am now satisfied that it is not possible to ask a first class orchestra to perform nightly for a month programmes containing no repetitions, lasting over two hours, and including novelties and works like Bartok's Violin Concerto. The Promenade programmes have reached a stage when only a drastic change of policy can possibly keep them going at the present level. From the audience point of view they are excellent, and this season has, if possible, been better than the last, but I have good reason to believe that even the keener part of the audience would welcome shorter programmes, and most of them are utterly impossible to perform without a great deal of slovenly work, which is incompatible with what I hope will be the standard for the rest of the year. I must therefore ask that the Prom programmes should be cut ruthlessly down to 95/100 minutes' music. This will involve a considerable change in programme plans. I am convinced that this is essential from every point of view. Three major symphonic works make an absurd programme and can be digested by nobody, particularly when the usual trimmings are added. I admit that the audience stops to the end, for the most part, but that does not prove that they would not have enjoyed a shorter concert better! The programme books of the last week contained an announcement of our first Symphony Concert. Can it be believed that any member of the average Prom audience will wish to hear a Bach Sinfonia, one of the less known Mozart Concertos played by Ida Haendel, and the Ninth Symphony with the same cast as at the Prom, and to pay ten shillings for the entertainment! For all these reasons then the Proms must be ruthlessly cut down.

But I am putting this forward mainly for orchestral efficiency. It may be said that what was done in 1938 can be done in 1947. I would reply that it was not done in 1938. The Orchestra took at least several weeks each autumn to recover its standard, and the Proms were not so exacting for a number of reasons.

2. Conductors

I wrote of my own position last year. I very much hope that this may be my last season, whatever decision is taken about the future of the Orchestra. I don't wish to be unreasonable about this, but I am convinced that new blood must come at once into the Proms. And I would urge that a second Associate be given at any rate one or two appearances in the January experiment, whether I appear in this or not (I hope not).

3. Programmes

I have already said that I think these have been splendid from the public point of view, granted that the public wish to be exhausted by their music. I am sure that there is plenty of evidence in favour of a desire for shorter programmes, and so I repeat here my firm conviction that every concert should be finished at or before 9.

There are other reforms which I consider worthy of consideration: the repetition of novelties: a five-day week, and others which would improve the series, even if they broke certain aspects of the Prom tradition. But the length of the concerts is the first and most important.

4. *Broadcasting*
It has been very satisfactory that part of almost every concert has been on the air. The absurdly meagre ration last year has been greatly improved. But an overhaul of plan which would be necessitated by a 9 o'clock finish might perhaps allow the broadcasting of more novelties.

5. *Organization*
Once again Mr. Thompson's Management has proceeded flawlessly, and the Library has also functioned not only without a hitch, but further with a gratifying readiness to meet any crisis that might occur.

6. *Soloists and choirs*
When artists like Menuhin, Szigeti and Jo Vincent are engaged from abroad it is a big responsibility for the Home Product that has to stand beside them. On the whole, our artists stood up to it well, but I should perhaps mention that I differed profoundly from Mr. Brosa's present (not his pre-war) outlook on Mozart; that I found Miss Shafir's brilliant technique utterly spoilt by her thoughtless and rhythmically spineless performance; that in a work like The Sea Symphony Mr. Roy Henderson's lack of volume cannot allow his performance to get across however artistically thought out it may be, particularly when his partner is Miss Baillie; and that that fine artist Mr. Pouishnoff – never a great exponent of Brahms – seemed more than usually out of his element in the B flat major concerto as he was still suffering from a slight concussion. I think we reached low water mark on September 18th in the performance of 'Belshazzar's Feast'. The problem was insoluble as it is manifestly impossible to expect any choral society, however many performances they have had in the past of a certain work, to give an unrehearsed performance. I had not been able to see them for a month, and Mr. Woodgate's absence for four weeks had naturally not improved their form. There were some very ragged attacks in the Vaughan Williams 'Sea Symphony', and there were very many more (pace The Times) in 'Belshazzar's Feast'. I would suggest that the whole work of the B.B.C. Choral Society be taken very firmly in hand and efforts be made to clear Mr. Woodgate's time in order that he may give his personal attention to the Choir throughout this season.

7. *Programme Books*
It was good to have the text of all vocal works printed in the programmes. A good many of Mr. Hull's Notes were good, but I was sorry that we were deprived altogether of the variety, and especially the interest of those written by Mr. Alec Robertson, Mr. Ralph Hill and Mr. Scott Goddard. I daresay that a single contributor made the difficult printing processes far easier.

8. *Conclusion*
I would ask then for a decision as soon as possible about the future of the Orchestra as rehearsal plans are already being made. I would further ask for a fundamental overhaul of our attitude to the Proms, which seem to me to have over-reached themselves to a dangerous degree. On paper, we are giving programmes of identical

calibre with our Symphony Concerts, at greater length and at half the price. Even the artists are now on the same plane. This is not only an absurd situation: it is dishonest, for the slipshod nature of our performances cannot be understood by most of that young audience, and even our professional critics seem to assume that we have three rehearsals for every concert. There are many things to be considered under this head, but I am satisfied that the shortening of programmes is the most important. If we do not take courageous action very soon there will be no future for our Symphony Concerts, and the Promenade performers will be unable to make the pace.

IV

PROMENADE CONCERTS BY VICTOR HELY-HUTCHINSON, DIRECTOR OF MUSIC

21st November, 1946

The layout of the 1946 Proms was very much on the lines of the 1945 Proms, except that the programmes were of a rather more symphonic type, and one or two foreign artists of international eminence were included in the programmes. Also an important new departure was made in the representation of Wagner, which was done by means of a few large extracts from the operas instead of by a fair number of what Tovey described as 'bleeding chunks of Wagnerian meat'. Before I proceed to recommendations about the 1947 Proms, perhaps I may comment on these three innovations. These comments and the recommendations which follow them are the result of consultation with Sir Adrian Boult, D.D.M., and Concert Manager.

I feel that the symphonic aspect of the programmes was rather overdone this year. The performance of all the Sibelius Symphonies *and* all the Vaughan Williams Symphonies, in addition to the usual repertoire of classical symphonies, overloaded the programmes, made difficult the suitable representation of artists, and limited the introduction of novelties. Also this preponderance of symphonies excluded a certain number of smaller works whose introduction would have given more variety to the programmes. I do not mean by this to criticise the programmes as a whole, which were unique in their combination of scale, scope and skill in construction; nor do I mean that it was not right to try the experiment; but having tried the experiment, I feel bound to admit that in my view it was only successful at the expense of other things which are of the least equal value to the Proms.

The introduction of international artists into Prom programmes, although of course immensely successful as regards the individual concerts, seems to me to fall outside the scope of the Proms. Concert Manager has pointed out to me that whereas no resident English conductor constitutes in himself a 'draw' at a Symphony Concert (at any rate to the extent of the seating of the Albert Hall), the thing which should differentiate the Proms from Symphony Concerts is the presence in the latter of great international artists, and the more we improve the standard of the orchestral playing at the Proms and the scope of their programmes, the truer this will be.

As regards Wagner, we are in a difficulty. Most of the usual Wagnerian excerpts are grossly inartistic when taken out of their musical context. Also, Wagner's music is stage music, and does not gladly suffer transplantation to the concert room. My feeling is that we are justified in carrying on with large-scale excerpts until Covent Garden gets going on Wagner as part of its repertoire, as we shall at any rate be giving people an opportunity to hear this music as it was meant to be heard. This seems to me to be in keeping with the progressively educational policy which has always been followed in the Proms – whether or not it has been openly announced as such.

I now come to recommendations for the 1947 Season. With the Proms as they now are, and with the traditional commitments of the programmes in various directions – not to speak of the necessity for keeping a reasonably sympathetic eye on the box office if the programmes are to be really varied and interesting, eight weeks is scarcely enough for the programme builders to "turn round in". I would like to see a nine or ten weeks' Season – preferably the latter. I am confident that with audiences as they now are (and I do not anticipate any falling off in the Prom audiences next year, whatever may happen to Symphony Concert audiences), this would be a popular move. I feel that the Proms should start on July 26th, and I have asked Concert Manager to ask Mr. Taylor at the Albert Hall to pencil the dates July 26th to October 4th inclusive for the Proms. We need not, of course, take up the whole extent of this period if we do not want to. (I understand that the Albert Hall authorities have now more or less abandoned their idea of carrying out repairs throughout August, and that in all probability we shall be able to start on July 26th.) I would suggest 7.30 p.m. as a starting time preferable to 7.0 p.m., although Concert Manager advises me that this is not likely to make much difference to the attendance. (The letter from the Public Relations Officer of the L.P.T.B.*, which you have passed to me and which I have sent on to Concert Manager, reinforces the argument in favour of 7.30 p.m.)

At present the overall length of most concerts is pretty well up to two-and-a-quarter hours; but I suggest that this should be an outside limit and that we should not shy at building programmes of just within two hours' overall length on certain occasions. This has, in fact, been done in the Winter Proms.

I think it is generally agreed – and it is certainly my own earnest wish – that Mr. Herbage should be asked to build the programmes for the 1947 Proms, although he will no longer be on the staff. This implies a big employment for him. He ought to begin by being in on the soloists' auditions (which we held in the Albert Hall in January and February). He would have to be in constant consultation with Concert Manager and Planners while the programmes were actually being built; he ought to be available before and during the preliminary rehearsals; he ought to attend all the concerts and keep an eye on them from the point of view of broadcasting, and also to write a report afterwards. In the past he has done as much of all this as has been possible, but his other commitments have got in the way. It would be amply worth while to give him a contract to secure his availability and services on this larger scale now that he can free himself (and is willing to free himself) from his other commitments in order to undertake the work. I have asked Concert Manager to discuss the question with him, so that we know just what will be implied.

I now come to the largest and most important question of all – the question of orchestras. The position is, of course, that the Proms are a survival from the days when the standards of orchestral playing and the expectations of the public in this respect were infinitely lower than they are today. Nowadays the amount of rehearsal needed and the additional fatigue caused to the players by the necessity of being always "on their toes" are far greater; also the repertoire is more exacting. Various

*L.P.T.B. = London Passenger Transport Board.

steps have been taken in recent years to meet this situation and to keep the standard of playing in line with current requirements. But it is still the case that performances are, on the whole and with a few notable exceptions, not up to the standard that an Orchestral Concert should attain. As to this, one can either take a defeatist attitude and say that a series of concerts which goes on nightly for eight or more weeks cannot be expected to maintain a fine standard all the time; or one can go all out to achieve that standard regardless of cost and trouble. The choice between these two attitudes cannot be divorced from considerations of cash; but the cash situation in regard to the Proms is extraordinarily good, and Concert Manager sees no reason to anticipate that it will get worse next year. So I suggest that we should now "take the bull by the horns" and book three orchestras – including our own – on a full-time basis for the 1947 Proms, and have a different orchestra playing each night. It does not necessarily follow that the rotation would be quite rigidly observed; so long as no orchestra plays on two consecutive nights, there would be room for some latitude in this. But the basis of the suggestion is that the three orchestras should take an equal share in the Season. If we were employing them all full time they would each be doing on an average two concerts a week, for each of which they would have not less than two rehearsals. This would take up four days of the week. On the remaining two days they would be available for studio work – which might also be extremely helpful to L.T.S., or might, alternatively, free our Orchestra to do some of the commercial recording for which H.M.V. have been clamouring.

As it would be implicit in the scheme that each orchestra should work with the same conductor throughout the Season, this necessitates a change of our view as to the use of conductors. This year and last year we had two joint Chief Conductors and one Associate Conductor. In 1947 – if this scheme is adopted – we should have three Chief Conductors, with an Associate not appearing on quite such a regular basis as Lambert did this year. On the assumption that the three orchestras concerned would be our own, the L.P.O., and the L.S.O., I recommend that the conductors should be respectively Boult, Cameron and Barbirolli. I have no doubt that Cameron would accept; but I am not so sure about Barbirolli. However, I think there is no doubt that he would be the best choice if he were available; and the fact that he was once a member of the L.S.O. might make him disposed to accept.

As to the identity of the Associate Conductor, I feel that in 1947 we should substitute Stanford Robinson for Lambert. I opposed this suggestion two years ago because Robinson was then specifically associated with the Theatre Orchestra; but now that he is associated with the Symphony Orchestra, I think it would be unjustifiable not to allot this work to him. How much he would have to do would depend on the requirements of the individual conductors, and would probably vary with each of them. But the programmes could be built in such a way as to make it clear that we had a 'stake' in the Season as a whole.

This recommendation does not imply a criticism of the work that Lambert has done in the last two years. His work on the whole has been very good, although he has not quite built himself up in the way that we hoped he would when he was originally appointed. In other words, I do not see Lambert developing into a Chief Conductor of the Proms one day, and there would certainly be no justification for putting him on a par with Boult and Cameron next year. It was made clear to him when he was first invited to join that the invitation was from year to year and not necessarily a permanency. I am sorry about Lambert, as the fact that we are dropping him – if this scheme is approved – is not due to any shortcomings of his, but to the fact that circumstances, both in regard to the Proms and our own Orchestra, have changed, and we must view the matter impersonally.

In the letter from Lady Wood which you passed to me, she urged that the same Orchestra should undertake the Proms throughout, as this was part of the character of the Proms (as I have returned the letter to you, I am quoting from memory; but that was, I think, the sense of her argument). I am not impressed by this argument; it might have been valid even ten years ago, but now that the Proms are so firmly established, I think their essential feature is not the sameness of the orchestral faces, but the scope of the programmes. This has extended out of all knowledge since the Proms were founded – but they are still 'The Proms', and I can see no reason why a corresponding expansion of the orchestral policy should destroy the character of the Season. In any case, to have the same orchestra throughout inevitably implies a poor standard of performance, and that, I have no doubt you will agree, is the thing we must at all costs set our faces against.

I attach a report which Sir Adrian sent to me just after the end of the Proms this year. Most of the points in it are covered either in this memo or in that on the 'BBC Symphony Orchestra'. In any case the terms of this memo are agreed by Sir Adrian. I should mention also that whereas he has been most unhappy about working in the Proms under the system of the last two years, he is very happy to continue on the basis proposed above, more especially as it gives him an excellent opportunity for training up the BBC Symphony Orchestra for the Winter Season.

The cost of the scheme which I have put up cannot be determined until we get down to detailed negotiations with the orchestras, and I am getting hold of Mr. Russell and Mr. Wood to ask them whether they would be prepared to collaborate in such a scheme as this; and if they are, I will hand them over to P.C.D. But Concert Manager believes that the Prom budget could stand this very greatly increased cost, provided the various Services contribute in respect of their use of the Orchestras apart from the Proms.

Names and Addresses of Copyright Owners

BAINTON, Edgar *and* Ethel

Helen Bainton
1/20 William Street
Double Bay
New South Wales 2028
Australia

BANTOCK, Sir Granville

Dr Cuillin Bantock
101 Crouch Hill
London N8 9RD

BAX, Sir Arnold

A. B. Rye
Rye & Leman
11 Golden Square
London W1R 4DU

and

Lewis Foreman
Music Trustee
Sir Arnold Bax Trust
22 Pheasants Way
Rickmansworth
Hertfordshire WD3 2ES

or

Sir Arnold Bax Trust
Wray, Smith & Co
1 King's Bench Walk
Temple
London EC4Y 7DD

BEECHAM, Sir Thomas

Shirley, Lady Beecham
c/o Stanley Sovin & Partners
182 Finchley Road
London NW3

BELL, W. H.

W. H. Bell's widow, Helen McEwen, a sister of the composer Sir John McEwen, is believed to have retired to England after Bell's death in 1946. His son died during the War. No direct descendent who might have an interest in his copyrights has been traced. His music is preserved at Cape Town University, who issue a typescript catalogue.

BLISS, Sir Arthur

Lady Bliss
The Bliss Trust
c/o Joynson-Hicks
10 Maltravers Street
London WC2R 3BS

BLUNT, Bruce

No direct descendent who might have an interest in his copyrights has been traced. Enquiries concerning Blunt and Heseltine should directed to:

Fred Tomlinson
25 Walnut Way
Ruislip
Middlesex HA4 6TA

BOUGHTON, Rutland

The Rutland Boughton Music Trust
Secretary: Mrs R. P. Campbell
Ashley Manor
Box
Wiltshire SN14 9AW

and

Michael Hurd
Music Adviser, Rutland Boughton Music Trust
4 Church Street
West Liss
Hampshire GU33 6JX

BOULT, Sir Adrian

All copyrights of material in the present volume are owned by the BBC.

BRAITHWAITE, S. H.

No direct descendant who might have an interest in his copyrights has been traced. Most of Braithwaite's music was in the possession of the late Freda Swain. Its present location is unknown.

BREWER, Sir Herbert

Capt Godfrey Brewer DSO RN
1 Granville Road
Limpsfield
Oxsted
Surrey RH8 0BX

BRIAN, William Havergal

Mrs Jean Furnival
24 The Meadway
Shoreham Beach
Sussex BN4 5RP

BRIDGE, Frank

The Frank Bridge Trust
Secretary: John Bishop
14 Barlby Road
London W10 6AR

BRITTEN, Benjamin, *Lord Britten*

The Britten-Pears Foundation
The Red House
Aldeburgh
Suffolk IP15 5PZ

and

Dr Donald Mitchell
3 Queen Square
London WC1N 3AU

BUTTERWORTH, George

A. J. Croft
George Butterworth Memorial Fund
c/o Clarendon Laboratory
Oxford

CHISHOLM, Erik

Mrs Sheila Smit
P.O. Box 101
Durbanville 7550
South Africa

The music is at: Stellenbosch University, South Africa

COATES, Albert

Miss Tamara Coates
83 Corringham Road
Golders Green
London NW11 7BS

The music is at: Cape Town University, South Africa

COURTAULD, Mr & Mrs Samuel

The Right Honourable Sir Adam Butler MP
House of Commons
London SW1A 0AA

DARNTON, Christian

Mrs Vera Darnton
Flat 3
66 The Drive
Hove
Sussex

DELIUS, Frederick *and* Jelka

Dr Lionel Carley
Archivist, The Delius Trust
16 Ogle Street
London W1P 7LG

DENT, Edward J.

The Residual Legatees of the Dent-Trend Estate
c/o Lloyds Bank
North Street
Broadway
Worcester WR12 7DR

DUNHILL, Thomas

Mrs Barbara Vincent
2 The Shrubery
Topsham
Exeter
Devon

and

David Dunhill
Beech Tree
Lydford
Oakhampton
Devon EX20 4AB

DYSON, Sir George

Miss Alice Dyson
1 St James Terrace
Winchester
Hants SO23 4PP

ELGAR, Sir Edward and C. Alice

Sir Edward Elgar Will Trust
The Royal Bank of Scotland
Trustee Division
Regent's House
P.O. Box 348
42 Islington High Street
London N1 8XL

FOULDS, John

Mrs Marybride Watt
2 Brasier Court
Minster
Sheerness
Kent ME12 3PW

GARDINER, H. Balfour

John Eliot Gardiner
3 Hauteville Court Gardens
Stamford Brook Avenue
London W6

and

Stephen Lloyd
85A Farley Hill
Luton, Beds

GIBBS, Armstrong

Mrs Ann Rust
Abbey Cottage
May Hill
Longhope
Gloucestershire GL117 0NF

GOOSSENS, Sir Eugene

Leon Goossens CBE
7A Ravenscourt Square
London W6

GRAINGER, Percy and Rose

Stewart Manville
7 Cromwell Place
White Plains
New York
10601
USA

and

Dr Kay Dreyfus
Grainger Museum
University of Melbourne
Parkville
Victoria 3052
Australia

GRAY, Cecil

Mrs P. K. Holdrup
(Pauline Gray)
4 Magnolia Wharf
Strand-on-the-Green
Chiswick
London W4 3N7

and

Trustees of the Estate of Cecil Gray
Dundas & Wilson, C.S.
25 Charlotte Square
Edinburgh EH2 4EZ

GURNEY, Ivor

Mr J. R. Haines
Haines & Sumner
Bastion House
Brunswick Road
Gloucester GL1 1JL

HADLEY, Patrick

Dr James Gibson
147 Petersham Road
Richmond
Surrey TW10 7AH

HARRISON, Beatrice *and* May

Miss Margaret Harrison
Hollesley Farm
Smallsfield
Nr Horley
Surrey RH6 JJ9

and

Mrs Patricia Cleveland-Peck
Harelands
Ashurst Wood
East Grinstead
East Sussex RH19 3SL

HARRISON, Julius

C. J. Harrison
Larkfield
St Christopher's Close
Little Kingshill
Great Missenden
Bucks

HARTY, Sir Hamilton

The copyright is vested in The Queen's University of Belfast:

Professor Adrian Thomas
Department of Music
The Queen's University of Belfast
Belfast
Northern Ireland DT7 1LS

HELY-HUTCHINSON, Victor

All copyrights in the present volume are owned by the BBC

HENRY, Leigh

Leigh Henry bequeathed all his music and his copyrights to Margaret Martyn, whom it has not proved possible to trace.

HERRMANN, Bernard

Norma Herrmann
9 Seymour Square
Brighton
Sussex BN2 1DW

HESELTINE, Philip ('Peter Warlock')

No direct descendent who might have an interest in the copyright can be traced. Enquiries should be directed to:
Fred Tomlinson
25 Walnut Way
Ruislip
Middlesex HA4 6TA

HEWARD, Leslie

Miss Karen Heward
185 Queen's Road
Norwich NR1 3PP

and

Lyndon Jenkins
3 Christchurch Close
Edgbaston
Birmingham B15 3NE

HOLBROOKE, Joseph

Gwydion Brooke
38 Carter Street
Fordham
Ely
Cambs CB7 5NG

HOLST, Gustav

Dr Colin Matthews
G. & I. Holst Ltd
79 New Cavendish Street
London W1M 8AQ

HOWELLS, Herbert

Mrs Ursula Pelissier
Plummers
Bishopstone
Seaford
Sussex BN25 2UD

IRELAND, John

The John Ireland Trust
25 St Mary's Mansions
St Mary's Terrace
London W2 1SQ

JAEGER, A. J.

Jaeger's widow became Mrs Hunter during World War I, and in the 1920s her daughter, Mary Hunter, was the private secretary to the Headmaster of Tollington School. Mrs Hunter died before World War II, and her daughter went to South America, where all attempts to trace her have failed. For practical purposes it presently appears impossible to resolve the copyright of unpublished Jaeger documents.

LAMBERT, Constant

Isobel Rawsthorne
Sudbury Cottage
Little Samford
Saffron Walden
Essex

LEGGE, Walter

Dr Elisabeth Legge-Schwarzkopf
Reghusstrasse 29
CH-8126 Zumikon
Zurich
Switzerland

LLOYD, George

George Lloyd
199 Clarence Gate Gardens
London NW1

MILFORD, Robin

Marion Milford
5 Wharf Close
Abingdon OX14 5HS

MOERAN, Ernest John

Walter Knott
2/10 Ormond Road
Ormond
Victoria 3163
Australia

NAYLOR, Edward

Naylor's son, the composer Bernard Naylor lived in Vancouver, Canada, and died in 1986. It is not known to whom Naylor's copyrights may have passed.

ORR, C. W.

After the death of Orr's widow, Helen Orr, his copyrights passed to the Musicians Benevolent Fund:

Martin Williams
The Musicians Benevolent Fund
16 Ogle Street
London W1

PARRY, Sir Hubert

Lord Ponsonby of Shulbrede
House of Lords
London SW1

QUILTER, Roger

Martin Williams
The Musicians Benevolent Fund
16 Ogle Street
London W1

RAWSTHORNE, Alan

Isobel Rawsthorne
Sudbury Cottage
Little Samford
Saffron Walden
Essex

RICHTER, Hans

David Loeb
83 Abingdon Villas
London W8

RONALD, Sir Landon

Ronald's son Vernon Ronald is believed to have died and his nephew Sheridan Russell cannot be traced. The most authoritative source is his biographer:

Bridget Duckenfeld
94 Station Avenue
West Ewell
Epsom
Surrey KT19 9UG

RUBBRA, Edmund

Edmund Rubbra died in 1986. Enquiries should be directed to:

Mrs C. Rubbra
Lindens
Bull Lane
Gerrards Cross
Bucks

SAMMONS, Albert

Mrs Alberta Hill
237A Carr Road
Northolt
Middlesex UB5 4RL

SMYTH, Dame Ethel

David Higham Associates Ltd
5-8 Lower John Street
Golden Square
London W1R 4HA

SOMERVELL, Sir Arthur

Elizabeth Jane Howard
28 Delancey Street
London NW1 7NH

STANFORD, Sir Charles Villiers

The Secretary
The Royal School of Church Music
Addington Palace
Croydon CR9 5AD

SWINGLER, Randall

Mrs Judith Williams
10 Cornwallis Crescent
Bristol BS8 4PL

THOMPSON, Herbert

Herbert Thompson died without children. His papers may be found in the Brotherton Library at Leeds University. No direct copyright owner is known.

TIPPETT, Sir Michael

Sir Michael Tippet, OM
48 Great Marlborough Street
London W1V 2BN

TOVEY, Sir Donald Francis

Trustees of Sir Donald F Tovey
c/o Messrs Skene Edwards & Garson, w.s.
5 Albyn Place
Edinburgh EH2 4NJ

VAN DIEREN, Bernard

*Van Dieren's son died several years ago. It has
not been possible to trace whether there is still any
descendant who may have a claim on the copyright. Contact:*

Alastair Chisholm
4 Frazer Street
Largs
Ayrshire KA30 9HP

VAUGHAN WILLIAMS, Ralph

Mrs Ursula Vaughan Williams
66 Gloucester Crescent
London NW1 7EG

WALFORD DAVIES, Sir Henry

The Trustees of the late Sir Walford Davies
c/o C. M. Wilson
White Goose Cottage
Kerswell
Cullompton
Devon EX15 2EL

WALLACE, William

*It has not been possible to trace whether there is
still any descendant who may have a claim on the
copyright*

WARLOCK, Peter *see* Heseltine, Philip

WALTON, Sir William

Lady Walton
La Mortella
80075
Forio D'Ischia
Italy

and

The Walton Foundation
Mrs Diana Rawstron
Goodman Derrick & Co
9–11 Fulwood Place
Gray's Inn
London WC1V 6HQ

WOOD, Sir Henry

The Principal
Royal Academy of Music
Marylebone Road
London NW1

WILLIAMS, Grace

Mrs Marian Glyn-Evans
23 Rushton Road
Wilbarston
Market Harborough
Leicester LE16 8QG

BIOGRAPHIES OF CORRESPONDENTS

Notes are provided on all of the writers. Recipients are only covered where they are the object of more than one item or where they are of considerable historical significance. In some cases more biographical or other information may also appear in the main text.

ALEXANDER, Arthur (1891–1969). New Zealand born pianist and teacher who lived in England for most of his life. A pupil of Tobias Matthay, he was pioneering in his repertoire. He was a personal friend of the Russian composer Medtner whose music he played. He married his pupil Freda Swain, pianist and composer, with whom he appeared as a well-known two-piano team.

ALLUM, Walter (1895–1986). As a composer and poet Allum was an amateur, but a talented one. His music includes a set of 24 Preludes for the piano.

ASHWELL, Lena (1872–1957). Musician and actress. Studied at the RAM, but became celebrated on the London stage during the 1890s and early 1900s.

BAINTON, Ethel. Wife of Edgar Bainton (1880–1956). Bainton was a pupil of Stanford. His music has been forgotten in the UK since his emigration to Australia in 1933, when he became Director of the NSW State Conservatorium, Sydney. He was principal of the Newcastle-upon-Tyne Conservatoire for many years, and while he was interned in Germany, at Ruhleben Camp, during World War I, his wife ran the Conservatoire virtually single-handed. She, too, had been interned at first, but the women internees were released after three months.

BALLING, Michael (1866–1925). German conductor: he was assistant conductor at Bayreuth from 1896, and Richter's successor in England, conducting *The Ring*, and the Hallé Orchestra, immediately before World War I.

BANTOCK, Sir Granville (1868–1946). Noted English composer, who in the mid-Edwardian period was often discussed in the same breath as Elgar, whom he succeeded as Professor of Music at Birmingham. The composer of orchestral tone poems, substantial choral works, including a complete setting of Fitzgerald's *Omar Khayyam*, and many songs, his output was very large. He was knighted, at Elgar's instigation, in 1930.

BARNES, George R. (b. 1904). Joined BBC as Talks Assistant 1935; Assistant Director Talks 1937; Talks Director 1941; Assistant Controller (Home) 1945. He became the Head of the Third Programme in 1946 and in 1948 Director Spoken Word.

BAX, Sir Arnold (1883–1953). Pupil of Corder and Matthay at the RAM (1900–5) and a brilliant sight-reader at the piano. He composed a substantial body of music at first subject to great Irish influence. Altogether he wrote 84 works requiring the orchestra, including seven symphonies, as well as a substantial body of chamber music, piano and choral music and over 100 songs. Knighted in 1937, he was appointed Master of the King's Musick in 1942.

BEECHAM, Sir Thomas (1879–1961). Celebrated English conductor and operatic impresario, well-known for his championship of various composers, including Delius, Sibelius, Strauss, Mozart and several French composers. Up to the 1930s it could be fairly said that he had done more than anyone living towards the establishment of Grand Opera in the UK. He founded the New Symphony Orchestra (1906), the Beecham Symphony Orchestra (1908), the LPO (1932) and the RPO (1946). His Covent Garden season of 1910 was epoch making and between then and World War 1, financed by his father Sir Joseph Beecham, he specialized in Wagner and a wide range of Russian music encompassing the Ballets Russes. The Beecham Opera Company did remarkable work during World War I and afterwards, and without its groundwork the British National Opera Co. could not have begun. Later he took control at Covent Garden during the years before World War II. Beecham succeeded brilliantly in his chosen repertoire over a long career, but was only ever willing to work from a position of total control, and thus when the BBC developed as a musical bureaucracy Beecham was not sympathetic. Sir Thomas was notoriously a bad co-operator in the radio studio. Although Beecham's last years succeeded gloriously in the recording studio, in the opera house they did not have the opportunities of his earlier career. He was knighted in 1914 and on his father's death became baronet in 1916.

BENNETT, George John (1863–1930). Organist and composer. Organist of Lincoln Cathedral and director of its Festival from 1905.

BLISS, Sir Arthur (1891–1975). After studying at Cambridge University and the RCM under Stanford, Bliss's early music did not survive World War I, and was withdrawn by its composer. He served successively in the Royal Fusiliers and the Grenadier Guards. Afterwards Bliss briefly became known as the leading British avant garde composer and a champion of the new. Yet his mature characteristics quickly became apparent in *Two Studies* for orchestra (1920) and *A Colour Symphony* (a sensation at the Gloucester Festival of 1922). His highly personal idiom has perhaps, only been truly appreciated since his death. 'Music must have panache' he said, and exemplified this in his ballets, his film music (probably the only timeless feature of the pioneering *Things to Come*), his opera *The Olympians*, and his choral works, especially *Morning Heroes*, his memorial for his brother and fallen comrades. He was Director of Music at the BBC 1942–4. Appointed Master of the Queen's Musick on Bax's death he was remarkably successful in re-establishing the ceremonial role of that office.

BLOIS, Colonel Eustace (1877–1933). After a military career during which he also studied music (including singing in Leipzig) he wrote an opera which remained in the repertoire of the Moody-Manners Company. He first worked for Covent

Garden in 1919, and joined the newly formed London Opera Syndicate in 1925 with Mrs Courtauld as Chairman. He became Managing Director in 1928 under the Chairmanship of F. A. Szarvasy.

BLUNT, Bruce (1899–1957). Journalist, wine importer, francophile and author of verse set by 'Peter Warlock' at the end of his life. Warlock and Blunt were regular drinking companions and in February 1927 were each fined 10 shillings for being drunk and disorderly together in Cadogan Street, London. Warlock set five poems by Blunt between 1927 and 1930, the first two twice ('The First Mercy', 'Bethlehem Down', 'The Cricketers of Hambledon', 'The Frostbound Wood' and 'The Fox'). Each contributor appears to have found a sympathy with his collaborator which gave a haunting if elusive quality to their work.

BOOSEY, Leslie (1887–1979). Music publisher. The firm of Boosey & Co. merged with Hawkes & Co. in 1930, and he remained with Boosey & Hawkes until 1963. Chairman of the PRS 1929–1954. By securing the lease in 1944 he saved the Royal Opera House from becoming a dance hall.

BORSDORF, Adolf (1858–1923). Celebrated horn player, born in Germany but settled in England and was a founder member of the LSO in 1904. He had a major influence on horn playing in the UK and was the teacher of both Aubrey and Alfred Brain.

BOUGHTON, Rutland (1878–1960). English composer. Taught at Bantock's Midland Institute School of Music (1905–11) and between 1914 and 1927 organized the Glastonbury Festival, inspired in equal measure by arts-and-crafts socialism and by the music dramas of Wagner. The main product of this movement was a series of operas uniquely involving the chorus as commentator and encompassing a cycle of five Arthurian dramas (the last two written later have never been performed). *The Immortal Hour* was first heard at Glastonbury in 1914 and made him famous with productions in Birmingham in 1921 and London in 1922 and 1923, when it had a record run. His orchestral music is only beginning to be known in the 1980s with broadcasts of the Second and Third Symphonies.

BOULT, Sir Adrian (1889–1983). Celebrated English conductor, to a large extent the architect of the received assessment of his own generation of British composers. Studied at the Leipzig Conservatoire and Christ Church, Oxford. He started as a disciple of Nikisch; conducted Diaghilev ballets and opera at Covent Garden in 1914. Established the City of Birmingham [Symphony] Orchestra 1924–30. Music Director BBC 1930–42. While DM he was notably wide-ranging in his sympathies, Berg, for example, writing on 15 April 1935: 'That my compositions are esteemed in England and not in my own home country ... makes me proud', after Boult had given symphonic excerpts from *Lulu*. A year before he had performed the opera *Wozzeck* and repeated it in 1946. Chief conductor BBCSO 1930–50, he became Principal Conductor LPO from 1950. Boult enjoyed an Olympian old age as a conductor, his stature accorded belated recognition through the sudden growth of recorded repertoires, especially of British music. Knighted in 1937 and appointed Companion of Honour 1969.

BRAITHWAITE, Sam Hartley ('Tim') (1883–1947). British composer and artist. Student of Corder at the RAM. He succeeded Holst as director of the Passmore

Edwards Settlement from 1910 to 1913, and was friend of Bax and his circle. Two of his orchestral scores, *Snow Picture* and *Elegy*, were published under the Carnegie Trust's publication scheme. Later Braithwaite abandoned music for painting and etching.

BREWER, Sir Herbert (1865–1928). English organist and composer. Born and died in Gloucester, and organist of the Gloucester Cathedral from 1896–1928. Identified with Three Choirs Festival. His oratorio *Emmaus* was scored by Elgar.

BRIAN, [William] Havergal (1876–1972). English composer and musical journalist, who quickly established himself before World War I. The loss of his patron and the changes brought by the War resulted in few performances taking place for 40 years. He continued composing, yet although his vast *Gothic Symphony* was published in 1932, it was not performed until 1961. Interest in his music was fostered by Reginald Nettel's book *Ordeal by Music* (1945) and by Robert Simpson at the BBC, who managed to have all 32 symphonies broadcast between 1954 and 1979.

BRIDGE, Frank (1879–1941). English composer, conductor, viola player and the teacher of Benjamin Britten. His music was at first romantic, the impressionistic suite *The Sea* being a notable success before World War I. Later he turned to expressionism as he attempted to articulate the pain of the War, a development crowned by his *Oration* for cello and orchestra. His later output was not appreciated in the 1930s, one critic accusing him of 'uglifying his music'. Even as late as 1960 one leading musician wrote to Britten seriously asking if some Bridge manuscripts were worth preservation. The revival started at the instigation of Britten and dates from the late 1960s. It was consolidated by recordings and the promotional activities of the Frank Bridge Trust. Bridge is now regarded as one of the leading British composers of his day.

BRITTEN, Benjamin (1913–1976). The most influential English composer of his day. Initially seen as a precocious youngster, his residence in the USA at the outbreak of World War II crystallized attitudes against him. He returned to England in 1942 and was established as a major figure by his opera *Peter Grimes* (1945). The establishment of the Aldeburgh Festival and his custom of writing for a circle of sympathetic performers, particularly his friend Sir Peter Pears, resulted in a clique of admirers who promoted his interests, and tended to cause some reaction after his death. The leading accompanist of his generation and a conductor of flair and insight, he would have been celebrated even if he had not composed. His operas were the first by a British composer to enter the permanent International repertoire, and his various other works, particularly for voice, stamped an indelible personality on British musical life. He was the last English composer to produce choral works that entered the regular repertoire of amateur choral societies with the great works of the past. He was created Lord Britten in 1976, and had been appointed a Companion of Honour in 1953, and to the Order of Merit in 1965.

BRODSKY, Adolph (1851–1929). Celebrated Russian violinist who gave the first performance of the Tchaikovsky *Violin Concerto*. The Brodsky String Quartet was one of the leading quartets of its day, dedicatees of the Elgar Quartet. Brodsky succeeded Hallé as Principal of the Royal Manchester College of Music in 1895 and held the post until his death.

BUESST, Aylmer (1883–1970). Assistant Music Director of the BBC 1933–5. Australian conductor and violinist. Studied at the Leipzig Conservatory, attending Nikisch's conducting classes. Conducted the Moody-Manners Opera Co., Beecham Opera Co., and the BNOC. After working for the BBC he was conductor of the Scottish Orchestra (1939–40).

BUSH, Alan (b. 1900). English composer and pianist. Studied with Corder at the RAM and later with John Ireland. As a pianist he first studied with Matthay whom he now regards as 'ruining English piano playing for 40 years'. His own technique was developed by his study with Benno Moiseiwistch whose assistant Miss Mabel Lander taught him the Leschetizky method systematically. Later went to Schnabel, another Leschetizky pupil. He studied in Berlin and embraced Communism. He at first composed in an idiom which reflected the latest trends from central Europe. Subsequently, in the 1940s, his style began to be simplified, exemplifying consciously 'English' characteristics. Bush has written in almost every form, though his operas have achieved greater success in Eastern Europe than in the West. He remains a major figure of his period who awaits adequate assessment.

BUSH, Geoffrey (b. 1920). English composer, teacher and musicologist. At the time of John Ireland's letter to him (p. 252) Bush was working at the Hostel of the Good Shepherd, Tredegar, helping to look after evacuated boys who for one reason or another were unbilletable in private homes. He studied at Balliol College Oxford taking the MA in classics and DMus both in 1946. Most of his teaching career devoted to extra mural lecturing at Oxford and London. Well known as a scholar specializing in British music, he has worked particularly on nineteenth-century composers including Sterndale Bennett, Stanford and Parry. His music includes operas, orchestral works including two symphonies, choral and chamber works, and a notable group of songs.

BUTTERWORTH, George (1885–1916). English composer, educated at Eton and Oxford. An early collector of folk-song and friend of Vaughan Williams. He left few works, these include settings of Housman's *A Shropshire Lad* poems. He took the theme from his song 'Loveliest of Trees' for his orchestral Rhapsody *A Shropshire Lad*. His other orchestral scores are *The Banks of Green Willow*, *Two English Idylls* and an orchestral version of his song cycle *Love Blows as the Wind Blows*.

CHAPMAN, Ernest (1914–1983). Largely self-taught writer and editor. Worked for Boosey & Hawkes 1934–47 and editor of *Tempo* 1939–47. Responsible for a lot of the ground-work in developing the Macnaghten Concerts. A personal friend of Bloch, he was the dedicatee of his *Fifth String Quartet*.

CHISHOLM, Erik (1904–1965). Scottish composer, pianist and conductor. Champion of Berlioz in the 1930s. Pupil of Tovey. He lived in Canada before becoming Musical Director of Celtic Ballet, then conductor with Carl Rosa Opera Co (1940–41) and Anglo-Polish Ballet (1941–44). Dean and Director of Music of the South African College of Music at Cape Town. His music includes 12 operas, six ballets, orchestral works including two piano concertos, a violin concert and two symphonies. His trilogy of three one-act operas *Murder in Three Keys* was televised by the BBC in 1953, and ran for 10 weeks in New York in 1954.

CHURCH, Richard (1893–1972). Poet, novelist and man of letters. At the time of Bax's letter (p. 146) he was, among other things, a columnist on the *Radio Times*.

CLARK, Edward (1888–1962). Musical administrator who studied in Vienna before World War I, and was on first-hand terms with Schoenberg and his circle. Worked for the BBC 1923–36, and was a champion of the European avant garde in the 1920s and 1930s. Husband of the composer Elizabeth Lutyens.

CLIFFORD, Hubert (1904–1959). Australian conductor and composer. From 1941–44 he worked for the BBC and was then a professor at the RAM. Musical Director of Alexander Korda's London Film Productions 1946–50. His music includes various orchestral works, film scores and a symphony (1940).

COATES, Albert (1882–1953). Born in St Petersburg and died in Cape Town, Coates was, nevertheless, British. Studied at the Leipzig Conservatory where he was influenced by Nikisch, under whom he became a repetiteur at the Leipzig Opera. At 29 he conducted *Siegfried* in St Petersburg and became the conductor of the Marinsky Theatre. Coates returned to England and in 1919 launched on an international career, giving a variety of premieres of British composers such as Bax, Delius, Holst and Vaughan Williams. He subsequently lived in the USA and from 1946 in South Africa. His compositions, by which he himself set great store, are highly proficient and informed by his time in Russia. He wrote nine operas, various orchestral works including *The Eagle* (a tone poem in tribute to Nikisch for chorus and orchestra (1925)), piano and cello concerti, three symphonies, two film scores and a variety of songs.

CONCORDE, R Norman-. Impresario and director of the Concorde Concert Control.

COOLIDGE, Elizabeth Sprague (1864–1953). American patron of music, whose generosity enabled composers of chamber music, many of them British, to write substantial works. In 1916 she found herself a considerable heiress. Establishing first the Berkshire Quartet and then a Berkshire Festival of Chamber Music, she quickly inaugurated a prize for new chamber music. She decided to give the 1923 Festival a British emphasis and commissioned a new piece from Eugene Goossens (his Sextet). Visiting London to research this project she met Frank Bridge, with whom she formed a close friendship. The Coolidge Medal and the Coolidge Foundation were other examples of her patronage which continued until old age, and, among British composers, after Bridge's death focused on the young Benjamin Britten.

CORBETT-SMITH, Arthur (1879–1944). Secretary General of the Naval and Military Musical Union and a gifted singer, pianist and lecturer. Under the pseudonym of Aston Tyrrold he composed popular songs. Promoted to Major he was invalided home from France in 1916. He published a number of books including accounts of the Marne and Mons, and later edited the National Opera Handbooks for Grant Richards.

CORDER, Frederick (1852–1932). English composer and teacher of composition at the RAM, where his pupils included Holbrooke, Bantock, Bax and (much later) Alan Bush. The earliest translator of Wagner's operas into English. He established the Society of British Composers (with Matthay) in 1905.

COURTAULD, Samuel (1876–1947). Industrialist and patron of the arts. With his wife he established wide-ranging and generous patronage of music and the visual arts. Their home at 20 Portman Square was a centre for artistic life in London. From 1925 to 1927 they were associated with the promotion of opera at Covent Garden. Mrs Courtauld was possibly better-known as a patron in her own right and in 1929 started the Courtauld-Sargent Concerts at London's Queen's Hall. She died in December 1931.

DALE, Benjamin J. (1885–1943). Composer and pianist. He studied with Corder at the RAM, who promoted his large-scale Piano Sonata (1905) which made his name. Later composed music for the viola and for the orchestra. He became warden of the RAM in 1937 and was on the BBC music panel from 1936 until his death.

DAMROSCH, Walter (1862–1950). Born in Breslau but became naturalized American. Celebrated conductor, initially specializing in Wagner. Relaunched the NY Symphony Society which he conducted for nearly 25 years, taking it on an extended European tour in 1920 to England, France and Italy. He was also a composer, one of his three operas being *The Man Without a Country*, briefly celebrated in the 1930s, as well as incidental music and choral works including a setting of *The Canterbury Pilgrims*.

DARNTON, Christian (1905–1981). English composer who at first wrote as a noisy aphoristic avant gardiste. Later, during World War II, he changed to a populist stance fuelled by his Communist beliefs, and works in the latter vein include his *Ballad of Freedom*. Of his *Third Symphony*, broadcast in 1945, Lennox Berkeley wrote in assessment (23/8/44) 'It strikes me as a big advance on anything I have seen or heard by this composer . . . I feel a struggle going on between his sense of tonality and a desire to free himself from conventional harmony . . .'. His opera *Fantasy Fair* (1947) is of the genre of Weill and Krenek. Later scores attempt a synthesis and broadcasts of his remarkable *Concerto for Orchestra* and *Fourth Symphony*, in 1975 and 1984 remind us that he is a figure of some stature who needs performance for a full evaluation. Darton was also a painter, and his book *You and Music* was published by Pelican Books in 1940.

DELIUS, Frederick (1862–1934). Celebrated English composer who lived most of his life abroad, successively in the USA, Norway, Germany and France. Many of his first performances came in Germany between 1900 and 1914. After the War he was more appreciated in England, and his music was championed by Beecham, his reputation finally crowned with the first Delius Festival, in London in 1929. The appearance of the Delius Society in the 1930s dedicated to recording Delius's music further assisted its dissemination. The Delius Trust from the 1960s onward (the Trust had been formed in 1935) used the royalty income to promote performances and recordings and these included all six operas and the art of Eric Fenby, Delius's amanuensis, as interpreter. In the early 1920s Delius began to show the symptoms of the progressive paralysis which resulted in him being blind and totally immobile for the last eight years of his life.

DELIUS, Jelka (1868–1935). More accurately Helene Sophie Emilie Rosen. She had been born in Belgrade, her parents coming from Schleswig-Holstein. Established as a painter in her own right before she met Delius, but after their marriage she subordinated her art in the interest of Delius's music.

DENT, Edward J. (1876–1957). English scholar and Professor of Music at Cambridge 1926–41. Founding President of the International Society for Contemporary Music 1923–37.

DIEREN, Bernard Van. *see* VAN DIEREN, Bernard.

DUNHILL, Thomas (1877–1946). English composer, pupil of Stanford, Assistant Music Master at Eton College 1899–1908. Has tended to be remembered for *Tantivy Towers*, one of the most successful British light operas from the inter-war period. He also wrote two other light operas, as well as chamber and orchestral music, and the celebrated song 'The Cloths of Heaven'. Author of several books including one on Elgar.

DYSON, Sir George (1883–1964). Composer and organist. Studied at the RCM. Taught at various public schools including Rugby and Winchester. Director of the RCM 1937–52. Compositions are mainly choral, including a noted setting of *The Canterbury Pilgrims*, but also include a symphony (1937). Knighted in 1941.

ECKERSLEY, Roger (1885–1955). After careers in law, the Foreign Office and farming, cut short by illness, he joined the BBC as Director of Programmes (1924–30); Assistant Controller (1930–39) and Chief Censor (1939–45).

ELGAR, Lady Caroline Alice (1848–1920). The daughter of Major-General Sir Henry Gee Roberts, she was nearly nine years Elgar's senior and was 41 when she married Elgar. Her marriage was opposed by her family on grounds of social station and religion (Elgar was a Catholic). Some of her verses are set by Elgar, notably in *Sea Pictures*. Elgar was desolated by her death 14 years before his own.

ELGAR, Sir Edward (1857–1934). England's major composer after Purcell. Son of a Worcester music dealer and piano teacher he was self-taught, his education being practical rather than academic. He gradually developed a provincial reputation as a composer until national recognition came with *Enigma Variations* in 1899. The great works of his maturity date from 1899 to 1913. *The Dream of Gerontius* (1900) was the climax of a series of choral works popular in the provinces, including *The Black Knight* (1892), *The Light of Life* (1896), *King Olaf* (1896) and *Caractacus* (1898). However, it was with his orchestral works that Elgar became famous, particularly the trio tune of his *Pomp and Circumstance* March No. 1, given added memorability for a mass audience by the words 'Land of hope and glory'. The *First Symphony* (1908) achieved over 100 performances in its first 12 months, including many on the continent and in North America. After *Gerontius* was hailed a masterpiece by Richard Strauss at the Lower Rhine Festival in 1901 his music was widely played in Germany until the War intervened. Knighted in 1904, appointed to the Order of Merit in 1911, appointed Master of the King's Musick in 1924 and created baronet in 1931. He was the first composer to preserve his own performances of most of his music on record.

EVANS, Edwin (1874–1945). Critic and writer on music. Championed young British composers and succeeded Dent as President of the ISCM in 1938.

FENNEY, William (1891–1957). Protégé and student of Bantock at Birmingham.

Influenced by Elgar, Bantock thought Fenney's style advanced. Later Fenney abandoned composition, feeling himself to be unsympathetic to postwar trends. He died in total obscurity and isolation, his body lying for some time before it was discovered. Only a few of his works (mainly chamber ones) have been published.

FOULDS, John (1880–1939). English composer and conductor who started professionally as an orchestral cellist in the Hallé Orchestra. Fould's *A World Requiem* was the equivalent to Britten's *War Requiem* for the 1920s, and became a regular if short-lived event at the Albert Hall on Armistice Night, drawing large crowds. In his day Foulds was best known as a light music composer. He became Musical Director of All India Radio in Delhi. Promoted to the Calcutta station in April 1939, he was dead within nine days of arriving there, apparently of cholera. His output is a substantial and important one; it is not possible to form a balanced view of British music in his time without experience of it.

GAISBERG, Fred (1873–1951). Recording impresario, American by birth, internationalist by profession but English by domicile. He grew up with the development of the gramophone and worked with Emile Berliner from the first days of recording. As the International Artists Manager to The Gramophone Company he was responsible for the many great names who appeared on the HMV label from the first, and by his friendship with Elgar ensured that for the first time a great composer's own readings of his own music be preserved for posterity.

GARDINER, H. Balfour (1877–1950). English composer. With his friends Percy Grainger, Cyril Scott, Roger Quilter and Norman O'Neill, referred to as the 'Frankfurt Gang', because they studied at the Hoch'sche Konservatorium. Financially independent, his patronage was directed to the less well-off members of his own circle (particularly Holst) and in later years he secured Delius his home. His series of eight concerts of the then new British music in 1912–13, effectively launched Bax, Holst, Percy Grainger and others as composers. He destroyed much of his own music, though, of his surviving short orchestral or choral works, *Shepherd Fennel's Dance* was very popular and is still occasionally heard.

GANZ, A. W. The son of William Ganz (1833–1914) who settled in London in 1850 and was a professor at the Guildhall School of Music. A. W. was prominent in London musical circles between the wars, though professionally a barrister. He was an early champion of Berlioz. He encountered George Lloyd when the young Lloyd's opera *Iernin* was given in 1935. Ganz attended most performances, commissioned a sculpture of the young composer and later championed Lloyd when during World War II the composer was almost fatally shell-shocked in HMS Trinidad.

GOOSSENS, Sir Eugene (1893–1962). English composer and conductor from a celebrated musical family. He studied composition with Stanford at the RCM. At first a rank and file violinist, he took up conducting and became Beecham's assistant during World War I. After conducting at Covent Garden he went to the USA (1923–46) and later to Australia. He composed extensively, including two symphonies and the operas *Judith* and *Don Juan de Manara*. He was knighted in 1955.

GOSS, John (1894–1953). English baritone, well-known as interpreter of English song. He was particularly associated with Heseltine whose *Sociable Songs* were dedicated to him.

GRAINGER, Percy (1882–1961). Australian pianist, composer and folk-song collector. Like Balfour Gardiner one of the 'Frankfurt Gang'. Celebrated in his lifetime as a pianist, his popular short compositions including *Shepherd's Hey* and *Country Gardens* earned him substantial royalties. His more extended compositions and experiments in pulseless sound ('free music') have only recently been accorded serious attention. His mother Rose Grainger (1861–1922) dominated his life until her suicide and unwittingly prevented him from becoming a normally adjusted person.

GRAY, Cecil (1895–1951). Musical critic and writer. Associate of Philip Heseltine and his biographer. His music, which includes three operas and orchestral works has been forgotten, yet deserves at least a hearing.

GURNEY, Ivor (1890–1937). English poet and song composer. A pupil of Brewer and Stanford (who once remarked to Herbert Howells: 'mark my words that boy will end up mad') who after war experiences, including being gassed at Passchendaele, was admitted to Dartford Insane Asylum (1922–37). His musical reputation was fostered by the work of Marion Scott, Gerald Finzi and Herbert Howells. His poetic output has been edited by Edmund Blunden and R. K. R. Thornton.

HADLEY, Patrick (1899–1973). English composer who lost a leg in World War I and whose brother was killed. He subsequently studied at Cambridge and at the RCM (the latter with Vaughan Williams). Professor of music at Cambridge (1946–1962). His output is comparatively small, showing the influence of folk song and Delius. He finds a passionately individual voice best heard in the cantata *The Hills* (1946), which celebrates the landscape of the Peak district.

HADOW, Sir [W.] Henry (1859–1937). Educationalist and writer on music. Lecturer at Worcester College Oxford. Vice-Chancellor of Sheffield University from 1919. Chairman of the Hadow Committee on education (report: 1926). His compositions are early and tend to be Victorian in sympathy.

HARRISON, Julius (1885–1963). English composer and conductor. Studied at the Midland Institute under Bantock, and assisted Nikisch and Weingartner in Paris in 1914. Conducted for the Beecham Opera Co and then BNOC. Conducted Hastings Municipal Orch from 1930, maintaining a final season after the outbreak of War in 1940. His earlier music was later withdrawn, but he produced several substantial works for chorus and orchestra, and popular orchestral works including the *Worcestershire Suite* and *Bredon Hill*. There were also chamber works, piano music, songs and part songs.

HARRISON, May (1891–1951). English violinist, sister of Beatrice and Margaret. Studied with Arbos and Rivarde at the RCM and in St Petersburg with Auer. She was celebrated while still in her teens, touring Europe. Later she became associated with Delius, Bax and several other British composers.

HARTY, Sir Hamilton (1879–1941). Ulster composer, conductor and pianist. First established as the accompanist of famous singers and gradually changed to conducting. He wrote an *Irish Symphony*, violin and piano concerti, short orchestral works, songs etc. Conductor of the Hallé Orchestra 1920–33. He was knighted in 1925.

HELY-HUTCHINSON, Victor (1901–1947). British composer and administrator, born in South Africa. First joined BBC in 1926. Professor of Music at Birmingham 1934–44. Director of Music BBC 1944–47. Best known for his *A Carol Symphony*.

HENRY, Leigh [Vaughan] (1889–1958). English composer and critic. Youthful works shown to Bantock when Leigh Henry was 16, elicited encouragement. At 23 he was appointed director of music in Edward Gordon Craig's School for the Art of Theatre, Florence. He was interned in Germany at Ruhleben Camp during World War I. Founded the magazine *Fanfare* in 1921 but it only lasted for seven issues. He was never established in the UK as a composer, but works include the *commedia dell'arte* ballet *The Rogueries of Corviello*, published in New York, the symphony *Llyn-y-Fan*, the opera *The Moon Robber*, and various other orchestral works.

HERBAGE, Julian (1904–1976). English broadcaster and musicologist. Joined the BBC in 1927 acting as Assistant Director of Music 1940–46. He worked on planning the Promenade Concerts from before the War until 1961, and from 1944 to 1973 introduced the weekly programme 'Music Magazine'.

HERRMANN, Bernard (1911–1975). American composer and conductor, best known for his film scores for Orson Welles and Alfred Hitchcock, and for his pioneering performances of Charles Ives. He had a unique sympathy among American conductors for British music, exploring a wide repertoire. In the latter part of his life lived and worked in London for long periods, becoming a significant influence on the appreciation of British music by broadcasting and recording works by Rubbra, Cyril Scott, Lambert and others. His own music includes an opera *Wuthering Heights*, two symphonies, a violin concerto, a cantata *Moby Dick*, and many orchestral scores including suites from his film scores.

HESELTINE, Philip (1894–1930). English composer and working musicologist. From a well-to-do background he inhabited the more Bohemian fringes of British musical life, encouraged by Delius and van Dieren, both of whom he revered. Composer chiefly of songs, and a pioneering transcriber of seventeenth-century song manuscripts. He founded the periodical *The Sackbut* in 1920 and was part of the circle which included Cecil Gray, E. J. Moeran and Constant Lambert. He first adopted the pseudonym 'Peter Warlock' in 1917.

HEWARD, Leslie (1897–1943). English conductor. He studied with Stanford who, his friend Donald Suddaley felt 'crippled Leslie as a composer'. Conducted for BNOC. Musical Director South African Broadcasting Commission 1924–7. Conductor City of Birmingham Symphony Orchestra 1930–43.

HIGGINS, Henry Vincent (1855–1928). Solicitor and businessman: Director of the Carlton and Ritz Hotels companies. Chairman of the Grand Opera Syndicate formed in 1896 on the death of Sir A. Harris, to carry on the business of promoting opera in London during the summer seasons.

HOLBROOKE, Josef [he later spelled it Joseph] (1878–1958). English composer and pianist. Unlike many composers of his generation, he came from a poor family background and had a hard struggle to establish a livelihood, as a pianist and gradually as a composer. During the Edwardian age he was thought of in British musical circles as a 'dangerously modern' composer. The works he wrote then have not lasted in the repertoire and it is difficult with justice to judge him, unheard. He came under the patronage of Lord Howard de Walden, whose Celtic liberetto he set in his operatic trilogy *The Cauldron of Annwn*. Holbrooke's late works have never been fully catalogued and most remain in manuscript. His huge output includes at least eight operas, three ballets, a large number of orchestral works, chamber and piano music and songs. He made a significant contribution to the establishment of the emerging British composers in the 1900s by promoting their music in his chamber concerts.

HOLST, Gustav (1874–1934). English composer whose family had come from Sweden three generations before, though Holst retained the 'von' in his name until World War I. He studied at the RCM with Stanford and became a lifelong friend of Vaughan Williams. At first he earned his living as a trombonist. Director of Music at St Paul's Girls School 1905–34 and Director of Music at Morley College 1907–24. Influenced by the folk-song movement and by Sanskrit literature. He took a long time to establish himself as a composer. Revived the tradition of Byrd and Weelkes. *The Planets* (arguably the most popular of any British music) was started before World War I and was completed in 1916. First played privately in 1918 under Adrian Boult's baton it was not heard complete in public until presented by Albert Coates in December 1920. Holst's later works, particularly his *Choral Symphony* and *Choral Fantasia,* were not fully appreciated by contemporary audiences.

HOWELLS, Herbert (1892–1983). English composer. Student of Stanford at the RCM and teacher of composition there for over 60 years, he was the last heir of Stanford and Parry. Chiefly known for his church and organ music, he also wrote a number of orchestral works, including two substantial piano concerti, and extended works for soloists, chorus and orchestra of which the best known is *Hymnus Paradisi*, a personal requiem for the composer's son Michael who died in 1935 aged ten. His *Stabat Mater* was revived in 1986 and a number of unfamiliar scores of very high quality will need to return to performance before an objective assessment of Howells's considerable stature can be made.

IRELAND, John (1879–1962). English composer and student of Stanford at the RCM. Professionally a choirmaster and organist for over 40 years. He taught composition at the RCM between the wars. His reputation was established with piano music, chamber music and a substantial literature of songs. He became celebrated, literally overnight, after the first performance of his *Second Violin Sonata* in 1917. Of his orchestral works *The Forgotten Rite* (1912) and *Mai-Dun* (1921) were both inspired by place, while his *Piano Concerto* (1930) was perhaps the best-known example by a British composer for two or three decades. He also composed church music, the cantata *These Things Shall Be* and the film score *The Overlanders*.

JAEGER, August J. (1860–1909). German-born employee of Novello and Co. whose influence played a significant part in promoting the careers of the emergent generation of British composers after about 1895, especially Elgar. He was 'Nimrod' of the *Enigma Variations*.

KELLY, Frederick Septimus (1881–1916). Australian born composer and pianist. Educated at Eton and Oxford, he was a renowned sportsman, rowing for England in the 1908 Olympic Regatta. Later studied at the Hoch'sche Konservatorium in Frankfurt. An Australian tour as a concert pianist in 1911 was followed by appearances in London. He was killed in action at Beaumont-Hamel in France in November 1916. His surviving compositions are few in number and include chamber music, songs and two for small orchestra: the five movement *Serenade* op 7 for flute and small orchestra (1911) and the *Elegy* for string orchestra (with harp) 'In Memoriam Rupert Brooke', written during the two months after Brooke's death in 1915.

KEYNES, Sir Geoffrey (1887–1985). Celebrated surgeon and man of letters, and a leading expert on William Blake. His brother was John Maynard Keynes who was married to the ballerina Lydia Lopokova. Gwen Raverat, the designer of Vaughan Williams's *Job* was Sir Geoffrey's sister in law, and cousin to Ralph Vaughan Williams.

KILBURN, Nicholas (1843–1923). A Sunderland iron merchant whose amateur enthusiasm for music led him to succeed at the highest academic musical qualifications. As a choral conductor he produced all Elgar's major works. The two men, introduced by Kilburn's enthusiasm for Elgar's music, remained friends until Kilburn's death.

LAMBERT, Constant (1905–1951). English composer, conductor and writer. His contribution to the development of ballet in the UK is an honoured one. His is a sad tale of youthful brilliance culminating through overwork and excessive drinking in his death two days before his 46th birthday. His output as a composer is small – 20 published works – but includes such celebrated scores as *The Rio Grande* and the ballet *Horoscope*. His ballet *Romeo and Juliet* was the first British ballet commissioned by Diaghilev and was produced when Lambert was only 21. His book *Music Ho!* was the most widely read volume of music criticism of its generation.

LEGGE, Robin H. (1862–1933). English music critic. Studied law at Cambridge and music at Leipzig (where he was a contemporary of Delius) and elsewhere on the continent. Worked on *The Times* 1891–1906. Music critic of *The Daily Telegraph* 1906–1931.

LEGGE, Walter (1906–1979). English recording producer and writer on music. Worked for HMV from 1927. Deputy music critic of *The Manchester Guardian* 1934–8. From then until the outbreak of war acted as Beecham's assistant artistic director at Covent Garden. Organized ENSA concerts during World War II. Founded the Philharmonia Orchestra in 1945, as an élite orchestra which established high standards of performance and interpretation. Married the singer Elisabeth Schwarzkopf in 1953.

LLOYD, George (b. 1913). English composer. His Third Symphony was broadcast by the BBC when he was 22, the year in which his opera *Iernin* enjoyed a London run. His second opera, *The Serf*, was commissioned for Covent Garden in 1938 (both operas to libretti by his father William Lloyd). His early success was cut short by the War in which severe shell shock caused a protracted physical collapse. He was commissioned to write a third opera, *John Socman*, for the Festival of Britain, and John Ogden took up his *First Piano Concerto* in 1964, but he did not establish himself with a wide audience until Edward Downes took up his music in 1977 and performed all his later symphonies. Now established in the repertoire again, Lloyd has preferred to conduct his own first performances and recordings, introducing his *Eleventh Symphony* in the USA in 1986.

LOPOKOVA, Lydia (1892–1981). Russian ballerina, who married John Maynard Keynes (brother of Sir Geoffrey Keynes) and spent the majority of her life in England. Danced with Diaghilev's Ballets Russes and later associated with the Camargo Society and the Vic-Wells Ballet.

MANNERS, Charles (1857–1935). The professional name of the Irish bass and operatic manager Southcote Mansergh. After an extensive singing career during which he married the soprano Fanny Moody (in 1890), they established the Moody-Manners Opera Company. Particularly associated with provincial touring they actively promoted new British operas.

MATTHAY, Tobias (1858–1945). English piano teacher of wide influence, long associated with the RAM, who later founded his own school.

MAWER, Sir Allen (1879–1942). University lecturer and professor of English in various universities and colleges. Between 1921 and 1929 Baines Professor of English Language at Liverpool.

MOERAN, Ernest John (1894–1950). English composer of Irish descent whose music was closely associated with Irish folksong and landscape. Wounded in World War I, a piece of shrapnel lodging in his head. This may have been the cause of later instability. He studied at the RCM before the War and afterwards took lessons from John Ireland. His style is uniquely forged from folk song and the idioms of several of his contemporaries, including Ravel, Ireland, Bax, Vaughan Williams and Sibelius, which in his finest works, such as the *Symphony in G Minor* take on a memorable personality, though all his later works took him extraordinary trouble to articulate on paper.

MURRIL, Herbert (1909–1952). English composer who studied and later taught composition at the RAM. His early works include the jazz-influenced opera *Man in Cage* (1930). By the time of his best-known work, the *Second Cello Concerto* (1950), he had adopted a rhapsodic style (here incorporating a Catalan folk song). He joined the BBC in 1936 becoming Assistant Head of Music (1948–50) and Director of Music (1950–52).

NAYLOR, Edward (1867–1934). English church music composer and organist whose ripe harmony is best heard in his celebrated anthem *Vox Dicentis* (1911). He composed a number of large-scale works, all published, of which the prize-winning opera *The Angelus* has not been produced since the 1920s.

O'NEILL, Norman (1875–1934). One of the 'Frankfurt Group'. English composer and conductor whose career was mainly in the theatre, particularly at the Haymarket Theatre, London. His fairly extensive list of compositions includes much incidental music.

ORR, Charles Wilfred (1893–1976). Lived in seclusion in the Cotswolds for most of his life, his reputation dependent on a tiny output, just 35 songs of which two thirds are settings of Housman, and a few instrumental pieces.

PARRY, Sir Charles Hubert Hastings (1848–1918). English composer and teacher of radical outlook but 'county' background, educated at Eton and Oxford. At first launched on a business career, he came under the influence of the illustrious pianist Edward Dannreuther (1844–1905), who was an ardent Wagnerian. Parry succeeded Grove as Director of the RCM in 1894 and was simultaneously Professor of Music at Oxford 1900–8. His musical output is large, including more than two dozen extended works for chorus and orchestra, five symphonies and other orchestral works, much church music and organ music, piano and chamber music and a large number of songs. The objective re-assessment of Parry as a composer only really got into its stride in the 1980s, and it is still difficult to arrive at an overall view based on performance. However, even on the basis of *Blessed Pair of Sirens* and *Jerusalem,* his reputation is secure.

PETRI, Egon (1881–1962). Celebrated German pianist, known as an interpreter of Busoni's music, whose pupil he was.

PIGGOTT, Patrick (b. 1915). English composer, pianist, writer and administrator. Concert pianist and university lecturer 1939 to 1965. BBC Midland Region Head of Music 1965–1970. He has withdrawn many of his early works; his compositions include piano and chamber music, vocal works and concerti for violin and for piano.

PITT, Percy (1869–1932). English composer, conductor and operatic manager. Studied in Leipzig while Delius had been there. Appointed organist, accompanist and repetiteur at Queen's Hall (1896–1902). Music adviser to the Covent Garden Grand Opera Syndicate from 1902, becoming Musical Director in 1907. Associated with Beecham's operatic activities. Artistic Director of the BNOC 1922–24. Music Director of the BBC 1924–30.

POCOCK, Guy Noel (1880–1955). Worked for the BBC from 1934 to 1940. First as Head of General Talks Department and later as Editor of Supplementary Publications.

POSTON, Elizabeth (1905–1987). English composer, writer and pianist. Studied at the RAM, and with Harold Samuel for piano. She spent most of the 1930s collecting folk songs abroad. During the War worked for the BBC's European Service using music to broadcast coded messages to the Continent. After collecting folk songs in North America she became involved in the start of the BBC Third Programme.

RADFORD, Robert (1874–1933). English bass. Debut 1899 at Norwich Festival, Covent Garden debut in 1904. A founder and director of BNOC in 1921.

RAWSTHORNE, Alan (1905–1971). English composer who was emphatic in his rejection of folk-derived styles. Rawsthorne's individual concept of tonality was strongly influenced by Hindemith in the 1930s. Coming to music fairly late he studied at the RMCM and later was taught piano by Egon Petri, briefly appearing on the concert platform in the 1930s, his repertoire including Falla's *Nights in the Gardens of Spain.* An overture for chamber orchestra appeared in a Lemare concert in 1936, and a now withdrawn Concerto for clarinet and orchestra in 1937. He made his name with his *Theme and Variations* at an ISCM concert in London in 1938, and with the *Symphonic Studies* at an ISCM concert in Warsaw in 1939. During the War he produced few concert works but kept up a steady flow of film scores, including *Burma Victory.* It is in abstract orchestral and chamber music that Rawsthorne has cast most of his major works and in the 25 years after the war he produced a distinguished body of work including three symphonies, various concerti, chamber music and a few choral works, of which the most extended is *Carmen Vitale*, a 45-minute setting for soprano, chorus and orchestra of early English lyrics (1963).

RICHTER, Hans (1843–1916). Austro–Hungarian conductor. Prepared the fair copy full score of *Die Meistersinger* (1866–7) and assisted in the completion of *The Ring* full score (1870), and took part in the first performance of the *Siegfried Idyll* at Wagner's home. Opera conductor in Munich, Pest and Vienna. Conducted the first *Ring* cycle at Bayreuth in 1876. From 1877 he was a regular visitor to England and from 1885 he became Music Director of the Birmingham Music Festival, settling in Manchester as conductor of the Hallé Orchestra (1897–1911). He conducted the first *Ring* cycle in English at Covent Garden in 1909. Elgar's *First Symphony* is dedicated to Richter.

ROBERTSON, Alec (1892–1982). English organist, critic and broadcaster. Worked for HMV record company in the 1920s and Head of Music Talks for the BBC 1940–53.

ROBINSON, Stanford (1904–1984). English conductor and administrator. Joined the BBC in 1924 as Chorus Master. He remained in various conducting capacities until 1966. He recorded brief choral extracts from Bantock's *Pilgrim's Progress* with the National Choir and BBC Orchestra for Columbia in the late 1920s, and a substantially complete *Elijah* with his BBC Chorus. Boult promoted him within the BBC as conductor and organizer of opera, which he remained up to 1952, during which time he produced a wide repertoire, including many of the British operas composed before 1939.

RONALD, Sir Landon (1873–1938). Born Landon Ronald Russell. English conductor, pianist and composer. Studied at the RCM and conducted Augustus Harris's touring opera company. He was Melba's accompanist on her US tour in 1894. He became famous as a song composer, and 'Down in the Forest' (No. 2 from his *A Cycle of Life*) and 'O Lovely Night' (Teschemacher) achieved almost embarrassing popularity. His briefly popular incidental music to Robert Hichens's *The Garden of Allah* (1921) he recorded on 78s (HMV: D 488/9). A well-known conductor, friend of Elgar (the dedicatee of *Falstaff*) and adviser to The Gramophone Company, Ronald had a rewarding career which masked a tragic personal life. He was knighted in 1922.

ROTHENSTEIN, Sir William (1872–1945). Celebrated artist and art historian. Professor of Civic Art (Sheffield) 1917–26. Principal Royal College of Art 1920–35.

RUBBRA, Edmund (1901–1986). English composer and pianist. From a poor, working-class background, he was taken up by Cyril Scott and subsequently won a composition scholarship to Reading University and thence to the RCM, where his composition teacher was Holst. Initially a freelance musician, recognition came quickly, once his *First Symphony* had been heard (1937). He lectured in music at Oxford (1947–68) and taught composition at the GSMD. A deeply spiritual composer, Rubbra was converted to Catholicism in 1948. His output includes 11 symphonies and a Sinfonietta, concerti for violin, viola and piano, many choral and chamber works, songs and music for recorder.

SAMMONS, Albert (1886–1957). Celebrated English violinist. Appointed by

Beecham to lead his orchestra in 1908, he quickly established a career including being leader of Diaghilev's Ballets Russes Orchestra from 1911. He was also well known as a chamber music player, and had a well-known long-standing partnership with the pianist William Murdoch. His recording of the Elgar Violin Concerto is the touchstone by which others are judged. He was George Lloyd's violin teacher.

SCOTT, Marion (1877–1953). English musicologist. Studied at and was associated with the RCM. Noted as a Haydn authority, she ensured the preservation of Ivor Gurney's music.

SEIBER, Matyas (1905–1960). Born in Hungary and died in South Africa, Seiber settled in England in 1935 and was naturalized in 1945. Stylistically influenced by both Schoenberg and Bartók, he became the most influential British composition teacher of the post-War period.

SOMERVELL, Sir Arthur (1863–1937). English composer. An early pupil of Stanford at Cambridge, he later taught at the RCM. Somervell's reputation has tended to be dependent on his work as inspector to the Board of Education, particularly in the 1920s. His music varies in impact but his song cycles are all vivid, especially *Maud* (after Tennyson); orchestral works, including a symphony, piano and violin concerti, deserve revival. He was knighted in 1929.

STANFORD, Sir Charles Villiers (1852–1924). Born and brought up in Dublin, Stanford went up to Cambridge in 1870. He quickly established a commanding reputation in music, and for 40 years was a major figure on the British musical scene. His lack of sympathy with developments in his declining years saddened him. As a teacher of composition at the RCM he is legendary, his pupils including almost all of the big names over two generations. He revolutionized the music for the Anglican ceremony, but it is only in the 1980s that the beginnings of a revaluation of his major secular works could begin, previous commentators being content to sneer without having heard the music. These include over 30 extended choral works and a similar number for the orchestra (including seven symphonies and over 10 for soloist and orchestra). His partsongs and solo songs have continued to be played and demonstrate the variable quality of Stanford's published works, with many fine examples rubbing shoulders with many which are, often because of their text, no longer viable.

STEIN, Erwin (1885–1958). Austrian musicologist and publisher's editor. A pupil and associate of Schoenberg and his circle, he was an adviser to Universal Edition in Vienna. In 1938 he emigrated to England and accepted a post with Boosey & Hawkes. A champion of Schoenberg, he soon became associated with Benjamin Britten, as his publisher, and an ardent champion of him.

THATCHER, Sir Reginald Sparshatt (1888–1957). English organist and educationalist. Music master at various public schools, before joining BBC as Deputy Director of Music in 1937. Resigned in 1943 to succeed Benjamin Dale as Warden of the RAM, becoming Principal in 1949. He was knighted in 1952.

THOMPSON, Herbert (1856–1945). English critic. He became music critic of the *Yorkshire Post* in 1886, a post he held for 50 years. An influential figure in musical circles, particularly before World War I, he was particularly associated with the Leeds Festival.

TIPPETT, Sir Michael (b. 1905). Since the death of Benjamin Britten, Britain's leading composer. Tippett had never heard an orchestra before he was 17, when Ravel's *Mother Goose* made a marked impact. He studied at the RCM but was dissatisfied with his own music. Before World War II Tippett took a variety of jobs giving expression to left wing politics and for eight years he was employed by the LCC conducting an orchestra of unemployed musicians that met at Morley College. In 1940 he joined the Peace Pledge Union, and became director of music at Morley College after the old building had been bombed. He thus became the focus for many of the activities and personalities who would flower after the War, including Walter Goehr, Matyas Seiber, Britten and Pears, the pianist Noel Mewton-Wood and the counter tenor Alfred Deller. As a composer Tippett developed slowly. Although his *First String Quartet* was played in 1935 he later replaced the first two movements by one, first performed in 1944. He received a three-month prison sentence for failing to comply with the conditions of his registration as a conscientious objector. His works were gradually played during the War. His *Concerto for Double String Orchestra* in 1940, the *Fantasia on a theme of Handel* in 1942, and the *Second String Quartet* and the solo cantata *Boyhood's End* in 1943. Perhaps most important of all was the oratorio *A Child of Our Time*, written in the first two years of the war, and first performed in March 1944. With the appearance of his *First Symphony* in 1945, he came of age musically speaking. Tippett's mature output followed at regular intervals over the succeeding years, comprising four each of operas, symphonies, string quartets and piano sonatas, his musical language showing a marked stylistic advance with each opera, crowned in 1984 by *The Mask of Time*. He was knighted in 1966, appointed Companion of Honour in 1979.

TOVEY, Sir Donald Francis (1875–1940). English composer, pianist and academic. Developed early and was associated with Joachim from childhood who took a personal interest in his musical education. First emerged as a pianist of the front rank and was associated with the Joachim Quartet from 1894 to 1914. His own music was mostly composed before World War I and shows a brilliant mind overawed by the great classical tradition, particularly of the music of Brahms. His later music comprises an opera *The Bride of Dionysus* (1929) and the 55-minute cello concerto he wrote for Casals (1935). Appointed Professor of Music at Edinburgh in 1914 he founded the Reid Orchestra in 1917 for whose concerts he wrote the programme notes from which selected items were later published as 'Essays in Musical Analysis'. Though enormously influential these reveal Tovey's prejudices, in particular his over-veneration of the classical masters, and his distaste for the Russians or for descriptive programme music (though writing memorably of Elgar's *Falstaff*).

VAN DIEREN, Bernard (1884–1936). Dutch born composer who settled in London in his twenties. He has tended to be known more by reputation than by first-hand knowledge of a small but complex output. He attracted an intense interest among an intellectual clique which included Cecil Gray, Philip Heseltine, the Sitwells, Gerald Cooper, Augustus John, Epstein (on whom van Dieren wrote a book), Lambert, Moeran and Hubert Foss. It is possible to take two diametrically opposed views on van Dieren. On the one hand he was venerated by a small circle of admirers: a devout Catholic who though often bedridden and in intense pain produced wonderful music. On the other hand he is seen as a persuasive but essentially destructive influence, and in this view it is noted that many of his admirers came to grief at a comparatively early age.

VAUGHAN WILLIAMS, Ralph (1872–1958). Probably the most celebrated British composer of his generation, was born at Down Ampney, Gloucestershire, the son of a parson. His formative years, however, were spent at Leith Hill Place near Dorking, for his father died when he was only three. A string player from an early age, he read history at Cambridge and studied at the Royal College of Music, with Max Bruch in Berlin, and with Ravel in Paris. Thus, he had one of the broadest based educations of any British composer of his generation.

It was with songs that he first found a public following , and *Songs of Travel* and *Linden Lea* first marked him out as a distinctive voice. His first contact with living folk song was probably in 1903, and, as Maud Karpeles wrote in a memorial tribute 'He found in folk song the affirmation of his musical philosophy: that music is a "spiritual necessity" and that the making of music is not just the prerogative of the chosen few.'

If the idiom of folk song became Vaughan Williams's point of departure, his work on *The English Hymnal* not only added to a growing reputation but contributed to the development of his style. His position as a composer of stature really dates from the appearance of the *Fantasia on a Theme of Thomas Tallis* and *A Sea Symphony* in 1910. *A London Symphony*, first performed in 1914, and the song cycle *On Wenlock Edge*, underlined this quickly growing reputation.

His seven remaining symphonies were more or less evenly spaced over the remainder of his long life, each of them springing surprises on their first audiences. Those dating from the period covered by the present book are the *Pastoral* (1922), the Fourth (1935) and the Fifth (1943).

His ability to write good memorable tunes, and the extent of his choral music (from every sort of occasional piece to the larger canvases of *A Sea Symphony*, *Sancta Civitas*, *Dona Nobis Pacem* and *Five Tudor Portraits*) has meant that choral societies have consistently performed it and it is therefore deeply implanted in the musical consciousness of the nation. Only Vaughan Williams could have carried off the *Thanksgiving for Victory* with such a sureness of touch.

It is typical of him that he should also have established that the British composer can write distinctively for the operatic stage, with five operas, ranging from the ballad style of *Sir John in Love* (1914) to the utterly idiosyncratic *The Pilgrim's Progress* (which, typically, Vaughan Williams referred to as 'a morality'). In the latter the preoccupations of a lifetime are brought together in one personal vision. His achievement is unique. He was appointed to the Order of Merit in 1935.

WADDINGTON, Sidney Peine (1869–1953). English teacher and composer. He was one of the foundation students of the RCM where for many years he was later Professor of Harmony and Counterpoint, and Master of the opera class.

WALFORD DAVIES, Sir Henry (1869–1941). Welsh-born composer, organist and broadcaster. Studied at the RCM with Stanford. Had various appointments including organist of the Temple Church, London, 1898–1918. Master of the King's Musick after Elgar (1934–1941). He was one of the first broadcast popularisers of music.

WALLACE, William (1860–1940). Scottish composer and musical administrator. He was also a qualified ophthalmic surgeon, practising at the beginning of his career and during World War I. He studied at the RAM. His six symphonic poems, strongly influenced by Wagner and Liszt, were proclaimed the first British examples of the Lisztian symphonic poem, though earlier examples are known. He was Secretary of the Royal Philharmonic Society (1911–13) at the time it received the accolade 'Royal'.

WALTON, Sir William (1902–1983). English composer. Born at Oldham, Lancashire, at the age of ten he became a chorister at Christ Church Cathedral, Oxford. Becoming an undergraduate at the age of 16, he never took a degree. While essentially self-taught as a composer, he received encouragement from various leaders of Oxford musical life, and was 'taken up' by Sacheverell Sitwell, and much of his later success stems from his association with the Sitwells.

The short choral piece *A Litany*, and his Piano Quartet, both date from his mid-teens, but he was established as a name by the succes de scandale of *Façade*, first heard in public on 12 June 1923. Walton's reputation as a significant composer dates from the Viola Concerto in 1929, but it was *Belshazzar's Feast* (1931) and the First Symphony (1934–5) which finally established him as a 'big' name.

Walton's popular audience grew with the success of his Coronation Marches and his film music. His later works, from the lyrical Violin Concerto of 1939 and his postwar opera *Troilus and Cressida*, seemed to some contemporary critics not to have built on the achievement of his earlier works. Walton always composed slowly, and it is only with the passage of time that the quality of some of his music from the 1950s onwards can be properly appreciated, though the earlier works have become established twentieth-century classics. He was knighted in 1951 and appointed to the Order of Merit in 1967.

WEBSTER, Sir David (1903–1971). Chairman of the Liverpool Philharmonic Society 1940–45. General Administrator of the Royal Opera House, Covent Garden (1945–70).

WELCH, Rev. James William (1900–19??). BBC Director of Religious Broadcasting 1939–1945.

WILLIAMS, Grace (1906–1977). Welsh composer. Studied at University College Cardiff and at the RCM (with Vaughan Williams and Gordon Jacob). She also studied with Egon Wellesz in Vienna (1930–31). During the next fifteen years she earned her living as a schoolmistress in London, returning to Wales in 1946.

WOOD, Haydn (1882–1959). English composer, a pupil of Stanford, best known as a popular songwriter. He established his reputation with songs such as 'Roses of Picardy' during World War I. He also wrote serious concert works including piano and violin concerti.

WOOD, Sir Henry J. (1869–1944). British conductor, who directed the Promenade Concerts from their inception in August 1895 until 1944. His range of sympathies and repertoire is unequalled, and his championship of new works by British composers play an essential role in the development of a significant number of British composers of stature. His own arrangements were once well known, and using the pseudonym 'Paul Klenovsky', he promoted his orchestration of Bach's *Toccata and Fugue* in D minor. Having worked most of his life in Queen's Hall, he lived to see it destroyed in an air raid in 1941. He was knighted in 1911.

WOODGATE, Leslie (b. 1909). Studied at the RCM. Assistant chorus master BBC

Chorus 1928–29. Founder and first conductor BBC Theatre Orchestra. BBC Chorus Master from 1934.

WRIGHT, Kenneth (1899–1975). Joined BBC as Director of the Manchester Station as early as 1922. Assistant Director of Music 1937. Overseas Music Director 1940; Deputy Director of Music 1944; Acting Director of Music 1947. Also known as a composer at the lighter end of the orchestral repertoire.

INDEX OF CORRESPONDENTS

There are two possible sequences under each name; the first those letters written by the name indexed, the second group — represented by numbers in italic — are the recipients of the item in question. Titles are given as appropriate, even though the main text titles are only used after the date on which they were conferred. References are to the number of the letter in question, not to the page.

GENERAL INDEX

All musical and literary works are entered under their composer or author, with the exception of hymn tunes, films and folksongs, which are entered under title. References to plates appear at the end of an entry and are to the plate number in *italics*. References are to page number; the *Index to Correspondents* should also be consulted, where reference is to letter number.

Whereas names are given in the text in the style the correspondents used at that particular date, in the index the final style, particularly in the matter of knighthoods, has been adopted, even if the honour postdates this book's time span.